Water Resource Economics and Policy

Water Resource Economics and Policy
An Introduction

W. Douglass Shaw
Professor, Texas A&M University, USA

Edward Elgar
Cheltenham, UK • Northampton, MA, USA

© W. Douglass Shaw, 2005

All rights reserved. No part of this publication may be reproduced, stored in a retrieval system or transmitted in any form or by any means, electronic, mechanical or photocopying, recording, or otherwise without the prior permission of the publisher.

Published by
Edward Elgar Publishing Limited
Glensanda House
Montpellier Parade
Cheltenham
Glos GL50 1UA
UK

Edward Elgar Publishing, Inc.
136 West Street
Suite 202
Northampton
Massachusetts 01060
USA

A catalogue record for this book
is available from the British Library

Library of Congress Cataloging-in-Publication Data
Shaw, W. Douglass.
    Water resource economics and policy : an introduction / W. Douglass Shaw.
       p. cm.
    Includes bibliographical references and indexes.
    1. Water resources development–United States–Economic aspects.
    2. Water-supply–United States–Economic aspects. I. Title.

HD1691.S53 2004
333.91′00973–dc22   2004058842

ISBN 1 84376 917 4 (cased)

Printed and bound in Great Britain by MPG Books Ltd, Bodmin, Cornwall

Contents

Preface and acknowledgements   vii

1   Introduction to water resources, water resource economics, and law   1
2   Review of basic microeconomics applied to water resources   35
3   Water quality issues   66
4   Water prices and rates for residential use   100
5   Water and agriculture   136
6   Uncertainty and risk in supply and demand of water resources   172
7   Groundwater   202
8   In situ uses of water: environmental and recreational values   251
9   Floods and droughts and the role of dams   287
10   Water issues outside the United States   319
11   Summary, suggestions for future work, conclusions   352

Index   361

Preface and acknowledgements

Economic issues arise in most water policy contexts today. Water becomes of most concern when it is scarce, as it is in the western United States, deserts in the Middle East, and many parts of Africa. But physical scarcity is often overcome as human beings move water from place to place, sometimes creating monumental structures. The role that cost and economic value play in water resource allocation is implicit, but often poorly understood, even by those who make critical allocation decisions.

When I looked around for a suitable textbook for a course in this subject I found some engineering books and a few other books that were written for that audience, even though economics often appeared in the title. There were none that fit the bill then, so I decided to fill this gap by writing this book. The book is intended for senior-level undergraduates and first year masters students in economics. It probably will not bore PhD economics students at all, but the book is meant to be accessible even for those with little knowledge of economics. Readers and students are expected to be comfortable with mathematics at the appropriate levels, and also with microeconomics, at least at the level of intermediate microeconomic theory typically offered to university undergraduates. Chapter 2, which is a review of basic microeconomics, is applied to water resource issues.

The approach is to offer material that can be applied in assessing water resource allocation problems. For examples, I mostly draw on my 22 years of experience as a resource economist in the western United States, but I hope that students in other parts of the US and in other countries find much of the material to be of some use. Chapter 10 specifically addresses select institutions and issues in nations other than the United States. Though the US will have its problems for sure, I believe other countries are where much of the attention of water resource economists will be focused in the future.

ACKNOWLEDGEMENTS

The person who introduced me to the broadly defined area of water resources as an undergraduate student in geography was Gilbert White, and similarly, I was introduced to water resource economics by John Morris, and later, by Charles Howe. Both John and Chuck are now officially retired from the University of Colorado, but the last time I checked, Chuck is reporting to work five days a week. I would especially like to thank him for all his support over the years I have known him.

I have learned about the institutions of water from the late Ernie Flack, who taught us some water law at the University of Colorado, and have benefited from working on water resource projects with scholars elsewhere, including economists Dave Lambert, Mark Eiswerth, Eric Huszar, Noelwah Netusil and Richard Woodward, and former science and hydrology colleagues of mine: Scott Tyler, Glenn Miller, Mark Walker, and John Tracy. In addition, I have benefited greatly from listening to other water resource economists talk about particular issues, including Bob Berrens, Rich Howitt, John Loomis, Ari Michelsen, Frank Ward, and David Zilberman.

Thanks are also due to Tom Cech for his encouragement to keep on going to get this book completed, as well as to Michael Hanemann for his equal enthusiasm. Michael wanted to join me in writing this book I think, but as an insanely busy mutual acquaintance of ours said, 'I don't even know what multi-tasking is compared to Michael'. So, to Michael – maybe next time?

I worked to finish this book while in my first semester at Texas A&M University, and there is no doubt the book would not have been finished without all the excellent help I received from Michele Zinn. Michele painstakingly went through all of the suggested edits the publishing staff at Edward Elgar made. Alan Sturmer at Edward Elgar Publishing encouraged me to keep going on the book even with my delays, and provided valuable early comments.

Finally, the 'gurls' – Lynn, Lucy, Elizabeth, and Nan – are publicly acknowledged for putting up with my constant trips to the basement of the house we lived in while on 2002–3 sabbatical in Boulder, Colorado to keep writing and rewriting parts of the book. This book is dedicated to them and to my late father, who liked nonfiction books, though he never got to read this one.

1. Introduction to water resources, water resource economics, and law

1.0 INTRODUCTION

This textbook provides an economist's perspective about the allocation of water resources, and other related topics. In this first lengthy chapter the student is introduced to water resources, law, and resource economics concepts. The last of these will constitute the material in most of the remainder of this book. Economics is of critical importance in determining the allocation of water: where it flows and how and when it is stored. Economics also has something to offer in solving the problem of how society can try to make water move from place A to place or point B, especially when point B is not a natural place for water to end up. By natural, I mean the water would not, by simple forces of nature, end up at point B. Economics also plays a role in determining existing levels of water quality for many water bodies, because society engages in certain economic activities that are polluting, and then must decide whether and how much of this pollution to clean up, given the cost of doing so.

Though it is often said that water flows 'toward money', one must start with the laws of gravity or physics in all this: the laws of gravity apply and as you will see in future chapters, water, even when underground, does actually generally flow downhill. Politics and political power held in the hands of a few suggest that select agents cannot be ignored in allocating water. Together, politics, institutions, and laws often lead to the protection of certain interest groups who would probably not get water in a purely economic scheme of things. In the United States, for example, agricultural interests put water to uses that are generally of lower value today than several other possible uses, and this is possible because of existing laws and political clout that agricultural users obtain via lobbyists in Washington, DC and in state legislatures throughout the country. As will be seen below, interpretation of water law often vests enormous amounts of power with existing water rights holders.

In many countries in the world institutional and legal systems are also critically important in allocating water. Much of this book focuses on institutions, providing examples of water allocation in the United States, and even more specifically, in the western part of this vast country. Whenever possible, examples from other regions and countries are offered. However, to fully understand institutions associated with water, one needs to carefully study all of the features of the locality. It is often not possible to generalize across countries and it is a mistake to do so, particularly when applying some of the material in certain chapters of this book to countries outside the United States that are just fundamentally different. For example, there is tremendous concern for water quality issues in countries outside the United States, but these issues are of a different nature in other countries, and take on a much different priority, as Chapter 10 will demonstrate. There is also concern over water quantity issues, obviously greater in those countries with arid lands similar to the western US desert regions, but again disputes over quantities might be cross-cultural and resolved very differently.

As a good example, very recently Wines (2002) documents problems in Uzbekistan, Turkmenistan, Tajikistan, Kyrgyzstan, and Kazakhstan, where growing populations and waste in irrigation have led to the demise of the Aral Sea, fed by the region's rivers, the Amu and the Syr. Under a scheme managed by the Soviet Union many years ago the rivers were diverted via canals and desert areas were watered so that rice, of all things, is grown in Kazakhstan. Today, of course, there is no Soviet Union and much has changed. Each separate country mentioned above is fighting for a share of the diminishing relative supply of water, and there appear to be few laws, regulations or other institutional features to help solve the problems.

Another example is found in India as recently as 1992: deaths and looting occurred after violence erupted over disputes related to the Cauvery River. The Tamil Nadu and the Karnataka peoples have argued for years over water rights issues in the river, exacerbated when the Karnataka built dams for irrigation, which the Tamil Nadu believed adversely affected their access to supplies. Probably more obvious and well known than the above are problems in the Near East and Middle East. These very often have their origins in issues over water. Negotiations over the Golan Heights regularly mention issues related to the Jordan River (see Chapter 10).

Finally, as many readers will already understand, law can be very complicated and water law is no exception. This book, and particularly this chapter, is not in any way a substitute for a water law text, and a good old standard in this regard is the book by Trelease (1979). The interested student could also consult Goldfarb's (1988) or Beck's (1991) edited text. As with institutions and the functioning of markets, water law differs by countries, from state to state in the US, and even within some regions of some states, so it is essential to scrutinize the geographical area or region of interest if one is to understand the water laws that help govern allocation. Below I revisit several of the ideas discussed below in more detail.

1.1 PHYSICAL CHARACTERISTICS AND DIMENSIONS OF WATER

1.1.1 Earth's Water Supply

The world's supply of freshwater is mostly in icecaps and glaciers (about 74 percent of the total freshwater in the world). A much smaller percentage is found in freshwater rivers and lakes (less than 0.01 percent), while the vast majority of all water on the planet is in the ocean (97.5 percent of the total). The distribution of precipitation is quite uneven in many regions of the world. For example, the average annual precipitation in the lower 48 states of the United States is about 30 inches per year, but varies greatly throughout the country.

1.1.2 Physical Scarcity

Though often nearly free in cost or market price, water is often quite scarce, again relative to the regional population's demand and in particular locations. Today more than 40 percent of the world's population lives in river basins where water scarcity is an issue (Revenga et al., 2000). These basins are often, but not always, in arid areas with little natural precipitation. Again, there may be reasonable precipitation in some areas, but population growth or degraded water quality have nevertheless led to scarcity problems. When comparing the resource to demands for it, economists and some scientists in other fields talk about relative, rather than absolute scarcity.

The American West offers many excellent historical examples of the concept of relative scarcity. Some historians believe that the evidence suggests that Native American tribes fought over the scarcity of resources such as water.[1] Struggles over scarce water became common in the US as people of European origin began migrating from the east to the west. The struggles were especially violent when the demand for water outstripped its supply. Often during the West's history, as so brilliantly described in Marc Reisner's book, *Cadillac Desert* (1993), droughts or too many people vying for too little water drove people back to the eastern regions of the United States. But once any particular drought event was 'over' the Federal government would encourage western settlement yet again. At least initially upon their return, there seemed to be no shortage of water, or so the new batch of settlers thought. Then another drought would occur, crops and livestock would die, and the migration process would begin again.

Today water is becoming relatively scarce in the western United States and concerns are even growing in the eastern US, as is national and regional media coverage of this issue. As a good example, Clark County, Nevada, which encompasses the sprawling metropolis of Las Vegas, has been the fastest growing in the United States over the past several years, yet the region is also the most arid in the country. Many have deemed Clark County's growth rates as being 'third world' and indeed a 4 percent or even 5 percent annual growth rate is equal to, or even faster than, the most rapidly growing population growth rates in developing nations (countries such as India) around the world. The strategy of the county has been to withdraw water from the Colorado River, which cuts through the lower southeast corner of the state, but as will be seen below and in other chapters of this book, this strategy will probably not work for much longer because competing demands on the Colorado River will not allow it. The county will have to find other sources, and it remains to be seen whether water will constrain further growth.

Such matters are no longer the sole domain of the arid West. The 2002 drought in the eastern US, including states as far north as Maine, and as far south as South Carolina, caused water planners, and lawyers, to question water rights (Jehl, 2003). Again, a growing population may quickly turn what appears to be an ample water supply into a relatively scarce one, but there are also concerns about the role that climate change and global warming might play in changing the frequency and duration of droughts throughout the United States.

It is certainly no surprise to most that water shortages are fundamental in explaining the poor human health conditions in many countries in Africa. Good health, especially for infants, begins with access to clean drinking water and sanitary conditions. As the reader will see in Chapter 10, economics is the key to differences between arid rural villages in Africa having no access to good drinking water and the Clark County government's ability to continue to provide water to the rapidly increasing population there, when the climates in both regions offer similar natural supplies of water.

These situations point out what seems to be a most interesting contradiction in economics. If water is so precious and important to society, why does it typically command such a low price? And, if water should appear to be a limit to growth, then why do some western world governments seem able to continue indefinitely in their quest to find adequate supplies of water in arid areas with explosive population growth rates?

The answers to this question are central to understanding water conflicts and the role that economics plays. To begin to understand these issues, we must first get familiar with some of the physical dimensions of water, including how water is measured.

1.1.3 Water Flows, Stocks

It is assumed that the reader is already familiar with the hydrologic cycle, the importance of rainfall and snow pack, and reliance on groundwater for much of society's water needs. Those who are not might wish to supplement this text with a book on the physical relationships involving water and water quality, such as Tom Cech's (2003).

All hydrologists have some things in common with electrical engineers. For one, they must learn some basic mathematics about flows, and that branch of mathematics involves dynamics. Rates of change in flows then involve differential equations, but this book is not the place to become an expert on this kind of mathematics. A very simple beginning for those who haven't this knowledge is to think of one's bathtub.

One may turn on the tap and water will flow out at a certain rate over time. Most taps allow some variation in the flow by turning the valve handle, but there is a maximum flow that accompanies the system. The flow out of the tap can be measured, but this is beyond the capability of most of our home measurement capability and technology: most of us could only distinguish between crude observations, such as a 'trickle' or 'gushing' water. The tub begins to fill up if the stopper is placed in the drain, and if the tap is left on, the tub will eventually fill, and may even overflow. Again, many of us could figure out a simple way to measure the amount of water in the tub, in gallons or quarts, at any point in time, after turning off the tap. However, once the tap is off, this quantity of water is no longer a flow, it is a stock. If the drain is stopped and the water turned off at the tap, then the stock may appear to be constant for a while; at home this could be quite a long time. However, anyone who has done the experiment knows that water can leak out of the drain even when it is stopped up, and it may evaporate into the air, so if left for long enough, the water level in the tub will fall, even when the stopper is firmly in place.

Now let's complicate things a little bit. Depending on the flow, this same tub above may never fill, provided that the stopper is left out of the drain. Water may continuously flow through the open system, with little or no stock ever being accumulated in the tub that is measurable in large quantities. Determining what one can see in the tub at any given time are the rates of inflow, what is coming out of the tap, and the rate of drainage, which of course is what flow is going down and out of the drain. Gushing water will allow some water to accumulate, even when the stopper is out. But a trickle of water will just go down the drain so that even with a positive, nonzero flow, the dynamic system that has been created leads to no accumulation of water in the tub.

The rough analogy we can make to watersheds, basins, and lakes, reservoirs and rivers is probably obvious to all, or at least most readers who have had some basic course in hydrology or geography. Water is an input into a basin or watershed, or lake or reservoir, via rainfall, snowmelt, or from the ground. Assume that only 'gravity rules' in allocating water, so water flows downhill from a high to lower point. This could happen quickly, or extremely slowly, taking years. Hydrographic regions have natural boundaries formed by mountains or natural drainage areas formed by underlying geologic formations. For example, the Continental Divide in the western United States is a common geographical landmark, as, to the west of it, freshwater generally flows to the west, and eventually to the Pacific Ocean. To the east of the Continental Divide water generally flows to the Gulf of Mexico or to the Atlantic Ocean.

Of course the analogy of the bathtub is only approximate, and the above discussion has greatly simplified things that occur in river basins. Such basins involve soils and rocks that have vastly different properties than our smoothly surfaced bathtub, and as mentioned, we have not adequately dealt with water that evaporates in great heat, nor have we discussed the role that plants play in absorbing water. Occasionally water that is west or east of the Continental Divide flows to a landlocked region and disappears under the ground, or to a terminus lake as it does in Nevada's Great Basin. Thus, carefully done hydrologic studies must consider geology, physics, and geography of any watershed to better understand what is going on in an area.

Even groundwater moves or flows, which many people do not realize, though it most likely will move very slowly in comparison to surface water. Flowing surface water can accumulate as measurable stocks of lake, reservoir or groundwater, and there is often a complicated connection between groundwater and surface water supplies.

1.1.4 Evaporation/Evapotranspiration

Lakes and reservoirs can flood when input exceeds storage capacity, but water can be lost because of evaporation and seepage. Evaporation is what we most often think of when we see a lake on a very hot day and know that the lake's volume is being depleted. Evapotranspiration involves the uptake of water by the roots of plants, and can be a substantial source of additional loss of a river's flow. It has been estimated that 72 percent of all earth's precipitation returns to the atmosphere by evapotranspiration, though naturally the estimates vary depending on where on the earth one is looking. Not all transpiration by plants is bad, but phreatophytes, which are plants that send roots deep into water sources, are notorious for the animosity mankind feels for them. They are thought to rob us of precious water in order to supply plant growth when these plants might be viewed as pests or invasive species: the tamarisk or salt cedar is an excellent example of this in the American West.

Earth's water balance is known as the hydrologic cycle, and scientists have been attempting to estimate a relationship between runoff and rainfall for a long while; one of the earliest known rainfall runoff models was by Meyer (1915). His modeling appears to be the first to develop a water balance based on precipitation, evapotranspiration, and soil storage. From the model, Meyer could estimate monthly and annual flow volume.

1.1.5 Water Balance Models

A water balance model has several key components. Figure A1.1 (see the appendix to this chapter) depicts some basic parts of the Stanford Watershed Model, which is one of the earliest formal models available in the US (see Linsley and Crawford, 1960). Based on the diagram in Figure A1.1, or more complex ones, a hydrologist can develop mathematical relationships (i.e. equations) that define available total withdrawals at given points in time. Alternatively, one can use such equations to estimate a piece of the puzzle for which data may be missing. For example, if we can measure flow at the headwaters and at the end of a system, we can often make some inferences about what happens at places on a river that are in between those points.

Such models are important because humans can change the water balance through landscape alteration or other activities such as withdrawals or diversions, and almost certainly, the importance of water in a particular watershed changes because of population growth. The science underlying calculation, prediction, and forecast of the relationships described above is of course known as hydrology and this book is no substitute for a good course or two in the hydrologic sciences (my hydrologic sciences colleagues would probably argue for many more such courses!), but I make an effort below to provide the most elementary knowledge about water for those who have had no such course.

Before continuing, it is worth a reminder that humans build structures to transport water, overcoming the laws of gravity using power and pumps. But the analogy to the bathtub is still somewhat relevant. Pipe sizes and pressure in those pipes determine flow rates, and of course the bathtub can be a storage reservoir. The next thing to get used to is how to measure water quantities. You may have seen, or at least will soon see, all sorts of ways to measure water that relate to economic activity, but most often there is the need to distinguish between volume (stock) and flow, a basic concept that requires familiarity.

1.1.6 Stock Measures

Stocks of water can be measured in several ways. The layperson is naturally mainly interested in small stocks of water and not large ones, so may not have encountered anything beyond a quart or gallon. In fact, do you even know how many gallons of water your bathtub holds? In Table 1.1 are some common units used in the United States, and translations to units used in the metric system most often used outside the United States. All but one are units of stock; the exception being cubic feet per second, which is actually a measure of flow.

An acre foot is a very commonly used stock measure in the western US, and it can possibly be visualized as the amount of water that would cover an acre of land 1 foot deep in water. Quite often one sees estimates of the volume of water in a lake in terms of acre feet (abbreviated af), but this measure can also be used to characterize the average flow of water in a river over the course of a year. One should use the units, acre feet per year, in that case, and the measure is really a flow and not a stock, because we add the time dimension. Nevertheless, some authors use acre feet to denote a 'volume' for a river, which sounds like a stock measure. For example, the Colorado River, the US's seventh longest river, has averaged about 15 million af since the year 1905. One can see that this is small when compared to the Columbia (192 million af) or the Mississippi, with average volume of about 400 million acre feet (Carrier, 1991). Still, when rivers are discussed, we usually talk about their flow.

Table 1.1   Measures of stocks of water

---

1 acre foot = 325851 gallons = 1235 m^3 (cubic meters)

1 000 000 gallons = 3.07 acre feet

1 cubic foot = 7.48 gallons, which weighs 62.5 pounds

1 miner's inch = 0.02 cubic feet per second, or 9 gallons per minute.[a] 300 miners' inches = 7.5 cubic feet per second

Acres – surface area of lakes. Sometimes it may be helpful to note that 1 acre is 4047 square meters

---

Note: [a]Cech notes that a miner's inch was defined in the 1800s as the rate of water discharge through an opening in a channel 1 inch square under a specified head of water. Many states in the western US defined the quantity of water slightly differently. For example, 1 miner's inch was 9 gpm in Idaho, but 11.2 gpm in California.

1.1.7 Flow Measures

A flow measure must involve a volume and some unit of time (t) because the volume of water only tells us the stock. Flow is not simply 'speed', or velocity, which the uninitiated often do not immediately grasp. It incorporates dynamics of movement, but also volumes, and the combination of movement and volume can be deadly. A very small amount of water moving very quickly does not cause great concern, but a large volume of water moving very fast destroys homes and property, and can end lives. To rely on a primitive example again, imagine being hit by a tiny stream of water that is moving very fast, the sort of flow that comes from a high-pressure toy squirt gun. No problem. Next imagine being at one end of a large swimming pool, and being hit by a very slow moving wave created by a person diving in at the other end. Again, no problem. Now imagine that much or all of the volume of water in the swimming pool hits you at the same speed as the water shot out of the high-pressure squirt gun. At the very least, you will be knocked down, and probably badly hurt.

Typical measures of flows are set out in Table 1.2.

Note that all of these flow measures do incorporate time, with a second, minute, or a day, or a year, but they also indicate the volume of water moving over the time period. In the first measure the standard large measure of the volume of standing water, an acre foot, is again translated into a flow by indicating how many acre feet move past some point every day. Remember the above visualization of an acre foot of water standing still, and now imagine it rushing toward you very quickly. This may help you get the notion that this is a tremendous amount of flow, and in fact it is used to describe flows for big rivers such as the Columbia River in the Pacific Northwest of the United States, and the famous Mississippi and Missouri Rivers.

A river or stream's flow at an *exact* instant in time can be somewhat difficult to measure, indicative of the property that stream flow has as a continuous random variable (see Chapter 6). More often data on historical

Table 1.2 Measures of flow

1 cubic foot per second (cfs) = 1.98 acre feet per day, or 449 gallons per minute (gpm), or 0.646 million gallons per day
1 000 000 gallons per day (mgpd) = 3.07 acre feet per day, or 694.4 gallons per minute, or = 1120 acre feet per year
1 cubic meter per second = 70 acre feet per day = 22.8 mgpd

flow levels are collected using stream gauges. The gauge data can give estimates of flow during a day, but the data are perhaps better used over some long period of time. Long series of data are used to generate estimates of a river system's average flow, as well as identifying what might be 'low' and 'high' water years. Today sophisticated simulation methods are often used to supplement traditional modeling of this data. Much more will be said on random variables and flows in Chapter 6, which deals with uncertainty and random water supplies.

1.1.8 Supply of Water and Runoff

'Runoff' is another important term, often defined as the net supply of liquid water available for withdrawal. It is also defined as the portion of precipitation draining through the land to all surface water channels, and Cech (2003) simply defines it as the amount of water that flows across the land after a storm event. Underground flow is sometimes included in the calculation of total runoff. Runoff does not necessarily indicate the potential supply of liquid water; rather, it only approximates the net supply under current conditions (Hirshleifer et al., 1960).

Table 1.3 may be startling to the reader because of the large percentages reported. How can total use be greater than runoff? Another very important concept that may be new to some readers is called *return flow* – the portion of water used in activity A that returns to the river course after a use. This returned flow can potentially be used again in activity B, C, etc., and of course B's use may also result in a return flow. Because of this return

Table 1.3 Annual water use as a percent of runoff in nine western river basins

Region	Dry year
Missouri	124.3
Arkansas, White, Red	225.3
Texas-Gulf	259.9
Rio Grande	180.6
Upper Colorado	112.3
Lower Colorado	238.3
Great Basin	158.1
Pacific Northwest	101.8
California	112.7

Source: US Water Resources Council, reproduced in Vaux (1986).

flow actually allows much more water to be used than the total annual runoff. For example, Table 1.3 shows that in several western regional river basins, annual water use well exceeds annual average runoff, as the percentages are all greater than 100.

1.2 HUMAN CONSUMPTION AND USE

Water may be delivered to various users. For example, delivery of water to a farmer is typically done by a water or irrigation ditch manager. The amount delivered to the farmer might be expressed as a flow, and is often expressed that way. For example, when I have talked to farmers, they might tell me that their water right entitles them to 4 cfs. But when accumulated over a period, the total flow indicates the farmer's legal right to a certain total amount of water, or the farmer's annual water right. All of us with houses on municipal water systems also have water delivered to our homes, though we do not often think about it unless our region is in drought. How is the water a consumer or producer uses measured? Or is it? These questions will be addressed again in Chapter 4, on residential water use.

1.2.1 Types of Human Use

Water is used by humans in any number of different ways, and for many different purposes. First, we have to have water simply to exist, because we can only survive for short periods of time without drinking it or other beverages made with water as the primary ingredient, and the food we eat depends on water as an input in production. We use water in agriculture to grow crops. Areas with ample precipitation may be good for growing some crops, but in arid areas virtually no crops are grown without irrigation, and livestock must also be watered. Chapter 5 focuses on water and agriculture. Beyond what we think of as 'needs', water is used in industrial processes and manufacturing (for cooling purposes), it is also used to bathe and to clean items, and we like to use water for pleasure: we irrigate our golf courses and lawns, fill swimming pools, and run water through decorative fountains.

How much water do you think you use every day? What do you use it for? Think about your drinking, bathing, dishes, cooling, and outdoor use (lawns). One acre foot of water is a typical water supply for five people for an entire year, presuming the five people consume 180 gallons per person, per day. Naturally they might use more or less, but the minimum amount of water a person needs for a healthy living standard is estimated to be about 23 gallons per day (United Nations). Many water planning agencies such as the former Nevada Division of Water Planning (NDWP),[2] plan on between 0.5 and 1 af per household, per year, but it is well known that the highest consumptive use for single dwellings is for outdoor uses, with peak demands observed in summer months. The amount of the household's water consumption that is drunk is actually quite small. For example, the average household in Arizona drinks about 0.5 percent (one half of one percent!) of their water used (Gelt, 1996).

Economists often do not recognize any 'want' as a 'need'. For some economists, there are no needs. This statement may seem to defy common sense and good physical science, especially biology. We die without water, but even with an important or essential commodity like water, economists are interested in the relationship between the price and the quantity demanded of the good.

Perhaps it will make more sense to think of the needs issue this way. Suppose we assume that the minimum amount for drinking and survival is not an economic decision. Any economist would agree that one's maximum willingness to pay could equal one's total wealth if one were dying of thirst and could buy a life-saving drink of water. This is fortunately, for those in the developed world, a silly example. As Chapter 10 shows, it is not at all a silly example in underdeveloped nations: impoverished people pay huge proportions of their annual income for basic goods such as water.

However, a demander's responsiveness to water's price is easy to imagine when we think of the water used in application to one's lawn or yard. Economists would argue that one does not 'need' one's yard. As will be seen in later chapters, in much of the United States this external use of water in a home is by far the largest portion of water used in many months of the year. However, watering the yard is a function of choices, including what type of grass, or ground cover, or trees and flowers one plants, and how often these plants are watered. Clearly, one does not need to water a lawn to keep Kentucky bluegrass bright green. This is the essential meaning of the 'need' issue.

Water use per capita in the US is estimated to be two to four times what it is in some countries within Europe. As we shall see in more detail later, water use depends on several things, and not least among them may be the rate water users pay. How much do you pay for your water? Do you even know the relevant units? Many people do not, and often do not even know where to look for the answer. Most of us pay for water on a utility bill, which is either an item along with other charges for electricity and natural gas, or appears as a separate bill from a water utility. Water rates vary across the United States, and some billing schemes used by the water supplier are complicated, so we will postpone further discussion until Chapter 4. However, many economists in the US and elsewhere believe that water, like gasoline and other energy resources, is underpriced; many Europeans pay 50 to 350 percent more for their water than customers in the US (Frederick, 1991).

Based on the discussion thus far, where do you think you would find most people living, and a related question is, would you expect prices of water to vary drastically across regions? One might assume people live where precipitation levels are high, at least if one has allowed for a long historical period of relocation or population migration. For a variety of reasons this is not so. Many cities in the Middle East receive fewer than 5 inches of precipitation per year, and western US cities such as Phoenix, Arizona receive fewer than 10 inches. Even less annual precipitation is recorded in Cairo, Egypt and in California's Death Valley, one of the driest places in the western hemisphere, with an annual average of about 1 inch. In contrast, places on the islands within the state of Hawaii receive over 400 inches of precipitation per year, and an estimated 523.6 inches per year falls on Lloro, Columbia (Cech, 2003). Naturally, not many people live in Death Valley, but Cairo is a city with a large population, and Phoenix is a rapidly growing city in the United States.

Look at one state in the United States as another example. The State of Nevada is an extreme, as it is the most arid of all the states in the country. We consider rainfall first, in average annual precipitation (inches), for a few locations in the state of Nevada.

Carson City	10.8
Reno	7.5
Las Vegas	4.2

Common sense might suggest that, if water supply is a driving force in location decisions, most people would choose to live in Carson City, but in fact, most of the people in Nevada, about 80 percent, live near Las Vegas, the driest location.[3] For the state, the average precipitation is 9 inches per year, but what is more startling is that Nevada loses 90 percent of this precipitation per year to evaporation and evapotranspiration.

Even though it is arid there are some lakes in Nevada, of course, and they vary in size. What is the 'biggest' lake? Typically one may look at total or active storage capacity to answer this question. In Nevada estimates of some of the largest lakes are:

Lake Tahoe, total storage capacity = 125 000 000 af; 'active storage capacity' = 744 600 af
Pyramid Lake, 1990 contents were 22 170 000 af
Walker Lake 1990 contents were 2 527 000 af

Compare these estimates to the estimated Nevada groundwater stored in the upper 100 feet of saturated valley fill, an amount equal to 250 000 000 af. As noted earlier in this chapter, it is well known that much of the earth's supply of freshwater is under the ground. However, we have incentives to look for groundwater only when we need it, so we simply do not know much about groundwater in many parts of the world. Finding and quantifying the volume of water in aquifers is the job of the hydrologist or hydro-geologist, and requires investment for the research supporting this investigation. Money is needed to test for and measure the presence of groundwater, often simply by drilling test wells, which can be expensive. We return in Chapter 7 to an economist's view of the appropriate manner in which to use develop and use groundwater, which some deem 'mining' an exhaustible resource.

1.2.2 Diversions: Unnatural Moving of Surface Water

The above discussion and examples point out that human beings today often locate where there is very little water. They of course do this because they desire certain locations for any number of other reasons than the supply of water, including the availability of good jobs and wages, a mild climate, and proximity to friends or relatives. Mankind has not been satisfied with the natural or existing location of water supplies. Huge engineering feats have led to diversions of water. These may be small, within a basin, or the diversions may be trans-basin, literally moving water through mountains where the headwaters are located, to lower plains areas. A good small-scale example is the Colorado–Big Thompson Project, which takes water from the headwaters of the Colorado near Lake Granby, pumps it uphill and through 13 miles of tunnel to the eastern side of the Rocky Mountains. The Colorado River obviously has a natural journey westward toward Mexico from the Continental Divide, but via this Project, water is moved to eastern slope cities like Boulder and Fort Collins, Colorado. A larger example is the massive amount of water being transported from northern and eastern parts of California to California's thirsty cities of Los Angeles and San Diego in the south.

Such diversions also lead to conflicts, though here it is not so much one farmer pitted against another, as one entire group of basin users versus another. All the farmers near Grand Junction, Colorado, which is near the western border of the state and well on the western slope of the Rocky Mountains or the 'Rockies', may well agree that the welfare of the farmers in Weld County (on the eastern slope of the Rockies) should come second to their own. Because of this sort of situation some states have water laws that do not allow out of basin transfers (Wilkinson, 1985). Next then, governing withdrawal of groundwater, and most water

Introduction to water resource economics and law 15

withdrawals and allocation in the United States, we must consider, albeit briefly, water laws.

1.3 WATER LAW

People have been fighting over water in the United States for hundreds of years, and in the world, for thousands of years. The fights have continued, though now they mostly take place in the legal setting rather than culminating as violent actions between two or more individuals. Naturally water laws are devised to help prevent conflicts and clearly establish property rights, whenever that is possible. A very basic principle in law is that rights are given to one party or another, and if those rights are violated, penalties may be sought. The risk of a penalty may act as a deterrent to those who may wish to ignore others on a water course. Another way of looking at water laws is that they may at least describe what society agrees are 'unlawful' acts, leading to a moral and legal code of conduct. For example, Nevada state water law defines the act of interfering with a lawfully established headgate or water box as a misdemeanor offense (NRS 533.465; NCL § 7940). Prior to establishing this law, it may have been possible to go to another user's headgate and close it, so that water continued downstream and the culprit might benefit from greater withdrawals for himself. Imagine the conflicts that might have arisen if one farmer or rancher went out and did this to another farmer's headgate.

Even though water laws have led to established and understood property rights, disputes or 'wars' continue (see Brothers, 2002 or Jehl, 2003), and their setting becomes the courts, though avoidance of courts may be causing people and entities to learn to cooperate. In some states, such as Arizona, litigation over water disputes is backlogged in the courts for years and years to come. Some legal disputes now occur between states, water districts, or counties rather than between individuals. For example, the US Supreme Court had to intervene in 1989 in a dispute between the states of Texas and New Mexico. The court ruled that New Mexico had deprived Texas of water that was legally theirs, and the case resulted in an ordered settlement where New Mexico had to pay Texas some $14 million. Other disputes, especially in the western United States, are between Native American Indian tribes, the federal government, and several other possible parties. One of the longest running disputes in the American West involved water in the Truckee River, which has Lake Tahoe as its headwater, flows back east into Nevada, and empties into the terminus, Pyramid Lake. The Pyramid Piaute Tribe sued the Federal government over issues relating to protection of an endangered species at Pyramid Lake. After 50 years in and out of various courts there is finally a settlement called the Truckee River Operating Agreement (see Branson, 1997). The settlement and its relationship to environmental protection is explored in greater detail in Chapter 8.

Water law in the United States can be very complicated. Laws vary across states and there are historical reasons for the tug of war between the states and the federal government. We will come back to some specific legal aspects throughout the book, especially when special topics arise that require careful consideration of relationships between law and economics. This book cannot possibly do justice to water law, but there are some basic themes that all need to understand. I start with one that immediately demonstrates the connection between law and economics, as a 'good' that can be property must be defined.

First, can we characterize the kind of economic good that water is? Water naturally provides value because we use it, as described above. But economists differentiate between private and non-private goods. In his water law text Trelease talks about the 'public interest' and the 'good of the public' when he begins to define water rights and laws. A quick digression is necessary to explain the difference between a private good and a public good.

Private goods involve two properties: rivalry and exclusion. Rivalry essentially means that if I consume the good you cannot. Exclusion means that if I consume the good you are excluded from any effects from that consumption: there are no 'externalities'. Public goods are non-rival goods: one unit of your consumption does not lead to me not getting to consume that unit. Public goods may also involve externalities. A nice city park full of flowers provides benefits to all who drive by and enjoy looking at them. A 'common property' resource also definitely involves externalities, but here the externality can be a dynamic one. For example, as seen in Chapter 7, a common pool groundwater aquifer may encourage present pumping (extraction) at such a fast rate that future users receive no benefits.

Now, is water a private or public good? It can be both, especially if we think in broad terms about water courses and the services they provide, as well as the potential harm from flooding and the public goods aspects of flood control. Property rights can lead to creation of a private good. My private property, such as a home, is protected via property rights established by laws. However, water rights are not typically defined in the same way as the property rights for one's home. Often, water rights are legal rights to use the water – the volume of water itself is not owned by the individual. The distinction may sound trivial, but the key difference is that if one fails to actually use the water, the right may vanish. In contrast, if one wishes to own a second home, but does not visit it for years, the property right associated with that second home remains sound.

When the first non-indigenous people came to the American continent they brought property rights laws with them, mainly from European countries. Many of these were the green and wet countries in western and northern Europe. As territories became states, the state governments began to adopt water laws. Today many states interpret water rights such that the ultimate ownership of these rights resides with the state (e.g. California). In such interpretations individual, 'private' property rights in water are constrained by considerations of what constitutes the 'greater' good for the people in the state or in that region. In other words, just because a water-rights owner has clear claim to an amount of water, this does not, in such states, mean that he or she can do anything she wants with respect to withdrawals. So-called 'third party' effects arise in nearly every water trade. An economist quickly recognizes these as being possible externalities (see Chapter 2). As will be seen below, many water laws require consideration of impacts on third parties before exchanges can be made.

Certain water laws work well in such countries as immigrants to the US came from, but they may not work well in all climates and geographical regions. As settlements on the east coast of the US developed in the late eighteenth century, water laws brought over from Europe initially worked fairly well. However, many parts of these laws are not applicable to dry, arid climates, such as are found in much of the western US. In fact, as a portion of the population migrated westward it became clear that there needed to be another basic set of principles underlying water law. This enormous climatic difference leads to two distinct types of water law found in the United States. First we briefly describe the system brought to the United States from England, known as Riparian Law. English common law evolved from the Justinian Code of Roman Law and French Common Law.

1.3.1 Riparian Common Law

A riparian area is the area adjacent to a surface water body. The Riparian Doctrine is quite old, dating back to the sixth century. Strictly speaking, the doctrine states that water in a river or stream belongs to the public and cannot be controlled by private individuals. However, Riparian Law more or less means if you live in a riparian area and have property there, you also have the right to withdraw and use a reasonable amount of water associated with the property. A riparian owner has a right whether the water is actually used or not, and it may be initiated at any time. But the water use must be made on the riparian owner's land and within the watershed. Some water rights came directly from England to the United States.

For example, in 1632 King Charles I granted Maryland the right to the Potomac River, a point being contested today by the state of Virginia (Jehl, 2003). In the seventeenth and eighteenth centuries, Riparian Law came into play in the United States because of the activities of mills, and conflicts between these and fishermen and navigation on rivers and streams (see Chapter 7 in Cech, 2003, for more discussion). By the mid 1800s Riparian Law[4] in the United States had evolved to include the following features:

1. Riparian water rights included rights to the center of non-navigable streams.
2. Navigable streams are owned by the public and cannot be blocked.
3. Riparian landowners on either side of a river or stream have the right to develop mills and mill dams, and can transfer this right to the buyer of the property.
4. 'Excess' water cannot be diverted from the stream.
5. Injured riparian landowners have to be compensated for injuries.

As the fifth point notes, all riparians are liable to all other riparians for any 'injury'. Another feature of the Riparian Doctrine today relates to the connection between the land and the right to use water. Typically, a landowner may not sell water rights unless the land is also sold. Finally, in many states the Riparian Doctrine has also integrated the principle of Correlative Rights. This principle basically requires riparian landowners to share the total flow of a stream. However, shares may not be equal. Rather, they are often tied to the proportion of use associated with the landowner's waterfront property. This principle is important, as it allows users to share in shortfalls under drought conditions. As you will see below, this is quite different under other legal water allocation systems.

As suggested above, what if you happen to own property, wish to use water, but there is no water adjacent to the land you own? Take a look at a map of most western states or if you are more interested in other countries, pick out a desert there and look at a map of it. In many regions of the world there are very few rivers and lakes, making large land areas inaccessible to a water course, and of course making access for people on those lands impossible. Barring possible uses of groundwater, do you think only those who live near a river or lake should be able to use water? If your answer is yes, you need to consider possible conflicts that will arise. Violence around the world can and does stem from conflicts over water in such situations. With government support, western settlers quickly realized that another water law system must evolve.

1.3.2 The Doctrine of Prior Appropriation

What evolved to supplement or replace Riparian Law is called the Doctrine of Prior Appropriation, developed in many western states in the late 1800s. This type of law again relates to economic activity and the historical development in the West. A major contributor to the settlement of the western US was mining: settlers came in search of gold, silver, and other valuable minerals. In the year 1848 the California gold rush began, bringing thousands of prospectors to the region. Early mining technology involved the use of water in sluice boxes. Miners in this period in the West were largely operating with no system of laws, but an overriding ethic was that the first miner to stake a claim had his or her rights protected.

As early as 1853 water law developed to accompany the very different hydrological and institutional features surrounding mining activities. In that year the California Supreme Court ruled (*Irwin* v. *Phillips*) that gold miners could divert water from a stream under a *priority* system, even if this might injure downstream parties. This ruling established the Doctrine of Prior Appropriation, and nearby states quickly followed. The first recording of the appropriation doctrine in Nevada was in 1866 in the Nevada Supreme Court case of *Lobdell* v. *Simpson* (2 Nev. 274 (1866)). The state of Colorado adopted the concept in 1876, eliminating the use of the Riparian Doctrine there. Essentially, this means: first in time, first in right.

As in many water law systems the user of water under the Doctrine of Prior Appropriation must typically show that water is being applied to a 'beneficial' use. Beneficial uses are often defined in a state's statutes pertaining to water law. For example, in Nevada, watering livestock is specifically declared as a beneficial use (NCL § 7979 – see Nevada Revised Statutes website). Here it is clear that water rights may be defined completely independently from the right to own land, and there are interesting implications of this for economic analysis (see Crouter, 1987).

The checkerboard pattern of land ownership that accompanied the railroad industry's drive to the West aggravated the situation with water. If a settler's homestead was one mile from the water course, but he could build a ditch to get the water to his land, the Doctrine of Prior Appropriation gave that settler seniority in rights to the water from that stream or river, but only if he got there first. This led to the common and easy-to-remember expression mentioned above, first in time, first in right.

As part of the Doctrine of Appropriation many states have language that suggests another principle that can be paraphrased as 'use it or lose it'. This is quite different from riparian water law systems. As is well known, many western miners failed miserably, and eventually abandoned their claims. In doing so, they may well have abandoned their withdrawals and the original uses of the water. These uses ensured basic survival for homesteaders and miners, as well as applying water in various early mining technologies. Those that remained after others left wanted to obtain the abandoned water, leading to the evolution of water law that allowed them to file for rights to it. Unfortunately, as water users became more sophisticated over time, they realized that they could be aggressive and file for abandoned water in many different situations, including those where it was not obvious that the original user had really departed or abandoned their activity. So, while the Doctrine of Appropriation might well have ended physical violence, or at least helped reduce it in the West, many disputes and conflicts, as stated above, are now fought out in the water courts, or at least between officials representing parties in arbitration.

Today one of the more important issues remaining in water law pertains to exactly how water is exchanged between parties. As the above discussion notes, to obtain a water right in a Riparian Doctrine system, one must purchase the owner's land. This is not so under the Doctrine of Prior Appropriation. Many cities today purchase water rights from agricultural and other senior appropriators, even when the seller wishes to keep lands to which the water was originally applied. Most states' governing water agencies may allow this, but will consider the change very carefully. For example, the historical consumptive use of the original user is considered so that downstream effects can be minimized. If the original party withdrew 400 acre feet per year, but 200 acre feet returned to the system, then a city purchasing the water could likely only transfer 200 acre feet per year to its municipal system. Cech (2003) suggests that the monthly pattern of withdrawals that were exhibited historically would also be a consideration in the city's new withdrawals, perhaps leading to exchanges being granted only when the timing of withdrawals under new uses mimics the old pattern of use.

1.3.3 Mixed Water Law Systems

Today most states in the US have no pure riparian or appropriation system. They have mixed systems. Trelease (1979) reports that there are nine states with 'Simon-pure' appropriation law: Alaska, Arizona, Colorado, Idaho, Montana, Nevada, New Mexico, Utah, and Wyoming. This strict interpretation of the Doctrine of Prior Appropriation is also called the Colorado Doctrine.

Ten states (California, Kansas, Mississippi, Nebraska, North Dakota, Oklahoma, Oregon, South Dakota, Texas, and Washington) have the California Doctrine, which is a mixture of both appropriation and riparian, with the first getting most weight. Besides these two groups, the rest of the

50 (31) are mostly riparian, but each state's water laws are more complicated than that because there are systems of 'administrative permits' and rule of capture (groundwater). An important feature of basic Riparian Doctrine states remains that water rights are tied to land, so water rights cannot be transferred unless the land is sold.

1.3.4 Continuing Evolution of Water Law

Despite the predominance of the mixture of the two basic systems above, water law is continually evolving. One of the biggest changes in recent times relates to instream flow protection. The Doctrine of Prior Appropriation does not specifically allow for instream flow rights, but because of environmental concerns and allocation between regions and states, instream flow rights have come into existence. This has not come without a great deal of resistance. For example, in the legal case, *United States* v. *Truckee Carson Irrigation District*, which was mentioned above, the Pyramid Piaute Indian Tribe eventually filed for instream flow protection (see Chapter 8). However, defenders of the status quo vehemently maintained that such claims were barred by *res judicata* and collateral estoppel, which are legal arguments protecting water users from having to participate in legal actions where such actions have occurred before.[5]

Legal issues pertaining to riparian or appropriation doctrines pop up in many of the chapters that follow. We'll also take a look at national, international, and interstate compacts. Some of the laws implied in the compacts override the water laws of states, counties, or municipalities, and especially individuals. This suggests the need to prioritize uses or needs. As will be seen in Chapter 4, for example, a very important thing to note is that many interpret water laws to indicate that the highest single priority for water is the city's need to provide water to its citizens for drinking and domestic needs (Trelease, 1979, implies this in his interpretation of US water law). A few of the many complex federal water laws are considered next.

1.3.5 Federal and Instream Flow Water Rights

Federal water laws stem from several pieces of legislation, including those implied under the 1902 Reclamation Act and the Federal Reservation Rights. The US government can withdraw water from streams passing through lands and take it from private appropriation under the Reclamation and Power Site Withdrawal Act (see *US* v. *Appalachian Power Company*, 311 US 377). Federal authority for protecting navigation (US Army Corps of Engineers) was granted, allowing instream flow in the case, *US* v. *Rio Grande Dam & Irrigation Co.*, 174 US 690 [1899].

Native American Indian rights are well known as they have related to issues over water rights. The Winters Doctrine (*Winters* v. *United States*, 207 US 564, 1908) was the first time the federal government gave Native Americans water rights corresponding to a Reservation Treaty. In this famous case one of the plaintiffs, Henry Winters, and other irrigators were diverting water upstream from the Fort Belknap Indian Reservation in Montana, injuring the tribe. As the date of the Treaty establishing the Reservation was 1888 and the irrigators were diverting in about 1905, the court ruled that the tribes' water rights were senior to Winters' and the others' rights.

At the end of the nineteenth and beginning of the twentieth century, several laws created conflicts between states and the federal government. In fact, though the federal government clearly has powers, in 1935 the US Supreme Court gave states the right to control the use of water right requisition on federal lands (*California Oregon Power Company* v. *Beaver Portland Cement Company*, 295 US 142 (1935)). This law may be the source of huge differences between states that still have the same basic water rights and legal system (Radosevich et al., 1973).

Finally, note that related federal, state, and local laws exist that now involve protection of wetlands areas and riparian zones. These include the federal Clean Water Act, the Federal Power Act, the Endangered Species Act, the Wild and Scenic Rivers Act of 1968, and the Federal Reserved Rights Act.

Many states in the US (Alaska, Colorado, Idaho, Nebraska, Utah, and Wyoming) now also have instream flow programs, which runs contrary to conventional Appropriation Doctrine-based water law in the western United States (see Ranquist, 1980; Dunning, 1989). For example, in Idaho the state legislature provided authority for rental of storage water to augment Lower Snake River flows during the migration of Snake River salmon.[6] Many of the latter instream flow laws are summarized by Lamb and Lord (1992). Next, the role that interstate and international law plays in allocation water must be considered.

1.3.6 International and Interstate Treaties

Several laws relate to allocation between the United States and other countries (Mexico and Canada) and some regard interstate allocation. For example, the Colorado River Compact of 1922 allocates that river's water between the upper and lower basins, and was supposed to establish a framework to allow sharing of the obligation the US has to Mexico across the two basins. The Mexican Water Treaty of 1944–5 is also supposed to apportion water from the Rio Grande, Tijuana, and Colorado Rivers,

Introduction to water resource economics and law 23

guaranteeing at least 1.5 million acre feet of water to Mexico, except in times of drought.

There are a host of interstate compacts in the United States. The best known in the West is the 1922 Colorado River Compact, which was the first interstate compact in the US agreed to for the purpose of allocating water.[7] This compact divided what was thought to be average annual flows in the river evenly between the Upper Basin states (Wyoming, Colorado, New Mexico, and Utah) and Lower Basin states (Nevada, Arizona, and California), such that each basin would receive 7.5 million acre feet. Under the Upper Colorado River Basin Compact of 1948, Arizona is guaranteed 50 000 acre feet a year, and Colorado (51.75 percent), New Mexico (11.25 percent), Utah (23 percent), and Wyoming (14 percent) would split the remaining available supply. But the 1922 Compact is an agreement fraught with problems today.

The area around Las Vegas, Nevada experienced astonishing rates of population growth between 1990 and 2000, nearly doubling the number of people there. By 2002, this area alone uses all of the entire state of Nevada's apportionment of 300 000 acre feet per year. Similarly, the state of California, originally entitled under the 1922 Compact to about 4.4 million acre feet, uses about 5.2 million acre feet per year today. In one sense this thirst for water drew together competing agencies within this area of southern Nevada and even led to cooperation between the states of Nevada and Arizona (see Brothers, 2002), but in another, there is a growing tension over violations of the Compact and competition between states in the Lower Basin, as well as between the newly formed Southern Nevada Water Authority and other water agencies in the state of Nevada. Institutions and arrangements are evolving to replace compacts and laws that are not working well, especially in times of drought. As an example of cooperation, Nevada entered into an agreement with the state of Arizona to store up to 1.2 million acre feet in Arizona's groundwater basins. This is a type of 'water banking', as is discussed in Chapter 9, and the transfer or exchange process is very briefly discussed below. Before leaving the topic of water law, I briefly consider laws pertaining to the allocation of groundwater.

1.3.7 Groundwater Law

Groundwater law is fairly recent because so little was known about groundwater quantities in the past. In fact historically, many areas in the world simply followed the *Rule of Capture*, which states that if a landowner digs a well he can thereafter extract the water from it at will. Such a rule may accompany the *Rule of Absolute Ownership*, which states that landowners have the right to all groundwater beneath their property. As you will see in

Chapter 7, aquifers that contain groundwater may lie beneath several landowners' property, so these rules may cause problems.

At the heart of groundwater laws are the purposes of:

(i) regulating the rate of depletion for aquifers with a low recharge rate, and similarly,
(ii) regulating the rate for aquifers with connections to the flow of appropriated surface water, and for areas with geologic stability issues;
(iii) regulation to protect aquifers from pollution.

As an example, in the year 2005 the state engineer of Nevada will have the power to make rules and regulations affecting extraction of groundwater in areas where, in his or her judgment, the groundwater basin is being depleted (NRS 534.120). As with surface water law, often a state engineer is given very strong powers to adjudicate water rights, and hence affect the allocation of water resources in a given state.

Many groundwater laws also protect aquifers from pollution (including federal law under the Safe Drinking Water Act). As an example, today most states in the United States are quite concerned about aquifers becoming contaminated from leaks from storage tanks and landfills that contain drums of solvents, paint, chemicals, and the like, and they have initiated laws to protect them.

In the United States groundwater law is again somewhat complicated and varies by state because the federal government has largely left policy and law regarding groundwater up to each state.[8] Federal courts have prohibited some attempts to export groundwater across state lines (see *City of Altus* v. *Carr*, 255 F. Supp. 828 (W.D. Tex. 1966), affirmed *per curiam* 385 US 35), using the regulation of interstate commerce to support their decision. Utton (1985) evaluates some cases up to that time, and discusses how the commerce argument is used (see *Sporhase* v. *Nebraska*, 458 US 941 (1982)). The federal government also has the right to prohibit pumping that may cause injury to species adversely affected by dwindling groundwater supplies (see the case of a cave-dwelling fish near a national monument in *Cappaert* v. *United States*, 426 US 129 (1976)).

There are four basic systems of groundwater allocation: (i) absolute ownership; (ii) the reasonable use doctrine; (iii) the correlative rights doctrine; and (iv) the doctrine of prior appropriation.[9] Under (i), the landowner is entitled to deplete all groundwater on his or her property without regard to the interests of other parties. Texas uses this system, and the effects of the system are to encourage rapid pumping rates so that a well owner can 'beat' a competitor in the race to use an aquifer. It appears to be the only state in the US that still uses this legal system to allocate groundwater.

Under (ii) a landowner makes reasonable use of groundwater at times of shortage. Arizona and Nebraska used this system, imposing some limitations on pumping rates and well spacing. System (iii) is practiced in the state of California, and it holds that all landowners have an equal proportionate right to groundwater, necessary to supply their needs, but subject to the requirement that appropriators have not invaded the supply through five years of adverse use.

Finally, under (iv) the system works as the surface water rights system does: senior (the earliest filed claims) wells may pump before junior well rights users may. The nine states in the US that use the Colorado Doctrine in allocating surface water also apply this doctrine to allocation of groundwater.

Another variation on the four systems above involves management of both ground and surface water, or 'conjunctive' management. When aquifers are closely tied to surface water flows, pumping rates can influence the rate of surface water flow, even drying up streams and rivers. As an example of the recent evolution of state law along these lines, Colorado passed its groundwater law in 1957. There it is the state engineer's office that is given responsibility for registering all existing wells and issuing permits for all new ones. Future permits are issued in accordance with the doctrine of appropriation. In certain instances a well owner must fully replace all depletions in surface water supplies caused by his pumping. However, some states (again including Colorado with a 1964 law) deem groundwater that is a tributary to a stream as part of the supply of the stream and distribute it accordingly.

Finally, local laws also play a role in groundwater allocation. These may involve legal procedures for injection, pumping rates, and well spacing, particularly in urban areas where there is concern for water quality and protection of drinking water. Next we turn to the role that economics and markets can play in allocating water resources.

1.4 ECONOMICS, MARKETS, AND WATER RESOURCES

Economics is primarily concerned with relative scarcity and allocating society's wants. Relative scarcity considers both the supply of any resource or commodity, and society's desire for it. A small amount of some commodity or resource is not alone of great interest to an economist. For example, many natural resources of great importance in the 1800s, such as some metals or minerals, may be in very short supply today, but society does not get overly concerned about this situation. Why? Because society's demand for some of these resources, for example copper or tin, has to some extent been replaced with technological improvements that allowed substitution to other resource uses that initially required use of it. A simple example is the replacement of reliance on tin containers with plastic ones of considerable physical strength.

The earlier topic of scarcity is only of interest to an economist when supply is short relative to demand. As you will see in Chapter 2, a key issue is substitution, meaning the ability for humans to switch from one resource to another, as above. For some uses such as drinking, water has no substitute that we know of, suggesting some minimum amount of water be available for survival. Some suggest that 2 to 2.7 liters per capita/per day is the amount required to sustain life (Ensminger et al., 1983). In other uses of water, such as providing ornamental decoration in a fountain, a substitute for water (or here, substitution for the fountain itself) may easily be found. In still other uses, such as growing water-intensive crops, substitution may be difficult, but also possible as technological solutions unfold. A good example might be technological innovations and breakthroughs applied to desalinization.

Economics has been used to assess the benefits and costs of water projects for a long time. In the early 1950s the US Bureau of Reclamation's commissioner, Michael Straus, testified before Congress that 'The second [standard] although not required by reclamation law, is the showing of estimated benefits and costs . . .' (82nd Congress, Second Session, House Committee Print No. 23, p. 11). Many now rely on guidelines set by the Water Resources Council (see WRC, 1983). Water clearly may also have a very critical role in any particular region's economy. Regional economists have attempted to model that role, specifying the role that water plays as an input into industrial, agricultural, and municipal needs (for example, Gray and McKean, 1975).

Economists that apply their trade to water resource issues typically care about only a few things. Probably the most important of these is efficiency. A loose definition of efficiency is that when resources are being produced or used efficiently, there is little or no waste. A rigorous definition is actually specifically called 'Pareto' efficiency: a resource allocation is Pareto efficient when it is impossible to reallocate resources to make an economic agent better off without making at least one economic agent worse off. The work done by those economists interested in efficiency analyses whether particular water resource allocation schemes are indeed efficient, and if not, how could they be improved to move in the direction of efficiency. Economists do not often concern themselves with whether a resource allocation is fair. In the jargon of economics, the fairness issue focuses on the distribution of resources or income. Unfair distributions require consideration of whether society wishes to make decisions to redistribute income, via taxes or transfer payments (for example, welfare or food stamp programs). While studies that examine efficiency in water resource use are abundant, there are indeed few that examine fairness or equity (one exception is by Dudek and Horner, 1981). Partly because of this view, a strong contingent of water economists favor water markets as solutions to many water allocation problems. In fact, research in the early 1990s indicates that water transaction characteristics (explaining just how water is transferred) help explain the price of water (Colby et al., 1993).

Perhaps one of the main messages that economists have delivered regarding water resource allocation all over the world is that true markets need to be developed to facilitate the efficient delivery and transfer of water between parties. The above discussion of water institutions shows that allocation often depends on water rights in a given state, and depends little on economics. Economists have proposed for years that, if possible, water be freely traded (see Anderson, 1967), moving from the lowest and worst, toward the highest and best economic use (for example, Howe et al., 1986a). In simple terms, in a freely operating water market, water could be temporarily transferred (rented) or permanently bought and sold, and water rights could be purchased by anyone willing to pay a given price in the market.

This type of transfer or exchange is indeed happening to an extent today. For example, in the state of Oregon, a conservation group and a cattle rancher have promoted efficiency in a market transaction (see Middaugh, 1995). The Oregon Water Trust leased water rights from a rancher to increase instream flows in Buck Hollow Creek, a tributary of the Deschutes River that provides critical habitat for summer steelhead. In Colorado, the Northern Colorado Water Conservancy District has been encouraging short-term rentals of water since the late 1950s (see Howe et al., 1986b). In California, southern cities were negotiating a deal for more water with farmers in the Imperial Valley, who hold 3.1 million acre feet (maf) of the state's total allotment of 4.4 maf of Colorado River water (Jehl, 2002). Failure to successfully negotiate a deal may result in the loss of about 600 000 acre feet by the end of 2002 because California, as mentioned above, has been overusing its allotment based on the Colorado River Compact of 1922.

By mid-December 2002, officials of the Imperial Irrigation District voted three to two against part of the deal, which involved transferring a small portion of their allotment of water to San Diego County for 75 years. Both the governor of California and the federal government were very concerned this could cause the negotiation to fail altogether (Murphy, 2002). Indeed by the beginning of 2003 the US Department of Interior had already ordered a shutdown on water pumped from Lake Havusu that would have flowed to California. Both the southern California cities and the Imperial Irrigation District were shocked by the decision. They faced a loss of water, totaling approximately 650 000 acre feet (Murphy, 2003b). By October the parties agreed to the negotiation and the Department of Interior immediately relaxed the hold on California's water for the time-being. This time the Irrigation District vote was three to two in favor of the deal.

In other states in the US deals have been worked out by groups such as the Environmental Defense Fund and the Nature Conservancy, to purchase instream flow rights. I also alluded to states working things out between them, as in Nevada and Arizona's exchange agreement. In that agreement the water that Nevada stores in Arizona's groundwater basins is not actually pumped out and used when needed. Instead, Arizona agrees to build up a surplus 'bank' of water underground. Nevada will earn credits for future use and when it wants the water in the future, Arizona will forgo using a corresponding amount of its share from the Colorado River, instead letting this amount go to Nevada, while Arizona instead uses the surplus groundwater.

Despite success stories like these some economic agents are still reluctant to see water markets take hold and there are many remaining barriers to achieving smooth trading and exchanges. First, because of the structure of institutions and laws regarding third party effects, the number of eligible participants in a rental or long-term market may be quite small or 'thin' (Saleth et al., 1991). These authors conclude that thin water markets are the rule rather than the exception, especially in arid regions where streams and rivers are over-appropriated. The problem is nicely depicted in Figure 1.1.

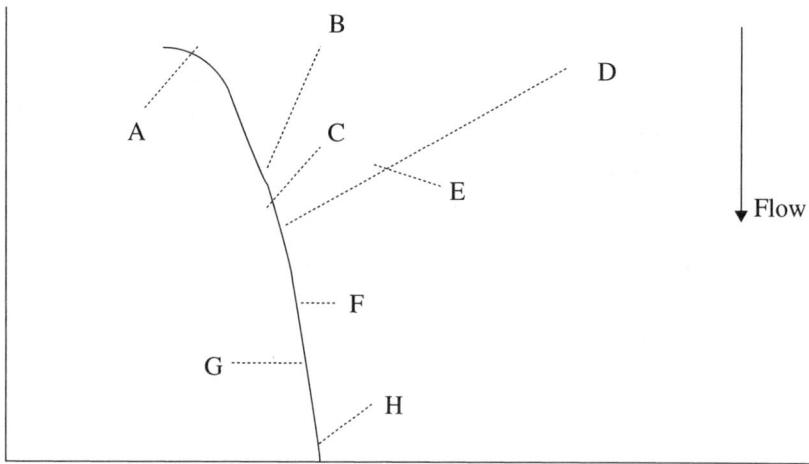

Source: Saleth et al. (1991).

Figure 1.1 Thin water market

In Figure 1.1 the river is the solid line, farmers are indicated by the letters and the dotted lines are withdrawal locations via diversions (ditches). In the figure, the location of the letters roughly indicates where stream gauges can be put to measure flows or diversions. Assume that farmers are certain about the total available supply, that water rights are strictly enforced and defined in terms of consumptive use rather than by diversions. This last definition should eliminate third party effects caused by the absence of adjudicating return flows. But a thin market may still emerge. Why?

Consider a transfer from A to D. If the availability of water at point D can support D's original withdrawal, plus the amount purchased from A, plus E's withdrawal, then the water transfer will not affect E's water right. But suppose that flow near D is only capable of supporting the original rights of D and E, then E will oppose this transfer. This is a case of binding flow constraints. As a solution to preventing transfers in the normal economic setting, Saleth et al. propose a multilateral bargaining game-theoretic model.

Transfers across users, between basins and states, can be very complicated, especially when interbasin transfers do not directly involve a transfer of water rights (see Chapter 4, NAP). Water banks are one innovative way to promote exchanges, but the design of these must be carefully done to try to eliminate transaction costs. Transaction costs, as the name suggests, are economic costs in money and/or time that add a burden to engaging in any economic transaction or exchange. The presence of transactions costs in water exchanges tends to favor the status quo, especially when the initial distribution of water (often in fixed supply) is such that trading is discouraged (see Stavins, 1983).

The executive director of the Idaho Water Users Association has noted that when other parties (such as the US federal government) demand a very large amount of water, fear of permanently losing farms and farmland will prevent willing sellers from materializing (Middaugh, 1995). This same fear of permanent loss has prevailed in the Truckee River Basin, as well as other parts of California and Nevada. Such fear leads to difficulty in getting temporary transfers (short-term leases and rentals) implemented. In addition, because return flows are typically not adjudicated in the legal system of water rights, some marketing schemes create negative externalities on third parties (see Howe et al., 1986a).

In fact, economists may oversimplify things when they advocate 'moving' water from lower to higher economic uses. Some water economists have concluded that the potential for markets has been overestimated, and now recommend slighter modifications to conventional water pricing schemes to achieve efficiency (for example, Griffin, 2000). Many practical issues may arise. For example, as will be seen in Chapter 9, during the reallocations accompanying the California drought and the state's creation of the Water Bank, the state successfully moved water from near the Delta to southern California. However, when some of that water was moved out of a particular ditch system, those remaining users of water in that ditch system may have been harmed. The reason for harm again relates to return flows, on which existing parties may depend, and also on the extent to which groundwater was recharged by the water diverted to southern California.

Not all water moves when people call for it. Lund (1993) reports that between 1981 and 1989 about 17 percent of temporary water transfer applications in California were rejected, and similarly, over 20 percent of Wyoming applications were denied between 1975 and 1984. MacDonnell et al (1994) conclude that removing legal impediments to water transfers will not alone succeed in changing the water resource allocation in the West. They too cite transactions costs and third party effects as further barriers to smooth transfers.

These realities require that exchange schemes carefully consider the timing of transfers, and also the possibility of requiring transfers to factor in consumptive use rather than a total diversion. There remains much work to be done before freely operating water markets become widespread.

APPENDIX

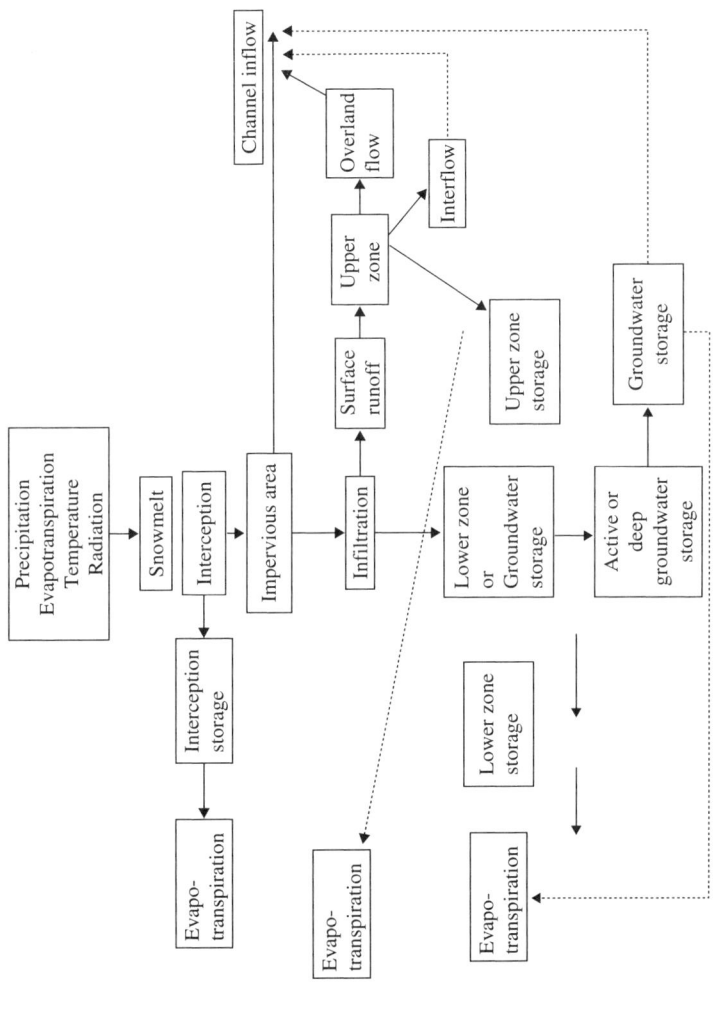

Figure 1-A1 Basic water balance model components

NOTES

1. For example, some scholars believe that the vanishing of Native American tribes near Mesa Verde in Colorado is due to conflicts over water.
2. As I was preparing this book, the NDWP was eliminated by state government administrators. The director at the time was Naomi Duerr and she graciously agreed to guest lecture in my water resource economics class and provide such information to a class. Naomi said that the Nevada state government saw the NDWP as unnecessary.
3. Obviously there are many factors in the decision to locate in one region rather than another.
4. The first court date was in 1827 (*Tyler* v. *Wilkinson*), and it involved protection of a downstream riparian landowners' right to flow. This ruling essentially defined the Riparian Doctrine in the US and set a precedent that water rights are *usufructory* rights, i.e. rights to reasonable use of something without actual ownership of it.
5. Ranquist (1980) considered whether these legal maneuvers could halt instream flow protection and concluded that they would not, though much legislative action would still be required. As it turns out, in many instances in the western United States, he was correct.
6. Several salmon species are threatened or endangered on the Snake and Columbia Rivers. See 1992 Idaho Sess. Laws, ch. 101, § 2, codified at Idaho Code § 42-1763A (Supp. 1993), as cited in MacDonnell et al. (1994).
7. Compacts on the Delaware, Potomac, and Savannah Rivers were adopted earlier, but for the purpose of navigation and fishing.
8. An exception regards federal reserved water rights. As with surface water rights, the federal government has recognized reserved rights for groundwater when resources need protection (see *Cappaert* v. *United States*, 426 US 129 (1976)).
9. See Clark (1977).

REFERENCES

Anderson, R.L. (1967), 'Windfall gains from transfer of water allotments within the Colorado Big Thompson Project', *Land Economics*, **43**(3) (August), 265–72.

Beck, Robert E. (1991), *Water and Water Rights*, vol 2, Charlottesville, NC: The Michie Company.

Branson, T. (1997), 'Better water management goal of operating agreement', *Sierra Sun*, 28 August.

Brothers, K. (2002), 'Water wars', *Urban Land* (September), 110–13, 143.

Carrier, Jim (1991), 'The Colorado: a river drained dry', *National Geographic* **4**, (June), 10.

Cech, Thomas V. (2003), *Principles of Water Resources: History, Development, Management, and Policy*, New York: John Wiley and Sons.

Clark, R.E. (1977), 'The role of state legislation in groundwater management', *Creighton Law Review*, **10**, 469.

Colby, B.G., K. Crandall and D.B. Bush (1993), 'Water right transactions: market values and price dispersion', *Water Resources Research*, **29**(6) (June), 1565–72.

Crouter, Jan P. (1987), 'Hedonic estimation applied to water rights markets', *Land Economics*, **63**, 259–71.

Dudek, D.J. and G.L. Horner (1981), 'Return flow control policy and income distribution among irrigators', *American Journal of Agricultural Economics*, **63** (August), 438–46.

Dunning, H.C. (1989), 'Instream flows and the public trust', in L.J. MacDonnell, T.A. Rice and S.J. Shupe (eds), *Instream Flow Protection in the West*, Boulder, CO: Natural Resources Law Center, University of Colorado.
Ensminger, A.H., M.E. Ensminger, J.E. Konlade and J.R.K. Robson (1983), *Foods and Nutrition Encyclopedia*, Clovis, CA: Pegus.
Frederick, K.D. (1991), 'Overview', in K.D. Frederick (ed.), *Scarce Water and Institutional Change*, Washington, DC: Resources for the Future.
Gelt, J. (1996), 'Consumers increasingly use bottled water, home water treatment systems to avoid direct tap water', *Arroyo*, **9** (March), 1–12.
Goldfarb, W. (1988), *Water Law*, 2nd edn, Chelsea, MI: Lewis Publishers.
Gray, S. Lee and John R. McKean (1975), 'An economic analysis of water use in Colorado's economy', completion report series no. 70, Colorado Water Resources Research Institute, Colorado State University, Fort Collins, CO.
Griffin, R.C. (2000), 'Pricing water as if all resources matter', invited paper, annual meetings of the Western Economic Association International, Vancouver, British Columbia, June 2000.
Heat-Moon, William Least (1999), *River-Horse: Across America by Boat*, New York: Penguin Putman Inc.
Hirshleifer, J., J.C. de Haven and J.W. Milliman (1960) *Water Supply: Economics, Technology and Policy*, Chicago: University of Chicago Press (out of print).
Howe, C.W., D.R. Schurmeier and W.D. Shaw (1986a), 'Innovative approaches to water allocation: the potential for water markets', *Water Resources Research*, **22**(4) (April), 439–45.
Howe, C.W., D.R. Schurmeier and W.D. Shaw (1986b), 'Innovative approaches to water management: lessons from the Colorado-Big Thompson Project and Northern Water Conservancy District', in K.D. Frederick (ed.), *Scarce Water and Institutional Change*, Washington, DC: Resources for the Future, chapter 6.
Jehl, D. (2002), 'Thirsty California cities covet the full glass held by farmers', *New York Times*, national edn, 24 September, A-22.
Jehl, D. (2003), 'A new frontier in water wars emerges in the East', *New York Times*, national edn, 3 March, A-21.
Lamb, B.L. and E. Lord (1992), 'Legal mechanisms for protecting riparian resource values', *Water Resources Research*, **28**(4) (April), 965–77.
Linsley, R.K. and N.H. Crawford (1960), 'Computation of synthetic streamflow record on a digital computer', *International Association of Scientific Hydrology*, (51) 526–38.
Lund, Jay R. (1993), 'Transaction risk versus transaction costs in water transfers', *Water Resources Research*, **29**(9), 3103–7.
MacDonnell, Lawrence J. (1994), 'Water banks in the west', with Charles W. Howe, Kathleen Miller, Teresa Rice and Sarah Bates, report of the Natural Resources Law Center, University of Colorado, School of Law, 31 August, Boulder, CO. Research sponsored by the US Geological Survey, DOI, # 1434-92-G-2253.
Meyer, A.F. (1915), 'Computing runoff from rainfall and other physical data', *Transactions of the American Society of Civil Engineers*, **79**, 1056.
Middaugh, Jim (1995), 'Water marketing: promise or peril?', *Northwest Energy News* (Summer), 19–23.
Murphy, Dean E. (2002), 'California vote threatens deal on Colorado River', *New York Times*, national edn, 11 December, A-23.
Murphy, Dean E. (2003a), 'Pact in West will send farms' water to cities', *New York Times*, 17 October, A-1, A-16.

Murphy, Dean E. (2003b), 'In a first, US officials put limits on California's thirst', *New York Times*, national edn, 5 January, A-1, A-14.

Radosevich, G.E., K.C. Nobe, R.L. Meek and J.E. Flack (1973), 'Economics, political and legal aspects of Colorado water law', completion report no 44, Colorado Water Resources Research Institute, Colorado State University, Ft. Collins, CO.

Ranquist, H.A. (1980), 'Res Judicata – will it stop instream flows from being the wave of the future?', *Natural Resources Journal*, **20**(1), 121–47.

Reisner, Marc (1993), *Cadillac Desert*, New York: Penguin Press.

Revenga, C. et al. (2000), 'Freshwater systems: pilot analysis of global ecosystems', World Resources Institute, Washington, DC accessed at http://www.wri.org/wr2000.

Saleth, R. Maria, John Braden and J. Wayland Eheart (1991), 'Bargaining rules for a thin spot water market', *Land Economics*, **67**(3) (August), 326–39.

Stavins, R. (1983), *Trading Conservation Investments for Water*, New York: Environmental Defense Fund.

Trelease, F.J. (1979), *Water Law*, 3rd edn, St. Paul, MN: West Publishing Company.

Utton, A.E. (1985), 'In search of an integrating principle for interstate water law: regulation versus the market place', *Natural Resources Journal*, **25** (October), 988–1004.

Vaux Jr, H.J. (1986), 'Economic factors shaping Western water allocation', *American Journal of Agricultural Economics, Proceedings Papers*, **68** (December), 1135–42.

Wilkinson, C.F. (1985), 'Western water law in transition', *University of Colorado Law Review*, **56**, 317.

Wines, Michael (2002), 'Grand Soviet scheme for sharing water in Central Asia is foundering', *New York Times*, national edn, 9 December, A-14.

WRC (US Water Resources Council) (1983), 'Economics and Environmental Principles and Guidelines for Water and Related Land Resources Implementation'.

SUGGESTED FURTHER READING

Anderson, T.L. (1983), *Water Rights: Scarce Resource Allocation, Bureaucracy, and the Environment*, San Francisco: Pacific Institute for Public Policy Research.

Committee on Western Water Management, Water Science and Technology Board, Commission on Engineering and Technical Systems (1992), *Water Transfers in the West: Efficiency, Equity and the Environment*, Washington, DC: National Academy Press.

Saliba, B. and D.B. Bush (1987), *Water Markets in Theory and Practice: Market Transfers, Water Values and Public Policy*, Boulder, CO: Westview Press, p. 269.

Sax, J. (1970), 'The public trust doctrine in natural resources law: effective judicial intervention', *Michigan Law Review*, **68**, 471.

Weil, S.C. (1908), *Water Rights in the Western States*, San Francisco, CA: Bancroft-Whitney, p. 974.

WEBSITE

http://www.leg.state.nv.us/NRS/NRS-533.html Chapter 533, Adjudication of Vested Water Rights, Nevada Revised Statutes.

2. Review of basic microeconomics applied to water resources

In this chapter the student can be introduced to or review material on basic microeconomic theory (see Varian, 1999, for an intermediate undergraduate text). The chapter may be skipped by more advanced students familiar with micro theory, but there are some fun applications to water problems for all readers. Microeconomics deals with the theory of behavior and markets for small agents, usually consumers, or firms that produce goods.[1] Often a farm is treated as a small firm. It is convenient, as well as natural, to discuss consumer theory and producer theory separately, but a few principles overlap. First, almost all of the discussion below presumes that water is a private good. Near the end of the chapter, we will re-examine the assumption that water is a private good, and revisit some of the important cases where water might be a public, or at least non-private or quasi-public, good. As a preview, remember from Chapter 1 that the return flow phenomenon, though not equivalent to 100 percent of the original amount of water in the river, suggests that many users can use part of the same unit of the good, which violates rivalry, a key property of private goods.

2.1 CONSUMER THEORY

The key consumer theory concepts that tie water use to consumption are utility maximization, preferences, budget constraints, marginal rates of substitution, demands, and price elasticities. Consumers often exhibit predictable patterns of behavior. You may wake up every day at about the same time, and begin a routine that might be followed each day, or at least on working days. You might regularly buy non-durable goods of the same brand, or at least category. As you will see, consumption or demand for water can be treated in some ways just as any other good for which individuals have a demand, but there are some interesting features of water that cause the need for slightly different treatment.

Practical or applied economists are concerned with how well economists can predict a person's or a market's consumption behavior. For example, if one three-person household with 2000 square feet uses 0.5 acre foot of water per year and another similar, even essentially identical three-person household uses 1.5 acre feet per year, we would like to be able to explain and predict these different demands for water. An economist will search for reasons why the second household uses an extra acre foot, as that is quite a large quantity of water. Similarly, if the market for water provided by agricultural water rights holders experiences a surplus, we would like to know what is causing this. We start with the utility or satisfaction that each consumer receives from one or more goods.

2.1.1 Preferences and Demand Functions

'Utility' is more or less the satisfaction of consuming a good or service. A philosopher at the turn of the eighteenth century, Jeremy Bentham, even thought that utility could be measured cardinally, as 'utils'. Bentham proposed the idea that one could measure the number of utils the first drink of cold water gave on a hot summer day, and considered that a second drink might yield fewer utils, and in introductory economics this example is used to explain diminishing marginal utility. More importantly, his utilitarian school of moral philosophy espoused the thought that the highest social good was the greatest happiness (utils) for the greatest number of people.[2] The implication is that cardinal utils can be measured and added to determine the greatest good.

Today the heart of modern consumer economics is the indifference curve, which indicates ordinal preferences for goods and services rather than cardinal ones. Modern economists mostly do not rely at all on cardinal measurement of utility, but the indifference curve has to meet certain properties for it to be helpful in predicting behavior. First, economists believe that indifference curves are downward sloping. Careful theorists avoid the terms diminishing marginal utility in favor of 'diminishing marginal rates of substitution'. Try drawing your own indifference curve, assuming that there are only two goods so that you can do this on a two dimensional graph. What is its shape and slope and what does this tell you? The marginal rate of substitution is the technical name economists give to the slope of the indifference curve. It tells us the rate of tradeoff between two goods at a variety of combinations of consumption.

Let the good Y on the vertical axis be a composite good that represents all other goods. Which of the illustrated indifference curves U_0 or U_1 makes more intuitive sense? Well, we have already noted the obvious point in Chapter 1: with very low quantities available, water becomes quite precious to us because we may literally die without it. The steepness of U_1 as we approach the quantity of water indicated by W_0 shows that an individual is willing to give up large quantities of Y to get a small amount of additional water. As the slope of U_1 is vertical at W_0 the amount of Y the individual is willing to give up approaches some infinite amount. As more water is obtained, the steepness is reduced, indicating less willingness to give up Y to get water.

A utility function, $U = U(Y,W)$, must take some specific functional (mathematical) form that leads to the shapes of the indifference curves. These in turn have shapes we expect conform to how we observe people behaving. As an example, though we observe some people in society with a strict diet consisting of one type of food (say, spam), most people are observed to eat a mixture of types of foods. As prices of spam decrease, holding other things constant, some utility functions would require consumers to eat only spam. Economists therefore make assumptions about the properties the utility functions have to have in accordance with commonly observed behavior. To consider this carefully, imagine what it would indicate about substitution if the specific mathematical form for the utility function was linear, as in $U = a + bY + cW$? (Hint: solve for Y to allow the function to be graphed in Y and W space).

Clearly rates of substitution vary above, depending on how much water is available and what the intended use is. Substitution is a very important concept when examining types of water use and the tradeoffs that consumers make. Why?

The student new to economics should practice what she or he has learned above. Try to show differences in the willingness to trade water for all other goods using the steepness of two indifference curves such as the ones above. There are no substitutes for all water consumed by living things, at least for that part pertaining to drinking purposes. Human beings drink things other than water all the time; still, as noted in Chapter 1, soft drinks, juices, beer, and wine are all products made using water as the primary ingredient. Still, for other purposes, such as watering the lawn, is there a substitute for water? And is it possible that some individual households would answer this question with a yes, while others might answer no?

To answer these questions we next have to go beyond looking at shapes of indifference curves that tell us about individual preferences. Though the reader is probably thinking about it, we have not yet said a single thing about the market price of water, or income, or any other specific good.[3] All economics involves consideration of resources, and for any household that consumes goods, the budget they have available is an essential determinant in modeling behavior.

Preferences can be coupled with the simple fact of economic life: scarcity means we all face a budget constraint because most goods are not free to us. Let *Inc* be income. A budget constraint for n goods (X) can be written as:

$$Inc \leq P_1 X_1 + P_2 X_2 + \ldots + P_n X_n \tag{2.1}$$

The above constraint holds as a strict equality if there are no savings and all income is spent on the goods consumed. As an inequality, equation (2.1) suggests that not all income during some period of time is exhausted on the goods above; it can be saved. To simplify things below we assume equation (2.1) holds as an equality. In addition, most simple presentations assume that the budget constraint is linear. In reality, as will be seen in Chapter 4, there may be kinks in the budget constraint, or non-linearities.

The two things you have learned about so far, utility functions and budget constraints, can be put together to yield the demand function for goods and services. If there are n goods and services, the demand function for good X is of a general form, with arguments as prices of all the goods, and income:

$$Q_x = f(P_1, P_2, \ldots, P_n, Inc) \tag{2.2}$$

where the prices of the other goods indicate the importance of the prices of substitute, as well as potential complementary goods. Note that other factors can influence demand, such as tastes, family size, and so on. How is this solution for the demand function obtained? The answer comes from solving a constrained maximization problem. To see how, let's return to the simple two-good world in Figure 2.1. First we need to solve a budget constraint such as (2.1) for Y, as that is on the vertical axis in Figure 2.1. With only the two goods Y and X, we obtain:

$$Y = \frac{Inc}{P_y} - \frac{P_x}{P_y} X \tag{2.3}$$

The first term on the right-hand side (RHS) is the vertical intercept and the second term is the slope parameter (the ratio of the prices) and the other good X. This is nothing more than the formula for a linear relationship: $Y = a - bX$, and it is graphed by a straight line, such as in Figure 2.1.

We expect that demand is a function of the prices of all goods and services and income. Again, tastes or preferences help exactly specify the demand function, and we have not specifically introduced these above, but when it is time to do empirical work, we usually do so. What other factors might affect a household's water demand? The household members' tastes for a garden, or big lawn with green grass, would certainly matter, as would their preferences for freshly washed cars, and whether each member desires a shower every day.

In a two dimensional world, the price for a good is plotted against the quantity demand of that good and the 'law' of demand holds: the quantity

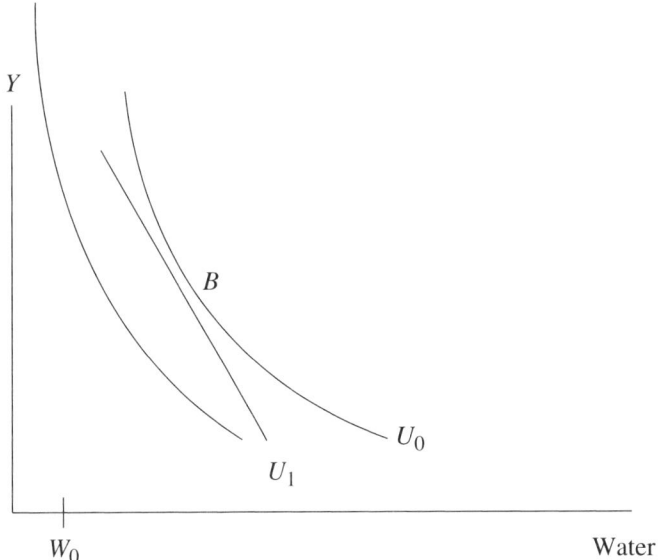

Figure 2.1 Indifference curves, budget lines and utility maximization

demanded of X or water (W) falls as the price of X or W rises, other things being held constant. Demand may or may not be derived above to yield a linear demand function, but Figure 2.2 shows the simple linear demand for water as a function of P, here the market price of water.

Figure 2.2 shows demand for water with the usual negative slope. Just how much water demand falls with a price increase is another specific issue. For those new to economics, it may be unusual to see the independent variable on the vertical axis, as you are probably used to $y = a + bX$ being graphed so that the dependent variable y is on the vertical axis. Convention in economics is to place P as above, but the functional relationship is as it appears in equation (2.2): we recognize that Q_w is expected to be a function of the independent price.[4]

How economists 'put together' utility functions and budget constraints to derive the demand Q_w is not voodoo or magic. The concept of constrained optimization is formally: maximize an individual's utility, subject to the budget constraint. This problem can be solved using the Lagrangian multiplier method, which relies on calculus. For that reason the utility function is typically assumed to be a smooth function that is twice differentiable. Students with a background in intermediate microeconomic theory will know that by introducing the budget constraint into the graph of preferences, and looking for a tangency point with the highest indifference curve

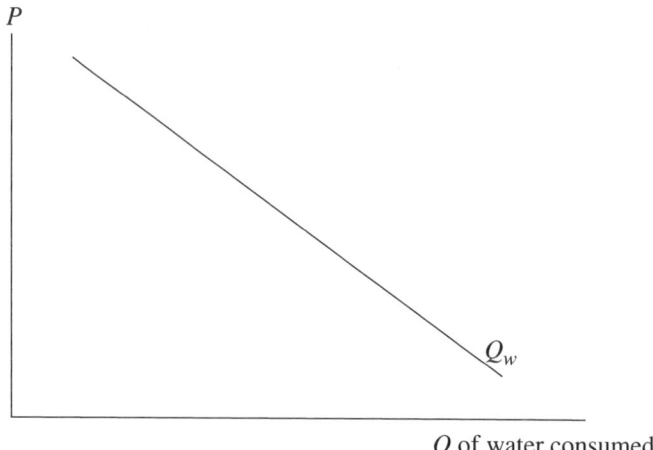

Figure 2.2   Water demand

(the most northeasterly in the quadrant), the optimal combination of two goods can be found for any combination of observed prices. I leave this as an exercise for review, but this is addressed in a slightly more advanced fashion below, specifically applying the Lagrangian approach.

Applied economists are interested in more than the abstract microeconomic theory that leads to being able to draw a particular demand function. They are typically charged with actually having to produce results that can be used in policy making. Any firm or policy-making body would be delighted to know the shape and location of a demand curve for a good or service because this knowledge provides them with information about what will happen in response to price changes. As a good specific example, consider the issue of the sensitivity of water demand to price, or price elasticity. Imagine how much a water utility would like to know their customer's price elasticity of demand for water.

2.1.2   Price Elasticity of Demand

A simple definition of the price elasticity of demand (ε) is:

$$\varepsilon = \frac{\%\Delta Q_w}{\%\Delta P} \qquad (2.4)$$

where %Δ indicates a percentage change in the variable. Recall that we wish to develop percentage changes because these are unit-less measures of sensitivity, and equation (2.4) provides a good approximation to this for ranges defined by any pair of prices and quantities. Though the slope of the demand function given by the derivatives is negative, we consider the absolute value of elasticity in our discussion. The simple idea is that if the price elasticity of demand is, in absolute value terms, a sufficiently 'big' number, then the demand is fairly sensitive (elastic) to price. What, then, is an elastic number?

More formally, one can replace the delta operators in equation (2.4) with derivative symbols and find values of elasticity for extremely small changes, or essentially point estimates of elasticity. A more formal definition or formula then becomes:

$$\varepsilon = \frac{dQ_w/Q_w}{dP/P} \qquad (2.4b)$$

Equation (2.4b) tells us the elasticity at any point on the demand curve. Elasticity is characterized as being inelastic when $\varepsilon < 1$, suggesting that in some portion of the demand function quantity is not very sensitive to price changes. Unitary elasticity is, as it sounds, when $\varepsilon = 1$, and consumers have an elastic response when $\varepsilon > 1$. Note that if a demand function is linear, elasticity will vary throughout the range of prices and quantities. This can be seen in equation (2.4b) rather easily, because a linear function has constant slope, but the weights of Q_w and P will change, changing the estimates of the elasticity at different locations on the demand function.

Sellers of a good are extremely interested in knowing whether the quantity demanded at some range of prices is inelastic or elastic because it tells them what will happen to their total revenue collected when price increases or decreases. Naturally, if nothing else changes, a seller hopes that *TR* will increase when price increases, especially if they have some market power and wish to raise price. But it can easily be shown that *TR* will increase with a price increase only if $\varepsilon < 1$. Table 2.1 summarizes relationships between elasticity and total revenue.

It is left as an exercise to demonstrate the relationship between total revenue and elasticity (see exercise 2.4). The key question that I hope is in the reader's mind is, exactly how does a policy maker or seller know what

Table 2.1 *Effect of a price increase on total revenue*

Elasticity (ε)	Total Revenue (*TR*) will . . .
$\varepsilon > 1$	Decrease
$\varepsilon = 1$	Stay the same
$\varepsilon < 1$	Increase

elasticity is? The answer is that they (someone at least) must estimate just what the market or individual's demand function looks like, using data. The shape then determines the elasticities at various quantities demanded. For that investigation we apply statistical analysis. In economics this kind of statistical investigation is known as econometric analysis.

Finding empirical estimates of elasticity
Suppose we wish to find out what the demand function for water looks like for consumers in the city of Albuquerque, New Mexico.[5] How would one go about the investigation? At a minimum, accurate data are needed that vary in some fashion for both the quantity of water used and for a host of prices. This creates a problem for water analysts because of the fact that while many consumers may desire or demand different quantities of water at a given price, they may all face only one 'market' price for that water. As Chapter 4 will illustrate, the rate that customers pay within a city or municipal region may be fixed at one point, and it may not vary much over short periods of time.

To do statistical analysis, one simply must have more variation than described immediately above. Variation in the data can be obtained in two or three ways: econometricians can do a cross-sectional, time series, or pooled cross-section and time series study. In cross-sectional data, data are collected that vary in many dimensions across the units of observation, that is if individuals or households are the units of observation, a good portion of them must face different prices and demand different quantities. If that is not the case, one may look for data from a cross-section of cities and towns where the rates or prices do differ in each city or town. The different locations may provide the needed variation in prices, but, again, unfortunately for the statistician, water rates for water customers in different locations are still often very similar, as will be seen in Chapter 4.

A time series is, as it sounds, a series of data that vary over time rather than across space or cross-sectional units. Cities probably have a local government or private water utility in charge of setting the price of water. This price probably changes over some period of time, again yielding the needed variation in the data. Given enough change over a readily observable period of time, it may be possible that the time series provides the needed variation to trace out a demand function and hence, the associated elasticities.

Finally, data could be collected over time and across cities or locations, and 'pooled' together to yield a larger data set that might vary in both a cross-sectional and time dimension. For example, one might obtain prices and quantities of water consumed for a 15 year period, for each of ten cities in a region or country. Pooled data have been frequently used in assessing the elasticity of demand for municipal water because such a data set can overcome the limitations in using data on residential households in one geographical area, or for a relatively short period of time.

Of course, no matter what type of data one seeks, the 'raw' data must first be obtained and put into a form usable by a statistician or econometrician, and this is no trivial matter. As many of us who do empirical research have to remind our colleagues who do not build up a data set, 'data do not grow on trees'. Think about how you would go about getting price and quantity data for water users. First, if a local water utility or government agency is in charge of billing residential customers, this entity probably has some data that is useful. Whether they do or not will depend on whether exact quantities of water consumed by each customer are measured. Often, they are not. Cooperation with such an agency is essential. Even when 'raw' billing record data is obtained, it often has to be put into the kind of shape that is required for use in statistical analyses. It cannot have missing records and most often needs to be systematically ordered to allow something like a simple regression to be estimated.

Once one has the data, it may be a matter of what some call 'curve fitting' to find the best functional form that fits the data well. Demands must be estimated using data by first introducing a source of error that turns observed price–quantity combinations into a predictable relationship. In other words, we add an error or residual term to our deterministic equation in recognition that Q_w is a random variable. A very simple way of doing this is to add an error term (μ) to the systemic or deterministic demand relationship:

$$Q_w = \alpha - \beta P + \mu \tag{2.5}$$

After introduction of the random term, Q_w will now follow the distributional assumptions in accordance with the choice of the probability density function underlying μ. For example, we might simply assume that μ follows the normal distribution, and in that case it can be shown that the demands, Q_w, follow this normal distribution also, though with a different meaning. The estimated parameters (estimates of α and β in the simple model above) in any relationship help to define the intercept and slope of a curve as in Figure 2.2, and depending on whether the form is linear or nonlinear, an elasticity formula finally emerges. For example, suppose that demands are linear, as in equation (2.5), then the slope is a constant equal to β, but elasticity changes throughout the range of points on the linear demand function, because the points Q_w and P are always different.

Using an empirical model, economists can collect the relevant and needed data and estimate the elasticity of demand for water or any other good, allowing prediction of response to price changes. Such estimation is

44   *Water resource economics and policy*

crucial to formulating water policy that is an effort to use pricing to change behavior, such as to get water users to conserve residential and industrial water. If price is to be an effective tool, then customers have to cut back considerably on their water use when water rates are raised: it remains an empirical issue as to whether water demand is indeed sensitive to water prices. In Chapter 4 we will return to, and more fully delve into, the issue of setting water prices and rates, and how rate setting might be related to elasticity, responsiveness, and the ability of water managers to use pricing to achieve conservation.

In the next section a very simple discussion of the producing firm's choice is provided, which has parallel features to the above discussion because of the similar use of the constrained optimization approach.

2.2   PRODUCTION

For the producer, the key concepts introduced will be output and/or profit maximization, technology and isoquants, marginal rates of technical substitution, cost constraints, cost minimization, supply functions, and factor demands.

2.2.1   Isoquants

There are many firms that we can think of that relate to water, but firms that actually produce water are somewhat complicated, so it is best here to think of a single farmer as a firm, producing a single output (one crop). I will assume away the farmer's important real-world problems, because an actual farmer faces tremendous uncertainty[6] and issues relating to uncertainty and risk in production are dealt with in Chapter 6. Here, making very simple assumptions, we can simply think about water as an input into a production process. Now, instead of indifference curves that indicate preferences, we want to look at isoquants, which illustrate technological relationships between inputs. A graph such as Figure 2.3 can be constructed that maps out combinations of two inputs and resulting outputs. These again show the tradeoffs, but this time between inputs used in the production of a given level of output (O_0), say labor (L) and capital (K).

In Figure 2.3 the curves that are convex to the origin look just like indifference curves, but they are called isoquants, showing possible combinations of K and L that can be used to yield a given level of output. As before, with consumer theory, the producer cannot simply produce whatever she likes. She is constrained again, this time by a cost level, shown above as the straight line labeled Cost. The goal is again to maximize

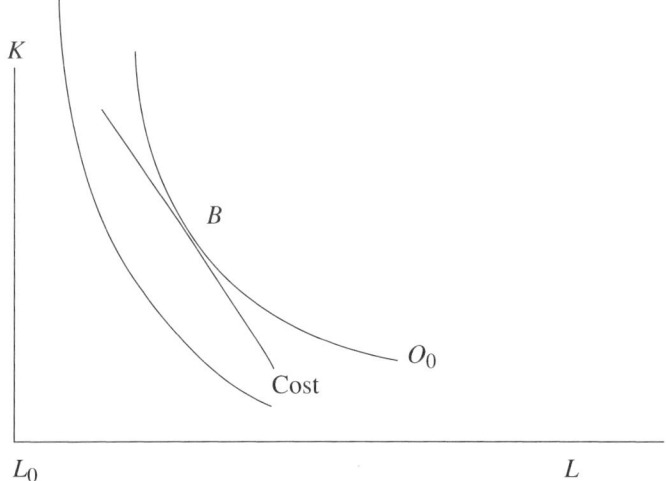

Figure 2.3 Isoquants

output, but constrained by the amount of cost or expenditure the producer has to spend on the inputs.

Naturally there are many inputs that might be considered as contributing to output, depending on what activity is under consideration. For example, suppose a farmer can grow alfalfa using water and another key input, say land. There are of course many more inputs a farmer in the real world deals with: the farmer's labor, his or her capital (tractors, etc.), fertilizers, and even some beyond his or her control, such as weather. Typically, economists focus on two key inputs to allow simple diagrams like the above to be viewed, or perhaps more believable, one key input is considered along with a composite of 'all other inputs'. Just how the farmer then bundles together the inputs to produce a level of crop output is mainly answered by considering the cost-constrained technology that determines input output relationships, so in a sense the isoquant and the optimal input choice may be something an engineer can deal with, but that is not the whole story. Beyond the technology, farmers have to consider market economic forces and decisions or they will quickly be out of business.

Technology may or may not vary from farm to farm, but there is no expectation that all farmers will face the exact technology, as the quality of land or soil that any farmer has can vary. As with the consumer example, the farmer's real problems of crop production cannot be considered without looking at some market prices, but in this case there are several prices to examine. First, the farmer may sell his output, again say alfalfa, for the price per unit that alfalfa will bring. Typically economists assume that farmers are quite competitive and hence, face a given market price that they cannot influence individually. In other words the farmer cannot dictate the per ton price of alfalfa. This output price per unit (P) multiplied by the quantity of alfalfa delivered to the market yields the farmer's total revenue ($TR = PQ$).

Formally, the inputs (k) have prices (P_k) also, leading to the cost or budget constraint the farmer faces:

$$C = P_L L + P_w W \tag{2.6}$$

Here, the left-hand-side variable is the same as the 'Cost' budget line above. Again graphically, solving for L and placing the resulting linear budget constraint on the graph along with isoquants, we can then find the optimal input mix given the prices and technology that farmers face. For the remainder of the book it is useful to examine two optimization problems that surprisingly tell us almost everything that the above solution could: constrained cost minimization and profit maximization. In addition, below we will drop the assumption that the only way a farmer views water is as an input into the production of a crop. I expand on this idea in Chapter 5.

2.2.2 Cost Functions

It may seem difficult for some to grasp at first, but all technology can actually be reflected in looking at a firm's cost function, which can be graphically represented by mapping the cost in dollars against the units of output (Q). Generally we say that $C = f(Q)$, but it is an empirical question as to what mathematical form this function takes.

A simple proportional cost function assumes that $C = bQ$, or perhaps with an intercept, a, it assumes the form of $C = a + bQ$, but economists often assume that cost functions are cubic in Q. Try graphing such a cubic function. It should look like the one in Figure 2.4, but ask yourself, what would it look like if it were quadratic instead of cubic?

We begin with the concept of fixed costs, which equal a capital stock (FC). What does the intercept imply in the cubic cost function above? It implies that even if $Q = 0$, $C = a$, and if $a > 0$, then there are costs even without producing a single thing. Once one decides to go into business, there is a cost that is assumed fixed, defining the so-called 'short run'. For example, the firm, property developer, or farm purchases water rights and land. The corporate farm must invest in and build storage facilities, farm equipment, and water delivery mechanisms such as pipes, pumps, and perhaps water quality treatment facilities. Even a small farmer must purchase land, or at least rent it, with some fixed term of lease. Whether the

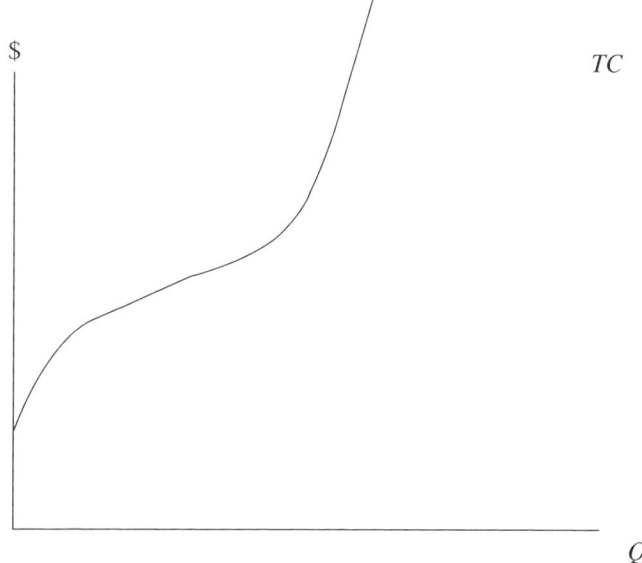

Figure 2.4 Typical total cost function, with assumed cubic functional form

agent exceeds all expectations for output or quits producing anything at all, it is stuck with those fixed costs.

Next, economists note that fixed costs can be spread out over output. Average fixed costs equal FC/Q. These are going to be falling because FC stays constant and Q increases over the range of output that is feasible for the supplier or producer. The more Q the firm produces, the more it can 'spread out' the fixed costs per unit.

Probably the most important cost concept to economists is that of marginal cost, equal to the cost of producing an additional unit (MC). Economists are very committed to the idea that agents should operate at the margin, even suggesting that fixed costs are 'sunk', and that sunk costs should be ignored in most decision making. It took years and years of communication between economists and airline managers for airlines to begin operating with this principle driving flight scheduling and staffing decisions. Key airline industry economists convinced managers that once the airplanes were purchased and leasing contracts for gates at airports paid, the airlines that have market power should price the ticket with the balance between marginal revenue and marginal cost in mind. Put simply, it is better to fly the plane if marginal costs and perhaps just a tiny bit of other costs are covered by the price than to leave it on the ground. Clearly, this

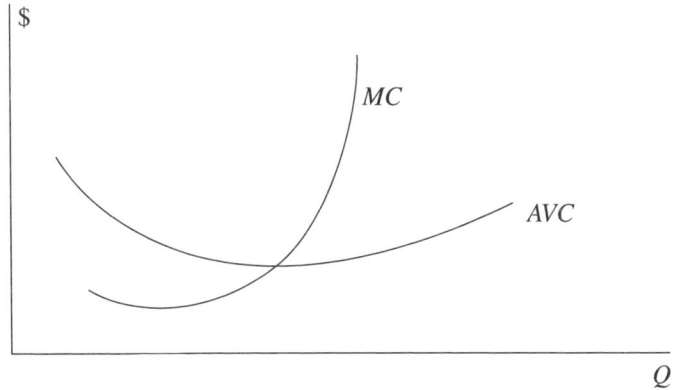

Figure 2.5 Average and marginal costs

marginal cost pricing scheme is potentially different from other possible pricing schemes, especially when an alternative scheme tries to set prices to cover fixed costs every time a flight is scheduled and seats are sold on that flight. Harkening back to a corporate farmer with some market power, imagine what would happen if they tried to operate so as to drive crop prices up to cover fixed costs.

Another important cost concept here and elsewhere in the book is that variable costs can be averaged to get average variable costs (*AVC*). These are the total variable costs averaged over the units of output, or *TVC/Q*. We can bring together all of these short-run concepts in one graph, Figure 2.5.

In Figure 2.5 *MC* must intersect *AVC* at the minimum point on the *AVC* curve because as marginal costs fall, so must *AVC*. As *MC* rises, so must *AVC*.[7]

We have said nothing so far regarding the period of production. In the long run there are no fixed costs. Firms can exit the market. The exiting firm will eventually get out of its commitments, sell off assets used in production and, thus, fixed costs will fall to zero.

On the positive side of course, successful firms can expand. Economies of scale are the economic advantages that firms receive by getting bigger, and producing more, which again is a long-run concept. Not all firms receive these, but if they do, the economies of scale are reflected in declining average costs. If *AC* are declining, then *MC* are falling even faster than those average costs.

The concept of scale economies may be quite important to providers of water, especially when domestic water must be treated for water quality problems. It is common in the United States for small rural water utilities to have difficulty providing treated water, and this part of their costs may fall with increasing size. We will come back to supply issues in Chapter 4, and some specific water quality issues are considered in Chapter 3. Next, a slightly more advanced discussion of some of the above concepts is provided. Mastering this material is beneficial to all who wish to read new research on water economics, which often appears in more technical journals.

2.3 A SLIGHTLY MORE ADVANCED MICROECONOMIC THEORY REVIEW

In this section the use of calculus is very simple, but necessary. Those who are rusty may wish first to review some rules of differentiation in their introductory calculus book. Several problems are outlined below, starting with the consumer's constrained optimization problem. The idea in constrained optimization is simple: we would like to maximize an objective function in one direction, but at the same time, minimize the influence of any binding constraint.

2.3.1 Constrained Optimization and the Consumer's Problem

Let the consumer be able to choose two goods with income constrained at level Y. The above intermediate theory showed that he will maximize utility (U), which indicates the structure of preferences for the two goods x_1 and x_2, subject to a budget constraint.

$$\text{Max } U(x_1, x_2) \text{ subject to } Y = P_1 x_1 + P_2 x_2 \tag{2.7}$$

Budget exhaustion is assumed here, but it doesn't have to be assumed in more complicated problems.

We typically assume that U is continuous and twice differentiable so that the calculus can be used with no suspicion that solutions are intractable. We use the Lagrangian multiplier method to derive the first-order conditions for a maximum (or minimum).

$$L: U(x_1, x_2) + \lambda[Y - P_1 x_1 - P_2 x_2] \tag{2.8}$$

Consumers choose the variables x_1 and x_2, and the λ is considered a choice variable also, so that its derivative gets you back to the budget constraint. To solve this problem first take the partial derivatives of L with respect to the choice variables and set them equal to zero. Why? Because these first-order conditions yield the first step in finding a maximum.

As a simple analogy think of looking for the top of the hill, or in minimization problems, the bottom of the valley. Suppose you are looking for the top, but can't see. How would you know, if you were blindfolded, where you were in relation to the top or summit? Not wishing to fall off the mountain, a cautious person would probably take a tiny step in each direction. Finding an uphill gradient would convince that person that he was not at the very top of a hill. Taking a sufficiently large number of steps in any direction, one might find that no more gain can be made. The slope at just the precise summit is zero, as it would be at the maximum for a function. Still, one could not be positive of being at the top. By only finding a downhill move was possible, a person might be quite tempted to believe the top had been reached. If indeed, it can be ruled out that the hill does not have several local peaks, then the mountaineer's 'false summit' problem can be avoided and the maximum is reached.

The constrained optimization problem above is in fact more complicated than is the mountain top search method described because it is as if the person has to find two optimal positions at once. This two point problem has been described as a saddle point: one can imagine viewing a saddle from the side, and again from the front of the horse. In one direction we want to find the top, but in the other direction (from the side) we may be interested in finding the bottom. The relevance to the above problem is that the consumer ideally wishes to maximize satisfaction from consumption, but wants the budget constraint to be the least binding it can be.

Proceeding to take the first derivatives with respect to all choice variables (a person is assumed only to be able to choose the amounts of the goods to consume) we get:

$$L_{x_1}: \partial U/\partial x_1 - \lambda P_1 = 0 \qquad (2.9)$$

$$L_{x_1}: \partial U/\partial x_2 - \lambda P_2 = 0 \qquad (2.10)$$

and we also need to consider the effect of the constraint here by taking the derivative with respect to the lambda term. This is L_λ: Note that this derivative gets you the constraint back again in the form:

$$Y - P_1 x_1 - P_2 x_2 = 0 \qquad (2.11)$$

The importance of this third derivative is that it is a way of recognizing that if the constraint were relaxed by one unit, the optimization problem would change. Just how it changes is exactly a function of the budget (or any) constraint. In words, the third derivative answers the question, what influence does it have on the problem if you can relax the constraint by one unit?

In the above context one asks, how much would it change the utility maximization problem if one had another dollar of income?

Rearranging terms, we see that:

$$\frac{\partial U/\partial x_1}{\partial \lambda} = P_1 \quad (2.12)$$

This relationship says that the dollar value of the marginal utility, or the marginal benefit or value (in monetary terms), equals the price of the good. If, as in competitive equilibrium, we assume that price is reflecting marginal cost, then marginal benefit equals marginal cost at the optimum consumption level. If there is only one price, then all consumers set $MB = MC$, so there are equi-marginal benefits in choosing consumption of the goods.

We use the three equations to solve by substitution for the equilibrium demands x_1^* and x_2^*. A specific example is perhaps the best way to show this. So, let $U = x_1 \cdot x_2$ which imposes a structure on preferences. The Lagrangian problem can be set up as above. Then, you have for the first-order conditions: $X_2 - P_1 \lambda = 0$, etc., and you end up with specific forms for the demand functions. If you attempt to solve this problem, you should get $x_1^* = Y/2 P_1$ and $x_2^* = Y/2P_2$.

In the next section we take up a new concept that turns out to be quite important in determining the value of a good such as water. The value of a good or service is the net benefit that good or service provides, known as the consumer's surplus.

2.3.2 Consumer's Surplus

Consumer's surplus (net benefit and hereafter CS) for price or quality changes tells us the value an individual has for those changes, or in the case where the change is detrimental to the user, the economic loss to the individual. Formally, CS is the difference between an individual's maximum willingness to pay for a good (WTP) and the good's observed market price. The standard measure of CS is called Marshallian consumer's surplus and it is the area under a demand curve. For a price change from p^0 to p^1 it is given by the formula:

$$\int_{p^0}^{p^1} Q(p, Y) dP \quad (2.13)$$

As a simple example, suppose again that the demand function is linear. Then the *CS* for a price change can be approximated from the formula for the area of a triangle. If the price of water falls, for example, the consumer benefits and the net benefit can be measured this way. Alternatively, a price increase reduces consumer's surplus. Here is a very simple example.

Consider the demand for a lake for a person who wishes to go fishing. Recall that any point on the demand function tells us the maximum willingness to pay a person has for a good. A lake, however, has no functioning market. Suppose we could nevertheless find out the relationship between a person's maximum WTP and trips taken to the lake, the relevant quantity here. With no price for the trip, the total consumer's surplus would then be the area under the entire demand function.

Sometimes it is possible to specify demand to be a function of quality. For example, suppose a household has a demand for water to drink, but that pollution can diminish the value of the water to that household. If the function can be specified we might envision a graph of the relationship between levels of quality, say dissolved oxygen, and demand. Then, the area under this function can be found, as in the above example of a price change.

Another way to examine quality changes is to treat the quality change as a demand shifter and to take the area under the curves in two states of quality, and subtract off the difference, or probably you are getting the area for a trapezoid, depending on the shape of the demand function.

The Hicksian measures of consumer's surplus

The Marshallian CS measure is criticized because it includes the effect of an income change (a complicated set of price changes can sometimes affect nominal, though not real, income). It is thought that if income effects can be removed, a better measure of welfare can be calculated than one that includes those income effects. Another way of putting this is that we would like to know only the true value of a price reduction, not the value of having more disposable income. The Hicksian measures of exact consumer's surplus are the compensating variation (CV), the equivalent variation (EV), and two other measures of compensating surplus for quality changes. These measures are found by examining the areas under the Hicks-compensated demand functions, which hold real income or utility constant. More advanced students may wish to consider and review the definitions of these in terms of either the conditional indirect utility functions, or the expenditure function in consumer theory.

Finally, it should be noted that the measure of value for a consumer may be somewhat different if uncertainty is introduced into the problem. Chapter 6 considers demands, under uncertainty, and the resulting welfare measures. Next, as promised, we consider aspects of water that may veer away from the assumption that water is strictly a private good.

Other chapters in this book examine the value of water, or its consumer's surplus. However, Diana Gibbons introduces both the elasticity and consumer's surplus concepts in a chapter of her book and it is worth briefly examining the consumer's surplus estimates here. Assuming that price elasticity is constant over some interval, Table 1.2 of Gibbons's chapter reports on the household WTP, or consumer's surplus, for a 10 percent reduction from a baseline of average use for various cities. She reports summer and winter estimates which range from $17 to $105, which isn't very meaningful at first because one does not know for what exact quantity changes the consumer's surplus is calculated. I make some assumptions to see what these consumer's surplus estimates might mean in standardized terms or usage units. One such unit is in terms of 100 cubic feet per month, or ccf, and another is the acre foot.

Converting acre feet to cubic feet, we get: 1 af = 43 560 cubic feet, or dividing by 100 = 435 ccf.[8] So, using ccf units, average water consumption levels in the late 1960s and 1970s are approximately 5.30 ccf to 16.43 ccf, or about 0.012 af per month, at the low end, which is 0.146 af per year. At the high end one arrives at a figure of about 0.453 af per household, per year. This indicates that average consumption is somewhat less than 0.5 acre foot per household, which might be a bit low for a desert city such as Reno, Nevada. Nevertheless, for a 10 percent reduction from this baseline level Gibbons might be looking at about 0.045 of an acre foot. Translating then, the marginal value for this amount of water, reported by Gibbons, is about $28.

The conclusion would be that the average consumer in Gibbons' cities would be willing to pay $28 rather than face a reduction of about 0.045 acre feet per year, or perhaps per season. If we could extrapolate linearly in consumer's surplus terms, or in other words convert smaller changes to larger units, we would be talking about a much larger sum of money as consumer's surplus. Unfortunately, we cannot make this simple extrapolation because of some of the assumptions apparently made by Gibbons.

2.3.3 Production: The Supply Side for Water

Water also might have a value to a producer of a good or service. In production, we can consider several other optimization problems including cost minimization, constrained maximization of output, and maximization of profits. Let profits be denoted as $\Pi = TR - TC$. Suppose the producer is facing perfect competition and that price is given to him. He does not set the price. This still might be true in some farming markets. If so, then the producer can sell his output (Q) at price P, and then $TR = P \cdot Q$.

To maximize profits, again we can look at the first-order conditions. Take the derivative of the profit function with respect to Q and set this equal to zero. We just get $MR = MC$, but since marginal revenue is the price, we have price $= MC$.

But let's suppose that total costs are $TC = \omega L + rW + \gamma K$, where each first term is the price of the resource being used, labor, water (W), and capital (K). We can just take the first-order partial derivatives again, and the farmer can only choose how much water, labor, and capital to use. Now, we have:

$$\Pi = P \cdot Q - [\omega L + rW + \gamma K] \tag{2.14}$$

But we know that $Q = Q(L, W, K)$ also. There is some technology for this, which imposes a shape on the isoquants (tradeoff curves between inputs). The partials yield the familiar:

$$P \cdot \partial Q/QL - \omega = 0 \tag{2.15}$$

$$P - \partial Q/\partial W - r = 0 \tag{2.16}$$

$$P - \partial Q/\partial K - \gamma = 0 \tag{2.17}$$

These just say that the resource is to be used up until this marginal product value is equal to its marginal cost. For water, the marginal revenue is the price, so $MPP_W = r$, the marginal cost of water, which could be the rental rate. Use water until the value of the marginal product of the water equals its rental price. Why? Common sense. If a farmer, for example, is getting more value from the last unit (acre foot) of water that she uses than it costs her, then she applies some more. Otherwise, she doesn't.

Now, many farmers think that because of their long-established water right (see Chapter 1), there is a *zero* marginal cost of the water. But if there is a market in water, they are wrong because they may be able to rent or sell that water to someone else rather than apply it to their crop. If there is no established market, and there is no opportunity cost to the water, they are probably correct. All of this begs the question though – what is the marginal product of water? The 'shadow' value of a resource comes from the production problem.

2.3.4 Producer's Surplus and Shadow Value

First, all intermediate level students should know that the area between two prices under the supply curve yields the producer's surplus. Let the *MC* curve be the supply curve, which is true for a farmer with a fixed 'plant'. The area u in Figure 2.6 shows the total producer's surplus at the initial price P^0. It is the difference between the price in equilibrium and the minimum price at which the producer is willing to sell output.

Review of basic microeconomics

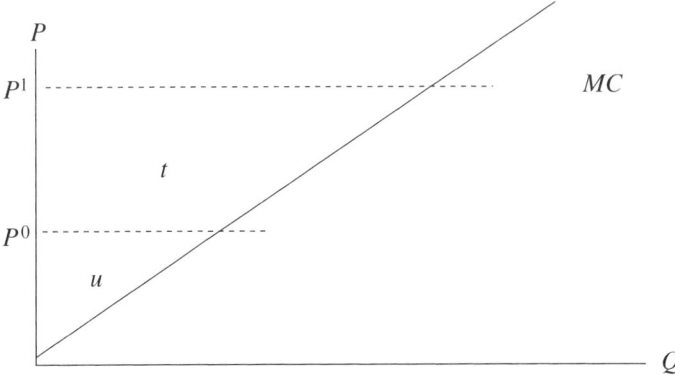

Figure 2.6.   Producer's surplus for a price change

If the price rises from P^0 to P^1, then the area t is the increase in the producer surplus for the price change. The total producer's surplus or quasi-rent is $(u+t)$. This is the farmer's willingness to pay for the privilege of selling output at the higher price.

We can also examine producer's surplus as the area between two factor prices above the supply curves (not demand curves) for two inputs, plus the 'quasi-rent' to the producer. This just means that, with a price increase, some of the rent goes to the producer, but some also goes to the input supplier.

Another way to look at this considers the value of the resource to the production problem.

$$\text{Max } Q(L,W,K) \text{ subject to the constraints, } L = L^0, W = W^0, \text{ and } K = K^0 \qquad (2.18)$$

The Lagrangian here is written:

$$Q(L,W,K) + \gamma[L^0 - L] + \lambda[W^0 - W] + \delta[K^0 - K] \qquad (2.19)$$

And the first-order conditions here give the marginal product of the resource equal to the Lagrangian multiplier. For the water variable, we have $\partial Q/\partial W = \lambda$, and the latter is the value to production of having one more unit of the resource, say one more acre foot. So, in equilibrium for the farmer the shadow value, or the value of having the constraint relaxed, is equal to the marginal product. A low marginal product means there is a low shadow value for the resource. Next we consider market aspects of water.

2.4 THE MARKET FOR WATER, AND PROBLEMS WITH EFFICIENT ALLOCATIONS

As stated earlier in the chapter, economists focus on efficiency over most other considerations. It is also fair to say that even politically liberal economists such as Paul Krugman, who writes a column for the *New York Times,* would believe that markets are generally a good thing. Markets do accomplish many allocation goals, at least under certain conditions. Many economists are especially fond of the notions that accompany two welfare theorems. Theorem 1 says that under certain assumptions, a competitive market equilibrium yields a Pareto-optimal allocation of resources. To understand this first theorem, first we consider the Pareto criterion.

2.4.1 Pareto Criterion

The following is based on the ideas of the economist, Vilfredo Pareto (1848–1923). To begin, assume there are two goods of importance, x and e, and let there be two preference bundles:

$$A^1 = (x^1, e^1); \quad A^{11} = (x^{11}, e^{11}) \tag{2.20}$$

For the group as a whole, a^1 is preferred to a^{11} if for every individual i, $U_i(a^1) \geq U_i(a^{11})$, and for at least one individual j, $U_j(a^1) > U_j(a^{11})$. In other words, one person strictly prefers a^1 and all others prefer it, or are indifferent. Meeting the Pareto criteria necessarily involves a unanimous vote, at least if one lives in a democratic, voting society.

The second welfare theorem says essentially that, given 'appropriate' initial distributions of resources, a competitive market can arrive at a Pareto-optimal allocation of resources through exchanges in production and consumption. What are the key assumptions made in such theorems?

1. Complete description of property rights for all goods and services.
2. Perfect knowledge and information for both the present and the future.
3. Atomistic participants – all agents are too small in size to affect the market.
4. No transactions costs.

The first of these assumptions implies that all benefits and costs in consumption and production accrue only to the agent that consumes or produces the goods. This rules out consideration of water as anything except a pure private good. The second implies that one can know the value of water, or more specifically its value or worth, everywhere, now and in the future. It also rules out uncertainty. The fourth rules out the use of water lawyers, as, in the absence of transactions costs, any exchanges in water can be done between two willing parties at no prohibitive cost.

2.4.2 Market Failures and Water

In their classic paper on the relationship between water rights and economics, Burness and Quirk (1979) laid out the basic model for efficient allocation of water. They concluded that 'in the absence of freely transferable property rights, the appropriative doctrine (see Chapter 1) leads to an allocation of water that is inefficient, but alternative schemes for assigning water rights are generally not incentive compatible with a competitive environment' (p. 27). The authors place at least part of the blame for this failure to reach efficiency on the fact that flows are inherently random. In addition, most water economists immediately see that water allocation involves externalities in consumption or production, or both.

2.4.3 Externalities in Consumption

An externality may occur when the actions or levels of consumption or supply of one agent affect the utility or production outcome for another agent. Whether an externality occurs or not depends on a variety of other issues, including whether there is compensation paid for the external effect. The potential for externalities turns out to be quite important in the agricultural use of water because what an upstream agent does can greatly affect the activities of the downstream agent. Imagine an extreme example, where an upstream agent takes all the water from a small stream, leaving none for the party below. Less extreme situations occur in most water settings.

Now, what if there is an externality? The economist can easily show that inefficiencies arise in the presence of an externality, leading to poor allocations of water. Say the externality is only working one way, with $U_B = U_B(x_1, x_2, U_A)$. This says that B's utility is a function of A's utility. One could also formulate this so that B's utility is a function of the amount of x_1 or x_2 that A consumes, but that is a different set up.

What if we maximize $U_B = U_B(x_1, x_2, U_A)$ subject to the usual constraint? Then, the first-order condition implies that:

$$\frac{\partial U_B / \partial x_1}{\lambda} = \left(1 - \frac{\partial U_B}{\partial U_A}\right) P_1 \qquad (2.21)$$

This is obviously quite different from the tangency condition for the consumer allocation problem above because it involves the term in brackets, which is absent in the first consumer problem considered earlier. We could, in any case, now consider water as being good x_1, and without the externality we can see that its value is the marginal benefit per dollar to the consumer. This is only one value determination, but clearly, the extra term in equation (2.21) is what leads to the inefficiency, unless it is somehow accounted for in the determination of prices that agent B pays.

2.4.4 Discounting: The Farmer, Water Value, and Uncertainty

As mentioned above, the hydrologic cycle involves precipitation and weather, which are typically treated as random variables. One can indeed say that flows of water are inherently uncertain, at least over some time period. We will say much more about uncertainty, the future, and water in Chapter 6, but it is worth mentioning something very important here in relation to farm production. In the production problem above we considered a farmer as an agent interested in water as an input, who makes decisions in the current period knowing everything he needs to know. One output was produced, which was a crop, and profits were maximized from the sale of that crop. This is just not the real problem that farmers face today, especially in the arid western United States, but probably, anywhere in the world.

As we will see later in the book, there are connections to the future, and much uncertainty that a farmer must cope with, but here we consider only one aspect. The modern farmer is not only a supplier of a crop. In the long run he or she may supply another precious commodity to other agents: water. The West has a long history of cities and industry forcefully or peacefully obtaining water from farmers. Today the owners of senior water rights are often second or third (or more) generation farmers. They face a long-run decision: at what point might water become so valuable that it pays them to give up farming alfalfa and sell water, rather than continuing to farm and hold onto their water? This decision involves the future and uncertainty, for no farmer can really know the future price of water.

For this reason current water markets are possibly distorted by speculation in water as an investment good. Recall that a farmer in an appropriative rights system may risk abandonment if she discontinues water use, so application to a beneficial use must continue, more or less, up to the point at which the sale of the water is made. One simple, though not entirely satisfactory, way of dealing with the future is to 'discount' it. As it is not assumed that the reader knows about discounting, I explain this below.

Discount rates and present value

Economists are always fond of discussing tradeoffs and trading the present for the future is yet another possible tradeoff that individuals face. Many consumers are more than happy to purchase items now rather than wait for the future, and often purchases are made at rates of interest that lead to a much greater total purchase price than had consumers been able to pay cash at one point in time. The willingness of an individual to trade the present for the future indicates several things about the individual's preferences for having something now, or in the present, versus in the future. Part of what determines this overall preference is called a 'time preference'.

The rate at which society as a whole is willing to trade the present for the future is called the social discount rate. This is not to be confused with the rate at which some central banks loan money to member banks, and note that it is quite possible that one individual may have a personal discount rate that diverges from society's. The discount rate also factors in technological changes that occur over time. We use the discount rate to calculate the present value of a good that has benefits (or costs) for many years into the future. The easiest way to see how this works is, in fact, to start backwards, by looking at a future value of something one has now. I simplify by first considering interest rates, rather than discount rates.

Suppose you have $1 at present. How much will this $1 be worth one year from now? We usually answer this question by considering the annual rate of interest, simplifying here by not considering complicated formulas for compounding. So, if the rate of interest is 10 percent, you can easily calculate the future value (one year hence) of the $1. You know it is $1.10. How did you get this? You implicitly or explicitly used the following formula:

$$FV = PV(1 + r) = PV + rPV \qquad (2.22)$$

If I ask how much the original $1 is worth two years from now, again using the simple 10 percent annual interest rate, most can easily answer again, $1.21. But again, you can use the basic formula:

$$FV(2) = FV(1)[1 + r] = PV(1 + r)[1 + r] = PV(1 + r)^2 \qquad (2.23)$$

This question and answer game can be continued for year three, four, etc., and many readers already know that for the simple interest rate we are considering, the future value in any year t then is simply determined by:

$$FV(t) = PV(1 + r)^t \qquad (2.24)$$

Now, we can reverse this entire analysis and ask a different question: what is the present value of $1.10 presented to us next year, and so on, for each year. The answer is found by rearranging our formula to solve for the present value (PV):

$$PV = \frac{FV(t)}{(1+r)^t} \qquad (2.25)$$

Intuitively, you know you would probably not want to accept $1 a year from now if you lent it to someone. You would like to get the $1.10 because if you don't, you have ignored the opportunity cost of using the $1 yourself, this year.

Discount rates are rather different from interest rates in theory, but the present value of some future value can be arrived at in the same fashion as the above, substituting a true private or social discount rate for some narrowly focused interest rate. As mentioned, there may be divergences between private and social discount rates, and when this happens, there may be problems and conflicts in evaluating private and public tradeoffs and decisions. Discount rates, especially social ones, do not simply reflect the opportunity cost of money related to forgone interest rates. As the above suggests, they encompass far more than that (see Portney and Weyant, 1999). To see their importance, consider two extremes, when the discount rate is zero, and when the discount rate is infinity.

Clearly, a discount rate of zero in the above formula for PV leads to the denominator being 1, as $1+0=0$, and 1 raised to any power is 1. Thus the PV is equal to whatever the FV is. This means that the present and the future are evaluated in equal terms. Some argue that the optimal social discount rate should be zero because of ethical and other reasons: the present generations need to consider the welfare of future generations, and treat it in the same way as our own.

In contrast, consider the case where the discount rate is infinity. Clearly, any infinite number in the denominator makes the right-hand side zero, meaning that the present value of anything in the future is worthless. Again, a private individual might have good reasons for thinking that the future is worth nothing to him or her. For example, a selfish person who does not care about anyone else, and who has found out he will die soon, might have no value for the future. Social discount rates of infinity might arise when all of society does not value the future.

This begs the question, how does society set or 'know' the discount rate? To answer this, let's look at a graph of society's consumption today, versus the level of consumption tomorrow (Figure 2.7). This presumes that we can somehow graph society's indifference curve for present and

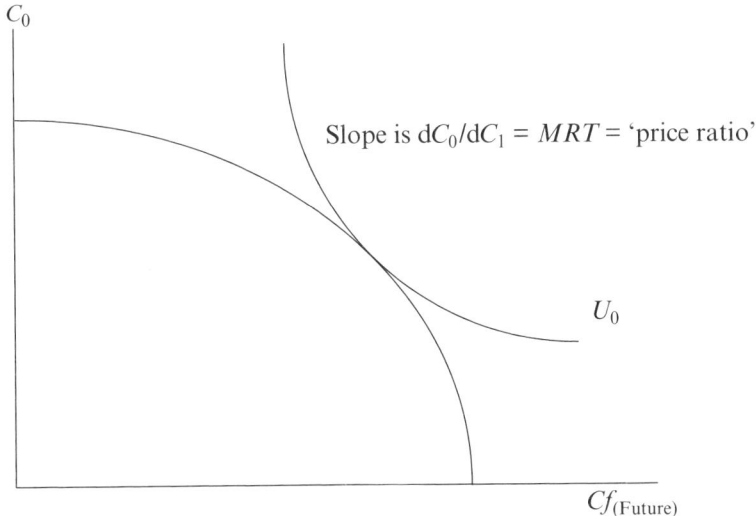

Figure 2.7   Present (C_0)/future tradeoff and the discount rate

future consumption, which involves various assumptions. But assume that these two goods can be treated like any other two goods we normally evaluate, and that society as a whole is capable of arriving at the rate at which it is willing to trade one good for the other.

This makes most sense when we think of members of society casting votes that involve investment of public funds with public benefits, particularly when expenditures in the present might be postponed to allow future generations funds to make future purchases. A very simple, and real, example arises when considering rolling over social debt, versus paying off that debt now so that future generations do not have to pay it.

In Figure 2.7, dC_0/dC_f = the slope of the indifference curve and the production possibilities curve, the *MRS* and the marginal rate of transformation *MRT* respectively. The optimal consumption point is at the tangency point above where *MRS* = *MRT*.

The slopes above are equal to the discount factor, β. The discount factor is determined here by two things: the consumer's rate of time preference (willingness to defer consumption) and the productivity of investments (the marginal productivity of capital). In other derivations, the factors that contribute to an explanation of a social discount rate are more complex (Arrow, 1966), and new ideas for special situations such as evaluating climate change, including 'gamma' discounting, have been proposed (for example, Weitzman, 1998).

Discounting in practice

The United States government does in fact use discount rates to evaluate public projects. The Office of Management and Budget (OMB) considers the appropriate discount rate for use by all federal agencies that must evaluate present and future benefits and costs, and then it issues a memorandum informing these agencies of the rate to use. These agencies include the Environmental Protection Agency, the Departments of Interior and Agriculture, and others. Obviously, the OMB does not have the ability to actually calculate the slope of the social indifference curve above, so how does it set the rate? OMB uses signals provided by other rates of interest to make a judgment. They factor in the inflation rate, so that a 'real' discount rate can be used, and they examine trends in long-term interest rates such as those on 30-year mortgages, 30 and 50-year bonds, and treasury bills. The rationale is that these long-term interest rates indicate society's willingness to trade future for present consumption, at least with respect to durable goods purchases. These rates obviously do not reveal all aspects of the tradeoff.

Discounting and uncertainty

Finally, we return to the farmer's problem about knowing the future, or more appropriately, society's uncertainty. Discount rates are often varied to reflect the amount of uncertainty there is about any project's benefits and costs. For example, one rationale for high discount rates is that the future is so uncertain that the benefits received at some distant point in the future are highly suspect. Some say, then, that a project with highly uncertain future benefits or costs should be discounted with a higher discount rate than other projects that have more predictable future benefits and costs. This line of thought is interesting when one contemplates large-scale water projects such as dams or wetlands restoration projects. As you will see in Chapter 9, many dams were built in the 1960s without careful consideration of the role that siltation would play in the future. As the years have passed, many dams' true benefits are being questioned because the silt that has accumulated at the base of the dams makes the future safety of them extremely uncertain. Had economists known of this uncertainty at the time the projects were being evaluated, they might have wished to increase the discount rate so that the benefits, most of which would accrue in the future, would have received less weight. The next section considers another topic at least partly related to uncertainty, focusing on whether water markets work, and particularly the role that transactions costs play.

2.5 WATER MARKETS AND TRANSACTIONS COSTS

Transactions costs are simply added direct and indirect costs that are associated with making any transaction. They may be easily observable and tangible, such as attorney's fees required in making legal arrangements, or they may involve great amounts of time, which some individuals may not notice. In water allocation decisions transactions costs are currently quite formidable. Because of inefficiencies associated with the institution of water many economists have promoted the development of active water markets, where water could be freely traded. Some federal legislation, such as the Reclamation Projects Act of 1992, at least tries to promote market reallocations.

Efficiency in the allocation of water has already been demonstrated for some states' water projects (see Howe et al.'s (1986) description of this in Colorado), but Colby et al. (1993) see water rights as a heterogeneous commodity, resulting in the need to expect different prices and arrangements depending on regional differences. Such differences can in turn lead to market inefficiencies, or at least difficulties in arriving at transactions. To demonstrate their concern about prices Colby et al. simply regress prices for 95 water transactions in New Mexico on some variables, finding that the priority of the water right has a positive, significant effect on the price, while the quantity has a negative effect. The seniority or priority effect may indicate a different perception of senior water rights than junior rights, making markets work less well with varying seniority of rights.

Howe et al. (1990) note that several types of costs may prevent buyers and sellers from completing a transaction or transfer of water. There can be physical barriers and costs, transactions costs, and costs associated with risk or uncertainty. Physical costs include the loss of water in transfer, the costs of transport, and possible pumping costs. Transactions costs include search costs, brokerage fees, public administration costs, research study costs, and externalities or impacts on third parties. Risk/uncertainty-related costs include those related to whether the water authority will actually allow a given volume to be transferred.

Howe et al. (1990) provide a small bit of evidence (nine cases were studied) on water transfers in Colorado and the transactions costs associated with them. The transactions costs range from a few cents all the way up to about $15 000 per acre foot. The authors tried to obtain information on court costs, as well as other administrative costs, to assess a relationship between these and other variables, such as whether one or more parties opposed the transfer. Their results are merely illustrative because of the small number of observations, but suggest a course of research to be pursued by other researchers in the future.

2.6 CONCLUSIONS

This chapter has offered a basic review of microeconomic theory concepts, and the student probably has many questions about applications in water at this point. It is fair to say that the answers to some of these questions require a lifetime of work, but it is hoped that others will be answered in later chapters. For example, the careful reader has figured out by now that the 'value' of water varies according to the type of use it is put to, and that there is no reason to think that the value will be equal in all places or in all uses. It is up to the mechanisms in a well-functioning market over the long run to arrive at equilibrium solutions that allocate water to its highest and best use in any region of the world. The discussion above may well cause one to question whether the most basic and simple assumptions often made in microeconomics are valid when it comes to the demand and supply of water.

SUGGESTED EXERCISES

2.1. Have all the graduate students in class do the teaching of the intermediate-level microeconomic presentation of consumer and producer theory.
2.2. Sketch out the preferences implied by the following mathematical form for a utility function with two goods, x_1 and x_2: $U = \alpha (x_1 x_2)^\beta$.
2.3. Consider the consumer's uses of water. Can economists examine preferences for water in all domestic uses using one indifference map? Why or why not?
2.4. Show that the relationships between price increases, elasticity, and total revenue hold. Hint: use the definition of elasticity in equation (2.4b) and the fact that $TR = PQ$.
2.5. Show that a double log demand function ($\ln Q = a + \ln P$) has a constant elasticity of demand throughout the range of prices and quantities. Hint: review your calculus of logarithmic functions and combine this with the definition of elasticity in equation (2.4b).

NOTES

1. Sometimes water resource issues are in the domain of the macroeconomist, for example, when two countries or states dispute water allocations between them.
2. Bentham lived from 1748 to 1832. See Varian (1999, fn. 2), p. 560.
3. For further comparison of the 'composite' good, a more advanced textbook is required.
4. The story goes that one of the early economists, Alfred Marshall, sent his draft book manuscript to the printer, but the printer switched the labels when setting the type, and

it was too expensive to correct the error. As an exercise, what difference does it make if we graph the same function, but switch the labels on the axes?
5. In Chapter 10 we consider the issues of estimating the demand for water in a very different country such as Kenya or Pakistan.
6. An interesting and amusing statement that reflects the difficulty for a farmer is that 'there is no such thing as good weather for a farmer'. The idea relates to uncertainty of weather, the farmer's planting decision, expected output, and the impact of market forces on the eventual selling price. Put simply, if weather is poor, expected output falls and reduces profits. If weather is good for all sellers, supply increases, but market prices may fall, again reducing profit.
7. Those wanting a numerical exercise to facilitate understanding of this point can find one in any good principles of economics textbook.
8. As you will see later in the book, ccf is a common abbreviation for hundred cubic feet.

REFERENCES

Arrow, K.J. (1966), 'Discounting and public investment criteria', in A.V. Kneese and S.C. Smith (eds), *Water Research*, Baltimore, MD: Johns Hopkins University Press for Resources for the Future, pp. 13–32.
Burness, H.S. and J.P. Quirk (1979), *American Economic Review*, **69**(1) (March), 25–37.
Colby, B.G., K. Crandall and D. Bush (1993), 'Water right transactions: market values and price dispersion', *Water Resources Research*, **29**(6), 1565–72.
Gibbons, Diana C. (1986), *The Economic Value of Water*, Washington, DC: Resources for the Future.
Howe, C.W., D.R. Schurmeier and W.D. Shaw (1986), 'Innovative approaches to water allocation: the potential for water markets', *Water Resources Research*, **22**, 439–45.
Howe, C.W., C.S. Boggs and P. Butler (1990), 'Transaction costs as determinants of water transfers', *University of Colorado Law Review*, **61**, 392–405.
Portney, P.R. and J.P. Weyant (1999), *Discounting and Intergenerational Equity*, Washington, DC: Resources for the Future.
Varian, Hal. R. (1999), *Intermediate Microeconomics*, 5th edn, New York: W.W. Norton & Co.
Weitzman, M. (1998), 'Gamma discounting for global warming', discussion paper, Department of Economics, Harvard University.

3. Water quality issues[1]

3.0 INTRODUCTION

This chapter addresses key issues related to water quality. We most often think of poor water quality as being caused by human beings polluting the waters, but natural or baseline water quality in the absence of mankind's activities may not be particularly good to start with. Just what is 'good' or 'bad' water quality can be assessed in a variety of ways, but a very broad categorization refers to toxicity. Pollutants can be toxic or non-toxic and toxic ones may impair the ecological and human services that water provides, if that their concentration levels are high enough. Simply defined, a toxic chemical is one that leads to harm (illness, mutation, or death) to a living organism if that organism is exposed at sufficient levels, for a sufficient amount of time. In contrast, an example of a non-toxic pollutant is simply sediment, or soil that erodes and makes its way into the watercourse. These types of pollutants may cause environmental problems, but they are not toxic to living things.

Often water quality and quantity issues in a geographical region cannot be separated from one another. After all, what good is an ample supply or volume of water that is too contaminated for any human or ecological use? Examples of large quantities of water that are of poor quality are fairly easy to find throughout the world: consider the lower Colorado River, loaded with some 9 million tons of salt each year (Lee and Howitt, 1996), the Mediterranean Sea in the bay near Barcelona, Spain, Saginaw Bay and Kalamazoo River in the state of Michigan, the Ganges and scores of other rivers in India and on the African continent; aquifers in many coastal areas contaminated by saltwater intrusion; and other groundwater supplies contaminated by industrial wastes and pollutants.

A timely example arises from the connection between quantity and water quality in the Salton Sea, generating controversy in southern California. This body of water, created by a flood of the Colorado River in 1905, has been replenished with 1.3 million acre feet of salt-laden irrigation water per year, resulting in an inland 'sea' 25 percent more saline than the Pacific Ocean. Four million tons of salt enter the lake each year (Gardner, 2002). Chapter 1 mentioned that Imperial Valley irrigators had refused to sign an agreement transferring water to southern cities until they were assured that they would not be held responsible for damage to the Salton Sea, and the resulting stalemate between the irrigators and state and federal agencies continued up until the end of 2002.

Ecological services provided by water include support of, and habitat for, aquatic life and riparian area animals and plants, and birds that feed on aquatic life. Surface water flow can provide a natural cleansing mechanism for some naturally occurring substances found in rocks and soils that find their way into the stream course (for example, arsenic and apatite), as well as providing other services to the ecosystem, such as diluting harmful human-caused pollutants in rivers and streams. In coastal areas freshwater may mix with saltwater forming estuaries that are the unique habitat for a variety of species.

Humans use water for drinking, growing food, cooking, bathing, other domestic uses, and for recreational activities such as boating, swimming, fishing, water-skiing. Humans sometimes just enjoy simply looking at, or being near, a water body. Economists often refer to these activities as water's *service flows* to humans.

Ample evidence exists that many ecological and human service flows can be disrupted by pollution of the groundwater or surface water. Economists often now conduct work that can be integrated with physical science that addresses the 'risk' and consequences of exposure to pollutants. So, early in this chapter I explore some of the physical science relating to water quality, albeit at a simple level, and later in the chapter, try to connect this to some economic analysis.

Some toxic or harmful substances and pollutants are easy to measure and have known health consequences. Others may be more difficult to understand, especially when uncertainty surrounds the consequences of exposure to humans and other living beings. An excellent current example of an uncertain effect is from exposure to methyl tertiary-butyl ether (MTBE), which is a fuel additive used to oxygenate fuels to decrease air pollution, but which is being found in groundwater supplies. In the past several years many states have banned the use of MTBE, but there is still debate about whether MTBE causes cancer or not (see Agapoff, 2000). This uncertainty recently led the then governor of California, Gray Davis, first to impose a deadline to phase out gasoline with MTBE near Lake Tahoe, but then later to drop this deadline (see Coleman, 1999). It is interesting to examine risk modeling in actual situations that demanded it to be performed, though a full discussion of risk and uncertainty must wait until Chapter 6.

Lichtenberg et al. (1989) model the excess cancer risks R, faced by an individual exposed to the pesticide 1,2-dibromo-3-chloropropane (DBCP) in the area near Fresno, California as:

$$R = G \times U \times A \times F \times Q \qquad (3.1)$$

where G is the lifetime time-weighted average concentration of DBCP in drinking water; U is the sampling error involved in estimating G from monitoring data; A is the lifetime time-weighted average consumption of water for individuals; F is a factor that transforms animal doses (used in experiments) into human equivalents, and Q is a dose-response potency parameter. Using predicted cancer risks, policy makers can decide what actions to take to reduce them, if any.

Another current example that illustrates risk is cryptosporidium. Toxicologists and physical scientists characterize health risks using a dose-response model. The dose-response model used to characterize the likelihood of infection from ingestion of water containing crytposporidium in the risk assessment and benefits analysis in this EA is taken from the work of Haas et al. (1996). The basic form of this dose-response model (see Cadmus Group, 2003) is:

$$PI(d,r) = 1 - e^{-dr} \qquad (3.2)$$

where $PI\,(d, r)$ is the probability of an individual becoming infected following ingestion of water providing an expected dose d (number) of organisms, each having the expected probability r of surviving to cause an infection. The 'expected dose' d of organisms is the product of the average concentration of organisms (oocysts) in the water being ingested and the volume of water ingested. An 'expected dose' of 1.0 oocyst might well mean that, for some portion of time, none would be consumed, and for the rest of the time, one or more oocysts would be consumed (see Cadmus Group, 2003). If the average crytposporidium concentration is measured to be 100 oocysts per 100 liters, or 1.0 oocyst per liter, and an individual consumes 1 liter of water, the expected dose d for the dose-response model would be 1.0 oocyst.

This type of uncertainty about the physical science relates directly to the task facing the economist who wishes to assess water quality issues. The better the economist's understanding of the pollutant, the better he or she is able to predict risk-averting (or taking!) behavior and calculate losses from water-borne pollutants.

3.1 WATER AND WATER POLLUTION

A common misperception among individuals uninformed about water quality is that a water body's color and appearance can simply tell us about a water body's quality and health. We often enjoy seeing or visiting 'clear' water or 'blue' water, such as Lake Tahoe or one of the famous lakes in northern Italy or Switzerland. Such features are well documented to be pleasing to the eye of visitors to Lake Tahoe. However, those familiar with Lake Tahoe know that its quality has been steadily declining in recent years, at a rather alarming rate (Murphy and Knopp, 2000).[2] Some of the lakes in the Adirondack Mountains of New York are lovely to look at, but they are aquatically dying or dead from acid rain. This is evidence that one cannot simply say that a clear, or clear and blue water body is ecologically healthy, and that a dirty brown water body is of very poor quality. Water quality scientists (biologists, hydrologists and hydro-geologists, chemists, etc.) look at the water's actual chemical make-up for clues as to the water's ability to sustain and support living organisms. A green lake that is pleasing to the eye may be full of plants and algae, which may not indicate health, and while a brown lake or river may indicate the presence of sediments, this may not indicate long-term ecological problems.

People again often judge water they drink or use in their household by its basic color (clear versus rust-colored or brown water frequently coming from the tap), its smell or taste, or some sense that their water is 'soft' or 'hard'. Rust may be leaking from corroding metal pipes, and there may be sediment in drinking water, depending on the supply source to the home. Some water smells slightly of sulfur or kerosene. The tap water here in College Station, Texas tastes quite salty to many people, especially those who just moved here from places with much different tasting water. No doubt all of us have visited places away from home that have softer or harder water than we are used to, but we may not know the cause of the difference. For example, have you been to a place where you took a shower or bath, and the soap seemed more difficult to wash off your skin (with soft water)? Or, where, no matter how hard you tried, you just couldn't get the soap to lather (as with hard water) when you washed with the water in a given geographical region?

These characteristics may well be indications of the hardness of the water. Hardness of water is in fact the amount of dissolved calcium, magnesium, and iron in the water. Hard water is difficult to get to lather or create soap suds, and is common in Florida and some other states. Hardness can be measured in milligrams per liter (mg/L) of calcium carbonate: very hard water contains 300 mg/L or more of calcium carbonate. Soft water is in the range of 0 to 75 mg/L. Table 3.1 lists several other measurable characteristics of water bodies that are used to measure water quality. The levels associated with a descriptive characteristic show typical measurable and reported units. It is useful to note that mg/L or milligrams per liter are equivalent to parts per million (ppm), and µg/L or micrograms per liter are equivalent to parts per billion (ppb). In his book, Tom Cech (2003) provides a useful description of the ppm and ppb measures that can be easily visualized: ppm is equivalent to the concentration if one put three

Table 3.1 *Water quality parameters/contaminants**

Physical Properties		
Temperature		
Conductivity/TDS		
Surface Tension		
Turbidity		
Chemical Constituents (CCs)	General Examples of CCs	Specific Examples of the General Examples of CCs
Inorganics (do not contain carbon)	PH (0, very acidic, to 14, very alkaline)	
	Dissolved Gases	O_2, CO_2 (mg/L)
	Metals	As, Cd, Cr, Hg, etc. (mg/L)
	Anions	Cl^-, SO_4^{-2} (mg/L)
	Nutrients	Nitrogen, Phosphorous (mg/L)
	Radionuclides	Radon (pCi)
Organics	Volatile Organic Compounds	Solvents, BTXEs, MTBE, etc. (ug/L)
	Synthetic Organic Compounds	Pesticides, Herbicides, etc. (ug/L)
		PCBs (ng/L), DDT, Dioxins (ng/L)
Biota		
Bacteria	Coliform, Giardia, Cryptosporidium	(cysts/L)
Algae	Blue-green	
Invasive Plants		

Note: *This is a partial list of parameters and contaminants. Note a pH of 7 is exactly neutral for water at 46°F. VOCs (Volatile Organic Compounds) are lightweight, easily evaporable compounds often found in solvents and plastics. The heavier synthetics can sink and may be found at the bottom of rivers and lakes.

drops of a liquid into 42 gallons of water, and ppb is equivalent to about one drop in 14 000 gallons of water. Coupled with suggested environmental standards, such an image makes it clear that toxic substances can be ingested in extremely small quantities before harm arises. One would certainly not be able to taste or smell some toxic substances at small doses.

Dissolved, suspended solids and solids that settle out are physical indicators of water quality. High total dissolved solid (TDS) levels suggest the presence of undesirable ions. Suspended solids include organic solids, viruses, bacteria, and algae.

Table 3.2 Some maximum allowed contaminant levels (MCLs)

Constituent	Maximum contaminant levels (MCLs)
Arsenic (ug/L)	10 (new std under Bush Admin, 2002)
Nitrate (N03-N) (mg/L)	10
Lead (ug/L)	15 (Allowable Limit)
Trihalomethanes (ug/L)	80
PCE (Tetrachloroethylene) (ug/L)	5
Total Coliform	<5% positive
Crytosporidium	Treatment technique required

Table 3.2 shows water quality standards set in the United States. These are maximum contaminant levels (MCLs) set by the US Environmental Protection Agency. These standards pertain to the National Primary Drinking Water Regulations, which are connected to prevention of human health risks. These apply to public water systems, not private ones; private wells are not regulated for water quality in the United States. Turbidity is a measure of the interference of the passage of light through the water, usually caused by soil runoff. Nephelometric Turbidity Units (NTU) are the most common measure. NTU standards are often set such that a maximum of 0.5 NTU in 95 percent of measurements taken each month must pertain. Adequate transmission of light is important in allowing one to see deep into a water body (it aids clarity) and is important to aquatic life that is searching for food. Without adequate light some species of predator fish cannot see their prey.

As suggested above, some water quality parameters relate to toxic substances and some do not, but non-toxic substances can still interfere with ecological and human service flows. The physical science in some cases of substances discussed above is somewhat debatable. For example, how significant trihalomethanes are in causing cancers is controversial and there is a similar debate as to the exact nature of, and details associated with, the health risks involved in ingesting arsenic. As will be seen below and in Chapter 6, there seems agreement that exposure to arsenic at some levels very likely causes bladder, lung, and skin cancer, but the magnitude of risk, as well as whether there are other concerns, remains the subject of considerable debate. Radioactive wastes have become an important problem in recent years. More complex issues and the ecological relationships with river and stream courses are explored in Spulber and Sabbaghi (1998; see their chapter 5).

A very common pollutant measure is the amount of oxygen demanded by a particular volume of effluent, and this is called the biochemical oxygen demand or BOD. When wastes are discharged into the water, many require a substantial amount of oxygen to decompose them. This 'demand' for oxygen is a measurement of instream water quality. BOD may be related to the amount of bacterial waste, and especially common are problems with fecal and total coliform.

Fecal coliform comes from untreated or inadequately treated human and animal wastes that are disposed of into surface waters and later ingested by humans. This pollutant leads to intestinal difficulties, which can be fatal, especially in small children. E. coli is another similar harmful waste, as is cryptosporidium, another microbial pathogen. Cryptosporidium is of great concern and is tied to treatment legislation (discussed below), though it cannot be removed using common disinfectants such as chlorine. The 5.0 percent figure in Table 3.2 indicates that no more than 5 percent of the samples taken in a month for total coliform may be positive.

Bacteria and other wastes increase BOD, or they decrease the level of dissolved oxygen (DO) available in the water column, which supports aquatic life. Dissolved oxygen is simply oxygen gas in water, necessary to support plants, fish, frogs, turtles, and so on in lakes and streams. Often, environmental characteristics are examined using the level of DO. For example, in concerns about Lake Tahoe, a recent report showed DO falling over the course of a few years, as shown in Figure 3.1. The downward sloping line is a regression line to fit the data, roughly reproduced from Murphy and Knopp (2000). DO can be affected by temperature, salinity,

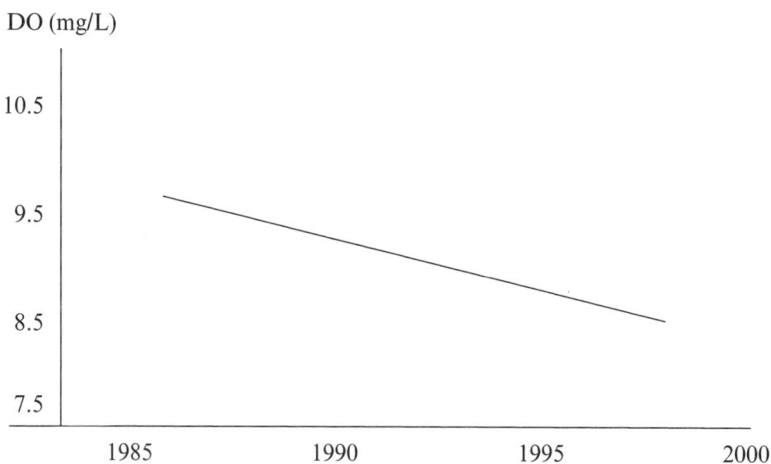

Source: Lake Tahoe Watershed Assessment, vol. 1 (US Forest Service).

Figure 3.1 Dissolved oxygen at Lake Tahoe, depth of 450 meters

atmospheric pressure, and the demand for oxygen by the stream or lake's aquatic life.

Finally, several other substances mentioned in Table 3.2 can cause cancers. As mentioned above, in high enough doses arsenic can cause skin damage, and may lead to an increased risk of bladder and lung cancer. Arsenic, as with many other metals (copper and cadmium) can be naturally occurring in rocks and soils, and erosion of these leads to concentrations in surface and groundwater. Nitrates come from fertilizer use, sewage, and may also be found naturally. They are another substance that causes debate in the health research community. They may cause 'blue baby syndrome' in infants under six months.

Nutrients are also important because they aid plant growth, and such nutrients include nitrogen and phosphorous. The source of these is often small farms and this has led to the area of concern called non-point source pollution. Farms apply about 11 million tons of nitrogen, 5 million tons of potash, and 4 million tons of phosphate to cropland each year (USDA, ERS, 1997). This is not just an isolated or local problem. As much as 15 percent of the nitrogen fertilizer applied to cropland in the Mississippi River Basin makes its way to the Gulf of Mexico, and siltation is considered the leading pollution problem in United States rivers and streams, creating damages in the range of $2 billion to $8 billion per year (see Ribaudo et al., 1999).

Soil erosion from farm and non-farm land results in costs to those using water, and can lead to ecological damage. Water treatment plants must use technology to cope with sediment removal: Holmes (1988) reports that an 80 million gallon (mg) per day water treatment facility spends $3.5 million ($120.82/mg) per year on removing sediments if conventional filtration systems are used. Direct filtration technology (discussed below) is slightly less expensive, resulting in $2.14 million annually ($73.36/mg) for the same scale of water treatment plant. Using a hedonic cost approach (see Chapter 8 for an explanation of this) Holmes estimates that the cost of sediment removal from 22 000 mg per day of surface water withdrawn is between about $460 million and $1.37 billion per year. This type of pollution has led to the formation of the Conservation Reserve Program of the United States Department of Agriculture (USDA), which removes 40 to 45 million acres of erodible agricultural land, subsidizing the farmers who plant trees or providing grants to reduce erosion that can lead to contamination of waters.

3.1.1 Fate and Transport

Finally, before turning to regulation of water quality, it must be noted that there is more to water quality management than simply knowing what concentrations of harmful substances are. The above discussion just scratches the surface. Fate and transport are the movement, disposition, and residence of the pollutants. If scientists are not aware of the movement of the pollutants, then they can predict neither the lessening nor increase in concentrations that might be due to mixing, temperature changes, and changes in a river or stream's velocity. All pollutants do not move in the same manner, nor do they reside in the same places in a water column or the sediments or banks of a water body. Thus, the study of fate and transport is essential to managing water quality, but as with many such issues, this is beyond the scope of this book.

3.2 HUMAN USE OF WATER BODIES

The number one area of social concern relating to water quality in the world is still unarguably to ensure human access to safe drinking water and sanitation (sewage treatment plants). In 1992 the World Bank estimated that one billion people were without access to safe drinking water. Chapter 10 elaborates on the fact that this is still the largest remaining problem for most rural areas in developing nations. Infant mortality in developing countries is still largely caused today by poor, or even by no access to safe drinking water supplies. This in turn is related to a variety of other problems, including adequate sanitation. The problem is simply that in many rural areas villagers rely on any water they can find that is close to the village, and this water is unlikely to be treated to reduce pollutant levels, and is very likely the outlet for human waste in the absence of sewer systems.

The United States has by no means solved all of its drinking water quality problems, though the US is far ahead of many parts of the world in this regard. Ingesting toxic substances can lead to death from cancers, mutations, blindness, and a host of illnesses. For example, in 1993 approximately 400 000 people became ill and over 100 died when cryptosporidium got into drinking water in Milwaukee, Wisconsin (see Cadmus Group, 2003; Innes and Cory, 2001). Drinking non-toxic substances can still lead to unpleasant consequences: bad smell or taste, indigestion, and minor gastrointestinal problems.

As suggested earlier in many, if not all water quality situations, health problems can only be characterized up to some degree. There is risk associated with particular health issues because there is no guarantee that health consequences will arise from exposures to toxic and other substances that are ingested. Risks arise for any number of reasons, as will be seen in Chapter 6, which focuses on risk and uncertainty. For now, consider that there is often difficulty in knowing exact levels of exposure, and exact linkages between ingestion of particular concentrations of pollutants and health consequences. To complicate the analysis, there is often a long lag in health consequences following initial exposure, known as the latency period.

Aside from drinking from surface water supplies, humans also consume fish and other aquatic species that live in freshwater and seawater. These may be commercially caught or harvested, or in developing countries the population may be dependent on fishing for their own food. The latter are often referred to as artisans or subsistence fishermen. When commercially harvested aquatic species become contaminated with pollutants they too provide a pathway for diseases: frequent consumption becomes unsafe and the commercial operation is jeopardized. Artisans may well ingest contaminated seafood unwittingly, and this has led to warnings given to those who may catch such fish and eat them.

Fish consumption advisories
In recent years in the United States many state and federal health agencies have imposed fish consumption advisories (FCAs) that warn consumers of potential health risks. The National Water Quality Inventory of 1998 showed 96 percent of the shoreline of the Great Lakes was impaired, based on the neighboring states' assessment of pollutants in fish tissue (Cech, 2003). FCAs are set to inform the public about risks of ingesting certain quantities of fish because of toxic substances found in fish tissues that are eaten. They can range from a total ban on eating all fish or at least particular species of fish, to limits on the monthly quantities of fish eaten, to limits on monthly quantities for certain kinds of people who are at risk. Some of the risks can be greatly reduced by simple removal of fat and skin of the fish, and various cooking methods. We return to these advisories below, but first consider other human uses of water.

Recreational aspects and ties to water quality
The above discussion conjures up images of people fishing, and many anglers are hoping to catch fish to eat. However, some anglers have no real interest in the food value of fish, and catch fish for the pure sport of it, as evidenced by the thousands of recreational anglers in various states who partake in 'catch and release' fishery activities. It is well known that water quality can affect the catch in such fisheries. Substances such as heavy metals (copper, cadmium) can kill fish in a river for a short, or long, period of time. An example is the Clark Fork River in Montana, once a place with an abundant number of sport fish. This river basin is where copper mining has been well documented to have severely reduced the number of fish. In fact, the mining in the Clark Fork Basin led to designation as the largest

superfund site in the United States, and most who know of it know of the infamous 'Berkley Pit', an enormous open pit which today contains contaminated groundwater.

Lakes, rivers, streams, and oceans are frequently a destination for non-fishing recreational outings such as boating, rafting, swimming, using the beach, simply walking along the shore or bank, or picnicking. The quality of the water has some direct connections to these recreational experiences. Eutrophication can lead to beach closures, as can oil spills. In 1998 the US Environmental Protection Agency reported that 40 percent of the streams, lakes, and estuaries assessed at that time were not clean enough for uses such as fishing and swimming. Less direct relationships may exist between boating and shore uses and many pollutants, and this area is ripe for new research. Next, several US federal regulations that attempt to control water pollution are examined.

3.3 REGULATIONS IN THE UNITED STATES

Almost every country in the world today has water quality regulations of some kind, but here the focus is on a few key US regulations. One of the first pieces of water quality legislation in the United States was the Water Pollution Control Act of 1948 (which allowed for federal funding of construction of wastewater treatment plants). This was followed by the Water Quality Act of 1965, the Federal Water Pollution Control Act of 1972, the Clean Water Act (reauthorized by overriding President Reagan's veto in 1987), and the Safe Drinking Water Act (SDWA) of 1974 and subsequent amendments, which govern public water supply systems. Other relevant legislation includes the Oil Pollution Act of 1990.

The National Environmental Policy Act (NEPA) was signed into law in 1969 and it created the US Environmental Protection Agency (EPA). EPA is mandated to address ecological and health risks and they propose standards and develop regulations according to goals related to acceptable risks, which must be passed into law by the US Congress. Any set of regulations may be fairly complicated, such as those tied to the Safe Drinking Water Act. For example, the SDWA sets pH levels between 6.5 and 8.5, and the early 1990s saw the EPA struggling to find SDWA standards and MCLs for toxic substances such as radon (see Raucher and Drago, 1992) and arsenic. Under the Safe Drinking Water Act Amendments of 1996, when proposing a national primary drinking water regulation that includes a maximum contaminant level, the US Environmental Protection Agency must conduct a health risk reduction and cost analysis (HRRCA).

Today the EPA is considering a new and more rigorous standard for arsenic in public drinking water supplies, reduced from 50 ppb to 10 ppb, based on new toxicology studies. The agency under President Clinton modified the regulations under the Safe Drinking Water Act, and the Bush administration, despite being generally viewed as anti-environment, has let the modifications stand.

Very recently, since the late 1990s, the US EPA has embarked on another water quality program: the watersheds approach, coupled with the Total Maximum Daily Load (TMDL) Program. This program addresses the problem that over 40 percent of the nation's assessed waters (some 20 000 lakes, rivers, and estuaries) still do not meet water quality standards set by states and other governing authorities. The program assesses the maximum amount of a pollutant that a water body can receive and still meet state and federal water quality standards.

The TMDL program stems from section 303(d) of the 1972 Clean Water Act, requiring governing agencies to develop lists of impaired waters. The TMDL also allocates pollutant loadings among point and non-point pollutant sources. The TMDL program is new enough that there are not many assessments of this program, but at present, a good deal of information can be found at EPA's websites. In particular, the Office of Water provides information at its website: http://www.epa.gov/owow/tmdl. What is known so far is that if the program is widely followed, a huge number (400 000) of assessments will have to be made, at great cost to society. Some have cautioned that many considerations must be made before blindly wading in and conducting these 400 000 TMDL studies (National Research Council). However, evaluation of some of the regulations is postponed until Section 3.4. Next, water treatment is examined, as it is such a basic, but important topic.

3.3.1 Water Treatment

Water 'treatment' is a broad term indicating some type of technological process to clean toxic and other substances from water, typically with the purpose of drinking. Private users of water can do this cleaning, but we most often think of public water treatment systems, or more likely in the US, people just take it for granted that the water they drink is clean and safe. Some water treatment approaches are quite simple, involving little technology. In fact one of the simplest treatment processes for drinking water simply involves holding the water in a sedimentation basin, first allowing the settling of large solids, and then using sand or another medium to further filter out finer and smaller particles of sediment. A host of technological options may be used to address the various pollutants. These include:

Chemicals – disinfection
Corrosion control
Membrane filtration systems
Reverse osmosis
Electrodialysis
Electrodialysis reversal
Adsorption
Chemicals – lime softening
Ozone systems
Sedimentation/filtering

The most common chemical used in the disinfection approach is chlorine, which attacks bacteria. In other chemical treatments, three types of chemicals are frequently used (Dearmont et al., 1998), including coagulants, other specific disinfectants, and pH adjusters. Coagulants, as the name suggests, bind with impurities to form particles big enough for removal by sedimentation and filtration. Disinfectants remove bacteria and the like, and lime can be used to remove acidity. Reverse osmosis treatment systems can be very small and simple, and may be installed in households.

Economics – monitoring and treatment cost
Economics is key in the determination of whether, and how much water quality improvement is actually done, especially in developing countries. In pollution control one must look at monitoring, as the first step to be taken, and then, depending on what concentrations of substances are observed, treatment.

Monitoring
No matter what regulation is contemplated, or for that matter, what economic scheme is considered, monitoring of water quality must be done by some agent in society. Economists often argue for market-based incentives in lieu of command and control regulation, but there is no getting away from monitoring, even with schemes that otherwise greatly reduce the administrative burden on the government. To know the level of water quality requires regular testing of source or output water, which is done in a variety of ways by a variety of government agencies, and sometimes by the polluter themselves.

In the US public water suppliers must monitor the levels of various potential pollutants to make sure they are in compliance with maximum contaminant levels set by the US Environmental Protection Agency. Monitoring may be made more efficient when the EPA can identify correlations between various types of pollutants. For example, if E. coli and

Cryptosporidium concentrations were strongly related, a water system operator might monitor one or the other only, and make inferences about both problems. Unfortunately, in this case in particular, such a correlation does not appear to exist (see Cadmus Group, 2003).

As an example, consider the new proposed regulations under the Long Term Surface Water Treatment Rule to lower the risk of illness and mortality from giardia and cryptosporiodosis, both of which are relatively new problems being addressed in the United States. Monitoring must be done before the rule takes effect, so that baseline levels can be determined. Under one of several possible assumptions, the EPA estimates that the present value of initial monitoring costs for small public water systems (those serving fewer than 10 000 people) will be $34.6 million, nationwide. Similarly, the EPA estimates that present value monitoring costs for larger systems will be $25.7 million (see Cadmus Group, 2003).[3] After the rule takes effect water systems must be monitored again, to ensure compliance. Under the same assumptions (see note 3) small system present value monitoring costs are estimated to be $23.5 million, and large system costs are $14.4 million.

Treatment

Using one or more of the above treatment approaches may cost the water supplier, and ultimately those living in the community served by the water supplier, a good deal of money. As mentioned above in the reference to Holmes's study of sediment loading, water treatment may increase substantially with the influx of contaminants. In a study similar to Holmes's, Dearmont et al. (1998) estimate the cost of treatment for 12 water treatment plants in Texas. Using a base of chemical treatment costs of $75 per million gallons, they find costs increase by $95 per million gallons in the presence of raw contamination of groundwater supplies. Extrapolating to other Texas cities, the authors suggest that a 1 percent increase in turbidity alone increases chemical treatment costs by 0.25 percent. Forster et al. (1987) also examine the change in soil erosion on treatment cost, this time considering a reduction in soil erosion for 12 Ohio communities in the corn belt. They find that a 10 percent reduction in soil erosion reduces treatment costs by 4 percent annually, and a 25 percent reduction in soil erosion lowers costs by $2.7 million.

In yet another, but different treatment cost example, Raucher and Drago (1992) estimated the cost of complying with EPA's proposed standard for radionuclides (radon) in drinking water in the early 1990s at more than $2.5 billion. These huge cost estimates caused policy makers to consider the nature of costs for water treatment facilities more carefully. How are such costs estimated?

Following Boisvert and Schmit (1997), who focus on the tradeoffs that rural water systems make between distribution and scale economies, let the total cost of treatment be a simple exponential function of output:

$$TC_t = \beta Q^{\alpha + \delta \ln Q} \tag{3.3}$$

where Q is output. Define economies of size (*SCE*) by the proportional increase in cost for a small proportional increase in Q, so:

$$SCE = 1 - \frac{\partial \ln TC_t}{\partial \ln Q} \tag{3.4}$$

The form in equation 3.3 allows economies of size to depend on the level of output, so that at some high level of output, the *SCE* can change. From equation 3.4 it can be seen that economies of size exist if $SCE > 0$, and diseconomies exist if *SCE* is < 0. Naturally, if $SCE > 0$, then average variable costs for the water treatment plant steadily fall with increasing size, at least up to a critical point where economies of size have a profoundly different influence. Ideally, if one is to allow for forms like this to exhibit economies of scale in water treatment plants, then one should also allow for differences in the types of treatment plant, that is, allow for differences in parameters among plants using different kinds of treatment technology. There is no reason to suspect that these parameters will be the same across types of treatment, and in fact, even for a small number of systems in rural New York, Boisvert and Schmit find different costs for systems that treat with use of slow sand, filtration, direct filtration, and aeration technologies.[4]

It is also fairly easy to imagine that different water quality improvement programs may result in different marginal costs of treatment for different industries and that is an issue in achieving efficiency in environmental policy. For example, Magat et al. (1986) estimate the marginal cost of removing set levels of BOD in water. One can see in Table 3.3 that these vary depending on the size of the plant and the type of industry.

Water treatment costs may also depend on the size of the water utility and its efficiency. It appears there is good reason to believe that rural water utilities are disadvantaged when it comes to dealing with several treatment issues (see Boisvert and Schmit, 1997; Bhattacharyya et al., 1995). As an example, the US EPA estimates that the total present value of capital costs associated with meeting the above-mentioned rule to reduce the risk of illness and mortality from ingesting cryptosporidium oocysts and giardia is $76.1 million for small systems serving fewer than 10 000 people, and $1.09 billion for larger systems serving more than 10 000 people. Obviously the larger of these numbers reflects the total population served by each.

Table 3.3 Marginal treatment costs of BOD removal (US dollars per kilogram of BOD removed)

Industry	Subcategory	Marginal Cost $
Poultry	Small plants (ducks)	3.15
Meat packing	Simple slaughterhouse	2.19
Meat packing	High processing packinghouse	0.92
Paper	Unbleached kraft	0.86
Paper	Paperboard	0.50
Poultry	Large plants (fowl)	0.10

Source: Magat et al. (1986).

However, it can reasonably be assumed that water systems will pass a considerable amount of increased capital and operating costs on to households and in this same case it is estimated that the average household cost is $4.61 per year for those on small systems, while it is only $1.68 for those on large systems. So, it appears that the small system water treatment-related capital costs are quite a bit higher, per household.

3.4 ECOLOGICAL AND AQUATIC SPECIES IMPACTS

So far the focus of this chapter has been on human service flows and impacts, but most of the above substances can cause impacts with the potential to harm all aquatic species if pollutant concentrations are sufficient, either killing them or leading to mutations, morbidity, and reproductive failures. Birds and mammals can also be harmed, especially as they may depend on aquatic species for food, that is, they are in the food chain. In a host of settings in the United States, there have been analyses of linkages between a pollutant, water quality, and impacts on animals. The Clark Fork example is given above, and one other obvious setting involves oil spills such as the Exxon Valdez in Prince William Sound or the Nestucca Oil Spill near Seattle, Washington (see for example, Rowe et al., 1992 or literature related to the Valdez spill). In large oil spills many fish, seabirds, and aquatic mammals have been killed or harmed.

Some 'ecological' economists have claimed that values for protection of species need to be calculated that are independent of human use or at least human beings' preferences. My view is that economic values are a human concept and construction and thus, placing values on ecological resources requires a tie to human preferences. But human values related to ecological protection are certainly plausible and ample evidence that these exist and are substantial is available in the literature (for example, Rowe et al., 1992). The case study on the Everglades provides a current example and Table 3A.1 (see appendix) summarizes the beneficial uses that may be impaired by a variety of contaminants. Next I consider how to assign economic values to these beneficial uses.

CASE STUDY 3.1   THE EVERGLADES RESTORATION PROJECT

The Florida Everglades suffered dramatically, with a reduction of this subtropical wetland by 50 percent from its original area. Phosphorus was identified as a major pollutant in the ecosystem. In addition, atmospheric deposition accounts for over 95 percent of the Everglade's external loading of mercury. Though there has been a significant decline in mercury found in largemouth bass and wading birds, fish consumption advisories remain in effect today for bass, gar, bowfin, and warmouth because of mercury concentrations higher than 1.5 ppm. Today, after passage of the 1994 Everglades Forever Act (Florida Statutes, Sec. 373.4592 (1) (h)), restoration efforts on a massive scale are under way. Six stormwater treatment areas are being constructed, with an area of 47 000 acres, capable of treating 1.4 million acre feet per year of stormwater runoff. Best management practices and a water quality regulation program are other parts of this program. The goal is to reach water quality standards by the end of 2006, and though progress is being made, this seems unlikely. A drought in 2001 complicated efforts.

Source: 2002 Executive Summary, Everglades Consolidated Report, South Florida Water Management District www.sfwmd.gov.

3.5   ECONOMIC ANALYSIS AND VALUATION OF WATER QUALITY IMPROVEMENTS

It is tempting to suggest that society must achieve the goal of meeting standards that prevent unacceptable health risks at any cost. Society may well decide that is the case, primarily for political reasons, but ignoring costs altogether is not an option in this era of tight budgets and the need to prioritize pollution abatement while considering all other types of expenditures (for example, expenditures on education, fighting crime, feeding people, and providing health care). And, so one may well ask, are these regulations effective, and more specifically, just what are the costs of water quality improvements, such as treatment?

First, some regulations have certainly improved our lives. The US EPA estimates that the Surface Water Treatment Rule (SWTR), which is part of the SDWA, helps avoid 90 000 cases of gastroenteritis per year, and that the lead and copper rule protects 140 million people (Innes and Cory, 2001). Changes are being considered today for the SWTR and how those changes will affect health and be assessed for their economic impacts can be quite complicated (see Cadmus Group, 2003). As these regulations change, it is most often the responsibility of state and local governments to keep up treatment practices and technology, and enforce the regulations. This can be quite expensive: it is estimated that full compliance with SDWA would cost $1.4 billion every year (Innes and Cory, 2001). As water treatment alone is quite expensive, it is worth focusing some discussion on water treatment and its economics.

The United States has typically tried to solve its problems by implementation of command and control policies, that is, the regulations and pieces of legislation to mandate controls or pollution standards that must be met by polluters described above. Economists have analysed water quality changes tied to several pieces of legislation in the United States, including the Water Pollution Control Act of 1948 (which allowed for federal funding of construction of wastewater treatment plants), the Water Quality Act of 1965, the Federal Water Pollution Control Act of 1972, the Clean Water Act reauthorized by overriding Reagan's veto in 1987, and the Safe Drinking Water Act of 1974. Other legislation includes the Oil Pollution Act of 1990. Economists have lately also examined water quality issues in developing countries. Before reviewing some of the analyses, I consider how households and individuals might respond to water quality changes and the health risks associated with them, in other words, how households behave in response in water quality changes.

3.5.1 Behavioral Responses

Human beings, and to some extent animals, have several possible behaviors they can take in response to water quality changes. It is an empirical issue which, among the suite of possible responses, human beings will take. We cannot predict a direction of response with certainty. For example, suppose an aquifer becomes contaminated so that drinking water poses a serious health risk. What can people do? They could do nothing, they could attempt to clean up the aquifer, treat the water from it, abandon the water supply in favor of another aquifer or surface water supply, or take actions such as drinking bottled water, or boiling the water that comes from the contaminated aquifer. Which action they take depends on the information given to them regarding the degree of safety they achieve via a particular action, as well as on the costs of any particular action. Some treatment schemes may work for particular contaminants, and others may not, and each comes at a perhaps quite different social cost.

Avoidance or mitigating behavior is not costless either. Boiling water, while not expensive as a directly observable cost, still has an energy or resource cost, and perhaps more importantly, involves use of the household's time, which can be quite valuable. Bottled water is enormously expensive as compared to the typical price of water delivered to a household, as much as 1000 times the price of tap water, but it is estimated that one out of every 15 US households now consumes bottled water. It is in fact possible to develop models that show that the optimal thing to do in some situations is to provide delivered water for non-drinking uses, while drinking water comes from bottled water (Innes and Cory, 2001).

3.5.2 Assessing the Economic Success or Failure of Water Quality Legislation

Non-economists largely agree that most pieces of major water quality legislation have been successful. Some of the assessments are qualitative, such as the report on the Clean Water Act in *Audubon* magazine, which mentions the vast improvement made on the Cuyahoga River in Cleveland, Ohio. The river burst into flames in 1969 because of the flammable contaminants there, and it is now much cleaner. The story also mentions the clean up of Lake Erie: bacteria counts and algae blooms dropped by 90 percent between 1968 and 1991. The author claims that 'All of this improvement and more is the result of the Clean Water Act' (Anonymous, 1997, p. 39).

Another success story is the Delaware Bay, where clean up efforts reduced oxygen depletion by half between 1958 and 1983. EPA states that 90 percent of pollution coming from point sources has been eliminated under the Clean Water Act. However, as recently as 1994 EPA estimated that 40 percent of the nation's surveyed rivers, lakes, and estuaries are too polluted for basic uses. Impaired waters include 300 000 miles of rivers and shorelines and 5 million acres of lakes. About 218 million people live within 10 miles of these impaired waters.[5] As a specific example, the Delaware is lined by more than 100 chemical manufacturing plants and oil refineries, posing the threat of toxic waste. In addition, agriculture is a 'non-point' source, and it remains the leading source of water pollution in the United States today because it is exempt from the permitting procedures the Clean Water Act established.

There are two basic approaches to economic analysis of pollution: (i) cost analysis of pollution control options and (ii) benefit or damage analysis. In the regulatory environment it may be fair to say that cost analysis is more important, at least to the regulators. However, economists are generally interested not in the results of a regulatory impact analysis (RIA), but in finding what plans achieve the maximum net benefits.

3.5.3 Control Cost Analysis

Note that here we are referring to the cost of pollution control in general, rather than the specific issue of water treatment cost that was discussed above. Assume that the regulatory environment for the United States applies generally. Costs are fairly easy to assess because of the accounting practices of government agencies. For example, it is estimated that EPA spent about $54 billion between 1972 and 1989 to implement the provisions of the Clean Water Act. A cost analysis is fairly straightforward in general terms. Assume there are n polluters who emit u_n units of pollution without control. Let the concentration at a receptor point R be K_R. Without control:

$$K_R = \sum a_n u_n + B \tag{3.5}$$

where B is the background concentration of the substance, and a_n is the transfer coefficient. The problem for the regulator if K_R is greater than some level that is the legal allowable concentration level is to minimize the cost of controlling pollution to get back to the legal level, say ψ. Let the level of control exerted for the nth polluter be q_n.

We can set this up as the usual Lagrangian problem:

$$\text{Min } \sum C_n(q_n) + \lambda \left[\sum a_n (u_n - q_n) - \psi \right] \tag{3.6}$$

The first-order conditions are such that:

$$\partial C_n(q_n)/\partial q - \lambda a_n \geq 0, n = 1, \ldots, N \tag{3.7}$$

This equation just says that the marginal cost of control should be greater than or equal to the marginal damage from emissions from the nth polluter. The strict equality holds except when a polluting source has a marginal cost of controlling the very first unit that exceeds the marginal damage.

If $a_n = 1$ for all polluters then we have 'uniform' contributions from each of them. In that case the marginal cost is the same for all polluters. If not, then polluters with bigger marginal damages at the receptor point allow higher marginal costs of control. This framework is used to develop, at least in theory, what might be optimal fees, charges, or taxes to be imposed on polluters.

For many years in the economic analysis of water pollution a comparison was made between command and control regulatory efforts and at least theoretical schemes to minimize costs. The latter included tradable permits and emissions charges or pollution taxes. The most famous of these studies early on was by Kneese and Bower (1968). They examined four methods to control water pollution: a uniform treatment (UT), least-cost ambient charge (LC), uniform emissions charge (UEC), and a zonal effluents charge (ZEC). Table 3.4 shows the alternative costs of treatment using each program. The zonal effluents charge comes closest to achieving the least cost approach, and the uniform treatment approach is over two times higher in costs.

A more recent example of examination of the costs was done to assess the 1987 EPA rule regarding the effluent guidelines for the organic chemicals, plastics, and synthetic fibers (OCPSF) industry. Caulkins and Sessions (1997) critique the RIA for this rule-making. They argue that because regulations sought implementation of best-available pollution control technologies, EPA made most of its decisions on the technological data and analysis, not on the economic impact analysis. They note that the benefit analysis performed for this RIA was not of interest to EPA, perhaps because some thought that scrutiny of benefits required by Executive Order 12291 was in contrast to the spirit of the legislation.

Analysis of the cost of compliance with federal standards is far from simple, especially when comparing across regions. For example, in 2001 one of the hot topics in water quality management was EPA's proposed new federal standard for arsenic in drinking water. The National Academy of Sciences reviewed the literature on arsenic's toxic effects and found in

Table 3.4 Costs of meeting DO objectives

DO Objective (ppm)	Program Adopted Costs: in millions of dollars per year			
	LC	UT	UEC	ZEC
2	1.6	5.0	2.4	2.4
3–4	7.0	20.0	12.0	8.6

Source: Kneese and Bower (1968).

a 1999 study that the chance of getting cancer was one in 100, over a lifetime of exposure at 50 parts per billion (ppb).[6] But based on new studies the Clinton administration had proposed a new standard of 10 parts per billion, down from 50 ppb, the standard established in 1942. Meeting this new standard immediately led to objections from many states and cities, and especially those smaller populations with water treatment systems inadequate to handle the new standard. Albuquerque, New Mexico, estimated that meeting the 10 ppb standard would cost them as much as $200 million (Egan, 2001). With these kinds of costs, one may well wonder what the benefits of reduced arsenic are, and while EPA commissioned a study to assess benefits from meeting the 50 ppb standard (see Abt Associates, 2000), more work is needed to examine the benefits of the new standard. A new study in progress, relating to this very issue, is described in Chapter 6.

3.5.4 Benefits Analysis

On the other side of the equation from costs are of course the economic benefits of regulatory programs. There are hundreds of studies that estimate the relationship between human uses and water quality, as well as the values or benefits from improvements. Many of these are recreational fishing studies. The idea in those studies is that as water quality is diminished, the stock of fish at a fishing site is impaired and the angler's ability to catch species is also impaired. Table 3.5 presents a table of fishing studies and gives an idea of the contaminant dealt with in each study.

Recreation values and motives for protecting water quality are but one part of the puzzle. Economists often seek 'total' values for resources,

Table 3.5 Recreational fishing studies related to water quality*

Study authors (date)	WQ measure
Englin et al. (1997)	Dissolved oxygen
Jakus et al. (1997)	Fish consumption advisories
Morey et al. (2000)	Copper, cadmium from mining wastes
Shaw (1985)	Acid rain
Jakus and Shaw (2003)	Fish consumption advisories

Notes: *Some recreational fishing study authors simply guess at the change in the angler's catch due to the water quality degradation and then calculate values based on that new catch rate.

Source: Agapoff et al. (2000). Note all references may be found there.

including water quality improvements. A recent example comes from California, the state with the largest population in the United States. Preliminary results of a survey of California households suggest that all California households would be willing to pay approximately $2 billion per year to fund efforts to improve state water quality so that waters were in compliance with current state regulations (Larson and Lew, 2001). The authors apply the well-known double-bounded dichotomous choice contingent valuation approach (see Chapter 8) to arrive at a figure in the range of $18 to $23 per household, per month, to improve water quality. There are about 10.4 million households in the state of California, and the per household numbers per month can be aggregated annually, arriving at a figure for the benefits of California water quality in the $2 billion range.

National studies/evaluation of the Clean Water Act

Many have asked in recent years whether the cost of the Clean Water Act was worth it. This is a difficult question to answer, but it might get asked as frequently as every five years, when Congress looks at reauthorization issues. The costs are felt by some to be easy enough to quantify. For example, Knopman and Smith (1993) put the cost of water pollution control from 1972 up to 1993 at $541 billion. There may be quibbling over the exact figure, but far more contentious are the estimated benefits of the programs that accompany such legislation.

A few studies are much larger in scope than the California study above and attempt to examine the benefits for the entire United States provided by specific or larger pieces of water pollution control legislation. For example, Levin (1997) reviews the RIA done to analyse the effects of the 1991 lead-in-drinking-water rule. Net benefits were projected to be $2.2 billion, annually.

Freeman (1990) estimated that the 1985 net benefit of conventional control is probably negative, using a comparison of the 1985 annual costs ($25 to $30 billion) and the annual benefits that year, which were around $14 billion. In contrast, Carson and Mitchell (1993) estimate positive current net benefits (about $6 billion for 1990), but warn that these may become negative as costs increase over time.

These overall studies are likely not convincing in their estimates. Carson and Mitchell's (1993) approach, for example, later became outdated as scientists from other disciplines criticized the hierarchy of water quality they used. Their assumption was that waters with 'Swimmable' water quality were better than those with 'Fishable' water quality and better still than 'Boatable' water quality waters. Later it was found that across states, this ranking scheme was inconsistent in the majority of US water bodies. Some rivers and lakes that could be fished are not safe for swimming.

Carson and Mitchell's very recent (forthcoming) study reexamines some water quality issues with a different ranking of the risks associated with water use. They explore the issues related to trihalomethanes (THM) in drinking water for a small town population. THM is created during the process of chlorinating drinking water, which is done to prevent biological agents (bacteria and viruses) from forming. Because it does provide the benefit of reducing biological agents, and because water treatment such as carbon filtration is relatively expensive for small towns, THM is controversial, but it poses a risk and standards are mandated under the Safe Drinking Water Act of 1974. Current estimates are that THM may kill between two and 100 people per year in the entire US population. Carson and Mitchell (forthcoming) conduct a survey to assess risks and willingness to pay to reduce them in Herrin, Illinois, to find out about values for drinking water improvements. The ultimate goal of the study is to find the sample population's maximum willingness to pay (WTP) to reduce risks related to THM.

Part of any exercise like this is to correctly and adequately communicate the risks that people face. Just how economists and others measure the risks is an entire science and the subject for a college course. Carson and Mitchell proceed in two ways. First, they use a risk ladder to communicate that the risks of doing some normal everyday activities are the same as some others. Examples are that the risk of being killed when flying a single regular flight is the same as the extra risk of smoking two cigarettes in one's lifetime (see Figure 3.2).

Using such a ladder, one can then use comparison events. For example, Carson and Mitchell (forthcoming) extend the lower, very low risk, portion of the ladder (below 25). They show the ladder indicating that the annual risks of dying in an automobile accident are at 21, just below being a police officer, above. They then put the annual risks of dying in the 'special risk' column on the right, for certain levels of lifetime cigarette consumption. For 443 cigarettes consumed, the risk is the same as the automobile accident. For ten trips taken on a commercial airline, the risk is one per 100 000, corresponding to 21 cigarettes smoked in one's lifetime, and so on, with a final focus on the risk of interest to them, THM exposure. Then they link this risk to the amount of money people have to pay to get insurance. For example, people would only have to pay $0.05 to get a $100 000 life insurance policy against being killed by lightning in any given year.

We have to use the risks of any 'person' dying per 100 000 from some situation. Sometimes it is difficult for people to separate out the impersonal risk and death from their own personal experience. Any of us, when faced with a question about our WTP to prevent our own death, would give up all the money we have.

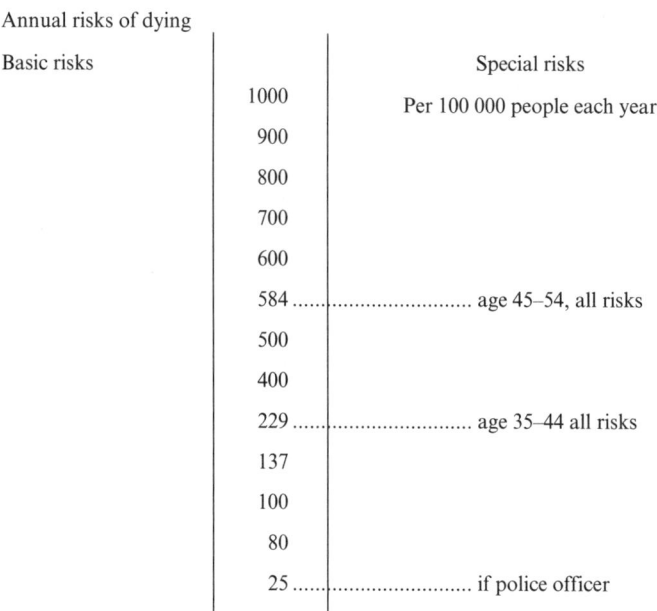

Source: Upper part, from Carson and Mitchell (forthcoming).

Figure 3.2   Risk ladder

The survey instrument uses an open-ended elicitation format, which Carson and Mitchell (forthcoming) say is known *not* to be incentive compatible: truthful preference revelation is not always an optimal strategy. The problem is that they ask about multiple levels of a public good, but only one level of the good can be supplied. In other words, they ask people to name the maximum amount they'd be prepared to vote for with each of three programs that vary the amount of THM reduction. Surveyors went door to door and got 237 completed surveys. Risk reductions would be brought about by increasing water bills to allow for new treatment systems or filters.

Economics predicts that WTP should increase with the increase in the magnitude of the risk reduction, but at a decreasing rate. To reduce the risk of death per 100 000 by 1.33 the estimated WTP is between $19 and $24 or so, and this falls quite a bit if the risk reduction is only 0.04 death per 100 000 (about $1 to $4). In another version the risk reduction is almost nine deaths per 100 000 and the WTP is in the range of $42 to $44.

These WTP per household can be translated into the expected value of a statistical life (SVL) using discounting (see Chapter 2) and the following formula:

$$E(SVL[r^*]) = (100\,000/r^*)(WTP[r^*]/2.86) \qquad (3.8)$$

where r^* is the risk reduction of interest, and $WTP[r^*]$ is the predicted WTP for the risk reduction at the level, and 2.86 is the estimate of the average household size for the sample in their survey. In 1989 dollars, the 1.33 risk reduction translates into between about $330 000 and $378 000, depending on the statistical model used. Such estimates are on the low side. However, the authors state that their estimate of the value of a statistical life falls within the range commonly estimated after one factors in the long latency period for THM to produce a health risk – about 20 to 30 years. If individuals discount over this long period, then the SVL estimates do fall within the range normally reported in the literature (see Horowitz and Carson, 1990).

Carson and Mitchell (forthcoming) conclude that it is possible to obtain WTP estimates for contaminants like THM, that is, ones with very low levels of risk and long latency periods. Risks so small are hard for people to understand. The authors believe that their survey worked well and confirmed expectations regarding the economic theory of risk.

CASE STUDY 3.2   FLUORIDE IN DRINKING WATER

On the ballot in Spokane, Washington in the fall of 2000 in addition to the historically important presidential election there was an initiative to put fluoride in the city's drinking water. The 'pro' side argued that fluoride cuts down tooth decay and the 'against' side argued that fluoride is poisonous and causes fluorosis of the teeth and bones. The pro side said that fluoride reduces cavities by as much as 65 percent. Economics could be used to assess the benefits of fluoridation versus the costs of the program ($1 million initially with about $300 000 per year in maintenance) and the costs in terms of increased risk of fluorosis of teeth and bones. Another possible cost relates to wastewater containing hydrofluorosilisic acid (HFS) and how this affects the aquatic environment once it makes its way into rivers and aquifers.

The US Center for Disease Control estimates that for every dollar spent on fluoridation, $80 is saved in dental treatment.

Source: Pia K. Hansen, 'Water Fight', *The Inlander* (November 2, 2000), pp. 9–10.

3.6 WATER QUALITY STUDIES IN DEVELOPING AND OTHER COUNTRIES

To conclude the chapter, I briefly discuss some water quality issues in other countries. Naturally water quantity problems arise in other countries, but it is fair to say that in many, water quality is a bigger issue than water quantity. European countries have had much longer than the US to dirty their waters and many of their issues have been studied. Canadian economists also investigate water quality problems there. For example, Brox et al. (2003) conduced a valuation study for clean up of the Grand River Watershed, an area just south of the urban portion of Ontario. Toronto, with a population of over 5 million, is just east of this watershed. Survey respondents are asked how much they would pay in their monthly water bill to recover the river's watershed water quality to meet water quality standards. They hypothesize, again using the contingent valuation method, recovery from a minor and major water problem, resulting in average WTP of between $4.56 and about $9.42 (in 1994 Canadian dollars). Brox et al. (2003) say that these estimates are compatible with other water quality valuation studies for United States waters, but these water quality problems are especially challenging for environmental and water resource economists in developing countries.

There is a growing number of studies on developing countries and their water pollution problems, and these are more extensively considered in Chapter 10. Whittington et al. (1991) provide a good example of problems relating to adequate supplies of safe water in Nigeria. Though one could view their study as about water quantity, it is clear that in many rural villages getting 'enough' water is not sufficient. Obtaining water safe for domestic uses is the key, so water quantity studies are still of interest in exploring water quality. Their analysis uses a contingent valuation survey to estimate the household's maximum willingness to pay for water in the city of Onitsha, a city of about 100 000 households. At the time of the study (1987) one-third to one-half of the population lived in conditions with no piped water or indoor toilets. Such a situation is not at all uncommon in the developing world.

Piped water in the city was provided by the local water authority, subsidized by the government, and insufficient resources existed to expand service. Instead, mobile water vendors took up the slack, and household members could either go to them, or if time were important, they could have the water delivered to their dwelling. Data suggested that households in Onitsha were paying about N120 000 (where N is the Nigerian currency, the Naira) per day to private water vendors in the dry season. At August 1987 exchange rates of $1.00 per N4.3, this meant an average of $27 096 per day for all households. If averaged over all households this works out to be about $0.28 per day, per household, or $8.37 per month, per household. This is not significantly different than the monthly bill for a low use household in a metered city in the US, but incomes are not nearly comparable, suggesting that residents of Onitsha are paying a much higher portion of their annual incomes on water.

Two hundred and thirty-five households completed a survey wherein they were asked if they would like to be connected to a new water supply service for a price of N1 per drum (one drum=45 gallons). If they said yes, they were asked the same question at a higher price and if they said yes again another bid was given, and so on resulting in a 'bidding game'. About 44 percent of households were willing to pay between N0.50 and N0.99 for a drum of water. During the dry season poorer households were actually paying up to 18 percent of their income for water, and this was borne out in results of the contingent valuation survey (CVM).

The results of the CVM study also showed that 99 percent of respondents would choose to connect to the new system at a price of N3 per 1000 gallons, and that with increases this percentage would fall, but not drastically. The study concluded that the local water authority could charge a price of the order of N8–10 per 1000 gallons, which would substantially increase revenue for them, but still be much less than the prices the local private vendors were charging.

In contrast to the study above, Lee et al. (1997) do not find significant effects of water supply sources on children's health in the countries of Bangladesh and the Philippines. However, their data do show that about 20 percent of those surveyed in Bangladesh get their water from a pond, river, or canal. Their sophisticated statistical analysis examines various effects on children's weight and survival, concluding that the most important variable is the household's wealth.

Torras and Boyce (1998) regress pollution variables across countries to explore the variation in these. Included in their exploration are two water pollution variables: dissolved oxygen and fecal coliform for various stations in 58 countries. They get their data from the Global Environmental Monitoring System (GEMS) data set.

The regressions performed indicate that income does have a positive relationship with the concentrations for these variables, which relates to the idea of an environmental 'Kuznets' curve. The environmental Kuznets curve idea was put forward by Grossman and Krueger (1995) and others, exploring per capita income's effect on environmental degradation. However, these results are obtained with exclusion of inequality variables such as a Gini coefficient, which measures the degree of an equal distribution of income within various countries. They find that countries with more equitable distributions of income tend to have better environmental quality.

Though Russia would not generally be considered a 'developing' country, in yet another study some economists (Larson and Gnedenko, 1999) examine drinking water quality and associated health risks in Moscow. Avoidance behavior is examined for 615 households surveyed, with findings that 88 percent of the sample regularly boil water. Avoidance decisions are related to income and city locations. Chapter 10 will take a longer look at water problems in other countries.

APPENDIX

Table 3A.1 *Beneficial uses that may be impaired by contaminants*

	Beneficial uses of Surface and Groundwater									
	Agri-culture	Cold fresh-water habitat	Wildlife habitat	Rare and en-dangered species	Drinking water supply	Ground-water recharge	Swim-mable	Fish consump-tion	Navigation and non-contact recreation	Hydro-electric power generation
Physical properties										
Temperature		X	X	X						
Conductivity/TDS	X	X	X	X	X					
Surface Tension/Detergents			X	X						
Turbidity					X					
Chemical Constituents										
Inorganics										
pH		X	X	X						
Dissolved Gases										
Metals		X	X	X	X		X	X		
Anions (SO4, Cl⁻)	X	X	X	X	X					
Nutrients		X	X	X	X	X	X			
Radionuclides					X	X				
Organics										
Volatile Organic Compounds	X	X	X	X	X	X				

Table 3A.1 (continued)

Physical properties	Beneficial Uses of Surface and Ground Water									
	Agri-culture	Cold fresh-water habitat	Wildlife habitat	Rare and endangered species	Drinking water supply	Ground-water recharge	Swim-mable	Fish consump-tion	Navigation and non-contact recreation	Hydro-electric power generation
Synthetic Organic Compounds		X	X	X	X	X	X	X		
Petroleum Hydrocarbons	X	X	X	X	X	X	X	X		
Oil and Grease			X	X	X					
Biota										
Bacteria										
Algae Blue-green		X	X	X	X		X			
Invasive Plants	X	X	X	X	X		X		X	

NOTES

1. I want to thank Betsy Fadali and Jean Agapoff for their contributions to a related report for the state of California, some of which I have incorporated into this chapter.
2. In this particular instance Lake Tahoe's famous clarity is also declining, so loss of clarity is correlated to a decline in water quality. Many readers will know that a 'blue' lake is one with characteristics that allow reflection of the sky color, and some 'green' lakes may simply be reflecting light and surrounding greenery.
3. These costs correspond to the assumption that the social discount rate is 3 percent and that the preferred alternative is the version of the rule met.
4. Feigenbaum and Teeples (1983) also investigate functional forms for the hedonic cost model of water delivery (rather than treatment), finding that the usual Cobb-Douglas specification is sensitive to the form of the model. They reject the hypothesis that ownership (private versus public) is an important determinant of costs.
5. Source: http://www.epa.gov/owow/tmdl/overviewfs.html
6. Is one in 100 a large or small risk? We consider the answer to this in Chapter 6.

REFERENCES

Abt Associates Incorporated (2000), *Arsenic in Drinking Water Rule Economic Analysis*, paper developed for the US Environmental Protection Agency, Office of Ground Water; and Drinking Water, EPA 815-R-00-026, Washington, DC. Accessed at http://www.epa.gov/safewater/ars/econ_analysis.pdf.

Agapoff, Jean (2000), 'A hedonic study of the impact of oxygenated fuels on water supplier's treatment costs', unpublished master's thesis, Department of Applied Economics and Statistics, University of Nevada, Reno.

Agapoff, Jean, Elizabeth Fadali and W. Douglass Shaw (2000), 'Summary of the literature on groundwater valuation', draft report to the California State Water Quality Control Board, Sacramento, CA.

Anonymous (1997), 'Clear progress: 25 years of the Clean Water Act', *Audubon* (September–October), 36–46 and 106–107.

Bhattacharyya, A., T.R. Harris, R. Narayanan and K. Raffiee (1995), 'Technical efficiency of rural water utilities', *Journal of Agricultural and Resource Economics*, **20**(2) (December), 373–91.

Boisvert, R.N. and T.M. Schmit (1997), 'Tradeoff between economies of size in treatment and diseconomies of distribution for rural water systems', *Agricultural and Resource Economics Review*, **26**(2) (October), 237–46.

Brox, James A., C. Ramesh and Kenneth R. Stollery (2003), 'Estimating willingness to pay for improved water quality in the presence of item nonresponse basis', *American Journal of Agricultural Economics*, **85** (2), 414–28.

Cadmus Group (2003), 'Economic analysis for the long term enhanced surface water treatment rule', draft report 68-C-02-02 to the US Environmental Protection Agency (EPA), Arlington, VA.

Carson, R.T. and R.C. Mitchell (1993), 'The value of clean water: the public's willingness to pay for boatable, fishable, and swimmable quality water', *Water Resources Research*, **20**, 2445–54.

Carson, R.T. and R.C. Mitchell (forthcoming), 'Public preferences toward environmental risks: the case of trihalomethanes', in A. Alberini, D. Bjornstad and J.

Kahn (eds), *Handbook of Contingent Valuation*, Cheltenham, UK and Northampton, MA: Edward Elgar.

Caulkins, P. and S. Sessions (1997), 'Water pollution and the organic chemicals industry', in R.D. Morgenstern (ed.), *Economic Analyses at EPA: Assessing Regulatory Impact*, Washington, DC: Resources for the Future, pp. 205–32.

Cech, Thomas V. (2003), *Principles of Water Resources: History, Development, Management, and Policy*, New York: John Wiley and Sons.

Coleman, Brooke (1999), 'Governor has deadline removed from MTBE bill,' *San Francisco Chronicle* (27 September), 22.

Dearmont, D., B. McCarl and D.A. Tolman (1998), 'Costs of water treatment due to diminished water quality: a case study in Texas', *Water Resources Research*, **34**(4), 849–53.

Egan, Timothy (2001), 'In New Mexico, debate over arsenic strikes home', *New York Times* (4 April), A-1, A-7.

Feigenbaum, S. and R. Teeples (1983), 'Public versus private water delivery: a hedonic cost approach', *Review of Economics and Statistics*, **65**(4), 672–78.

Forster, D.L., C.P. Bardos and D.D. Southgate (1987), 'Soil erosion and water treatment costs', *Journal of Soil and Water Conservation* (September–October), 349–52.

Freeman, A.M. (1990), 'Water pollution policy', in Paul Portney (ed.), *Current Issues in US Environmental Policy*, Washington, DC: Resources for the Future, pp. 97–149.

Gardner, M. (2002), 'Time runs short over Salton Sea', *The San Diego Union-Tribune* (30 December), A-1 and A-10.

Grossman, G.M. and A.B. Krueger (1995) 'Economic growth and the environment', *Quarterly Journal of Economics*, **110**, 353–77.

Haas, C.N., C.S. Crockett, J.B. Rose, C.P. Gerba and A.M. Fazil (1996), 'Assessing the risk posed by oocysts in drinking water', *Journal of American Water Works Association*, **88**(9), 131–6.

Holmes, Thomas P. (1988), 'The offsite impact of soil erosion on the water treatment industry', *Land Economics*, **64**(4) (November), 356–66.

Horowitz, J.K. and R.T. Carson (1990), 'Discounting statistical lives', *Journal of Risk and Uncertainty*, **3**, 403–13.

Innes, R. and D. Cory (2001), 'The economics of safe drinking water', *Land Economics*, **77**(1) (February), 94–117.

Jakus, P. et al. (1997), 'Do sportfish consumption advisories affect reservoir anglers' site choice?', *Agricultural and Resource Economics Review*, **26**(2) (October), 196–204.

Jakus, P. and W.D. Shaw (2003), 'Perceived hazard and product choice: an application to recreation site choice', *Journal of Risk and Uncertainty*, **26**(1), 77–92.

Kneese, A. and B. Bower (1968), *Managing Water Quality: Economics, Technology, Institutions*, Baltimore, MD: Johns Hopkins University Press for Resources for the Future.

Knopman, D.S. and R.A. Smith (1993), 'Twenty years of the Clean Water Act', *Environment*, **35**(1) (January–February), 17–25.

Larson, B. and E.K. Gnedenko (1999), 'Avoiding health risks from drinking water in Moscow: an empirical analysis', *Environment and Development Economics*, **4**(4) (October), 565–81.

Larson, D.M. and D.K. Lew (2001), 'Cleaning up surface waters in California:

how much is it worth?', paper presented at the Western Economic Association international meetings, San Francisco, CA, July.

Lee, Donna and R.E. Howitt (1996), 'Modeling regional agricultural production and salinity control alternatives for water quality policy analysis', *American Journal of Agricultural Economics*, **48** (February), 41–53.

Lee, Lung-fei, M.R. Rosenzweig and M.M. Pitt (1997), 'The effects of improved nutrition, sanitation, and water quality on child health in high-mortality populations', *Journal of Econometrics*, **77**, 209–35.

Levin, R. (1997), 'Lead in drinking water', in R.D. Morgenstern (ed.), *Economic Analyses at EPA: Assessing Regulatory Impact*, Washington, DC: Resources for the Future, pp. 205–32.

Lictenberg, E., D. Zilberman and K.T. Bogen (1989), 'Regulating environmental health risks under uncertainty: groundwater contamination in California', *Journal of Environmental Economics and Management*, **17**(1) (July), 22–34.

Magat, W.A., A.J. Krupnick and W. Harrington (1986), *Rules in the Making: A Statistical Analysis of Regulatory Agency Behavior*, Washington, DC: Resources for the Future.

Murphy, D.D. and C. Knopp (eds) (2000), *Lake Tahoe Watershed Assessment: Volume 1*, general technical report PSW-GTR-175 US Forest Service, Pacific Southwest Research Station.

National Research Council (no date) 'Assessing the TMDL approach to water quality management', Washington, DC: National Academy Press, accessed at http://books.nap.edu/books

Raucher, R.S. and J.A. Drago (1992), 'Estimating the cost of compliance with the drinking water standard for radon', *Journal of the American Water Works Association* (March), 51–65.

Ribaudo, M.O., R.D. Horan and M.E. Smith (1999), 'Economics of water quality protection from nonpoint sources: theory and practice', economic research service report no. 782, US Department of Agriculture, Washington, DC.

Rowe, R., W.D. Shaw and W.D. Schulze (1992), 'The Nestucca Oil Spill', in J. Duffield and K. Ward (eds), *Natural Resource Damages*, New York: John Wiley & Sons, Chapter 2.

Spulber, Nicolas and Asghar Sabbaghi (1998), *Economics of Water Resources: From Regulation to Privatization*, Boston, MA: Kluwer Academic Publishers.

Torras, M. and J.K. Boyce (1998), 'Income, inequality, and pollution: a reassessment of the environmental Kuznets Curve', *Ecological Economics*, **25** (May), 147–60.

USDA Economic Research Service (1997), agricultural resources and agricultural indicators.

Whittington, D., D. Lauria and X. Mu (1991), 'A study of water vending and willingness to pay for water in Onitsha, Nigeria', *World Development*, **19**(2/3), 179–98.

WEBSITE

http://www.epa.gov/safewater/mcl.html.

4. Water prices and rates for residential use[1]

4.0 INTRODUCTION TO WATER RATES ISSUES

This chapter considers water prices or rates for residential customers: how are these determined, and are they like any other market good price?[2] Special pricing issues for rural area customers do not get much attention, though special ones are arising today (see Chapter 3's description of rural water treatment problems, for example, which may lead to special water pricing issues). A few key issues included below are applicable to rural areas, but as small rural water systems are often fundamentally different from larger urban ones, the discussion is mostly geared to urban areas where water is provided to customers by fairly large-scale private firms or government utility companies. It is worth remembering from Chapter 3 that large water supply systems often exhibit economies of scale, and they don't often have to cope with issues related to delivery to remote and scattered customers. As a preview of what is to come, some readers may be surprised to see how moderately or even cheaply priced water is in many urban areas today, including areas that would be characterized as arid.

In October 2003 farmers in the arid south of California agreed to transfer water to residential consumers in the San Diego urban area for about $250 per acre foot (Murphy, 2003). Can we safely say, by observing this one price, that $250 per acre foot is *the* price, or at least what water costs a consumer? Definitely not, but the question of the prevailing price is not an easy question to answer, and in fact I phrased the question in two parts because the price and cost of water are not the same thing to an economist, as should be clear from Chapter 2. We look for answers to both questions in the water economics literature, especially that which is empirical; an empirical study uses actual data on prices and quantities to estimate demand or supply functions and sheds light on costs and prices.

Brookshire and his colleagues (Brookshire et al., 2004) recently provided an estimate of the average price per acre foot of water in three markets, Arizona, New Mexico, and Colorado. The average price per acre foot varies from $613 per acre foot in Arizona to $5312 per acre foot in Colorado. The authors of this study look for explanations of the variation in the number of water trades that take place, noting that Arizona trades are far fewer than in Colorado. Such analyses of market prices are rare.

In fact, most of the empirical economics literature on water demand that informs us about water rates comes from studies of residential customers. This is quite simply because a modern urban water supplier typically has easy access to data on its residential customers and economists have talked them into sharing it. For one reason or another economists do not have easy access to data from other sources, including rural water suppliers and industrial users. This is likely because rural areas may have many households on private wells, and many water utilities (both urban and rural) do not wish to disclose the data on industrial customers.[3] Residential customer data may include the volumes of water used in the household over some time period, but sometimes consists only of total billing data (i.e. the total amount of money the customer was charged). Both types of data may be used to estimate a model of the household's demand for water, or at least the demand a city has for water, but only if the latter data can be used to reveal quantities used.

In the early 1990s tap water for the typical consumer in the United States was priced between $0.45 and $2.85 per thousand gallons, a large range (Allen and Darby, 1994). In his recent book Tom Cech (2003) offers estimates of the annual cost per customer for three cities, Los Angeles, Lincoln, Nebraska, and New York. They are $534, $249, and $455 per year, respectively. But these costs are not the price that customers pay. For example, in New York the rate customers pay is about $1.31 per hundred cubic feet (per 750 gallons). Some residential prices are reported in different units. Residential water shares may sell for as much as $10 000 per acre foot in one area of Colorado, and for about $1000 in another area of Colorado (see Howe and Linaweaver, 1967). Why is the 'price' of water ten times higher in one part of the state than another, or in one region versus another? The consumer's cost of bottled water (is *priced* at) much more: in 1990 a single gallon was priced at $0.90, on average (Allen and Darby, 1994), and of course consumers often pay more than that at a retail outlet (a store, a shop, or vendor in an airport, etc.). We don't often think of water as having such a high per unit price, and many economists agree that the price of water has historically been too low from a social point of view. As will be seen below, low water prices may not continue to be the norm (Mann, 1987).

To clarify all of this, we begin again with some theory. Economists suggest that the price of water should be, from the point of view of economic efficiency, tied to the marginal cost of supplying it. As a quick reminder from Chapter 2, in a competitive market, the price of a private good should be set to the marginal cost of providing that good, $P = MC$.

At this point economic efficiency is achieved, and this is consistent with a competitive market equilibrium. The simple rule gives way to what is commonly known as 'marginal cost pricing'. A classic argument for short-run marginal cost pricing was made in the late 1970s by the deregulation economist Alfred Kahn (1988), who more or less encouraged a motto in the airline industry that can be paraphrased as: 'no airplane should ever take off with empty seats as long as there are customers who would be willing to pay the short-run marginal costs associated with giving them a ticket'. Even in the airline industry short-run marginal cost pricing is often difficult to accomplish and it is still subject to short-run fluctuations in input prices.[4]

This is all well and good, but it begs the question as to exactly what marginal cost is. Many involved in the water industry realize that marginal costs may be hard to identify and so some economists and policy makers may substitute 'average cost' pricing for marginal cost pricing rules. It now sounds as though it is all figured out, but not so fast.

Water rates in the 'real' world

Those familiar with what a private or public supplier of water does may wonder what in the world I am talking about here, for the above jargon may have little to do with setting water 'rates', which is the key word used in the water industry. Prices of water (P) and 'rates' charged for water are in fact not the same thing. A rate-setter may be used to thinking about accounting costs and trying to set rates to recover some of these accounting costs using a rate that will be politically acceptable. Why is this so?

If a water supplier has market power (ability to influence prices, at least locally), it may not be a price taker, and can set price above the point of marginal revenue, MR. In this type of market setting, the optimal pricing implies that MR (not P) = MC, and typically the price will be set much higher than in a competitive market. In the typical United States city the water supplier is a monopoly, and because of this strong market power is most often regulated by government. I suppose that this is one example of where the economics profession has influenced government such that much of society might favor monopoly regulation.

In many cities the water and electricity supplier are one and the same private utility company. Imagine how unpopular they would be if they could raise the price of electricity and water in any fashion they chose. Clark and Stevie (1981) state, without reservation, that 'the local water utility is ordinarily a pure monopoly except to the extent that industrial customers of water may furnish their own supplies' (p. 18). The 'price' the customer pays is most often the rate that the water supplier is allowed to charge by its regulator, either a state, county, or some other government oversight or regulatory agency.[5] We have nearly all picked up a local newspaper and

Water prices and rates for residential use 103

seen articles about controversies stemming from the utility company asking for a rate hike, often featuring an interview with someone from a household who feels that they just cannot afford this rate increase. With enough negative press, a utility sometimes has to back away from a rate increase request. All water rates are the result of a political-economic process and because of this, are different from prices determined in equilibrium in a well-functioning market. Still, it is worth pausing at this point, and quickly reviewing the basics for a well-functioning market, so that there is some substance and theory behind the claims above.

4.1 BACK TO BASICS: SUPPLY AND DEMAND

At its most fundamental level, water, like everything else, has a price that depends on the relationship between supply and demand. We begin with a fairly exhaustive discussion of supply.

4.1.1 The Supply Side

As mentioned in Chapter 3 in the context of treatment, a water supplier may have several tasks, but basically must secure and probably store a raw water supply, and then treat it for it to be of acceptable or legal quality, and finally, deliver it to households. A supplier has some reservation price, that is, the minimum price at which he or she is willing to sell a volume of water. This price of course depends on costs, as do all supply schedules.[6] Costs again include all operating or variable costs, such as labor and energy, but also include fixed or capital costs: the cost of a treatment facility, storage capacity, and distribution systems. In fact in their article on water supply Clark and Stevie (1981) suggest that the two important components for water suppliers can be split into (i) treatment, and (ii) transportation and distribution. (This ignores the first component above, the 'acquisition', or the securing of a source of water in the first place, either from surface water supplies, which might involve storage in reservoirs or tanks, or groundwater supplies.) Treatment and distribution involve capital costs for equipment, pipelines, and facilities (pumping stations, water tanks) and variable costs like labor and the energy used for pumping.

Often, large water suppliers experience economies of scale, where average costs decline as the firms get bigger. 'Big' here translates to an expanded market, and likely a larger service area. However, a key problem for the supplier stems from the fact that the distance from their plants of households wanting water affects the marginal cost of supply. This is of course for various reasons: pipeline amounts increase as distance increases,

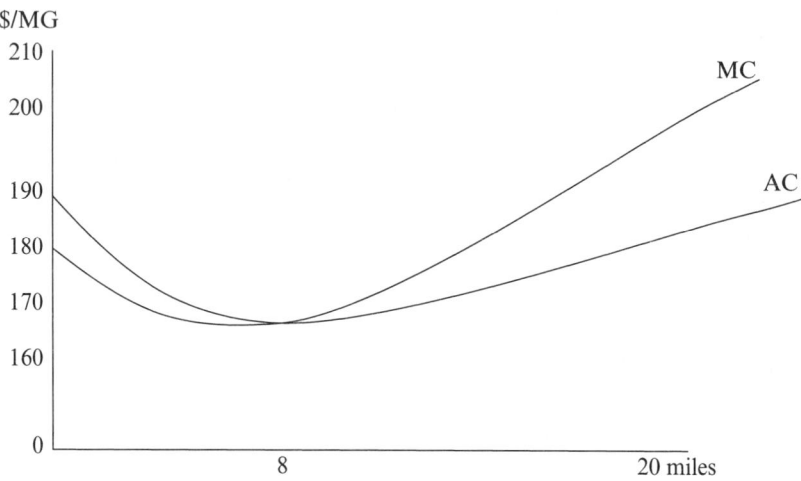

Figure 4.1   Unit and marginal costs for water utilities (capacity of 150 gallons/capita/per day), with distance

energy costs increase with distance, and so on. This suggests that there are tradeoffs between a water supplier's size (see Chapter 3) and distribution costs, and in fact, economists have modeled the 'optimal' distance of suppliers away from population centers, taking this into account. Clark and Stevie (1981), using data for 12 water utilities, find that as population densities decrease, the 'least-cost' distance from their customers increases for utilities of a given size. Using their data, they are able to estimate shapes for marginal and average cost curves over distance such as are reproduced in Figure 4.1. The data suggest that the minimum average cost, in dollars per million gallons, comes when customers are about eight miles away from the plants, at least for plants that provide about 0.018 million gallons per capita per year (150 gallons per capita per day).

This brief exploration allows the reader to see that water supply decisions are not as easy as it at first seems they might be.

Costs of providing dependable water supply have risen dramatically over time because of issues in providing reliable storage, and may continue to do so. As an example, one of the better known water economists in California, Henry Vaux, illustrated the rising capital cost per acre foot of annual dependable yield from several dams in California. Capital costs rose from $415 per acre foot of annual dependable yield in 1968 to over $2 400 per af for a project with a proposed completion date of 1998.

Economists stress efficiency in the water industry, in both the long run and short run. The difference between the short- and long-run outcome

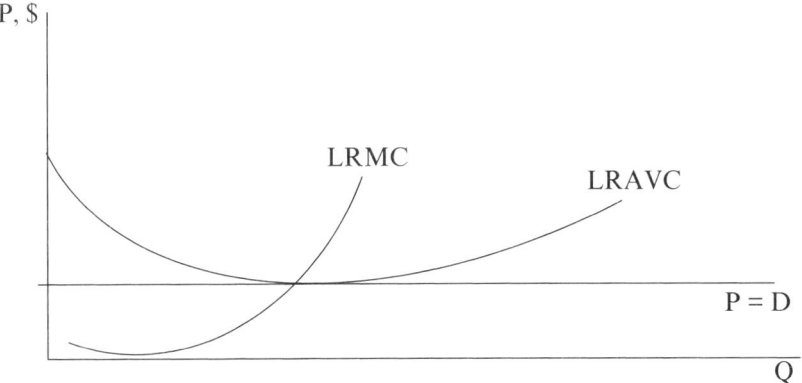

Figure 4.2   Long-run costs and competitive markets

may be tantamount to considering whether key features of the water industry allow adaptability and flexibility. Economists want to see policy makers move toward maximization of social net benefits. With perfect competition in the market place, the long-run equilibrium solution requires that P = LRMC, where LRMC is long-run marginal cost. Remember that in the true long-run world of the economist, there are no fixed costs.

Figure 4.2 depicts the usual long-run cost relationship in a competitive market. At the long-run equilibrium point in Figure 4.2 LRMC = LRAVC (long-run average variable cost), so we know that total revenue equals total cost, and, by the economist's definition, profits are zero. Recall from Chapter 2 that this is brought about by the absence of market barriers: there is no entry or exit problem. If long-run profits are in excess for some firms, new firms that want to supply water would enter the market, driving down profits to zero.

The water utility as regulated monopolist
Much of the analysis above is helpful as a starting point, but the introduction to this chapter suggests that it does not represent what we see in the real world of water supply because of the nature of the market. As stated above, the water utility is typically the only water supplier for residential users in a region, or at least is one of only a few. As mentioned above regulatory oversight is common. Water utilities are unusual in that they may not set output, the amount of water they desire to provide, nor do they set the prices their customers should pay for that water. Chapter 2's discussion of the competitive firm, some of which is repeated above, suggests that the usual competitive firm would choose output in accordance with a level that maximizes profits. However, many water utilities are required by regulators

to satisfy the demands of their customers. It is often politically unacceptable to allow water suppliers to cut supply to customers. Output is considered 'exogenous' to the supplier and it shows up as a variable in a cost function, along with the prices of inputs (see Crain and Zardkoohi, 1978). Even when the water utility would like to minimize the costs of producing a given amount of water for those in the community, and so takes this first step toward maximizing profits, they will likely find that their prices or rates are regulated and, to a degree, beyond their control.

The degree to which the regulator controls the water rate in a region or community varies. Have you heard of the water supplier and then the public utility commission (PUC) representative testifying at a rate hearing in your state or region? It is with this agency that troubles often begin for the utility company. The water utility cannot simply set prices, as a pure, unregulated monopolist would, because of the power of the PUC. Consider that an economist that works for the PUC would wish to set P = LRMC if he or she believes in the virtues of perfect competition. This may not at all be the price that the monopoly would choose, were it able to set rates, because they would set marginal revenue, not price, equal to LRMC and sell at the corresponding higher price. If the PUC has public support and a good deal of political power, it will deny the rate hike the utility seeks, if they believe it is way out of line with a competitive price, or would result in abnormally high profits.

Water rates that are approved by PUC and appear on one's bill, and competitively determined economic prices are actually two different things, and rates may even be different than the price determined in a monopoly pricing model. Economists are most often thinking of the competitive price of a good or service as in Figure 4.2. Prices in markets are determined by equilibrium of supply and demand, but depend on degrees of competition on the supply side. When introducing little or no competition Figure 4.2 is modified to allow a divergence between MR and demand, and the general result is that compared to a perfectly competitive market, a monopolist will under-supply and over-charge for the good. Figure 4.3 demonstrates this: compare Q_m to Q_{pc} and P_m to P_{pc}.

A natural monopoly

Another problem arises in the real world that relates to rate setting. What if there are decreasing average costs and the regulator tries to force the monopolist to accomplish the marginal cost pricing scheme? For the natural monopolist the MC schedule is always declining and always below AVC. Price can never cover AVC, and thus the natural monopolist is always unable to cover total costs if they set P = MC. If they are forced to pursue this goal, one would simply expect this supplier eventually to get out of the business altogether, unless some economic assistance can be provided to

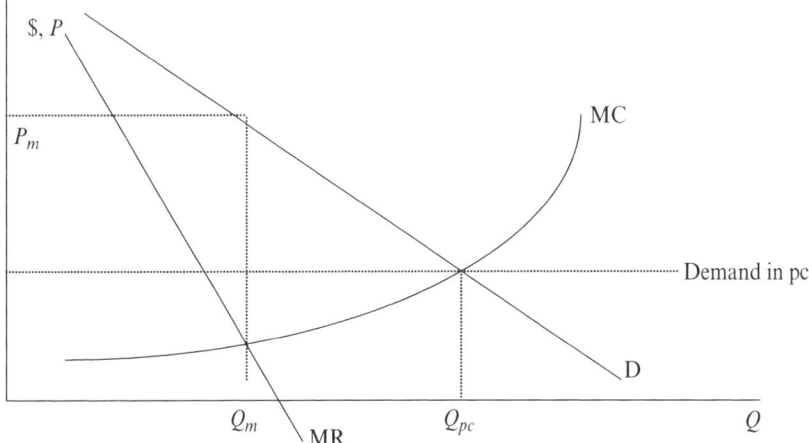

Figure 4.3 Monopolist versus competitive long-run equilibrium

keep them operating. Thus, there is a dilemma here for the natural monopolist that involves short-run and long-run planning, and long-run attainment of equilibrium conditions. The message is that the regulating agency cannot simply try to enforce the goal of setting P = LRMC for a natural monopolist. It is, however, usually up to the monopolist to demonstrate convincingly to the regulator that they are indeed a natural monopoly. Antitrust cases and history such as the break up of the giant telephone company into the 'baby Bells' suggest that they will not have much success in this regard. The reason the antitrust laws are popular with politicians is because of the perception that customers at the mercy of the monopolist will not fair well, so the public will support these types of laws and government intervention.

For all of the above complicated reasons, many private companies today shy away from the business of providing water to residential or other customers. Instead it is quite common to see public entities providing water in residential areas. As an example, in recent years the private utility in the Northern Nevada region, Sierra Pacific Power, got rid of its water supply division (see the case study below), and this division became one of several public entities that provide water, one of which is a regional water supply agency, and two of which are county government operations. Whether the public agencies provide water as efficiently (that is, at as low cost) as a private water supplier is a matter of debate (note, that an older study by Crain and Zardkoohi, 1978, suggests not).

Finally, as if all of the above is not complex enough, a further complication for the water supplier is predicting the reliability of precipitation which may fundamentally determine their raw water supply. No water supplier really wants to be caught short during a drought. In the past, many suppliers didn't use sophisticated models of storage under uncertainty. As you will see below, many now go to great lengths to model the risks of supply that stem from uncertainty of weather and precipitation (see Chapter 6).

4.2 RATES AND RESIDENTIAL WATER SUPPLY

Rates simply begin with costs to the supplier, and then the firm (the water utility) marks up or tacks on some additional cost increase that results in the 'rate' that the customer pays. It may strike the reader as odd, but in fact mark-up pricing is not too far distant from the way that Karl Marx suggested prices were determined at the time he lived. The relevant costs here are those accounting costs that the utility thinks are important in both the short-run and long-run supply of water. Often, a water utility will have a civil engineer and/or an accountant in charge of the rate-setting division, not an economist, and one hopes from the community's point of view, that this person, or group of people, is indeed thinking about long-run supply issues.

In the late 1990s the typical water-supplying monopolist in the western US wanted to make a profit, but still had to have a good plan for the future because of high, expected population growth rates. The country was experiencing a significant amount of out-migration from the northeast and Midwest, and substantial in-migration into Nevada, Arizona, Utah, Colorado, and California. Regulatory commissions in the modern era will let the monopolist who sells water make a small profit. They do that by regulating rates carefully, allowing for the excess over costs that leads to an acceptable accounting profit. As costs increase, a utility will ask for higher rates.

With a growing population and a constant or increasing demand per customer, the utility or water supplier has obviously had to try to secure more water unless they face the luxury of having a large excess supply in reserve. Today the supplier may wish to secure water supplies that are not needed, at least in the short run, but which under current projections of growth may well be needed in the future. Capital investment will be needed for storage facilities, historically a dam and reservoir, but also including underground storage, or above-ground storage tanks, depending on the supplier. A new distribution system may have to be built, again with costs being borne by the utility, which no doubt hopes to pass on these costs to its customers.

Water suppliers have to know very well what the actual relevant costs are, or will be, in the future, or they cannot plan and ask for rate hikes accordingly. A problem is created when they do not know. Some costs relate to long-run supply issues and these future costs may not be known with certainty. Thus, if a supplier is uncertain and worried that costs may rise (as in fact the introduction to this chapter suggests is true), they may have a strong incentive to overstate accounting costs in the hope that the regulator will set higher rates leading to higher profits. Such situations create a contentious environment in which to operate.

Short-run versus long-run rates
We return to a key question: should the PUC approve rates in a carefully calculated plan to provide water in the short run, or the long run, or put another way, should rates be based on long-run, or short-run, costs? The answer is not simple. It is complicated by the fact that, as time goes on, new water supplies may be more expensive than old water supplies were because of potential relative scarcity and competing demands, as well as simple cost increases. If the regulator sets prices too high in the current period because they want to let the utility save current profits for reinvesting in the purchase of new supplies and delivery systems, the public (the current residential customers) will get angry about short-term rates being too high. If the utility regulator sets rates low, to offset current short-run costs the utility may not invest and plan for expansion or unusual situations. But if a drought occurs, or growth occurs so quickly that water supplies run short, the affected set of residential customers will also get angry, blaming the water supplier for its failure to adequately supply them in times of shortage.

A common scheme observed in the arid western United States during droughts is to ask customers to voluntarily limit watering their lawns to only two or three days per week, and the voluntary restrictions become mandatory rationing schemes during the droughts. Rationing is hardly ever popular with such customers because they believe they are entitled to as much water as they want, whenever they want it. The problem for the utility is to convince the public, as well as the regulator, that they can only have this package of unlimited quantity and timing if they are willing to pay higher rates today, to build in a lot of capacity that might be in excess during normal times in the current period. The need for integrating the long run into rate-setting is discussed again below, after reviewing several types of rates.

4.3 PURPOSE AND TYPES OF RATES

There are many purposes of setting particular water rates, including: (i) generation of income/revenue to allow self-sustaining operations; (ii) allocation costs among types of use and users; and (iii) providing incentives to customers. Water rates have to allow revenue that is sufficient to cover:

- operating costs, taxes, energy costs
- capital replacement costs, or acquisition (purchase of water rights)
- planning costs
- labor costs (salaries)
- system expansion costs

As mentioned above, the water utility may have joint costs. For example, a water supplier's neighborhood distribution network has to provide fire protection as well as regular daily or monthly service. Peak loads for summer may also provide off-peak winter demands. The supplier may wish to allocate the costs of fire protection and provide for peak load supplies in setting the rate. This is complicated, so is there a solution to the joint cost problem? Some say yes: for example, many economists have proposed a two-part tariff or rate structure as a solution to the joint cost problem. In such a scheme the utility combines marginal cost pricing with a fixed charge (service or connection charge). The latter raises the needed additional revenue to cover total cost.

Administrators at water supply companies very likely intuitively understand that long-run capacity considerations should influence pricing decisions, though they may not couch the decision in terms of economic jargon. Marginal cost pricing first began to be viewed favorably in the electric utility industry in the mid 1970s, but I doubt that it has spread widely in the water business. The reader needs to remember that in some areas of the US there are still many residential customers who don't even have water meters, making it impossible for suppliers to even measure a household's water use accurately. This would make it less likely that the supplier would engage in sophisticated demand or supply analysis. In wet areas water utilities may not normally face the storage and capacity problems that the arid region utilities do, thus affecting short-run versus long-run costs, so again the suppliers in these areas may not adopt marginal cost pricing either.

A municipal region supplied by a single water supplier can of course change its rate structure. For example, after long struggles over the best, and politically acceptable, way to change rates, in 1977 the city of Los Angeles finally abandoned a decreasing block rate structure.

Returning to the idea that $P = LRMC$, or $P = SRMC$, note that, by definition, the relevant SRMC is always less than LRMC. The higher the level of capital intensity, the more pronounced the difference between the two. For the water industry, the estimated ratio of required assets per dollar of revenue is $10:$12, a much higher capital intensity than for other industries

Block 1 Use: zero to 525 gallons per day at rate of $1.71 per hundred cubic feet (ccf)
Block 2 Use: 526 gallons to 1000 gpd at rate of $3.25 per ccf
Block 3 Use: Above 1000 gpd at rate of $4.25 per ccf

Figure 4.4 Hypothetical example of block rate prices

(Mitchell and Hanemann, 1994). If costs do not vary at the margin over different blocks of use, then marginal cost pricing implies use of only one per unit water rate or charge, rather than something like decreasing or increasing block rates.

A changing block rate is one where the supplier defines a 'block' of usage from a low water volume used (for example, a baseline of 100 gallons per day) to some upper use amount (for example, 500 gallons per day) then defines a new block between this first upper bound and a new higher upper volume (500 to 1000 gallons per day), and so on, with all customers who use water at a level within a block facing one rate (see Figure 4.4). Though marginal cost pricing isn't exactly consistent with dynamics (incorporating changes over time), an increasing block rate structure can be justified by using a dynamic model of water system costs (see Dandy et al., 1997).

In practice, the rates that the water supplier sets that earn them some profit may simply be a rate that is fixed per month for all consumers, or fixed per month but varying across different types of consumers. Such fixed or flat charges are independent of the quantity of water that is used. The company does not need a water meter, or any device that measures actual use by a household or business, to charge a flat rate. The rate is often the same, regardless of the season. Without doubt this practice is quite profitable for the supplier during the months when actual demand is low (winter), but it quite possibly encourages waste of water, and may be a boon to high-demand users in summer months.

In contrast, the supplier must have a water meter in order to charge by volume used. Surprisingly, many household members do not really know much about their water meter.[7] There are also sophisticated rate structures when metering is possible, and many suppliers now charge initial hook-up fees. Table 4.1 below shows types of rates typically seen in the US and western countries. These vary from simple flat rates to fairly complicated mixed rate structures.

Table 4.1. shows many existing rate systems from a variety of places in the US, but it is increasingly common to see water suppliers, particularly in arid and rapidly growing regions, moving away from flat rate pricing and toward some scheme that is consistent with long-run marginal cost pricing.

Table 4.1 Types of water rates

Flat	Doesn't vary with quantity of water. Example: in 1996 Northern Nevada's Sierra Pacific Power charged customers with a 3/4 inch pipe $43.13 per month, and those with a 1 inch pipe $59.74 per month
Seasonally differentiated	Varies by season, in recognition that summer use is higher
Uniform rate variable charge	A variable charge; amount paid per unit of consumption is the same over all units consumed
Block rate variable charge	Variable charge where the unit charge varies, either decreasing with the amount consumed, or increasing with the amount consumed
	Examples: in 1990 Denver switched from a declining block to an ascending one, charging $0.71 per 1000 gallons for the first 15 000 gallons per month, $0.89 per 1000 for use above that, plus a $6.00 service charge every two months
	In 1992 Houghton, Michigan charged $0.75 per hundred cubic feet, with a separate, higher wastewater charge
	In 1996 Sierra Pacific Power (Reno, Nevada) charged $1.55 per 1000 gallons for the first 6000 gallons used, and $2.11 for each additional 1000 gallons
	In the year 2000 Lincoln, Nebraska charged $0.90 per hundred cubic feet (a 'unit') for the first 800 cubic feet used,* $1.11/unit for the next 1500 cubic feet used, and $1.55/unit for each additional hundred cubic feet used
Connection, facilities, or capacity charge	One time charge for hook up. An example here is that Sierra Pacific Power charges $10.02 per month for metered customers with a 3/4 inch pipe, and $10.61 per month for 1 inch pipe metered customers
Lifeline charges	Targeted for low-income customers

Note: * Recall that 100 cubic feet (hcf) equals 750 gallons. One can then see that rates per 1000 gallons allow a larger volume consumed per rate charged, so adjustments must be made to compare rates in each case.

Sources: Cech, 2003 (for Lincoln, Nebraska rates); Joyce and Merz, 1994 (for Houghton, Michigan rates); Morris, 1990 (for Denver rates).

Recall the discussion about costs and capacity. If a supplier purchases storage via a large reservoir, but only uses a small part of it now, then their average costs look big because the current output (Q) is small and of course AVC = TC/Q, and the small denominator makes AVC look larger. The greater the use of the water, the more AVC falls, simply because the costs are spread out as Q increases. However, short-run MC may also be falling for other reasons. These factors are important in the above debate about whether prices should be set to short-run or long-run marginal costs.

All of these factors complicate the water supplier's task of assessing long-run production and costs. At present, there is only general agreement among water and energy economists that a utility's prices or rates should never be set below short-run marginal costs. It would be nice to think this were true, but in fact most large utility companies provide many things (electricity, water, natural gas) simultaneously, and this puts them solidly into the world of joint production and allocating joint costs, which was briefly discussed above. The modern utility probably cannot even identify one simple marginal cost. So, what is done in the real world by the complex water supplier or general utility company (one that probably provides electric power) that happens to supply water to residential customers? Most likely, they use an embedded cost rate structure.

Embedded cost rate structures

The embedded cost rate structure approach is the most commonly used rate schedule method used by retail water agencies. There are dozens of possible methods, but the most common are the Demand/Commodity and Base Capacity/Extra Capacity methods. Often state and local public utility commissions require investor-owned utilities to calculate rates this way. The methods generally share four steps:

1. Determine the utility's annual revenue requirement (annual costs). This includes a return on invested capital. For example, the utility may be allowed to earn 5 percent on its invested capital.
2. Allocate the revenue requirement to functional cost categories. Once allocated, charges can be set to recover these. They include base capacity costs (this includes variable costs of water service), extra capacity costs (includes a fixed cost of system capacity portion and this is where they try to measure the costs of capacity to meet peak-load demands), customer costs (includes metering, billing, administration), and firefighting costs.
3. Distribute functional costs to customer classes according to usage characteristics (for example, industrial, single-family residential, multiple-family dwelling, and so on.)

4. Design the rate schedule to recover distributed functional costs. Set so that when multiplied by total use by that class, the total revenue equals the share of functional costs.

Mitchell and Hanemann (1994) say that this embedded cost-rate (ECR) scheme may be 'fair' because it attempts to allocate costs to that class that creates the need for the supply. However, these two economists also note that when commonly applied, ECR does not meet all of the typical objectives a water utility has (providing a break-even revenue and accurately reflecting the costs of service). Moncur and Fok (1993) say that utilities often make mistakes in this sort of calculation and typically under-price the cost of service. Part of the mistake may be due to the fact that accounting costs may be what they call 'book costs', which are the value of the asset when purchased, not replacement cost. Moncur and Fok suggest that use of market, rather than book, values of assets may result in an increase of water rates of up to 50 percent for some cities. In addition, ECR methods do not properly allocate joint costs and likely work best when costs are stable, not when they are unstable.

Long-run average cost pricing
In contrast to, and critical of, embedded rate structures, economists like Alfred Kahn harp on the fact that for efficient pricing, prices must be set equal to some sort of average long-run incremental cost expected for an incremental block of sales. The inference is that the water utility does not want to set price equal to the average cost of both the old and new source supplies, which is consistent with the embedded cost approach. Problems abound when there are decreasing average costs, because setting price equal to long-run marginal costs will lead the water supplier to never be able to cover costs.

Alternatives: two part tariffs, Ramsey pricing, and peak load pricing
One solution to the complex job of rate-setting is to allow for a two-part tariff. This is exactly what is becoming increasingly common in practice: one part of the tariff is a fixed charge relating to connection to a water system, and the other part is related to the marginal cost associated with actual delivery and use. This two-part tariff is still subject to criticism and many economists imply that it is a second-best alternative (Mitchell and Hanemann, 1994).

Ramsey pricing In 1927 the economist Frank Ramsey formulated ideas on optimal pricing that recognized difficulties with simple marginal cost pricing when there might be natural monopolies. Ramsey pricing is another possible solution to falling long-run average costs and the dilemma facing utilities wishing to set rates efficiently. Ramsey added an explicit constraint to pricing that forces the pricing decision to be a break-even one for the supplier. Prices are adjusted away from marginal cost in inverse proportion to the elasticity of demand (Mitchell and Hanemann, 1994). Ramsey pricing is very often offered as a solution to problems in the electric utility industry (for example, Berry, 2002), and it may be appropriate for many water utilities as well.

Peak Load Pricing There may be one area where utility staff persons and expert rate economists agree a great deal, and that is on the point that pricing should be done so as to be able to meet peaks in demand. Studies of observed water uses, such as the pioneering study by Howe and Linaweaver, consistently show economists that residential demand is largely for outdoor uses, which in turn is higher in summer than winter (lawn/garden irrigation), and also higher at some times during the week and during one point in the day than at others. The water supplier's problem is that it must meet demand at any time of the year, week, or day, not just at average use times. Clearly, the supplier must build in capacity to meet the peaks, leaving a good deal of excess capacity at low demand periods.

This leads to the rule for pricing capacity: capacity costs should be levied only on utilization at the peak. No part of these costs should be levied on off-peak users. The theory underlying this result is presented for the benefit of readers interested in the water industry by Mitchell and Hanemann (1994), but they borrow from Kahn (1988), noting that the peak of most interest in the water industry is clearly the summer season peak. One may conclude that a good case might be made for charging seasonal rates, and many city water suppliers now do just that.

Again, based on his work in airline deregulation, Kahn eventually concludes that economic efficiency may be a dynamic goal (one obtained over time) and that with changing conditions we might well expect that rates should change. But he adds that the dilemma is that the typical water rate design is probably going to be politically infeasible. This is first because the utility simply cannot change rates continually or even with some regularity. They would have to go before the public utility commission each time they changed rates.

Though focused on airline service, Kahn's suggestions imply that during droughts a really perverse thing might happen. During a drought period the supplier could encourage conservation with high prices, as in the Los Angeles (LA) experience, but then if customers over-react (cut back significantly) the supplier will lose money, leading them to want to raise rates. However, if they raise rates during a drought this is likely going to lead to political suicide. Consider this within a block rate system. The 'break point' for block rates is the usage level just below the point where the rate will increase in the next block. The lower the break point, the more conservation the supplier can encourage. If the supplier sets the break point price at too low a use level, revenues may fall precipitously, and this could encourage the problem described above. This sort of thing does happen.

So, what can the utility or water supplier do? California State University economist Darwin Hall's experience on the mayor of LA's Blue Ribbon Committee leads to some interesting recommendations for water rate reform (see Hall, 2001 and case study 4.1 below). In the 1990s the committee designed a two-tiered increasing block design with (i) a changing tail block rate, (ii) a changing break point, and (iii) flexibility in the initial block rate. A water rate setter might well use the marginal cost calculation for (i), but uses politics to determine (ii), and uses the revenue requirement of the utilities to determine (iii).

The 1993–94 Committee recommended a rate design that set the number of billing units for the break points depending on season, lot size, and temperature. The break point within each class is 120 percent of the median use during a drought.

CASE STUDY 4.1 LOS ANGELES RATE SETTING

Following a serious drought in 1991 the mayor of Los Angeles, Thomas Bradley appointed a Blue Ribbon Committee to consider the Los Angeles Department of Water and Power (LADWP) water rates, which were, at that time, flat rates. The Committee wanted to send the message that new rates were to promote conservation, not to generate more revenue. They decided on an increasing block rate structure. They also proposed seasonally varying rates, with high summer peak-season rates set to cover certain capacity costs of treatment, transmission, and distribution. Rates were also structured differently, depending on the type of residence.

One of the most difficult aspects is to decide where the switch or break point is for a two or more tiered rate structure. One idea is to consider the break point at just above the normal, average indoor household use for a family of four: around 250 gallons. The Committee also wanted to establish different rates for normal precipitation and drought years.

The LADWP Blue Ribbon Committee proposed a price of $1.71 per hundred cubic feet (ccf) for use up to 525 gallons per day for single-family residential homes. For use above that level, they proposed a winter rate of $2.27 per ccf and a summer rate of

> $2.92/ccf. For multi-family and non-residential uses, they proposed a switch point of 125 percent of winter use. Drought rates were dependent on the amount of the anticipated shortage in a drought year, and the switch points were lower, with rates in the peak blocks quite a bit higher than proposed for normal years.
>
> In January 1993 the LA City Council adopted a new rate ordinance, closely following the Committee's recommendations. The main departure from those recommendations was a higher switch point for single family residents, differentiated by seasons (575 gallons per day for winter and 725 gallons per day for summer). The Council predicted that 71 per cent of single family homes would face a lower average annual water bill under the new rate structure. At the beginning the new rates appeared to be both effective and politically acceptable. However, a new mayor of Los Angeles was elected in the Fall of 1993 with support from residents of the San Fernando Valley, known to be hotter, and with larger lots than average area residents. They pushed the new mayor to reconsider the rate structure to make it more favorable to them.
>
> *Source:* Mitchell and Hanemann (1994).

Finally, it is therefore worth carefully considering to what signals the residential customers are responding, harking back to the demand side.

4.4 BACK TO THE DEMAND SIDE

The residential demander has some maximum willingness to pay (WTP) for that same volume of stored water depicted in the supply stories above. When a market exists that brings together the suppliers and demanders, we expect that equilibrium can be achieved, and a market price and quantity can be determined. However, as we shall see, this simple achievement of equilibrium may or may not be the case. One simple reason relates to market information. An equilibrium solution implies that the market clears at well identified prices, but residential customers may not even know the price or rate charged for the water they consume.

4.4.1 What Price?

At this point it is interesting to ask again, just what water 'price' do residential customers pay attention to? Before continuing, the reader should try to answer this question for him or herself. Do you even know the price or rate you pay for say, 1000 gallons of water delivered to your home? Most students I have taught over the years do not know the answer to this question. The reasons for this are many, including the simple possibility that one may not actually receive a water bill because water is part of a fixed monthly rent on an apartment. Another reason is that a large utility that sells electricity, natural gas, and water, may send one utility bill to the household, and the household member who pays the bills may just not look very closely at the water portion of that bill. There is frequently the perception that it isn't worth worrying about the amount of the water bill, or that there is nothing one can do about it anyway.

Remember that, historically, many or all cities in the United States have not used meters on residential dwellings (some still do not), so there was of course no way for customers of a water utility to know exactly how much water they were using. In fact, in one of the early cited water demand studies, the city of New York had been contemplating building a new dam, but the mayor's office recommended the use of water meters in lieu of the dam. This was in 1949. A proposal was made that New York City customers would pay 15 cents per hundred cubic feet of water, and this was initially well-received. After study of the metering proposal, the city changed its mind and decided to build the dam. Subsequently, economists at the Rand Corporation studied this case to see if the correct decision had been made (see chapter 10 in Hirshleifer et al., 1960). Assuming linear demand functions for water, the economists estimated the loss in consumer's surplus from the rate hike under metering. This, added to the actual costs of metering compared to the actual costs of building the dam, suggested that the city would have been better off metering than building the dam (see also Hirshleifer and Milliman, 1967).

The above discussion of rates makes clear that in many homes the consumer may be able to influence the total water bill he or she pays because of a varying rate structure. In other words, a careful household can conserve (water the lawn less, use low flow showerheads, and so on) and avoid the higher priced tier, making their total bill smaller than if they consume a good deal of their water in that higher-priced tier.

One can model this using the simple indifference analysis that was introduced in Chapter 2. Griffin and Martin (1981) draw a diagram (Figure 4.4), which they say represents the multiple tariff (another phrase for two- or more tiered pricing) model of Taylor (1975). On the vertical axis M is money spent on other goods each month, and on the horizontal axis q is water consumed in hundred cubic feet (ccf) units.

In Figure 4.4 (1) is the region where marginal price, $p = \$0.30/\text{ccf}$, for quantities demanded between 0 and 10 ccf per month. Region (2) is where

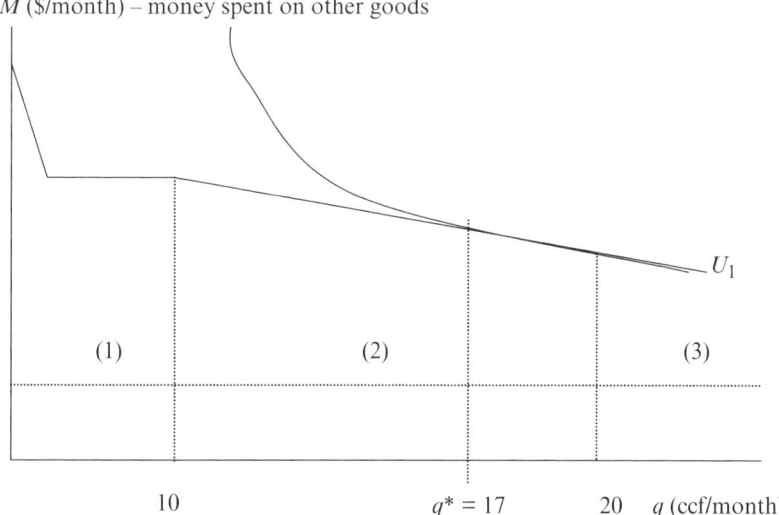

Source: Adapted from Griffin and Martin (1981).

Figure 4.4. Budget line and consumer facing multiple-part tariff

$p = \$0.60/\text{ccf}$, between 10 and 20 ccf per month, and Region (3) is where $p = \$0.90/\text{ccf}$, for all units consumed over 20 ccf. The higher per unit rates are charged to encourage conservation and are assumed to relate to outdoor uses for the household. The budget line in Figure 4.4 assumes income in units per month and that there is a fixed charge of $4.00 per month for any water service at the house. Suppose the tangency position leads to an optimal amount of water, 17 ccf per month consumed. Clearly, in a two-tiered system of water rates, the first block of units consumed might be cheaper than the second block, suggesting that savings to the household can be obtained by avoiding a large demand in that second block, and here the actual total bill is $4 + $3 + $4.20 = $11.20. The calculation reflects the fixed charge of $4, the total bill in the first block ($0.30 × 10 ccf) and the total bill in the second block ($0.60 × 7 ccf).

Using the numbers accompanying Figure 4.4, suppose one knows that monthly income is $1000. Then the amount the consumer has to spend on everything except water is easy to calculate by taking monthly income, and subtracting the actual billing amount (our $11.20), leaving $988.80. This naturally presumes we know the exact total bill for each household. If we do not, and use the observed marginal price and quantity only to calculate the amount due, a mistake is made. For example, if one incorrectly assumes that the water price per unit is $0.60 for each unit of water consumed, this implies that the expenditures on water are $10.20 ($17 \times \$0.60$), which is actually $1 too high. We return to this type of model below, but for now, suppose that this $1 difference is called '$D$'. In other words, the value D is the difference between the total bill calculated using the second or 'marginal' rate and the total bill factoring in the first, lower rate and quantity consumed in that block as well as the marginal rate.

There are now different price structures in demand modeling that allow for such two-tiered prices. For example, in 1975 Lester Taylor, usually credited as the economist who developed the model underlying Figure 4.3, was working on multiple tariff rate structures for the electricity market, rather than water. Nevertheless, his results can easily be applied to water, and he showed that the amount of water purchased by a consumer facing a multiple-part tariff can be expressed as a function of the marginal cost or price and a quantity, defined as the difference between the consumer's bill as determined by the cost/price schedule, and the product of the marginal price and the amount of water purchased. This is, of course, also the 'D' variable we described above, and it is used in the demand analysis to incorporate the two-tiered price structure. Billings and Agthe (1981) used this model to attempt to estimate demand for residents in the city of Tucson, Arizona. Their model of monthly water use (Q) is simply:

$$Q = f(P, D, Y, W)$$

where P is the marginal price of water for the typical consumer, adjusted by the consumer price index (CPI), D is the actual water bill minus $P \times Q$, adjusted by the CPI, Y is average inflation-adjusted income per household, and W is evapotranspiration less rainfall. Using this equation the authors estimate an equation using ordinary least squares (OLS) regression, and from it they obtain estimates of price elasticity of demand. However Griffin and Martin (1981) criticize the study as being biased because of the form the rate schedule took when the empirical work was done.[8] The issue is simply that the D variable is endogenous to the individual because it involves the optimal quantity consumed, q^*, which is really what is used in the above calculation of $P \times Q$. When it is used on the right-hand side in a regression, it may well cause problems. Despite some econometric issues, the Billings and Agthe (1981) paper appears to be the first attempt at actually estimating the Taylor demand model using data.[9]

These more complicated models now also include the 'Shin' pricing models (see Agthe and Billings, 1980). The 'Shin' pricing models allow tests of whether consumers react to average or marginal prices (see Shin, 1985). The formal Shin models are correct ways of incorporating more than one price, but the person paying the water bill may not even notice that the higher use (for an increasing block rate structure) has a higher rate than the rate in some first, lower block. Whether the household is sensitive to marginal rates in any geographical region remains a key empirical issue that the wise water supplier had better sort out before setting the upper and lower bounds and block-specific rates, and certainly before trying to change them to encourage conservation.

Estimating demand with a block-rate structure

As Figure 4.3 illustrates, the consumer facing a block-rate price structure faces a kinked or non-linear budget constraint. This fact should be taken into account when doing the appropriate econometric analysis to estimate demands. One must allow for differing marginal prices in the demand model. One way to do this is to have a two-stage econometric model, where the consumer first selects the block, and then maximizes utility subject to a budget constraint, choosing the optimal amount of water to consume within that block. More elegant empirical models have recently been estimated that incorporate this feature of residential water pricing (for example, Hewitt and Hanemann, 1995; Schefter and David, 1985). Martínez-Espiñeira (2002) estimates what is perhaps the first correct price model under block or multi-tariff pricing for Europe.

Martínez-Espiñeira specifies his model for the individual consumer as follows:

$$x = \beta_1 x_1^*(P_1, I - d_1) + \ldots + \beta_m x_m^*(P_m, I - d_m) + c_1 X_1 + \ldots + c_{m-1} X_{m-1} \quad (4.1)$$

where $1 - d_1 = P_1 x + y$ if x falls within the first block segment, and so on, with subscripts i through m. I is income, P_i are the marginal prices for each ith block, x is the amount of water demanded, y is a vector of all goods apart from water, d_i is the difference between the actual bill and the product of the amount of water used and the marginal price, x^*, is the optimal amount of water consumed conditional on being located in the particular segment, and X_i denotes the upper limit of each segment. The way that the model's equations work together to get the desired result is a little complicated, but note the following definitions allow for the kinks in the budget segments:

$$\beta_1 = 1 \text{ if } x_1^*(P_1, I - d_1) < X_1; = 0 \text{ otherwise} \quad (4.2)$$

$$\beta_i = 1 \text{ if } b_{i1}, b_{i2} > 0 \text{ and } \beta_i = 0 \text{ otherwise } (i = 2, 3, \ldots, m - 1) \quad (4.3)$$

$$\beta_m = 1 \text{ if } X_{m-1} < x_m^*(P_m, I - d_m) \text{ and } \beta_m = 0 \text{ otherwise} \quad (4.4)$$

$$c_i = 1 \text{ if } C_{i1}, C_{i2} > 0 \text{ and } c_i = 0 \text{ otherwise } (i = 2, 3, \ldots, m) \quad (4.5)$$
$$b_{i1} = X_i - x_1^*(P_i, I - d_i) \quad (4.6)$$
$$b_{i2} = x_i^*(P_i, I - d_i) - X_{i-1} \quad (4.7)$$
$$C_{i1} = x_i^*(P_i, I - d_i) - X_i \quad (4.8)$$
$$C_{i2} = X_i - x_{i+1}^*(P_{i+1}, I - d_{i+1}) \quad (4.9)$$

All of these definitions are used by the author in an aggregated, as opposed to household-specific, econometric model by summing over all of the users in each municipality over each month (her chosen time period to allow for seasonal effects.) I will report some of the results and a few elasticities from this model in the update on them in Section 4.4.3, below.

4.4.2 Elasticities

Chapter 2 introduced the reader to elasticity as a unitless measure of the responsiveness of demand to price or any other factor, such as income. One of the first empirical studies of both indoor and outdoor uses and their responsiveness to price was by Howe and Linaweaver, published in 1967. In the homes within selected regions actual flows into the household for a period of several years were recorded using water meters. The study showed that most of the real variation in demand was for outdoor uses and the conclusion was that indoor uses, as well as winter demands, were insensitive to price and metering. However, outdoor uses did respond to variation in price: not surprisingly, changes in the demand for watering lawns and gardens were more substantial than changes in demands for drinking water, bathing and showers, toilet use, and washing dishes.

The evidence today still suggests that the price elasticity of demand for residential water is inelastic, as most (90 percent) of the studies reviewed recently reported estimates of elasticity between 0 and 0.75, or less than one in absolute value terms (Espey et al., 1997). A rule of thumb is that a 10 percent price increase results, on average, in a 2–5 percent decrease in residential demand (Mitchell and Hanemann, 1994). Morris and Jones (1980), however, found that in the Denver, Colorado area outdoor demand fell an estimated 7 percent in response to a 10 percent increase in price. Some of this analysis suggests that water rates may not generally be a powerful tool to use in reducing residential water demand, but one should not be so hasty as to jump to the conclusion that water rates never work in this regard.

First, every successful student of an introductory economics class knows the difference between changing 'demand' and changing the quantity demanded. A change in price or a rate possibly moves the customer along his demand curve; it does not shift it (changes in tastes and income might). If conservation is the long-run goal for a community or water planning agency, it is clear that the goal is to shift the entire demand function down, reflecting the fact that the customer's taste for water has been reduced. Suppose that originally price is raised, but there is also a fundamental change in tastes by educating the public about alternative landscaping that uses less water than conventional methods. If prices go back down after the shift, we may again see an increase along this new demand curve, but the public education program may still have led to conservation overall. If the public education is skipped there may be no shift at all, and water use may be right back where it started. Energy economists worry that gains made in energy conservation in the transition to smaller, more efficient cars in response to Opec-induced oil price (gasoline) increases in the 1970s were offset by falling real prices in oil in the 1980s. Clearly, for a long-run energy management plan, it is long-run tastes and preferences that matter. Such thoughts are echoed in water studies that estimate both short- and long-run demand; Agthe et al. (1986) found that residential long-run demand for water for Arizona residents was almost twice as elastic as the short-run demand.

Still, many water planners may be attempting to shift demand down using short-run pricing, and this may come about in the long run, much as the early and late 1970s oil shocks may have reduced the demand for big cars and gasoline for much of the 1980s. It appeared for a while that US gasoline consumption may have been reduced because of relatively high oil prices.

Today many water suppliers use estimated demand models to sort out the issues they face, though they often call these 'forecast' models because they forecast future consumption trends. Examples are the IWR-MAIN forecasting model, adapted and used by the Metropolitan Water District of southern California (this version is called MWD-MAIN).[10] Such models allow prediction of single family or multiple dwelling residential demand, or at least aggregated demand across many such households, and how this use might change in response to key explanatory variables such as changing precipitation. Good models allow forecasts of total demand in the face of growing urban populations However, they can be misused by agencies, and such misuse has been criticized.

4.4.3 Update on the Price Elasticity of Demand for Residential Customers

To hammer a central theme point home, most water managers agree that water demand is not very sensitive to water price. However, one should be careful when reviewing the literature on water price elasticities. Espey et al. (1997) remind us that the assumed functional form for demand has implications for the elasticity of demand. Double log models lead to constant elasticity of demand, which is certainly convenient, but highly restrictive. In contrast, linear demand models have a changing range of elasticities and what we know from any particular study depends on the range for which elasticity was reported. Hanemann (1998) shows the mathematical forms that price and income elasticities have in linear, double log, and two semi-log forms: the log-linear and linear-log forms. Presuming that assumptions about the existence of an aggregate commodity (all other goods) have been met and that the price of these goods can be normalized so that the price of the aggregate or composite commodity equals unity, then all these types of demand equations can be made consistent with economic theory (that is, constrained utility maximization).

Under these conditions (Hanemann, 1998) the elasticity formulas shown in Table 4.2 have legitimate meaning. Because of these differences and the fact that the water quantity x or y (income) may enter the formulas, it is often conventional to report elasticities at the means for the data, that is, the mean quantity and price in the sample from which the data are generated. Otherwise one wonders at what value of x or y the elasticity is relevant.

Martínez-Espiñeira (2002) uses the equations derived above and data on three Spanish municipalities over the period of January 1995 to June 1999 to estimate coefficients for the model, which lead to reported elasticities. In the aggregated version of the model the proportions of each municipality are used as weights for average marginal prices. The empirical results indicate that income and average temperature have a positive effect on the proportion of users moving into higher blocks, which is intuitive. Correct theoretical marginal prices are used to estimate the conditional demands, that is, the demands conditional upon block choice. The mean marginal price (deemed WEMAP), weighted in each block by the proportion of users falling into the block, is significant and negative. Because of the

Table 4.2 Elasticities for various water demand (x) models

	Own price (p) elasticity	Income (y) elasticity
Linear demand	$-\beta p/x$	$\gamma\, y/x$
Double log demand	$-\beta$	γ
Semi-log (I) $\ln x =$	$-\beta p$	γy
Semi-log (II) $x = \ldots \beta \ln p \ldots$	$-\beta/x$	γ/x

Source: Hanemann (1998). The γ coefficient here is the coefficient on the income term in the demand function. Similarly, the β term is the coefficient on the water price.

nature of the model and the richness of the data, the author is able to provide a range of estimates for the price elasticity. A central estimate of the WEMAP elasticity ranges from 0.312 (in absolute value terms) for those facing low water prices to 0.659 for those facing the highest prices in the sample. As all such estimates are estimated with a degree of confidence, Martínez-Espiñeira notes that the highest price elasticity could be as high as 2.204. This nicely illustrates the importance of considering different prices when reporting elasticity estimates, while supporting the hypothesis that even for European cities, the demand for water is likely to be inelastic.

Espey et al. (1997) review many studies of residential water demand and do this by undertaking what is called a Meta Analysis.[11] In this type of simple empirical analysis all the results reported in a variety of studies are gathered together and the investigator tries to explain their variation using a regression model of some sort. The idea is to try to discover some factors in the studies and the study settings that lead to particular outcomes. For example, one might hypothesize that elasticities are higher in some places or situations than in others, say where incomes are larger in comparison to one's water bill, or where differing block rate prices are used rather than one simple one. Or, one might use meta analysis to test the hypothesis that a double-log specification for demands leads to lower elasticity estimates than other forms. The reason might be that the double log model's assumed constant elasticity might be too low in comparison to one at higher price levels.[12]

Note that Espey et al. find that when water demand studies include the average, D price or Shin price rather than just the marginal price, more elastic estimates are obtained than otherwise. All D and Shin price parameters are positive and significant in the semi-log and Box-Cox models reported by Espey et al., and the D price is significant and positive in the linear model. This suggests that multi-tariff water pricing leads to more price responsiveness. However, it may not be wise to conclude that metering and imposing an increasing block rate is a strategy water suppliers should pursue.

To meter or not to meter?
Finally, in light of the above we end with a discussion of whether it is worthwhile for the water supplier to install water meters, for they are not costless. In practice, when switching from flat to metered rates, what happens? One of the first economists to answer this question was Steve Hanke, in his uncomplicated (1970) survey of Colorado residents who had switched to a meter. He surveyed 180 water customers in 1969 in the city of Boulder, where meter installation had begun in 1961. Hanke found that 68 percent of sample respondents increased their concern for water use

after metering. The types of responses to metering that Hanke found included homeowners using their sprinklers more conservatively, permitting their yards to turn brown, and reporting that they had reduced use. He concluded that respondents clearly altered behavior in response to meters, in the manner that was anticipated.

In another Colorado study that considers Denver's water pricing and needs for conservation, Morris suggested there might be savings of 20 to 25 percent or more from metering (Morris, 1990). Denver is an important, growing city situated in the arid West, and it is situated where the plain begins, just east of the Rocky Mountains. In the 1970s Denver had strong hints of coming water shortage problems, but the managing entity, the Denver Water Board, managed to get around them. In this later water study Morris suggested that moving the service or hook-up charge from a flat rate fee to one tied to actual use could increase the water savings from metering even further. In 1990 the hook-up charge for a 3/4-inch tap in Denver was set at $2730 inside the city, and $3820 in areas just outside the city. Although this cost was mostly incorporated into a homeowner's mortgage, an annual payment of $400 was calculated, implying that much of a Denver resident's actual annual water rate was still fixed cost, not tied to use rates. A Denver economist, John Morris, remained critical of the Denver Water Board's policies for years, but was likely influential in getting them to at least move in the right direction before he retired recently. For an even more recent examination of metering issues, see case study (4.2).

4.4 MUNICIPAL WATER SUPPLY TODAY[13]

Today water supply is complicated by many factors, including growing populations, environmental regulations, and the possibility of increasingly unstable weather and climates. Many people want to live in areas where it is warm and sunny, even in the winter, and unfortunately these areas (such as the arid American West) may not be particularly abundant in water resources. Storage and groundwater become more important and water suppliers have got increasingly sophisticated in their analyses and plans. New planning approaches are often used. Probably the two most important changes from past ones used by cities are to develop more sophisticated models that incorporate uncertainty, and to directly involve the public much more in ratemaking decisions.

As the first example, the Metropolitan Water District of Southern California (MWD), exactly such an arid location with a large and growing population, today uses integrated resource planning (IRP), which they

CASE STUDY 4.2 METERING IN RENO, NEVADA

Vossler et al. (1998) obtained a small sample (350) of residential customers in the Reno/Sparks Nevada metropolitan area from the water utility, Sierra Pacific Power Company. At the time of this analysis (1996) 70 percent of residences in the Reno metropolitan area (Reno and its neighboring city, Sparks) were still paying a flat rate depending on the size of the pipe delivering water to their home. Those with a 3/4-inch pipe paid $43.13 per month and those with a 1 inch pipe paid $59.74 per month at the time of the study. Homes built after July 1, 1988 have water meters and pay a metered rate (Bremmer).

When asked, 205 of the 350 respondents to the brief survey questionnaire (60 percent) said they would accept the utility's offer to accept free installation of a water meter, while 135 rejected the offer. It was explained to the customer as best as possible in the short survey that, for most of them, moving from a flat rate to a water meter would result in savings. For example, their letter showed that those on a 3/4-inch pipe would have an average bill of $19.32 per month in winter months, and $44.64 in summer months, including a $10.02 monthly customer charge. Those with a 1 inch pipe faced similar bills by switching to metering.

The curious thing is why a customer would reject such an offer. The authors asked customers to agree or disagree with the following statements:

(a) I do not believe this will really be 'free' for me to do.
(b) I know the cost in dollars is zero, but I don't want to spend the time doing this.
(c) I think I will pay more under a metered system than our household does now.
(d) I suspect that the utility is really up to something that will not be good for me later.
(e) Other.

Of these choices, 54 households agreed with option (a), but 114 households agreed with option (c), and 94 agreed with option (d). There would seem to be some sentiment that customers do not trust the water utility, or that they fear that under metering there will be a rate increase. In fact, in the long run there was no reason that the water utility could not raise the flat rate, and in fact Sierra

Pacific asked the Public Utilities Commission for an increase in the flat rate and obtained it just two years after this study. The higher 1 inch flat rate rose to over $70 per month.

Whether the utility expects to obtain conservation via pricing in the short or long run, there are several reasons why they may wish to go ahead with a metering plan. First, as in the Reno/Sparks area, utilities without meters installed simply do not have good information on which to base decisions and adding meters will increase precision in estimating future demand. Second, meters can allow more sophisticated analysis of the timing of demand and linkages between houses and types of properties to be performed. Some, however, have been critical of using metered water rates to raise funds for capital improvements, suggesting that property taxes may have better outcomes for residents in the long run (Joyce and Merz, 1994).

The Reno story does not end with the above. The cities of Reno, Sparks and the county (Washoe) eventually adopted permanent (not temporary) lawn watering rules – twice weekly. Meters for all homes were seen as a solution, or a way to end mandatory restrictions (see Bremmer, 1996). The utility, Sierra Pacific Power, asked in late 1997 for a water rate hike, seeking an increase of about $15 per non-metered single family home, or a 20 percent increase. Justification for the water rate hike was Sierra Pacific's claim that it had to comply with the US Safe Drinking Water Act and build a new water treatment plant, increasing costs. Some customers were outraged (Mullen, 1998). The Nevada Public Utilities Commission denied the hike, giving them only about an 8.6 percent increase (*Reno Gazette Journal*, 1998). In their ruling, the PUC denied Sierra Pacific about $8 million that the utility wanted to include in its rate base.

Finally, in 2001, in the wake of the California energy crisis, Sierra Pacific Power got out of the water business altogether. The county and the two cities, fearing that a French multinational water supply company would take over water service for the area, formed a joint power agreement culminating in the Truckee Meadows Water Authority. Today, TMWA provides the water service for the area. The residential flat rate for a 1 inch pipe is $68.14.

borrowed from the power industry. MWD must provide water to many of California's over 30 million people, and this is accomplished through water imports from the Colorado River and northern California.

IRP is a dynamic planning process that incorporates least-cost planning. The steps used in IRP (Rodrigo et al., n.d.) are:

1. develop a forecast of water demand;
2. estimate current and future water supplies;
3. estimate the variation in demand and supply, with randomness assumed dependent on weather and hydrology;
4. estimate the effectiveness of demand side management (DSM);[14]
5. estimate the cost of water supplies and demand side management programs;
6. assess the risks associated with the development of supplies coupled with DSM programs.

DSM programs are relied upon today by several water agencies in the United States. They include pricing schemes such as increasing block rates, but also non-price policies, such as public education, rationing, water use restrictions, and subsidies for water-efficient technology adoption. The latter may include rebates for installing low-flow toilets, and distribution of free low-flow showerheads (see, for example, discussion in Renwick and Green, 2000). Always at issue, similar to the debate over the effectiveness of pricing strategies for conservation, is the question of whether DSM schemes actually work. Renwick and Green develop an eight year (1989–96), eight urban community model to test the effectiveness of water conservation programs. Their data come from urban communities in California, including San Francisco, San Diego, Los Angeles, the East Bay, San Bernardino, and Santa Barbara. Monthly use in these areas ranged over the period from about 600 cubic feet (ccf) per single family residence, to approximately 25 ccf. Prices also range greatly from $0.49 per ccf (San Bernadino) to $3.78 per ccf for the Marin County water district.

These authors have helped to solve some of the sticky issues involved in estimating demand models with block rate pricing structures and other possible endogenous variables. The model includes two price equations used in a first state: one to explain the variation in the marginal price of water over time and across the cities, and the other to explain the 'D' variable mentioned above. The first-stage model also includes climatic equations with adjustments for seasonal variations using a Fourier series of sine and cosine terms, as well as a second-state water demand equation. The first-stage predicted values are used in the water demand equation, purging the endogenous variables of their offending statistical properties. The

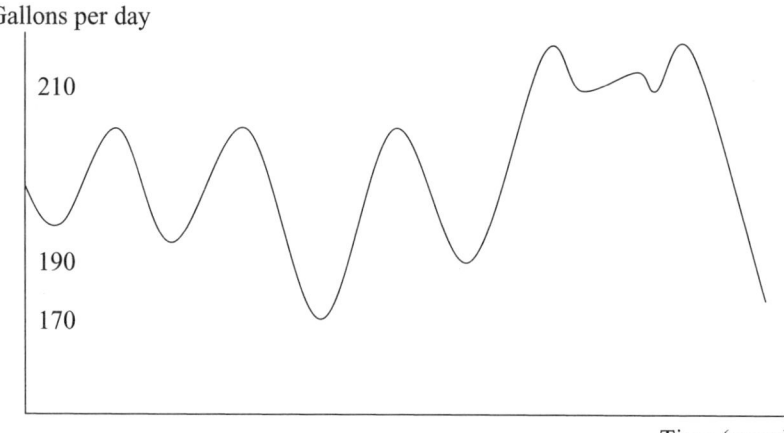

Figure 4.5   Urban per capita use

authors find expected negative influences of the marginal price and DSM variables on water demand, and these are significant. Resulting own-price summer elasticity of demand is about −0.20. Not surprisingly, the most strongly significant DSM policies are the mandatory ones, rather than the voluntary measures.

Both water demand and storage issues involve multiple types of risk and uncertainty, and without uncertainty modeling, past water suppliers often assumed that the only unknown they needed to account for was population growth. A usual assumption was that per capita water use would stay the same over time, and the only job they faced was to predict population growth rates over some period in their market area. However, predicting gallons per person per day does involve taking into account random weather patterns (see Figure 4.5).

The peaks in Figure 4.5 may indicate drought years, and the troughs may indicate wet years, or years when for some other reason (tastes change, time spent watering falls), demand falls quite steeply. For example, outdoor (lawn watering) use is low during wet years (one hopes!), so the troughs above may be indicating this decline in the most significant portion of residential use.

Using the above concepts and close scrutiny of long-run weather patterns, water suppliers must next consider the reliability of their storage. When droughts occur, water stored in reservoirs or underground provide a supply that can be used to mitigate the drought. The demand for that stored water will be high in the years of the drought, perhaps with several months lag. If a drought continues for a long period, renewing the stored supplies will be unlikely at precisely the same time that stored supplies are being drawn down, exacerbating their problems. Calculating recharge rates using surface and groundwater hydrologic models is a key component in long-term planning, so that water suppliers can know how quickly supplies can be restored when wet weather comes.

By using the knowledge of random demand and supply modern water suppliers can better plan for long-run needs. Water suppliers can calculate the probability of excess demand (more demand relative to supply) or excess supply, painting a picture of the cumulative probability of either shortages or surpluses. With such knowledge available, it still remains for them to set targets of reliability. For example, do they desire to supply 100 percent of the water demanded in all years in the planning horizon, or is some level less than 100 percent an acceptable risk? That is a question they must answer based on the company's goals and the feedback they get from the community, for increased reliability comes at higher costs.

Though bureaucracies often move at glacial speed, water utilities and departments seem to have learned, at least in many regions of the United States, that they cannot blindside the public when it comes to setting rates. Public outcry can be tremendous, resulting in backlashes such as removal of politicians from office. The Blue Ribbon California panel's issues were highlighted above. Another good example comes from the lessons learned by the Tucson Water Department as it developed a new water rate structure in early 1976. Two weeks after billing at the new rates, a recall petition for Tucson City Council members was circulated and by early January of 1977 all those Council members who had voted for the new rates were defeated by opponents who promised a rate rollback (Mitchell and Hanemann, 1994, p. 100). Similar problems for water agencies and politicians have arisen in other parts of the arid western United States. It is therefore very important for water agencies to involve the public early on, providing a good source of information on why rates must increase, and how.

4.5 SUMMARY

Water suppliers or utilities may have finally got the message from economists that marginal cost pricing is efficient, but they may simply see too much fluctuation[15] in short-run water use to make short-run variable-cost pricing feasible. They do not want revenue to swing up and down with water use, arguing that they should charge a fixed rate to ensure their own revenue stability. But this is not consistent with the economist's desire to price at marginal cost, leaving the need to solve both of the efficiency and stability problems. Politically, raising rates to offset long-run cost increases and provide a hedge against uncertainty in supplies may be very unpopular with the public. Some private utility companies have simply got out of the water business, leaving the tricky issues of water supply to a county or local government. For these non-profit entities the politically and economically viable solution likely rests in a combined rate structure that mixes both variable and fixed cost pricing.

PROBLEMS

4.1. As suggested in the text above, as a practical exercise go home and look at your water bill. Where did you find the explanation of your water use and rates, or could you in fact find it at all? What rate does the water supplier charge and in what units is this expressed? Is this a declining, fixed, or increasing block rate? Can you tell from looking at the bill you received?

4.2. Some say that marginal cost pricing is impossible to achieve. What do you think the practical obstacles to this type of pricing scheme are?

4.3. Under what conditions would raising water rates lead to 'conservation'?

NOTES

1. Thanks to Hope Lewis for her valuable comments on this chapter.
2. Rates for farmers are addressed in Chapter 5.
3. When industry is small and competitive, a particular firm may fear that disclosing data may lead to the risk of other firms learning something that may be used to their competitive advantage. Hence, small firms often will not share data with researchers. I found this to be true with the gold mines in Nevada (see Chapter 8).
4. In their report Mitchell and Hanemann (1994) point out that the airline industry is possibly a bad example for the water industry because airlines can price discriminate by setting airfares differently depending on the amount of time the ticket is purchased in advance and whether the customer is staying overnight on Saturdays.
5. In many states this is called something like the State Public Utility Commission or 'PUC'.
6. Recall from Chapter 2 that the supply curve is in fact a portion of the marginal cost curve.
7. As an interesting practical exercise, go home and see if you can locate a water meter in your yard, or connected to the building in which you live. Technology is changing to make it more convenient for the company employee to read the meter.
8. In their reply to Griffin and Martin (1981), Billings and Agthe (1981) say that the true error term is perhaps positively correlated with the marginal price variable, but show that the bias is small.
9. Below, see the Renwick and Green (2000) version of the modeling, which may correct for some of the problems mentioned here.
10. This is the Institute of Water Resources Municipal and Industrial Needs water and demand forecasting system.

11. Their review obviously does not include the most modern studies conducted after their analysis.
12. A good modeler would test for the appropriate functional form underlying the demand function.
13. This section follows presentation of operations described by Rodrigo et al. (n.d.).
14. DSM programs encourage conservation of power and water via measures that households can adopt that result in their savings. They were popular in the electric power industry in the 1990s, but fell out of use as energy prices fell.
15. For example, Chesnutt et al. (1993) show that residential water use for the Los Angeles area fluctuated by 100 percent from the lowest to the highest month of use in 1985.

REFERENCES

Agthe, D.E. and R.B. Billings (1980), 'Dynamic models of residential water demand', *Water Resources Research*, **16**(3) (March), 476–80.

Agthe, D.E. et al. (1986), 'A simultaneous equations demand model for block rates', *Water Resources Research*, **22**(1).

Allen, L. and J. Darby (1994), 'Quality control of bottled and vended water in California', *Journal of Environmental Health*, **56** (April), 17–22.

Beecher, J.A. and A.P. Laubach (1989), 'Compendium on water supply, drought, and conservation', report prepared by the National Regulatory Research Institute, Columbus, OH, October.

Berry, K. (2002), 'Generation search costs and Ramsey pricing in a partially deregulated electric utility industry', *Journal of Economics and Business*, **54** (May–June), 331–43.

Billings, R.B. and D.E. Agthe (1980), 'Price elasticities for water: a case of increasing block rates', *Land Economics*, **56** (February), 73–84.

Billings, R.B. and D.E. Agthe (1981), 'Price elasticities for water: a case of increasing block rates: reply', *Land Economics*, **57** (May), 276–8.

Bremmer, F. (1996), 'Water Meters Hot Item', *Reno Gazette-Journal*, 1.

Brookshire, D.S., B. Colby, M. Ewers and P.T. Ganderton (2004), 'Market prices for water in the semiarid West of the United States', *Water Resources Research*, **40**, W09S04, doi: 10. 1029/2003WR002846.

Cech, Thomas V. (2003), *Principles of Water Resources: History, Development, Management, and Policy*, New York: John Wiley and Sons.

Chesnutt, T.W., A. Bamezai and W.M. Hanemann (1993), 'Proposal to examine revenue instability induced by conservation rate structures', working paper no. 695, Department of Agricultural and Resource Economics, University of California, Berkeley.

Clark, R.M. and R.G. Stevie (1981), 'A water supply cost model incorporating spatial variables', *Land Economics*, **57**(1) (February), 18–32.

Colby, B.G., K. Crandall and D. Bush (1993), 'Water right transactions: market values and price dispersion', *Water Resources Research*, **29**(6), 1565–72.

Crain, W.M. and A. Zardkoohi (1978), 'A test of the property-rights theory of the firm: water utilities in the United States', *Journal of Law and Economics*, **21**, 395–408.

Dandy, G., T. Nguyen and C. Davies (1997), 'Estimating residential water demand in the presence of free allowances', *Land Economics*, **73**(1) (February), 125–39.

Espey, M., J. Espey and W.D. Shaw (1997), 'Price elasticity of residential demand for water: a meta-analysis', *Water Resources Research*, **33**(6) (April), 1369–74.

Griffin, A. and W.E. Martin (1981), 'Price elasticities for water: a case of increasing block rates: comment', *Land Economics*, **57**(2) (May), 266–75.

Hall, D. (2001), 'Politically feasible marginal cost water rates', discussion paper, Department of Economics, California State University at Long Beach, presented at the annual meetings of the Western Economics Association, Vancouver, British Columbia, June, 2000.

Hanemann, W.M. (1998), 'Determinants of urban water use', in D. Bauman, J. Boland and W.M. Hanemann (eds), *Urban Water Demand Management and Planning*, Los Angeles: McGraw-Hill.

Hanke, Steve H. (1970), 'Some behavioral characteristics associated with residential water price changes', *Water Resources Research*, **6**(5) (October), 1383–7.

Hewitt, Julie and W.M. Hanemann (1995), 'A discrete/continuous approach to residential water demand under block rate pricing', *Land Economics*, **71**(2) (May), 173–92.

Hirshliefer, J. and J. Milliman (1967), 'Urban water supply: a second look', *American Economic Review* (May), 169–78.

Hirshliefer, J., J. Milliman and J. DeHaven (1960), *Water Supply*, Chicago: University of Chicago Press.

Howe, C.W. and F.P. Linaweaver (1967), 'The impact of price on residential water demand and its relationship to system design and price structure', *Water Resources Research* (1st quarter), 13–32.

Howe, C.W., C.S. Boggs and P. Butler (1990), 'Transaction costs as determinants of water transfers', *University of Colorado Law Review*, **61**, 392–405.

Joyce, B.P. and T.E. Merz (1994), 'The pricing of water in a university town: an economic analysis of draining a cash cow', *Water Resources Research*, **30**(10), 2807–11.

Kahn, A. (1988), *The Economics of Regulation: Principles and Institutions*, Cambridge, MA: MIT Press.

Mann, P.C. (1987), 'Reform in costing and pricing water', *Journal of the American Water Works Association*, **79**(3), 43–5.

Martínez-Espiñeira, R. (2002), 'Estimating demand under increasing-block tariffs using aggregate data and proportions of users per block', in P. Pashardes, T. Swanson and A. Xepapadeas (eds), *Current Issues in the Economics of Water Resource Management: Theory, Applications and Policies*, Dordrecht: Kluwer Academic Publishers, chapter 2.

Mitchell, D. and W.M. Hanemann (1994), 'Setting urban water rates for efficiency and conservation: a discussion of the issues', draft report prepared for the California Urban Water Conservation Council (June), available from M-Cubed, Oakland, California.

Moncur, J. and Y.S. Fok (1993), 'Water pricing and cost data: getting the right numbers', University of Hawaii, Water Resources Center.

Morris, J.R. (1990), 'Pricing for water conservation', *Contemporary Policy Issues*, **8** (October), 79–91.

Morris, J.R. and C. Jones (1980), 'Water for Denver: an analysis of the alternatives', report to the Environmental Defense Fund, Boulder, Colorado.

Mullen, Frank (1998), 'Customers outraged: Sierra Pacific defends water rate increases', *Reno Gazette Journal*.

Murphy, Dean E. (2003), 'Pact in West will send farms' water to Cities', *New York Times* (17 October), A-1, A-16.

Ramsey, Frank (1927), 'A contribution to the theory of taxation', *Economic Journal*, **37**, 47–61.

Reno Gazette Journal staff writers (1998), 'Regulators slash water rate hike', *Reno Gazette-Journal* (3 April), 1.

Renwick, Mary E. and Richard D. Green (2000), 'Do residential water demand side management policies measure up? An analysis of eight California water agencies', *Journal of Environmental Economics and Management*, **40** (July), 37–55.

Rodrigo, D., T.A. Blair and B.G. Thomas (no date), 'Integrated resources planning and reliability analysis: a case study of the Metropolitan Water District of Southern California', discussion paper, Metropolitan Water District of Southern California, Los Angeles, CA.

Schefter, J. and E. David (1985), 'Estimating residential water demand under multi-tariffs using aggregate data', *Land Economics*, **61**(3) (November), 272–80.

Shin, J. (1985), 'Perception of price when information is costly: evidence from residential electricity demand', *Review of Economic Statistics*, **67**, 591–8.

Taylor, L.D. (1975), 'The demand for electricity: a survey', *Bell Journal of Economics*, **6** (Spring), 74–110.

Vaux Jr, H.J. (1986), 'Economic factors shaping western water allocation', *American Journal of Agricultural Economics, Proceedings Papers*, **68** (December), 1135–42.

Vossler, C.A., J. Espey and W.D. Shaw (1998), 'Trick or treat? An offer to obtain metered water', *Journal of the American Water Resources Association*, **34**(5) (October), 1213–20.

SUGGESTED FURTHER READING

Parker, M., J.G. Thompson, R.R. Reynolds Jr and M.D. Smith (1995), 'Use and misuse of complex models: examples from water demand management', *Water Resources Bulletin*, **31**(2) (April), 257–63.

WEBSITE

http://www.usbr.gov/wrrl/rwc/pricing/index.html. Here you can find the 'Incentive Pricing Handbook for Agricultural Water Districts', April 1997.

5. Water and agriculture[1]

5.0 INTRODUCTION

In this chapter we dig deeper into the agricultural sector's use of water, if you will excuse the pun. Growing crops is one of the older activities of mankind in the world, and it is still a prominent, if not dominant activity in many geographical regions. Agriculture takes many shapes and forms in the modern era. Still, whether the farm has a few acres or a corporate farm has 100 000 acres, all agricultural producers must have water to grow one or more crops, or to water their livestock. Where they get that water is a key issue, and it may surprise some readers to learn that agriculture is very prominent in areas with little natural precipitation, necessitating the irrigation of crops.

In Chapter 2 I used the farm as an example of a profit maximizing firm, in business to sell harvested crops at a profit. In such a simple framework water is an input in the production process and the basic economics of water use in this context is fairly straightforward. As will be seen below, more modern approaches to incorporating sophisticated irrigation methods increase the modeling complexity for the economist who wishes to predict the farmer's behavior. Still, from Chapter 2 the basic behavioral decisions pertain to choosing the optimal mix of inputs, and with some market power on the part of each farm, at what price to sell one's crops. As will be seen, many agricultural economists now break the input choice into two distinct parts: whether to allocate land for planting some crop at all, and if so, which crops to plant on this allocated acreage.

At the end of Chapter 2 it was also mentioned that, because they are the owners of senior water rights, modern farmers in the American West are likely to be involved in a complicated tradeoff between present returns from crop sales and potential future returns from the sale of water (and land) to other types of user. As mentioned earlier in the book, note that farmers in California's Imperial Valley, who typically pay about $15 per acre foot for delivered water, recently agreed to sell water to municipal users in the area around San Diego for about $258 per acre foot. This kind of profit on their water asset is not trivial. In the first part of this chapter we assume the simple standard framework with water as an input, and the last section examines the farmer as investor, where water may become an asset of considerable value regardless of its application to any crop.

Crop output (Q) typically depends on combining land quality and quantity, water (W), labor, energy, capital, fertilizer and other inputs. (For the remainder of this chapter I'll use crop farming rather than livestock production for most of the examples, noting that livestock can often be grazed on land unsuitable for other agricultural production. More sophisticated farm production models might allow the farmer to choose between allocating land to a crop, versus allocating it to grazing.) Technology is used to accomplish the growing of crops, and the nature of that technology determines the shapes of isoquants, as shown in Chapter 2. In the real world output is of course also subject to random fluctuations in the weather and a host of other factors related to sunlight and climate.

Did you know that rice is grown in parts of Texas and that fruits are grown on the arid western slope of Colorado? Food is grown in many regions of the world where one might not expect it. Irrigation is often used to grow extremely water-intensive crops, even in fairly wet regions. In very arid regions farmers simply must obtain water and irrigate in order to grow even the least water-intensive crops. Irrigated land provides more than one-quarter of the crop value for the United States and in many states agriculture is the dominant user of water in that region. In western states agriculture may be a very important component of economic activity (for example, in the state of California, agriculture is key, and this state represents the fifth largest economy in the world) and it is virtually impossible without irrigation.

In the 1980s irrigation in many western states, including California, Nebraska, Idaho, Kansas, Colorado, Oregon, Washington, and Montana, accounted for over 90 percent of total consumptive use of water. Irrigation in some eastern states also accounts for over 50 percent of consumptive use; this is true in Florida, Georgia, Mississippi, and Louisiana. California remains the state with the largest amount of irrigated land, at over 9 million acres and with a total of about 32 million acre feet a year in surface and groundwater withdrawals. For the US in the 1980s, about 55 percent of the water used by irrigators was consumed. This fact is partially explained by farming's higher consumptive rate for its withdrawals as compared to, say, urban uses. Consumptive use in irrigation varies according to soil, climate, and other geographic characteristics of the farms in a region. To better understand the connections between agriculture and water we begin by reviewing the basic role water plays as a factor of production.

5.1 WATER AS FACTOR DEMAND

A farmer demands water to grow crops, and economists assume that she or he, like every other economic producer, is driven by the desire to maximize profits from the sale of those crops. The water used by a farmer as an input is similar to other inputs such as land, capital, fertilizer, labor, and sunlight, in that different crops may require different amounts of water. For example, US crops such as corn, pinto beans, and alfalfa require about 20 to 25 inches of water per year (this requirement is in consumptive use terms), while wheat, oats, sorghum, and sunflowers may require 12 to 18 inches per year. When water supplies are scarce, perhaps in a given year, a farmer has a choice of planting a given crop as opposed to one he or she had planted previously. Predicting droughts and the period they are expected to last becomes a crucial part of the farmer's planting decision, or their optimal 'crop mix'.

Too much water may be a bad thing, and long before flooding has destroyed crops, water may exhibit diminishing marginal returns (see Figure 5.1). Recall that marginal returns just measure the amount of increase in output from applying the last unit of an input. Economists most often assume that there are diminishing marginal returns to any input in at least some relevant range of application: when one more unit of one input is added while holding other inputs constant, we expect that eventually any increases in output will be negligible, or even negative. The graphed line in Figure 5.1 doesn't turn down, but it does flatten. As one of my own economics professors used to say, 'otherwise you could grow the world's food supply in your flower pot'.

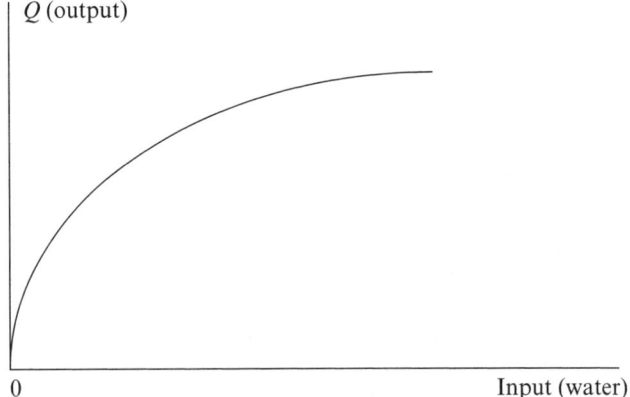

Figure 5.1   *Output as a function of an input*

Water and agriculture

For some inputs there is a well-functioning market and for others there is not. For example, large farms may rely on laborers outside the family,[2] and the wage paid to farm laborers is determined in a well-functioning market. The use of immigrant labor, in recent times sometimes illegally, complicates examination of this market. The factor payment paid to capital is often just assumed to be the market interest rate for loans on equipment and buildings, and land's rent may also be market-driven. The modern farmer may be quite sophisticated in managing to use other inputs provided by nature (sun and water), but there may be no market, or at least greatly distorted ones.

To review key modeling results in Chapter 2, in competitive factor markets the farmer may be able to influence only one thing related to the market: the amount of the input she or he applies. The farmer takes the factor or input price as given. We showed in Chapter 2 that the optimal amount of the jth input then applied is determined by setting the value of the marginal physical product ($P \times MPP_j$) of the input equal to its factor price (p_j), where P is the output price. Recall that, formally, we can arrive at this key optimality result using the usual profit maximization problem. The specifics can be handled in one of several ways because of the dual relationship between production and cost minimization (see an advanced microeconomics textbook on duality).

For example, a necessary condition for profit maximization is that the cost of producing a given level of output is minimized, subject to constraints on the farm's output target or constraints on total resources. To review, let profit (π) equal total revenue less costs ($TR(Q) - TC(Q)$) and the first-order condition for a maximum is simply:

$$dTR/dQ - dTC/dQ = 0 \rightarrow MR = MC \qquad (5.1)$$

To make this problem reveal the desired first-order conditions that we want to see if truly interested in the details related to factor prices, we have to let Q in turn depend on inputs (assuming second-order conditions are satisfied), say w and k. To do so, let total cost be $p_j w + rk$, where p_j is the price of w and r is the cost of capital. Suppose the farm is a price taker, so $TR = PQ(w, k)$. Then the problem becomes:

$$\max \pi = \max_{w,k} \{PQ(w, k) - p_j w - rk\} \qquad (5.2)$$

The farm can choose w and k and the first-order conditions now imply the above condition where the value of the marginal physical product is set to the input price ($P \times MPP = p_j$). The reader may convince him or herself of this by doing the mathematics. If w is the volume of water applied, then $P \times \partial Q/\partial w = p_j$, where p_j is the price of water.

Though delivery charges are paid to irrigation companies by farmers today, water was often nearly free to many US family farmers who inherited water rights from grandparents or great-grandparents. Traditional arrangements in the United States are that farmers often contract at the beginning of the growing season with an irrigation district, agreeing to pay a fee per acre of land to the irrigation district for the option of delivery, or a 'standby' charge, followed by a charge upon delivery of water to that land. In areas with high valued crops these charges have recently risen to cover costs and fees paid by the districts to the US Bureau of Reclamation. For example, in the Arvin Edison Water Storage District in the Central Valley of California prior to 1995, irrigators paid a standby charge of $118.25 per acre of land, and a delivery charge of $45.30 (see Schuck and Green, 2004). These traditional arrangements may be changing as agencies attempt to build in conservation pricing. The idea of course is to change the structure of pricing so that the fixed portion (the standby charge) takes a smaller role than a charge per volume of water actually delivered.[3]

Put simply, note that the above factor price optimization rule implies that if $p_j = 0$, and price of the crop is positive and non-zero, then the farmer must drive the *MPP* to zero to achieve an efficient level of production and profit maximization. This in turn implies high water use applications, if other factors are held constant. This doesn't necessarily mean that water will be disposed of in a manner consistent with a zero price because of the law of diminishing returns and because the delivery charges may accumulate, mounting to a considerable cost. However, the consensus still seems to be that the demand for irrigation water among farmers is price-inelastic.

An example in California, the Broadview water district, shows that, in contrast, when farmers do have to pay substantial charges for delivered water they will respond to these fees by changing their application rates. Because of environmental problems associated with drainage, the Broadview area water district announced a new water delivery rate structure to take effect in October 1989. They had been charging $16 per acre foot of delivered water, plus a fixed assessment of $42 per acre served by the district. It subsequently adopted a two-tier water rate structure (see Chapter 4), with water in the first block priced at the original $16 per af, but water in a second block priced at $40 per af. Switch points were set for each crop grown in the district. Table 5.1 shows that this new two-tiered system did accomplish a change in water use as anticipated: applications fell in 1990, especially as compared to average use during the 1986–8 period.

In the real world there are offsetting institutional features that limit what can happen in response to changing prices. Even farms with secure water

Table 5.1 Crop-specific use, Broadview Water District

Crop	Average use 1986–8 (af/acre)	Switch point (af/acre)	Average use 1989 (af/acre)	Average use 1990 (af/acre)	% Change between 1986/8 and 1990
Cotton	3.20	2.90	3.34	2.84	−11%
Tomatoes	3.22	2.9	2.73	3.03	−6%
Sugarbeets	4.58	3.9	3.73	2.54	−45%

Source: Adapted from Mitchell and Hanemann (1994). Original source: Dennis Wichelns and David Cone, 'Irrigation district programs motivate farmers to improve water management and reduce drain volume'. Presented at US Committee on Irrigation and Drainage, Technical Conference on Irrigation, San Francisco, November 1991.

rights frequently face constraints on the total amount of water that can be applied in a given year, especially at times of drought. Experiments suggest that, as economists expect, diminishing returns hold for water, but at what application rates? Accurate data for farms in regions around the US are difficult to come by and these would be needed to map exact relationships between crop output and water use. Water policy makers desire means of determining the value of water in agriculture because it is important in analyzing farm behavior and the forces that change the allocation of water in a region. As will be seen below, the 'value' of water in agriculture is not readily available in any region of interest.

5.1.1 Approaches to Finding the Value of Water

If it is possible to estimate a production function using empirical data, the value of water can be found, at least if one assumes equilibrium factor market conditions. This is much easier said than done. Imagine the necessary data one would need, and how one would obtain them. As an alternative to doing experiments to quantify production relationships, in many states agricultural researchers have estimated what are called farm crop budgets. These can be used to estimate the maximum revenue share for the water input, which is often of more interest than the actual physical productivity relationship. One can simply estimate total revenue from a crop, and subtract off all input costs to the farmer. Typically the researcher employs a linear programming method to accomplish this task. This analytical method will show net revenue per crop and if one divides this by the total quantity of water used to grow the crop, it yields a measure of the average value of water in applications to the crop. Average values are not of as much interest to economists as marginal values, but can be used to approximate the firm's (i.e. the farm's) willingness to pay for water for any given crop.

Yet another means of approximating the marginal value of water in crop production is to compare net revenue for the same crop for both dryland and irrigated farming. However, the underlying assumption here is that the farms are similar in all other aspects except the amount of water used, which may or may not be true.

How much water a farmer demands in a given year depends on many decisions and factors, but one of the most important of these is the exact crop (or crops) that is to be produced and brought to market. So far we have assumed that there is a generic 'output', but this is far from the real world of agriculture. Different crops naturally have different values in the market for agricultural commodities, and these values may change from year to year and vary across regions of the US and the world. The cost of cultivating these crops may be different, as may the amount of water each crop uses on a given acre of land. Table 5.2 demonstrates this nicely, even though the price and yields are based on ten-year averages (see Schuck and Green, 2004).

Table 5.2 1998 Data for Arvin Edison Water Storage District (Central Valley of California)

Crop	Price per ton ($)	Yield (tons)/ per acre	Water consumption/ per acre	Cost per acre (4)	Acres
Alfalfa	91.83	7.90	3.96	285	2009
Almonds	2461.82	0.74	3.46	1596	1760
Carrots	117.89	29.48	1.49	3772	1151
Citrus	366.09	12.31	2.80	4243	10034
Cotton*	0.87	1183.98	2.57	580	3637
Peaches	979.93	6.57	3.37	9495	3501
Grains	121.79	2.65	1.85	214	3372
Melons	133.42	22.93	1.91	1594	1096
Onions	63.89	21.40	2.31	589	2226
Potatoes	188.20	17.93	1.73	582	7785
Tomatoes	62.83	36.03	2.14	1246	2369
Vine	431.46	8.67	2.30	5764	10631
Fallow					1222

Note: *Note that for cotton, price and yield are per pound of lint, not per ton (personal communication with Eric Schuck, June 7, 2004).

Source: Schuck and Green (2004). Costs taken from University of California crop budgets. Consumptive water use requirements taken from District records.

Note from Table 5.2 that even though the price per ton of alfalfa is low in comparison to several other crops, the amount of water used to grow an acre of alfalfa is relatively high.

In a practical sense, there are many more complicated decisions a farmer must make than simply how much water to apply to a single crop. Many farmers choose to grow different varieties of crops (actually wheat is not wheat, as they might say), and they may rotate crops in different years, or even choose to grow more than one crop in a given year on different parcels of land. One may think that this does not complicate modeling greatly, presuming that prices for different crops brought to market are well known to the farmer. We could assume that he or she simply compares expected profits based on different choices of crops to be produced. This, however, ignores a huge part of any farmer's life: risk and uncertainty.

5.1.2 Uncertainty

Chapter 2 did not address uncertainty and I postpone extensive discussion of it until Chapter 6, but something must be said about it when writing about farming. Typical growers have to make decisions about what and how much to plant in the absence of information on market conditions that will exist at the time of sale. Will the market support key prices at the time the crops are harvested and brought to market? What will the demand for the crop be? Will there be the usual amount of rainfall in the summer months? The farmer cannot know the answers to these questions in advance, with certainty. In other words, while the optimal demand for inputs depends on supply decisions, which in turn depend on the market price of the crop, many or most farmers do not know what the market price of the crop at the time of sale is going to be. Imagine the list of things that determine the price of wheat or corn, or beef, six months from now: in 2003 a single cow in Washington State that had 'mad cow disease' greatly disrupted the market for beef and cattle for a time. This could not have been anticipated by any beef producers.

The farmer faces an inevitable degree of risk about the crop's future price. There is also the risk he faces relating to severe weather events that can ruin the crops, making them worthless in any event. These events include drought and too much intense heat, flood, a freeze or late frost, too much rain, and infestation by pests and diseases. As farmers say, there is no such thing as 'good' weather if you are a farmer.

5.1.3 Government Intervention

Because any nation depends on farmers for a stable food supply, and because there is general awareness of the uncertainty problem for the

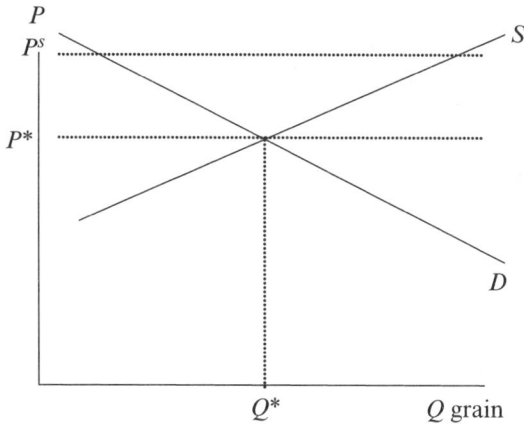

Figure 5.2 Surplus situation

farmer, there is often a good deal of market intervention by governments. In the US and in many other countries around the world, the federal or central government supports many individual or even corporate growers with price supports or subsidies. The supports are guarantees that the farmers can sell the amount of crop they harvest at a guaranteed price, and subsidies may be tax cuts or transfer payments given to farmers for growing certain volumes of certain crops. Many countries also engage in import or export control policies, most often adding tariffs to, or quotas on, imported crops or agricultural produce. In addition to price support programs, futures markets have been organized for many crops, providing ways to hedge against uncertainty for anyone willing to participate in these markets. However, these may not require any government intervention once they have been organized.

Price supports are relatively simple to analyse. They are often criticized by economists because they can lead to shortages and surpluses, depending on whether the supported price, P^s, is above or below the equilibrium market-clearing price, P^*. Figure 5.2 shows a situation that leads to a surplus of grain, which has been a common situation for the US in the late twentieth century. Figure 5.3 shows the alternative, which leads to a shortage of grain.

Next, we develop some more formal models of agricultural production, relying heavily on the work of David Zilberman, a University of California-Berkeley agricultural economist, along with several of his colleagues. The chapter finishes with a discussion of some issues related to water quality, and a look at some causes of agricultural market failure.

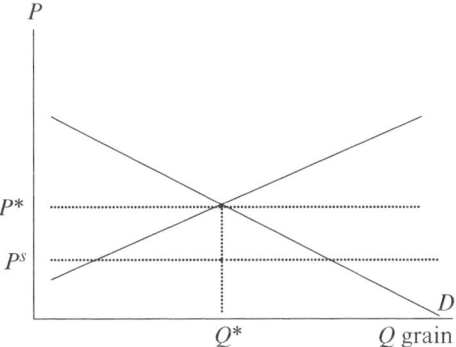

Figure 5.3   Shortage situations

5.2   MODELING PRODUCTION AND IRRIGATION TECHNOLOGIES

Thus far we have used very simple concepts in our discussion of the choices that farms must make: the main theme has been how much of the inputs land, labor, capital, and water to use, in turn leading to the crop supply or harvest decision. We can capture these simple concepts using any number of simple mathematical functional forms for the production function. Because it is simple, the Cobb-Douglas form is often used. In earlier chapters we ignored the problem that a farmer must decide to plant a certain amount of a certain crop well before the crop can be brought to market, and perhaps before the market price of the crop is known. However, we could write a Cobb-Douglas production function as:

$$Q_{t+1} = \alpha_0 l_t^{\alpha_1} k_t^{\alpha_2} w_t^{\alpha_3} v_{t+1} \tag{5.3}$$

where l, k, and w are acres planted, variable inputs such as capital and labor, and water used at time t, respectively, and v_{t+1} is a random variable. When we make the parameter restrictions: $\Sigma \alpha_i = 1$, and $0 < \alpha_i < 1$ ($i = 1, 2,$ and 3), the function in equation (5.3) is known as a Cobb-Douglas, which exhibits constant returns to scale (CRS). Note that in the production relationship above a time lag is introduced. We can find the marginal physical product by taking the partial derivatives of Q_{t+1} with respect to any of the inputs. For example, the marginal physical product of water is:

$$\partial Q_{t+1}/\partial w_t = [\alpha_3 \alpha_0 l_t^{\alpha_1} k_t^{\alpha_2} w_t^{\alpha_3} v_{t+1}]/w_t \tag{5.4}$$

which is equal to $\alpha_3 Q_{t+1}/w_t$. CRS in production means that if we increase inputs by some factor, output increases by the some proportion, that is, doubling inputs leads to a doubling of output. This is often an assumption that is not borne out in the empirical evidence and causes objections when it is just assumed without any testing of the validity of the assumption.

A more realistic farm production model than in equation (5.3) allows the farmer to produce multiple outputs (a vector of crops l) using inputs that imply joint production. The usual duality results do not apply (see Chambers and Just, 1989). Instead, one can set up the restricted profit maximization problem (following Schuck et al., 2000) as:

$$\max s_k, g_k \left\{ \sum_{k=1}^{K} [p_k f(l_k, \delta(s_k + g_k); \theta) - rs_k - hl_k] - p_e \Gamma \left(\sum_k g_k; \theta \right) - C \left(\sum_{k=1}^{K} (s_k + g_k); \theta \right) \right\} \quad (5.5)$$

where s_k and g_k are surface water and groundwater applied to crop k respectively, and surface water charges are r. The price of the crop is p_k, $f(\cdot)$ is the production function for crop k depending on the 'effective' water applied (captured by the $\delta(\cdot)$ function), technology e, less a water fee tied to acreage (h). The last two terms are the energy (Γ) and irrigation system costs (C), where the former of course relates to the price of energy (p_e) in determining groundwater pumping costs. We won't go through the mathematics of the solution to this problem here, but I will highlight the important outcomes from it.

First, this problem emphasizes the point that the farmer makes two decisions: how to allocate acreage, and then, conditioned on this given acreage, how much water to demand from its sources (groundwater and surface water). This is presumed in equation (5.5) above because total acreage is fixed ($l = \Sigma_{k=1}^{k} l_k$), or held constant. In reality acreage is of course a choice farmers can make, usually determined in advance of the time when crops are brought to market.[4] As such the acreage decision is treated as a long-run adjustment process.

In empirical studies it is often found that when the price of water changes, perhaps because the irrigation company raises the delivery price r charged to the farmer, the farmer will not change his or her use of water very much at all. Instead a farmer will reallocate acreage planted. The solutions to the problem above yield the farmer's demand functions for surface and groundwater. Because of the jointness of the problem the demands are not broken down for specific crops (Schuck et al., 2000), but each demand function depends on prices of the water source, technology, and the total amount of acreage used by the farmer. Perhaps surprisingly, technology has an indeterminate effect on water demand. Therefore, we might think that a technological advance would lower demand for water, but this is not necessarily the case. Technological advances can result in greater productivity for water, and hence, demand for water might actually increase. Schuck, et al. note that in Kern County, California the Arvin Edison Water Storage District adopted a new water rate structure for growers there, but 'the effects of the rate change are not obvious' (2000, p. 14).

In the remainder of this section we re-address some of these concepts and explore the way that water really does enter production decisions for farmers, recognizing that modern agriculture involves complex technological innovation and institutions, as well as uncertainty. We begin by assuming that farms are located in arid regions, and must irrigate.

Caswell and Zilberman (1986) provided the first model of irrigation technology choice, integrated into a reasonable empirical model of crop production. They begin by recognizing that a farmer does not simply employ an amount of land; he can influence an acre of land quality using different types of irrigation technology. Older irrigation systems simply rely on flood, level border and furrow methods, and gravity often results in uneven distribution of water on the planted soil, affecting the soil's 'irrigation effectiveness' in growth. Soil is a reservoir for the plant, and its characteristics affect the marginal productivity of several inputs. Modern irrigation technologies include drip systems that continuously and evenly apply water to crops, or a bit more basic: sprinkling systems. We show the model developed by Caswell and Zilberman (1986), assuming that irrigation water is provided via groundwater, requiring pumping.

Assume output per acre using technology $i(Q_i)$ is produced in a constant-return-to-scale manner, depending on *effective* water and land as inputs:

$$Q_i = f(e_i) \tag{5.6}$$

where e_i is effective water, or the amount of water (in acre feet) effectively used by the crop, per acre. Output is often called the yield per acre. For example, in California's San Joaquin Valley the average yield of cotton is about 1100 pounds per acre (see Caswell et al., 1990), which is about the same as reported in Table 5.2.

The production function in the above equation looks too simplistic because it appears to only have one argument (e_i), but as we will quickly see, this functional relationship incorporates most of the usual factors of production. First, this effective water in turn depends on land quality (α) and well depth (γ) in feet. Next, irrigation is going to come at a cost, and the cost per acre for a particular technology (again denoted by i) is:

$$C_i = I_i + \{v\beta(\gamma + \psi_i)a_i(\alpha,\gamma)\} \tag{5.7}$$

where I_i is the fixed irrigation cost per acre, and this includes the cost of labor and annual equipment costs that are incurred whether the farmer produces a single unit of the crop. The entire group of terms inside the $\{\}$ brackets on the right-hand side denote the energy costs for pumping and pressurization. Breaking them down: v = the energy price, in \$/kw; β = the amount of energy required for lifting one unit of water one unit of distance (kw/acre foot per foot); $\gamma + \psi_i$ = distance of lift equivalence required by technology i, given that some irrigation technologies require energy for pressurization; others require the same energy for a given well depth only; a_i = the acre feet of applied irrigation per acre for a given land quality and well depth.

Next, we put what we know from the above into a per acre rent-seeking, or profit maximization problem. Let output price be P, and the rental rate of land $r(\alpha, \gamma)$. The farmer's expected behavior suggests that, for a given location, the manager or farmer makes decisions in two stages. First, the manager selects the optimal water use for each given irrigation technology, and estimates his profits per acre. Then, in the second stage, the profits of alternative technologies are compared, and the farmer decides which technology to use for a given location. Obviously, for a farmer with a large parcel of land, with varying quality of that land, the right water choice and technology may vary over the entire parcel. To write this out completely requires one more definition, the irrigation effectiveness of technology i, which is:

$$h_i(\alpha) = \frac{e_i(\alpha,\gamma)}{a_i(\alpha,\gamma)} \tag{5.8}$$

The first-stage water use choice problem for a given technology is then:

$$Profit_i = \text{Max} Pf[h_i(\alpha)\, a_i(\alpha,\gamma)] - I_i - \{v\beta(\gamma + \psi_i)a_i(\alpha,\gamma)\} \tag{5.9}$$

The left-hand side can be viewed as quasi-rent per acre for a given technology. The farmer is maximizing here simply by choosing the amount of applied water per acre for that technology. Taking the first derivative of equation (5.9) with respect to a_i and setting it equal to zero yields the first-order condition:[5]

$$Pf'h_i - v\beta(\gamma + \psi_i) = 0 \tag{5.10}$$

This can be interpreted best by moving the second term on the LHS to the RHS and dividing by h_i. The result is just the usual first-order condition, that the value of the marginal product, in this case of effective water, is equal to its price. The price of effective water is thus $\nu\beta(\gamma + \psi_i)/h_i$. In Chapter 1 and above I have suggested that water was nearly 'free' for many farmers, especially in the western US, because it is passed down from generation to generation. However, the above problem and derivation of the price of effective water notes that in the context of groundwater as the source of irrigation water, this is not true. Here the true water application price depends on lift technology and energy used, as well as per unit energy prices.

Caswell and Zilberman go on to show that the framework above leads to some interesting comparative statics analysis: we can show the response of water use, energy use, quasi-rent per acre, and output to changes in land quality, well depth, output price, energy price, and the lift technology. As will be seen in Chapter 9 there is a drought under way in several parts of the United States today, and the framework allows examination of drought-related responses. By enriching the simple production model to allow for more complex factors, agricultural economists are able to explore real world issues such as this.

5.3 EMPIRICAL APPLICATION OF AGRICULTURAL PRODUCTION MODELS

As mentioned above, the first thing an agricultural modeler must decide is what form the production function should take. We begin with some intuition regarding the shape of the production, that is, input-output, relationship, as seen above in Figure 5.1. Mathematically, we impose a functional form on the production function that is consistent with logic, laws of physics, and what we know regarding the real world of agricultural production. We do not believe that continued application of an input w yields a constant yield. In other words marginal physical product, $\partial Q/\partial w$, does not equal a constant, say b, from $Q = a + bw + cOI$, where OI is all other inputs. We know this simply because continuously increasing applications of water have diminishing returns. So, economists generally believe that marginal productivity has three phases in production, as seen below in Figure 5.4. We again rely on the model from Caswell and Zilberman (1986), so that the input is effective water, e_i.

From the origin to point A we have phase 1, where marginal productivity is positive and increasing. In phase 2, between points A and C, small input levels lead to positive, but decreasing MP, and in phase 3, after point C, marginal productivity is negative, as would likely be the case with large

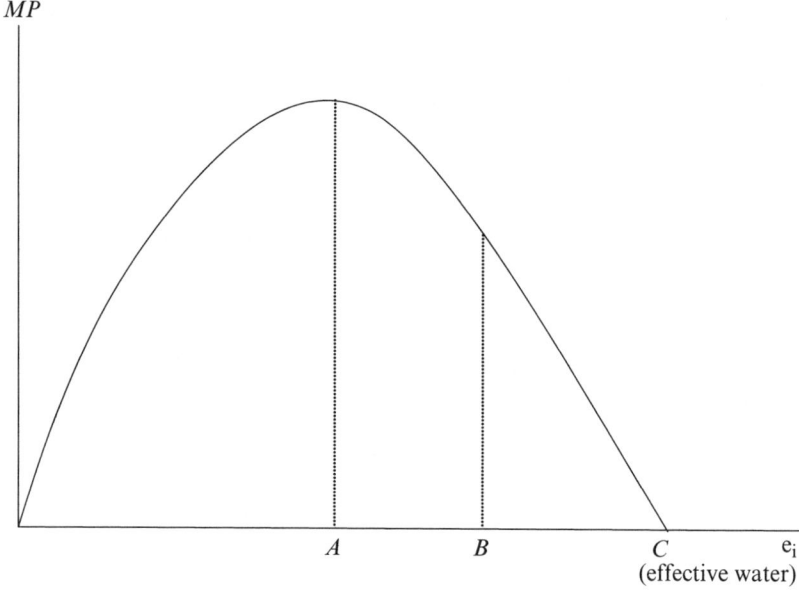

Figure 5.4 Marginal productivity and the three phases of production

input levels. For phase 3 one can imagine flooding a field so much that the plants are destroyed.

Next, what are the steps in modeling the above relationships using some kind of data, so that we can learn about the parameters? First, we might assume a particular functional form that matches our intuition on the marginal productivity relationships in Figure 5.5. We know that this curvature means that the slope of the production function in the basic Figure 5.1 cannot be constant, and possible forms are then the quadratic and Cobb-Douglas. Caswell and Zilberman use a variety of assumptions and observations from field studies in California to arrive at a quadratic production function:

$$Q = -6 + 10.68\, e - 1.78\, e^2 \quad (5.11)$$

Alternatively, a Cobb-Douglas yields:

$$Q = A e^{\psi} \quad (5.12)$$

where ψ is the output elasticity of effective water.[6] Despite the fact that the Cobb-Douglas is one of the most widely used forms in econometric studies of production, it is flawed for the purposes of the investigation in the

Caswell and Zilberman study. The Cobb-Douglas is quite restrictive in the technology and input substitution patterns it implies.

Caswell and Zilberman make some assumptions so that they can proceed with an empirical example. After all, the end goal for many is to get real answers to the tough questions. Some questions that may occur to you are: (i) How many acre feet of water should be applied to a given crop, and does this vary by crop? (ii) Does the 'best' technology in irrigation change across regions and crops? (iii) Exactly how much does irrigation improve land quality? (iv) How would Caswell and Zilberman's model change if surface water is used in irrigation instead of groundwater? There are countless others. To begin, a modeler has to impose a specific structure on the equations being modeled, meaning that even if there is confidence in the quadratic form, exact parameter values are needed. How do we find such parameter values?

The empirical researcher has several possible methods for finding parameter values, including the programming method we alluded to above, as well as to go out and collect data to fit an econometric model. In some states there just are no good data. Sometimes, casual empiricism is used, relying on the literature. For example, Caswell and Zilberman say that 0.2 is a reasonable estimate of the output elasticity of effective water. They then take estimates of water applied to growing fruits and vegetables in arid areas of Southern California. These are between 3 and 5 acre feet per acre, per year. But such applications result in effective water yields under traditional irrigation technology of between 1.8 and 3 acre feet. They assume that 50 percent of effective water produces about 60 percent of maximum yield. These assumptions lead to the quadratic equation in (5.11).

Using an approach such as this the modeler can find answers to comparative statics questions by making a few more final assumptions. Data suggest that traditional irrigation technology leads to land quality effectiveness at about 0.6, while sprinklers boost this to 0.85 and drip technology yields about 0.95. Data must be collected on the energy price and the lift and pressurization to implement the Caswell and Zilberman model. In the 1980s, the authors report that the cost of lifting an acre foot of water 1 foot was about $0.20 (this is the term $\nu\beta$). Pressurization in traditional irrigation technology is nil because those systems mainly rely on gravity, so that ψ is about zero for this technology, while for sprinklers a pressurization equivalent is 120 feet, and for drip, about 70 feet. Once these assumptions are put into the model, a host of results are forthcoming. There are too many results to review here, but, for example, Caswell and Zilberman report that using the quadratic model, the increase in profits by using drip irrigation, as opposed to traditional technology, could be $60 to $90 per acre, at well depths of 300 to 400 feet. That is the main point of such investigations.

5.4 ESTIMATED VALUES FOR WATER IN AGRICULTURE

The fact that water adds value to agricultural land is obvious, especially in agricultural regions that would be characterized as arid. At the extreme, poor quality land in desert areas is probably worth very little, at least in agricultural use. As with other inputs it is interesting to explore the marginal product (MP) of water, in dollar terms and its relationship to applications of certain amounts of water. The dollar MP is the value of the marginal product of VMP. Figure 5.5 shows the VMP for Arizona cotton.

One can see from Figure 5.5 that the VMP falls as water is applied, which is consistent with the usual assumptions economists make regarding falling marginal physical products. Of course one cannot conclude that there is one value per quantity applied when water is used as an input based on the above. Crop prices, soil conditions, the crop grown, and a host of other factors all cause variations in the value of the marginal product of water. In fact water's value is particularly high in growing cotton, as opposed to many other crops.

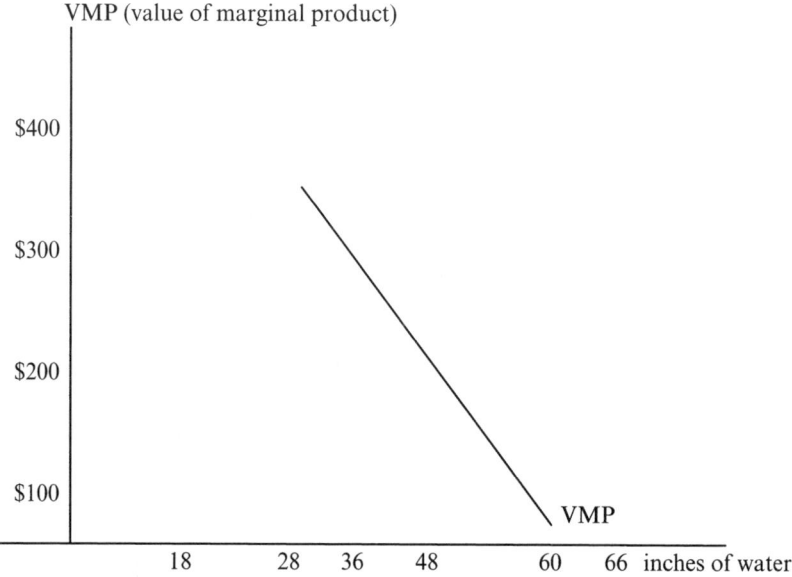

Notes: Marginal physical productivity measured as pounds of lint per acre for medium-textured soil.

Source: Based on Harry W. Ayer and Paul G. Hoyt. 'Crop-water production functions: economic implications for Arizona', University of Arizona, September 1981.

Figure 5.5 VMP ($/acre foot, 1980 dollars)

How do economists find estimates of monetary values for irrigation water? To begin, one might think of a simple economic analysis: examine the observed prices of agricultural land with irrigation water applied to grow crops, and then examine observed prices for agricultural land in the same region, with similar characteristics, but without irrigation water available. The difference in observed price might roughly proxy the value of irrigation water. The assumption is that the increased value of the crops from irrigation is capitalized into the land's price. Making this observation is more easily said than done, for it is often difficult to find agricultural land without irrigation water and observable market prices for this land in arid regions. Whatever the shortcomings, in this vein one can use a method called hedonic price analysis, which sorts out the effects of certain characteristics of a market good (here agricultural land) on the good's price.

Using this hedonic approach Faux and Perry (1999) specify a model where the price per acre of agricultural land is a function of the time (month) of sale, the class of the land (its quality, more or less), distance to towns, assessed value of the buildings per acre, and number of permitted residences per acre. They estimate the value of irrigation water for 225 properties in a county in the state of Oregon, finding that the value varies from $9 to $44 per acre foot. The range is for the least productive land irrigated, up to the most productive land, and the prices included all sales between 1991 and 1995. This is very useful information, but one might expect that irrigation water values may vary greatly by geographic region. Faux and Perry also remind us that the value revealed has to do with the market value of the land, and not exactly with the value of agriculture's value in production because markets clear demand and supply factors. The point is that there may be speculative or other reasons for market values for land that cannot be captured in the analysis.

Gibbons (1986) reports several estimates of the marginal value of water for certain crops, mostly based on studies done in the early 1980s by Harry Ayer and his colleagues for USDA. These estimates are based on crop-water production functions estimated in 1980. Gibbons's table is reproduced as Table 5.3, but needs to be viewed with a bit of caution. In all instances except for potatoes, the national average price for the crop is used to derive the marginal value of water. Second, the values are for a 10 percent reduction in the number of acre inches of water applied from the maximum yield point for the crop in the experiment. Because of this, the estimates do not perfectly conform to one another; Gibbons mentions that if low valued crops like alfalfa require more water than high valued crops, this feature heightens the disparity in values between the high and low valued crops. With these caveats in mind, the range of marginal values across crops appears to be fairly large. However, it is fairly consistent across

Table 5.3 Marginal water values from crop-water production functions, 1980 (dollars per acre foot)

Crop	Value					
	Idaho	Washington	California	Arizona	New Mexico	Texas
Grain sorghum				<15		113
Wheat		$59		22		35
Alfalfa				25	25	
Cotton			71–129	56	61	
Corn					52	57
Sugarbeets		144				
Potatoes						
Tomatoes	698	282	390			

Source: Gibbons (1986, chapter 2, table 2.2), based on various studies done by Harry Ayer, Paul Hoyt, Jane Prentzel, Sharon Kelly, David Miller, Mark Lynham, and T.S. Longley.

states, for a given crop, with the exception of grain sorghum in Texas and Arizona.

An alternative method of valuing agricultural water, and probably the more usual one in practice, is to use farm crop budgets to make inferences. There are two methods of analysis, one which yields on-site values for water, and the other which allows net returns to be comparable to instream water values. The difference between the two methods centers on whether the costs of water in the locale are included or not, because local water costs make the value most relevant to the farm site. Lacewell et al. (1974) used the farm crop budget method for the Texas High Plains and found values in the rather wide range of $15 to $101 per acre foot, depending on the crop. The high was for soybeans and is an on-site value, and the low was a net value for wheat.

Shumway (1973) used a regional linear programming (LP) model in California's San Joaquin Valley to derive long-run values for water for various crops. The values for water range from $22 per acre foot (in 1980 dollars) for barley to about $40 per acre foot for dry beans and for melons in one area. There are several other LP modeling studies that yield values for water in the production of crops in other states, but most of these date back to the 1970s or 1980s.

Table 5.4 presents a host of other estimated values reported in various sources.

Some studies try to estimate the value of water across all crops. Again, these seem to be 20 or more years old and may not still be relevant today,

Table 5.4   Estimates of water values in agricultural production

Crop, location	Estimated value in dollars per acre foot of water
Wheat, Texas	$8
Alfalfa, Washington	$10
Wheat, Arizona	$18 (averaged across counties in 1980 dollars)
Alfalfa hay, California	$26
Cotton, California	$37
Rice, Arkansas	$49
Corn, Texas	$57 to $76 (1980)
Cotton, Arkansas	$64
Soybeans, Texas High Plains	$72 (short run)
Apples, Washington	$86
Vegetables, Arizona	>$117

Note: All dollars converted to 1980 values using individual crop indices.

Sources: These vary but are found in various agricultural technical reports from Texas A & M, the University of Arizona, Washington State University, and, for California, see Shumway (1973).

but they are cited and summarized in Gibbons's (1986) chapter on irrigation. Robert Young (1984) concluded that though some crops suggest that water commands a high marginal value (as Table 5.4 shows), most crops translate to a value of water per acre foot of less than $30. With changing agricultural practices, a changed market, and changes in water institutions it appears that researchers should revisit the issue of the value of water in agriculture. However, it must be said in conclusion here that a complicating factor, in the western US at least, is the price at which the farmer expects he or she can sell water to a municipality at some point in the future. Speculative values certainly may be driving what the farmer is doing today. That is, we should not assume that the actual value of water as it pertains to agricultural production of one crop or the other explains whether a farmer uses more or less water, keeps a farmer growing certain crops, or drives the farmer to sell water and get out of farming altogether. Next I look at water quality issues for the agricultural sector.

5.5   AGRICULTURE AND WATER QUALITY

Chapter 3 focused on water quality issues, and mentioned that siltation from eroded farmland and non-point source pollution are among the biggest remaining water pollution problems in the United States. A few special problems relating to agriculture are expanded upon here. Irrigators cannot escape the issues of water quality, and even are part of disputes over endangered species that are found on their lands (see Revkin, 2002). As with other productive uses of water, agriculture can contribute to pollution or diminished water quality in both surface and groundwater, and in many cases agricultural runoff is the sole cause of certain types of water pollution.

Water applied to crops can evaporate, be taken up by all sorts of plants (evapotranspiration), it can percolate down into the soil where it may eventually return to the surface water course, or it can drain back to the surface water as runoff. In these processes water can become polluted with fertilizers, chemicals, and salts in the soils. The most frequently cited agricultural water quality problems in the United States are increased salinity and nutrient loading from use of fertilizers: 45 of the 50 states reported in 1994 that pesticide and fertilizer applications were responsible for groundwater contamination. Because there are so many farms and their individual contributions are hard to identify this has led to increasing concern about non-point source pollution.

5.5.1 Non-point Source Pollution

Chapter 3 notes that non-point source pollution (NSP) from farms has been deemed the largest unsolved water quality problem in the United States today. To recap, NSP is pollution where individual output sources are difficult or impossible to find, and loads are the outcome of contributions from many small individual polluters. NSP includes nitrogen, salinity, and heavy metals.

Farm runoff finds its way into groundwater and surface water supplies through natural drainage. In the late 1990s then president William Clinton directed the Environmental Protection Agency to tackle this problem head on, as part of his Clean Water Action Plan. The pollution addressed takes several forms, but nitrates can cause ecological and human health concerns and they are a primary concern. A notorious ecological situation in California involved contamination of the Kesterson Wildlife Refuge by agricultural drainage.

Nitrogen and phosphorus also accelerate algal production in surface water. Algal production may in turn lead to clogged pipelines, and mortality of fish and other aquatic species. The problem is greatest in lakes and estuaries, but can be found in rivers and in coastal waters (Ribaudo et al., 1999; EPA, 1998). Dinar and Xepapadeas (1998) report on NSP in Kern County, an unfortunate receptor because it hosts the Kern County Water Bank in the form of a rechargeable aquifer.

The debate that raged in the 1990s concerned whether national and local policy should address erosion at the farm, or issues away from the farm site, most likely downstream on a river (see Kozloff et al., 1992). Those in favor of on-site policies argue that what is happening on the farm is easiest to discern and manage, while those who argue for off-site policy management rely on the usual spatial impact arguments: it is just too difficult to regulate each farm's emissions. The latter group basically tries to demonstrate that the contribution to ambient downstream concentrations is the most important determinant of assessing marginal damages from any farm.

Salinity

Salinity is also a problem that stems from farming practices. Put simply, many farms produce crops on saline soils. This is because salts remain in the root zone after water is transpired from plants or after it evaporates. Depending on the adequacy of drainage, flushing or excess irrigation of that soil may leach out the salts, depositing these into surface and groundwater supplies when the water returns. Salinity problems on the Colorado River were so severe[7] that Congress enacted Public Law 93-320, the Colorado River Basin Salinity Control Act in 1974, in an effort to control salinity there (see Gardner and Young, 1988). More than 50 percent of the basin's 3.1 million irrigated acres are classified as saline (with soils in excess of 1300 mg/L of total dissolved solids or TDS), and this salinity lowers crop yields to the tune of millions of dollars in the Lower Colorado River Basin. Gardner and Young estimated that a rise in input water salinity from 800 mg/L to 1100 mg/L would cost Imperial Valley (in California) producers $13.88 million.

Using an optimization model Lee and Howitt (1996) find the optimal reduction in salt in the Colorado River to be about 1.3 million tons per year. This would allow salt levels at Imperial Dam to fall from 753 to 600 mg/L. The effects of a salt reduction program are simulated by taking Upper Colorado River Basin agriculture out of production, but implementing an actual program would be no trivial political task in the real world. Supposing that somehow this could be accomplished, the losses to agriculture in the Upper Basin would be $16.27 million, but the gains to the Lower Basin are about $95 million ($1.61 million to the agricultural sector and $92.8 million to industry), so the net benefit to society is about $55 million per year. Could this really be a feasible solution to the salinity problem? Probably not, as will be seen below.

5.5.2 Solutions to Agricultural Pollution Problems

Like most environmental problems in the US, agricultural pollution is still mainly handled through federal and state government regulatory efforts.

All regulatory efforts (and market-based incentives for that matter) involve monitoring, and it should be remembered that detailed monitoring cannot really be accomplished easily in the case of non-point source pollution. In other words, no government agency is going to monitor emissions from every farm in the country. Monitoring is especially complicated for groundwater contamination, which requires drilling a test or monitoring well at a considerable fixed and variable cost. One can easily imagine that if the geographical area in the questionable region is large and varies in water quality, a large number of wells might be required and, therefore, monitoring costs would be considerable. In addition, if the aquifer is depleted and falls, for example, the test well might not be deep enough to monitor and cannot be easily drilled to greater depths.[8]

Ribaudo (1989) estimates that in the US agricultural runoff causes about $9 billion per year in damage to surface waters. As is usual in the US, state and federal regulations or 'command and control' programs have been proposed and adopted to attempt to cope with the problems. There are current federal public standards set by the US Environmental Protection Agency on 15 agricultural chemicals, including nitrate (with an MCL of 10 mg/l), and the herbicides alachlor (0.002 mg/l) and atrazine (0.003 mg/l).

As mentioned above, the US Congress established water quality standards for the Colorado River allowing maximum salinity levels of 723, 747, and 879 mg/L at Hoover, Parker, and Imperial Dam, respectively. To ensure quality standards are met however, the federal government (i.e. the US taxpayer) would have to be paying hundreds of millions of dollars (Lee and Howitt, 1996).[9] The cost of meeting these standards via federal expenditures is prohibitive: the 'second best' solution Lee and Howitt suggest to removing Upper Basin agriculture from production involves an annual federal expense of $37.5 million, yielding a net benefit of about $4.3 million per year (Lee and Howitt, 1996). Salinity issues on the Colorado River between the United States and Mexico are supposed to be handled in international law. But these standards and laws may be difficult to enforce, and some public water treatment systems may be lagging behind in meeting them.

Meanwhile, it is up to each state to provide regulations to attempt to deal with agricultural pollution. Table 5.5 shows some states that do have a nutrient plan requirement based on 1998 data; other states do not.

Other states had a comprehensive water quality plan and most had plans to deal with disposal of animal wastes. Still, it is easy to see that most states, such as Nevada, did not have regulations in place to deal with possible agricultural runoff. Naturally, some states have little agricultural production, so agricultural runoff there currently does not pose a problem that would require restrictions or regulations, but states with a large agricultural sector continue to experience problems.

Table 5.5 States that had a nutrient plan requirement or pesticide restriction in 1998

Nutrient Plan Requirement	Pesticide Restriction
Arizona	Arizona
Colorado	California
Delaware	Iowa
Iowa	Kansas
Maryland	Montana
Montana	Wisconsin
Nebraska	
West Virginia	
Wisconsin	

Source: Ribaudo et al. (1999).

Probably the biggest recent US agricultural regulatory program initiated to address non-point source pollution is the Conservation Reserve Program (CRP). It offers farmers annual rental payments to remove erodible land from crop production. In return farmers also agree to cover the land with vegetation to reduce erosion for a period of ten years. Specific parcels of land can be targeted for this purpose. Kozloff et al. (1992) use a simulation model in a Minnesota watershed to achieve results in an evaluation of micro-targeting and they conclude that it is cost-effective. However, they are cautious in noting that administrative costs are substantial, and gains (savings over regional CRP programs) fall as more land is targeted. Clearly, the need for economists to provide innovative economic solutions is present.

Economic solutions and market-based incentives
A market-based incentive is one where a producer directly experiences monetary incentives (either positive or negative) that motivate a change a behavior. For example, the use of taxes has been proposed as a tool for dealing with non-point source pollution. At the theoretical or methodological level it is certainly possible to factor environmental damage into economic models of agricultural production, thereby internalizing this damage in the optimization problem. Ribaudo et al. (1999) show that an ex ante optimization problem that includes risk or uncertainty can be specified that maximizes expected net surplus: quasi-rents minus environmental damage costs. Farmers are assumed to obtain profits from the use of inputs applied to cropland using choices that are best described as discrete ones.

A discrete choice might be the choice to produce corn with no-till tillage versus the production of corn via a crop rotation and using mulch tillage. The choices affect the amount of runoff, which in turn determines the amount of damage that may be imposed on others. The mathematics is skipped here, but the usual first-order conditions yield the rule that marginal private benefits from the use of inputs should be set equal to the expected marginal external damages from their use. Ignoring the externalities results in too much of an input being used, which is what we observe in farming today.

A specific example of an economic model incorporating environmental quality is Caswell and Zilberman's (1986) model of agricultural production and choice of irrigation technologies, modified to include water conservation and environmental quality concerns. In fact, adding a co-author as a colleague, the authors did just this. The expanded model will not be reproduced here, but the idea is simply to include a pollution coefficient for each acre of land used, and to see what the effect of internalizing the cost by charging a pollution tax would be (see Caswell et al., 1990). Their modeling of cotton growers' behavior suggests that a pollution tax on drainage may encourage adoption of more modern irrigation technologies, as well as helping to achieve conservation of scarce water resources. There is additional support for this idea. Using computer simulations Dinar and Xepapadeas (1998) show that in theory, pollution taxes can be applied along with individual monitoring to achieve a reduction in NSP related to an aquifer.[10] However, I know of no situation in the US where a tax program has actually been applied to NSP situations.

Another market-based incentive that has been proposed to alleviate the salinity and fertilizer loadings problems is the use of tradable permits. The concept is borrowed from the general literature in environmental economics, which has now been applied to EPA's program to reduce acid rain (sulfur dioxide permits), originally implemented under the 1990 amendments to the Clean Air Act. The idea in theory is to allow point sources to purchase allowances from non-point sources to meet their emissions reductions requirements. Trading is possible when the pollutants are common to both parties. Gains can be obtained when it is less expensive to reduce non-point source loads than point sources. However, allowances are not feasible for trading if the non-point source emissions cannot be measured with a reasonable degree of accuracy (Ribaudo et al., 1999).

Point/non-point trading experimental programs have been set up at several places in the United States, including the well-known Dillon Reservoir in Colorado. Here the point-source polluters purchase emissions allowances from non-point polluters. The marginal phosphorus abatement cost for point-source polluters in the Dillon Reservoir instance is in the range of $860 to $7861 per pound, while the same abatement cost for non-point source polluters is only $119 per pound (Malik et al., 1992). Reductions for non-point source polluters are accomplished via implementation of best-management practices (BMPs) and nutrient management plans. As of 1997, no trades had actually occurred (Hoag and Hughes-Popp, 1997), but at the time of writing some trading in Colorado has begun.

5.6 MARKET FAILURES, UNCERTAINTY AND AGRICULTURE

Price distortions and uncertainty are briefly introduced above, but below we revisit these concepts, adding some evidence on the problems these cause. In particular, the concept of expected profits is introduced, though a fuller explanation comes in Chapter 6, which focuses on uncertainty.

5.6.1 Price Distortions and Subsidies

There is a good deal of rhetoric regarding the economics of agriculture and farmers in the United States, and much of it is negative. The administration of George W. Bush initially pledged a return to free markets for agricultural commodities, and less government intervention. As time passed, the administration fell back on the usual agricultural support programs in order to gain political support in agricultural states. It seems that in the United States farmers are never satisfied with their situation and demand more help and attention, while at the same time mainstream economists always chime in with protests against government interference. It should be remembered that the current generation of consumers do benefit when prices are kept low, so policies that affect food prices do matter to consumers.

The theory is that, left to itself, the market will provide for a Pareto-optimal allocation of all resources, including food (see Chapter 2). When there are government price supports or subsidies many economists will immediately and continuously call for their removal. They note that price supports cause the market to veer from its natural equilibrium, and depending on the level of the subsidy, lead to surpluses. These price supports are typically thought of as price floors for a particular crop such as wheat or corn. They may also take the form of a government guarantee to purchase any surplus supplies. In 1997, about 36 percent of the 1.9 million farms in the US received government subsidies of some kind (see www.ewg.org).

Another subsidy goes largely unnoticed in the parlance of Washington DC and the media. That is the original subsidy on water that agricultural users obtained, sometimes well over 100 years ago, as well as existing irrigation-related costs that are still subsidized by the government today. Settling the American West was often encouraged with promises of free land and water. Given the difficulties of easily applying surface water that likely was at a great distance from a parcel of land, the US federal government also began to supply public distribution systems, or publicly funded irrigation projects.

Put simply, many irrigation systems, including storage reservoirs and irrigation ditches, were financed by the US federal government. Upon completion of the irrigation project, farmers who wanted water were often given it at no initial cost, or asked to pay back loans at a greatly reduced fee relative to the true cost. The first who came were the first served. Some farmers were asked later to take over maintenance of irrigation facilities such as dams and reservoirs, but today most often a federal or state government agency continues to foot maintenance bills on facilities. It is fairly common to observe farmers stating that water from a federal project is theirs, but also observe that an agency such as the US Bureau of Reclamation, and ultimately the taxpayer, is paying for the upkeep of facilities that are part of that project.

Some argue that if one factors out government subsidies of water projects, few water projects today that rely on agricultural benefits would pass the benefit-cost test (Foster et al., 1986). For example, Levy (1982) estimated that the true cost of delivered surface water in 1978 for the Central Valley Project in California was about \$20 per acre foot, while the state of California charged an average delivery price of \$8 per acre foot, giving a \$12 per acre foot subsidy. In their analysis of water subsidies Foster et al. (1986) analyse the California market for rice, a very water-intensive crop. They estimate a rice supply function (S) for states other than California to be:

$$S = 26844 + 2526P + 25949TE \tag{5.13}$$

where price is dollars per cwt, and TE is a dummy variable representing new technology developed in the early 1960s, including second-crop rice production in Texas. Supply is measured in 1000 cwt. Demand for California rice production is estimated to be $D = 283002 - 30628P$, again measured in 1000 cwt. These equations are used to estimate the change in consumer's and producer's surplus resulting from changes in the price of water facing California rice farmers.

The idea is to examine the effect of prices of water that are above the subsidized price of \$7.84 per acre foot which farmers were being charged for surface water in 1978. Using a programming model the authors simulate the effect of rising water prices leading to California rice farmers producing less rice, so that the price of rice rises and affects supply in equation (5.13). They illustrate the fact that consumers gain from the subsidy initially. But as California water prices are raised, the producer's surplus for rice growers elsewhere increases, while the consumer's surplus for US rice decreases. In their simulations using the programming model, total consumer's surplus falls from $184 081 (at the subsidized water price of $7.84) to $158 584 when the price is about $19.60 per acre foot. However, because the producer's surplus for rice growers outside California rises at the same time, the indication is that the optimal subsidy in terms of total surplus (producer's plus consumer's surplus) is near $0.00 per acre foot. This is consistent with the economist's notion that subsidies are inefficient.

All of these issues have caused some to claim that a farmer is potentially the ultimate welfare recipient in the United States, which causes anger in many quarters. This is controversial, and one may well ask the question, why do governments offer such subsidies to farmers? There are many different answers to this question, and probably the most important ones fall into the category of politics. However, it is possible that the reason is that agricultural markets, if left to their own devices, would fail to provide the amount and quality of food that the public demands. In short, perhaps agricultural markets without government intervention are not perfect markets at all, largely because of the farmer's problem of uncertainty.

5.6.2 Uncertainty, Agriculture, and Expected Profits

One could hardly find a more compelling case for introducing the economics of uncertainty and risk than in producing crops. Uncertainty is taken up in detail in the next chapter, but it must be addressed in the context of agriculture.

As discussed in the introduction to this chapter, a farmer has to plant his or her crop, well before knowing market conditions at harvest time, and before knowing how the growing season will be. Poor weather brings crop failures and good weather, when widely spread geographically, brings a bumper crop and the market ends up with an excess supply, so that the crop's price generally falls, leading to lower profits than expected. I can easily imagine that most farmers think the usual joke ('no such thing as good weather' mentioned above) is hardly worth much laughter.

Farmers may be uncertain about the results from applying inputs, so it is thought that a risk-averse farmer will apply more water than necessary to maximize yields. Another important area of risk management for farming in modern economies relates to environmental risk. Most farmers, as noted above, face issues of erosion or water pollution, and perhaps the issue of harming endangered species.

Some believe that the farmer will almost certainly not be in complete compliance with environmental regulations. Therefore, they recommend a 'safety-first' concept be used in agricultural management. The concept essentially means that the decision maker focuses on the probability of falling below some critical target level, say, of compliance with clean up (Qui et al., 2001). Safety-first rules can be modeled by programming in constraints that involve this probability. Early literature in economics introduced what are known as lower partial moments to evaluate economic (financial) risk (see, for example, Fishburn, 1977), but Qui et al. (2001) adapt the concept to the introduction of upper partial moments to impose environmental safety-first constraints.

More generally, modeling risk in economic models goes back more than 50 years (for example, Friedman and Savage, 1952) and flows from models conceived of in the 1940s by the mathematicians, von Neumann and Morgenstern (1944). Though much early work focused on managing a portfolio of investment alternatives, each with a different expected return, agricultural models of production and profit maximization under risk were soon to follow in the 1960s (for example, McFarquhar, 1961; Halter and Dean, 1971).

A simple way of introducing this risk and uncertainty is to let the farmer's utility depend on expected income and the variance in that income.[11] The departure from the conventional problem with certainty begins with the definition of profit. Usually we think of utility $(u) = u(\pi)$, where π is known profit, $= TR(Q) - C(Q)$. However, risk and uncertainty can stem from a variety of sources. As above, weather may lead to uncertain harvests, so π becomes a random variable because Q is a random variable. It may also be that the profit function can be written:

$$\pi_{t+1} = P_{t+1}Q_{t+1} - C(Q_{t+1}) - TFC \tag{5.14}$$

where $t+1$ indicates the future period, when harvest is in, and TFC are total fixed costs. The problem for the farmer is that the planting decision is made in period t, not period $t+1$, and thus, a very obvious issue is that at planting time the future price (P_{t+1}) is uncertain (see Helmberger and Chavas, 1996). Thus, this profit maximization cannot be solved because the value of output cannot be determined at the time the decision to produce a certain amount is made. So again, to accommodate this uncertainty, one simple approach is to let the farmer's utility be a function of expected income and the variance or standard deviation on that income, that is (following Helmberger and Chavas, 1996):

$$u_t = u\{E_t(\pi_{t+1}), [V_t(\pi_{t+1})]^{1/2}\} \tag{5.15}$$

where here $E(\ )$ denotes taking the expected value of future profits, and $V(\ )$ denotes the variance (see note 11). Suppose that the farmer knows whether he is risk averse, risk neutral, or loves to take risks, and assume that the farmer can know the probabilities of forming an educated guess about expected future income and the variance on that income. Then, in general, it may be possible to find the output the farmer with a particular risk preference chooses to produce, given these combinations of preferences and sources of randomness, coupled with the information pertaining to risks.

Recently, this sort of risk modeling has also incorporated risks the farmer faces from things that damage crops, such as bad weather or pests. For example, Archer and Shogren (1994) model the risks of damage from invasive, harmful weeds. Such weeds can reduce yields to various crops, but the farmer can self-protect or insure, by applying herbicides that control the weeds. Archer and Shogren show that an expected profit model can be modified to allow for the impacts of weeds (monetary damages that reduce profits), as well as the cost of applying herbicides. Alternatively one might, rather than letting utility be a function of expected future profit or income, let the farmer maximize expected utility itself. We return to that concept in Chapter 6, which explicitly deals with uncertainty.

One of the most important outcomes of this research is the development of futures markets in agricultural commodities. Trading, mainly related to the Chicago Board of Trade, involves the use of futures contracts to hedge against uncertainty. The modern farmer almost certainly trades in futures at some point (Turvey and Baker, 1990). Futures are discussed in the next chapter.

5.7 THE FARMER AS SPECULATOR OR INVESTOR

Before concluding this chapter, I promised a brief exploration of an additional interesting modern complexity related to water and agriculture: a speculative role for the farmer. In the 1970s, farmland in the United States increased in value fairly rapidly because of encroachment of growing cities and towns, causing many to consider the capital gains that farmers were receiving simply by holding onto their land for potential sale to residential developers (see, for example, Melichar, 1979). Similarly, a senior water rights holder in a system of prior appropriation must now view water in two ways: one of these is that water is simply an input that enhances the quality of land; the other is that water itself is an asset, which may have increasing value as time goes on.

A good example of this was mentioned in Chapter 1, that of the growing power of farmers in the Imperial Valley to negotiate a price for their water in sales to southern California cities. It is well known that California has been using more than its fair share of water allocated to it under the Colorado River Compact of 1922. The overuse came from shares legally held by the upstream states of Arizona and Nevada, but these states' populations have been growing rapidly and now they want to take their fair share of the Colorado's water. Arizona is in a position to do so because of completion of the enormous Central Arizona Project.

President Clinton set several key due dates for California to show progress in complying with cutbacks in their withdrawals, and an important one was the end of 2002 (Jehl, 2002). One part of the 2002 negotiations in fact allowed farmers to obtain $50 million in financial incentives, while requiring farmers to fallow as much as 10 percent of their fields. This part of the negotiations relates to environmental concerns in the Salton Sea, and the need for runoff to reach the lake to reduce salinity there (Jehl, 2002).

Any financial asset may be treated as part of an investment portfolio and a resource such as water or farmland is not much different. Under very simple assumptions, models of portfolio management under risk lead to one important rule of investment: a simple version of the rule is that an investor should 'harvest' or 'extract' a natural resource such that its price rises at the going market rate of return on other potential assets. Simply put, suppose a farmer has water and an expectation that its price will rise in the future. At any time a farmer can close the farm and sell the water, reinvesting the profits from sale in another asset, say the 'stock market'. The farmer must consider the loss of income in farming, but if more money can be made in the stock market, he or she will sell the water and invest. Conversely, if the farmer can earn a higher rate of return by waiting and holding onto the water, she will hold her wealth in the form of water.

This is all quite similar to the simple problem of deciding to be in farming to begin with (see Helmberger and Chavas, 1996), and we modify the usual discussion to examine the decision at a point in time to sell the water versus keeping it and continuing to farm. Suppose, for example, that a farmer has 1000 acre feet of senior water rights and that the current price per acre foot is $100. The farmer wishes to retire at time T. Assume all is certain, that T is 20 years from now, and that the farmer has no assets other than the water.[12] Also assume that the farmer can earn a rate of return of r in the stock or money market. The farmer can make decision A, sell the water now, or B, keep farming. Under option A, the value of the water at time T is:

$$V_T = \$100\,000\,[1+r]^T \qquad (5.16)$$

If, for example, $r = 0.05$ and T as we said is 20, then the $100 000 is worth $265 333 at the end of year 20. Alternatively, suppose the farmer wants to consider option B. He can reinvest all of the profit or quasi-rent he earns at the end of each year, and again we assume he reinvests this money in the stock or money market with rate of return r. Assume that annual quasi-rent is constant, at QR. At the end of period T, the farmer will have farming income (FM):

$$FM = QR(1+r)^{T-1} + QR(1+r)^{T-2} + \ldots + QR(1+r)^{T-T} + S = QR\Sigma_{t=1} (1+r)^{T-1} + S \qquad (5.17)$$

where S is the salvage value of the farm, including what he obtains for the water at the end of period T. Now assume that there is some particular value of QR that satisfies $FM = V_T$, so that the total value at the end of T is the same in each case, say QR^*. We can then solve for what is known as the 'user cost of capital',

$$QR^* = V_T - S/[\Sigma_{t=1}(1+r)^{T-t}] \qquad (5.18)$$

Clearly, if all is known, the farmer will stay in farming as long as the rate of return from doing so is greater than or equal to the user cost of capital. Unfortunately the trick in such decision making is that the farmer may not know the exact rate of return in the stock market or the salvage price of assets she will receive at time T by holding on to her assets, such as the water. So, the farmer has to maximize utility from the uncertain income on these investments, and this leads to the expected utility framework (see Chapter 6). Recognize that in the modern era, especially in the situation described above, any farmer must trade off the current returns in farming a crop and using water as an input against the future returns of water as an asset. Naturally the wise farmer assesses the future market for her water by looking at potential future buyers. Who will be wanting her water at some point and when will that be? Cities and counties are the obvious source of demand, so if residential population growth is strong, here is where the intelligent farmer will be looking. But that farmer still cannot know with certainty when the exact right time to sell will be and this fact has caused several scholars to consider and discuss the development of options markets in water (for example, Howitt, 1998). We take this up again in the next chapter.

PROBLEMS

5.1 Suppose the production function is quadratic for an agricultural producer: $Q = a + be + ce^2$. At what point does output per acre peak?

Is this function of constant elasticity? Is it consistent with the figure showing the phases of marginal productivity in the chapter, Figure 5.4? Explain your answers.

5.2 Explain why Caswell and Zilberman might reject the Cobb-Douglas production function.

NOTES

1. I thank my former student, Flint Wright, who, as an aide to an agricultural lobbyist, had familiarity with real US agricultural issues and provided valuable comments on this chapter.
2. Helmberger and Chavas (1996) offer a model of the family farm, where labor is provided by those within the family. They show that a family's own capital could be invested in the farm or any other asset and that the decision to farm can be treated as an analysis of long-run returns.
3. Schuck and Green (2004) note that shifting from per acre of land fees to volumetric fees changes the problem from an extensive margin (the acreage decision) to an intensive margin one (whether crop A or crop B should be planted on that acreage).
4. This suggests use of an uncertainty model, where acreage depends on expected profits.
5. Caswell and Zilberman (1986) show the second-order condition, ensured by concavity in the production function.
6. For the student new to economics, this tells us the percentage change in output for a percentage change in the input. In Caswell and Zilberman's model the output elasticity of effective water for a given technology is $\psi I(e) = -f'(e_i) \, e_i/f(e_i)$.
7. Estimates in 1975 were that salt content at the Imperial Dam with the control program was over 1200 parts per million (ppm), and the US EPA had indicated that this posed a 'high' hazard to most crops.
8. As the discussion above shows, drilling costs increase with depth because of the extra energy needed to lift the water from greater depths.
9. They suggest that federal projects to reduce salt loadings cost between $4.44 and $300 per ton of salt to improve irrigation water use.
10. The authors consider the possibility that farm-specific monitoring could work in the region, as opposed to centralized monitoring.
11. Chapter 6 will show that the expected value of x, $E(x)$, equals the sum of probability of x times its outcome, for a discrete random variable. The standard deviation is the square root of the variance.
12. To keep things simple assume the farmer doesn't wish to sell the farm property itself.

REFERENCES

Archer, David W. and J.F. Shogren (1994), 'Nonpoint pollution, weeds and risk', *Journal of Agricultural Economics*, **45**(1), 38–51.

Caswell, M.F., E. Lichtenberg and D. Zilberman (1990), 'The effects of pricing policies on water conservation and drainage', *American Journal of Agricultural Economics*, **72**(4) (November), 883–90.

Caswell, M.F. and D. Zilberman (1986), 'The effects of well depth and land quality on the choice of irrigation technology', *American Journal of Agricultural Economics*, **68**(4) (November), 798–811.

Chambers, R.G. and R.E. Just (1989), 'Estimating multi-output technologies', *American Journal of Agricultural Economics*, **71** (November), 980–95.

Dinar, A. and A. Xepapadeas (1998), 'Regulating water quantity and quality in irrigated agriculture', *Journal of Environmental Management*, **54**, 273–89.

US Environmental Protection Agency (1998), *National Water Quality Inventory: 1996 Report to Congress*, EPA 841-R-97-008, Office of Water, February.

Faux, J. and G.M. Perry (1999), 'Estimating irrigation water value using hedonic price analysis: a case study', *Land Economics*, **75**(3), 440–52.

Fishburn, P.J. (1977), 'Mean-risk analysis with risk associated with below-target returns', *American Economic Review*, **67** (March), 116–26.

Foster, W.E., L.S. Calvin, G.M. Johns and P. Rottschaefer (1986), 'Distributional welfare implications of an irrigation water subsidy', *American Journal of Agricultural Economics* (November), 778–86.

Friedman, M. and L.J. Savage (1952), 'The expected utility hypothesis and the measurability of utility', *Journal of Political Economy*, **60** (December), 463–74.

Gardner, R. and R.A. Young (1988), 'Assessing strategies for the control of irrigation induced salinity in the Upper Colorado River Basin', *American Journal of Agricultural Economics*, **70** (February), 37–49.

Gibbons, Diana C. (1986), *The Economic Value of Water*, Baltimore, MD: Resources for the Future Press.

Green, G.P. and D.L. Sunding (1997), 'Land allocation, soil quality, and the demand for irrigation technology', *Journal of Agricultural and Resource Economics*, **22**(2) (December), 367–78.

Halter, A.N. and G.W. Dean (1971), *Decisions under Uncertainty*, Cincinnati, OH: South-Western Publishing (out of print).

Helmberger, Peter G. and Jean-Paul Chavas (1996), *The Economics of Agricultural Prices*, Upper Saddle River, NJ: Prentice Hall.

Hoag, D.L. and J.S. Hughes-Popp (1997), 'Theory and practice of pollution credit trading in water quality management', *Review of Agricultural Economics*, **19**(2), 252–62.

Howitt, R.E. (1998), 'Spot prices, option prices, and water markets: an analysis of emerging markets in California', in K.W. Easter, M. Rosegrant and A. Dinar (eds), *Markets for Water: Potential and Performance*, Boston, MA: Kluwer Academic Publishers, Chapter 8.

Jehl, D. (2002), 'Thirsty California cities covet farms' full glass', *New York Times*, Western edn, 1.

Kozloff, K., S.J. Taff and Y. Wang (1992), 'Microtargeting the acquisition of cropping rights to reduce nonpoint source water pollution', *Water Resources Research*, **28**(3) (March), 623–8.

Lacewell, R.D., J.M. Sprott and B.R. Beattie (1974), 'Value of irrigation water with alternative input prices, product prices, and yield levels: Texas High Plains and Lower Rio Grande Valley', Texas Water Resources Institute technical report no. 58, College Station, Texas A & M University.

Lee, D.J. and R.E. Howitt (1996), 'Modeling regional agricultural production and salinity control alternatives for water quality policy analysis', *American Journal of Agricultural Economics*, **78** (February), 41–53.

Levy, Y. (1982), 'Pricing federal irrigation water: a California case study', *Federal Reserve Bank of San Francisco Economic Review* (spring), 35–55.

Malik, A.S., B.A. Larson and M. Ribaudo (1992), 'Agricultural nonpoint source pollution and economic incentive policies: issues in the reauthorization of the clean water act', staff report AGES 9229, US Department of Agriculture, Economic Research Service, Washington, DC.

Markowitz, H.M. (1952), 'Portfolio selection', *Journal of Finance*, **7**, 77–91.

McFarquhar, A.M.M (1961), 'Rational decision making and risk in farm planning – an application of quadratic programming in British arable farming', *Journal of Agricultural Economics*, **14**(4), 552.

Melichar, Emanuel (1979), 'Capital gains versus current income in the farming sector', *American Journal of Agricultural Economics*, **61** (December), 1085–92.

Mitchell, D. and W.M. Hanemann (1994), 'Setting urban water rates for efficiency and conservation: a discussion of the issues', draft report prepared for the California Urban Water Conservation Council (June), available from M-Cubed, Oakland, California.

Qui, Z., T. Prato and F. McCamley (2001), 'Evaluating environmental risks using safety-first constraints', *American Journal of Agricultural Economics*, **83**(2) (May), 402–13.

Revkin, A.C. (2002), 'Study discounts halting irrigation to protect fish', *New York Times*, 5 February, A-16.

Ribaudo, M. (1989), 'Water quality benefits from the conservation reserve program', agricultural economic report no. 606, US Department of Agriculture, Washington, DC.

Ribaudo, M.O., R.D. Horan and M.E. Smith (1999), 'Economics of water quality protection from nonpoint sources: theory and practice', Economic Research Service report no. 782, US Department of Agriculture, Washington, DC.

Schuck, E.C. and G.P. Green (2004), ' "Cash and carry" irrigation water prices in a cost-contained world', *AERE Newsletter* essay, spring issue.

Schuck, E.C., G.P. Green and D.L. Sunding (2000), 'Irrigation water rate reform and endogenous technological change', Paper presented at the Western Agricultural Economics Association annual meetings, Vancouver, British Columbia, (June).

Shumway, C.R. (1973), 'Derived demand for irrigation water: the California aqueduct', *Southern Journal of Agricultural Economics*, **5**(2) (December), 195–200.

Turvey, C.G. and T.G. Baker (1990), 'A farm-level financial analysis of farmers' use of futures and options under alternative farm programs', *American Journal of Agricultural Economics*, **72**(4) (November), 946–57.

Von Neumann, J. and O. Morgenstern (1944), *Theory of Games and Economic Behavior*, Princeton, NJ: Princeton University Press.

Young, Robert A. (1984), 'Direct and indirect regional economic impacts of competition for irrigation water', in Ernest A. Englebert (ed.), *Water Scarcity: Impacts on Western Agriculture*, Berkeley, CA: University of California Press.

SUGGESTED FURTHER READING

Boggess, W., R. Lacewell and D. Zilberman (1993), 'Economics of water use in agriculture', in G. Carlson, D. Zilberman and J. Miranowski (eds), *Agricultural and Environmental Resource Economics*, Boston, MA: Oxford University Press.

English, B.C., G. Smith and G.E. Oamek (1986), 'An overview and mathematical representation of the National Agricultural Resources Interregional Modeling System', staff paper, Center for Agricultural and Rural Development, Iowa State University, Ames.

Helmberger, Peter G. and Jean-Paul Chavas (1996), *The Economics of Agricultural Prices*, Upper Saddle River, NJ: Prentice Hall.

Young, R.A. (1978), 'Economic analysis and federal irrigation policy: a reappraisal', *Western Journal of Agricultural Economics*, **3**, 257–67.

6. Uncertainty and risk in supply and demand of water resources

6.0 INTRODUCTION

This chapter addresses the problems that risk and uncertainty create for producers who wish to supply water or consumers who demand water for various reasons. As indicated in previous chapters, it is quite difficult to characterize completely models of behavior relating to water resources without taking a look at risk and uncertainty. There is both a quantity and quality dimension that involve risks. Risk is especially inherent in the agricultural producer's world. Any business activity dependent on weather involves risk because forecasting the weather is inherently risky. Because agriculture's decisions affect water markets, this gets more attention below. Howitt (1998) states that static analysis is 'unable to address the central driving characteristics of water markets that are first, uncertainty about supplies and prices . . .' (p. 125).

To begin, an economist differentiates risk from true, total, or complete uncertainty. Risk can be characterized using a probability distribution and it has a long-standing role in financial economics and investment (for example, Markowitz, 1952). With total uncertainty one might not even know what the probabilities of random events are. This type of total uncertainty was discussed by Frank Knight in 1921, and it is also known as ambiguity (see Riddel and Shaw, 2003). Economics is a reasonable discipline for dealing with risk, but has little to offer in explaining how truly uncertain events affect decisions. Unfortunately, some believe that true uncertainty in our society may now be the norm (see Woodward and Bishop, 1997, for example.) To proceed, those students who are a little weak in basic statistics might wish to dust off their basic statistics text and do some revision before diving into this chapter.

Random Variables
When there is risk it is because a variable is random (or we are uncertain about its values) and this random variable has an effect on a producer's or consumer's decisions, which might be difficult to discern. In sum, water supplied in various places on the earth is ultimately dependent on weather

Uncertainty and risk in supply and demand of water resources 173

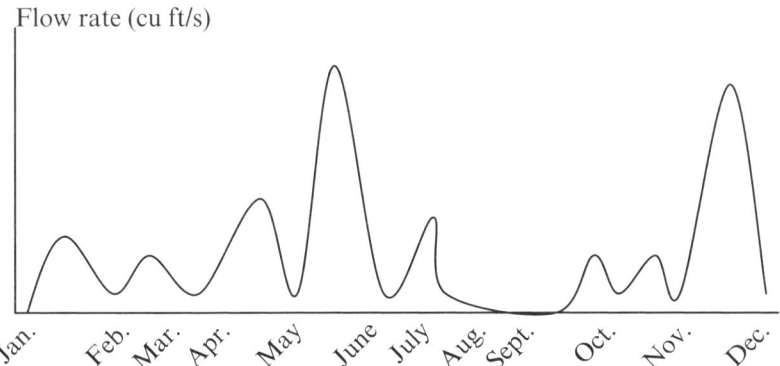

Figure 6.1   Random monthly flows

patterns, and often these are unique to a very small geographical area. Rain and snowfall are by their very nature random, as are extreme heat, drought, wind, and other descriptors of climate. The amount of water available at any given time is also dependent on evapotranspiration, evaporation, and soil and bedrock characteristics. This means that anyone or any thing dependent on water faces risk in being able to ascertain its availability, at least over some time period. A picture is worth a thousand words, so imagine you are relying on the flow from a river with a year's monthly flows (in cubic feet per second) plotted as in Figure 6.1.

Worse still, the figure above might fundamentally change from one year to the next. Risk is not just introduced via the randomness of weather and climate and their relationships to water supplies, it can relate to water supply or demand for other reasons.

Agricultural producers of crops face multiple sources of risk because of the nature of their decisions and the market. They also face risks in determining the future rate of return on water as an asset, and they face risk in investments in technology and pollution-reducing methods of production. Even households face some risks in determining the demand for water. For example, suppose a household must decide whether or not to let the delivery company deliver water with an installed meter, or stay on a fixed monthly rate (see Chapter 4). The company usually tries to encourage the household to install the meter, suggesting that there will be savings to the household, but this depends on the likely future rates charged for that water, which are probably uncertain. In addition, as will be seen below, households often face health risks associated with particular water quality levels.

Because it is virtually impossible to talk about risk and uncertainty without them, a few simple concepts from statistics are worth reviewing.

First, a random variable X takes on n distinct values. The probability that $X = X_i$ is denoted p_i, or often as π_i, though this Greek letter is used for profit elsewhere in the book. The specific values for the probabilities from the probability distribution or probability density function (pdf) that underlies X are usually assumed to be well known. We also know that if we have carefully laid out all the possible probabilities underlying values that X may take, they must sum to 1.

Generally, a pdf is given for a continuously distributed random variable (r.v.) and a probability distribution function is given for a discretely distributed r.v. The mean of a discrete r.v. can be defined using the definition for the expected value:

$$E(X) = p_1 X_1 + p_2 X_2 + \ldots + p_n X_n \tag{6.1}$$

When the r.v. is a continuous variable bounded only by negative and positive infinity, the probability of a distinct value for the r.v. is not meaningful and the definition of $E(X)$ incorporates the pdf:

$$E(X) = \int_{-\infty}^{+\infty} Xf(X)dX \tag{6.2}$$

The variance of X, $V(X)$ is given by

$$V(X) = E[X - E(X)]^2 \tag{6.3}$$

which in turn implies that $V(X) = E(X^2) - [E(X)]^2$.

Finally, the covariance of two random variables, Y and X, $Cov(Y, X)$ is given by:

$$Cov(Y, X) = E[(Y - E(y))(X - E(X))] \tag{6.4}$$

which in turn implies that $Cov(Y, X)$ is $= E(YX) - E(Y)E(X)$. There are times when we wish to have a unitless measure of variability so that we can compare different random variables to one another. A common measure of this type is the coefficient of variation, CX. It is defined by:

$$CX = \sigma_x / E(X) * 100 \tag{6.5}$$

where the numerator in the ratio on the right-hand side is the standard deviation of X, or the square root of the variance. The coefficient of variation indicates the deviation as a proportion of its expected value, scaled by 100 to yield a percentage. These formulas are likely to be quite useful in examinations of risk and uncertainty and in what follows below. In the next section we examine models of supply or production and demand that incorporate risks. As always, the focus is on applications to water resource issues.

6.1 DEMAND AND SUPPLY UNDER UNCERTAINTY

In this section we take up the two sides of a market again, but this time we allow for uncertainty in the decision-making process for those who demand and supply water. Sometimes economists just refer to 'price' uncertainty rather than demand or supply uncertainty, but in fact variability in price is obviously due to either shifting demand or supply, or both. For example, supply could start at S_o and shift up to S_1, then back down to S_2 in Figure 6.2, and all of this could happen quickly. Imagine what the situation might look like for a market if demand (D) is also shifting around fairly quickly. Rapid movements cause fluctuating prices, making any knowledge of a single, stable equilibrium market price nearly impossible. In the next sections I consider demand and supply uncertainty more specifically.

6.1.1 Consumer Demand

We can make demand stochastic simply by introducing a random variable. Following Helmberger and Chavas (1996), let the demand for an agricultural good be represented by the equation

$$P = 10 - Q \qquad (6.6)$$

where P is the price and $Q = H$, where H is the harvest of the good or crop. Suppose that we know that there are two discrete outcomes for H, making

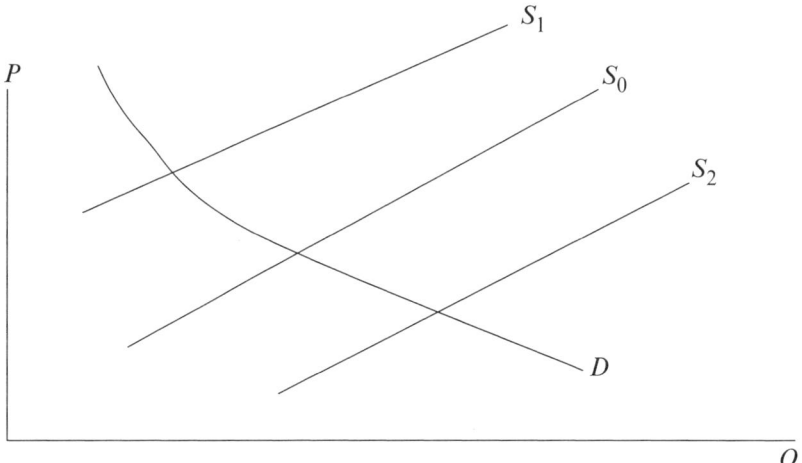

Figure 6.2   Price variability

it a random variable as well as Q. Imagine that we know that $H = 8$, so that $Q = 8$ with probability $= 0.50$, and $Q = 4$ with a probability also equal to 0.50. We can now determine the expected price and the variance of the price, or demand. From equation (6.6) we know[1] that $E(P) = 10 - E(Q) = 10 - \{0.5(8) + 0.5(4)\} = 4$. I leave it to the student to see if they can show that the variance of P is equal to 4.

We have simply shown that demand, given by the price equation in equation (6.6), can be made stochastic, and that the relevant concept is to examine expected price, not just price. The randomness in H may be due to weather, and therefore, in this specific case, we can say there is risk associated with the price. We characterized the risk using a very simple probability distribution. The harvest followed a discrete probability distribution with two outcomes, and two probabilities, much like a coin toss: two sides, two probabilities. However, we have done nothing so far to develop an underlying model of behavioral demand under conditions of risk.

The expected utility model

Recall that, in Chapter 5, we let a farmer's utility be a function of expected future profits and the variance on those profits. This is one simple way of letting risk enter a decision problem, but many economists are agreed that there is a better way of introducing risk and uncertainty into the analysis of a consumer's decision.

All of us are consumers of something. When perfect certainty is assumed, economists assume that consumers make their decisions by maximizing utility subject to constraints. Chapter 2 has several examples of this. The solution to a constrained utility maximization problem yields the optimal demands for goods. Now suppose that something makes utility uncertain. In other words, utility has a probability attached to it because we do not know something completely and this influences utility. For example, we invest in an asset that has a likely return, but we cannot know for certain what this return will be. In other words, we take a gamble. Traditional analysis follows development of game theory and modeling of gambles, developed by the mathematicians von Neumann and Morgenstern in the 1940s. Over the years many economists have contributed to the development of the conventional model of utility maximization under uncertainty: the expected utility model, or EUM.

The following is known as a state-dependent utility model. To keep things simple, suppose there are two possible states of the world dictated by a random variable, q. An example is some outcome that is dependent on a process such as a coin toss. Say that q is the quality of a groundwater aquifer. It can become contaminated (denoted by q^1) or not (q^0), and whether this happens is random. Utility is a function of income (y) and q, and the probability of no contamination is π, while the probability of contamination is $1-\pi$. Expected utility is defined as the sum of the probability-weighted utilities in two states, U_1 and U_0:

$$EU = \pi U_0(y, q^0) + [1-\pi] U_1(y, q^1) \qquad (6.7)$$

The probabilities are determined above by the nature of the random variable q. We can now maximize expected utility subject to the usual constraints on income or resources. We won't go through this here, but note that the result will yield optimal 'expected' demands rather than just the optimal demands under certainty, where the probabilities enter into the definitions of the demands.

Equation (6.7) can be modified to let risk or uncertainty influence any variable in the utility function. The traditional economics model is based on the finance literature and lets income be the source of randomness or risk, not q. It is important to note that if y is random, equation (6.7) is still quite different from letting certain utility be a function of expected income and the variance of income, the approach Helmberger and Chavas (1996) suggested (see Chapter 5) as a way of incorporating risk for farmers.

The expected utility equation above assigns a level of utility to the gambles. How much satisfaction does any one individual get from the gamble? The answer to this depends very much on what we assume about the individual's preferences for risk. Some of us detest any risky situation, while others simply love it. Others are neutral regarding risk. We can learn about an individual's preferences for risk (whether risk lover, risk averse, or neutral) in a variety of ways. Formally, economists make an assumption about the shape of the utility function with respect to the risky variable. Typically, assumptions are also assumed to hold across all risky situations, though this may not be true. For example, I would not gamble with money, but am quite willing to take risks in some of the sports I do, so my preferences for risk-taking would be quite different over the two sets of risks.

As an example of a money gamble, let y be random because a gamble is involved in determining income and consider the following game. Suppose a coin is tossed. If the coin comes up heads, you receive $1. If the coin comes up tails you receive nothing. To play the game requires that you pay $0.50. Would you like to play, or not? If the coin is a fair coin then we know that the probability of a head is 0.5, and a tail has the same probability of 0.5. From the introduction, we can then say that the expected payoff of this game is $0.50. Why? Because $E(y) = 0.5(\$1) + 0.5(0) = \$0.50$.

If economists analysed risk simply in terms of expected payoffs, then most would agree that a logical person would be indifferent to playing the game or not at the cost of $0.50 (on average, the player has $0.50 by playing and $0.50 by not playing). However, some who are reading this chapter might be unwilling to play this game. This is true because many are risk averse. In contrast, suppose the game is exactly as above but costs $0.55. Will some people play? The answer is yes, and the reason is because they obtain more utility than others from this gamble, that is, they are risk lovers and get excited at the chance that paying $0.55 might fetch them $1.00, or if 'excitement' is overstating it for these small stakes, imagine a situation where if they pay $550, they have a chance of immediately getting back $1000.

The classic exposition on risk taking measures risk of an asset estimated using the variance or standard deviation of the return. For example, suppose asset A has an expected return of 5 percent, while asset B has an expected return of 12 percent. If everything else were equal any logical person would choose to invest in asset B. But typically the asset such as B will have a higher variance or deviation on the expected return. Suppose that asset A's 5 percent is in fact going to hold, but with a lack of certainty: it could be that the actual rate of return will be plus or minus 1 percent. Asset B might have a 12 percent rate of return, but plus or minus 10 percent.

Again, risk-loving individuals still might dive into a portfolio heavily weighted with assets with characteristics such as B has, while risk-averse individuals choose a portfolio with assets that may even have a lower variance than A. One cannot say that the risk lover is a fool, only that she is a risk lover. In fact, we are all envious of the risk lover who receives a 22 percent actual rate of return! Next, let's operationalize these concepts and consider application to a water consumer.

Demand for water in the context of risk

As suppliers use demand models to predict future demand and adjust plans for long-term supply accordingly, they had better be aware of the random and uncertain components of demand. There are at least two simple examples of consumer's water quantity demand that seem germane under this topic, but if water quality issues are considered (as opposed to only considering water quantity issues) there are many, many more. Certainly one random component, the weather, can be incorporated into a model of demand, particularly as household demand largely consists of outdoor uses such as lawn watering that depend on precipitation and temperature. However, some modelers believe that simply incorporating variables that exhibit randomness as explanatory variables of demand does not go far enough in modeling.

Ng and Kuczera (1993), for example, discuss true uncertainty, that is, situations where we know there is randomness, but we do not even know the nature of the probability distributions for these variables. They cite distant future demand uncertainty, and uncertainty about future climatic conditions that make forecasting much more difficult. In the former case, they probably mean that tastes may be very different far into the future, but we cannot determine how at the present time. In the latter context involving climate, total uncertainty likely implies that we do not have the capability of parameterizing relationships between earth's future surface temperature and climate, and precipitation. To deal with either situation Ng and Kuczera propose using simulation methods to allow for many different possible scenarios, each with different possible probability distributions. At the heart of this type of analysis is the fact that a deterministic (non-random) model can be used to predict outcomes, and then the difference between actual observed outcomes and predicted ones portrays the remaining uncertainty, or residual. Naturally, observing outcomes suggests that models must be calibrated using past or existing data.

The simulation approach that Ng and Kuczera propose generates several possible future scenarios. For example, a future scenario involves a time series, or a series of data points that pertain over time and relate to possible future demands. Socioeconomic factors (income, unearned income, house or lot size) may determine present and future demands. Monte Carlo simulation techniques can be used to generate a time series of these socio-economic factors, as well as future stream flows, and ultimately demands. With many such scenarios being generated, they can be averaged, yielding measures of the predictive power of the models. Though there is uncertainty here, Ng and Kuczera really do not consider the details about uncertainty from the point of view of the water customer. Next, I consider a simple concrete example of another source of uncertainty, but from the viewpoint of the household.

Consider the household that is on a fixed water rate per month, but is asked by the water supplier to install a meter in the home. Suppose that the household will bear the cost of installation, at $1000. The household is told that it may save money on its monthly water bill, and that this will be especially or certainly true if fixed water rates go up in the future. Note that the household is supposed to think that the metered (rather than fixed) water rates won't rise in the scenario. The water supplier strongly suggests that fixed rates may increase, but won't say for certain, and won't say how much they will increase. This of course makes future fixed water rates something that should be characterized using a random variable. Resource price uncertainty is the topic of many economics papers, so this can be dealt with using standard economic approaches.

To let price be the variable that is random, again we must introduce a probability distribution for it. The household wants to know how to make the decision to install the meter or not. If prices or water rates in the future could be known with certainty, the calculations would be straightforward. The investment problem at the end of Chapter 5 is a simple way of comparing the tradeoffs. But, with the future price unknown we do best to let the household's problem be the one above: to maximize expected utility subject to its constraints on income or the household budget.

Assume that there are two outcomes regarding future prices for fixed rates. The first is where future rates exceed some level of increase, say that they double. The second case is where rates may rise, but they do not rise by as much as this. The household somehow knows that the probability that rates will double (denoted by p^1) is π, and the probability that they will not (denoted by p^0) is $1 - \pi$. Let utility be a function of income (y), and a vector of goods, x, and then the indirect utility function is a function of income and prices, p.

Let the optimal payment for the installation of the meter be WTP and if the meter is obtained let variable $m = 1$ (otherwise $m = 0$). We can analyse this problem again using the expression for expected utility in two states, where one state pertains to prices increasing (I) and the other does not (N), but we are also allowing for a difference in utility due to making the payment. The problem for the household is that it doesn't know which state will pertain, but has to make the payment in advance of the uncertainty being resolved. This is called an ex ante payment.

This is a classic situation and problem leading to development of an ex ante welfare measure. The ex ante payment is exactly that which equalizes the risky utility with and without the payment:

$$\pi U_I(y - WTP, p^1, m=1) + [1 - \pi]U_N(y - WTP, p^0, m=1)$$
$$= \pi U_I(y, p^1, 0) + [1 - \pi]U_N(y, p^0, 0) \qquad (6.8)$$

The zeros in the utility functions on the right-hand side denote $m = 0$, or that metering has not been adopted or installed. When a consumer is facing this problem it is possible to obtain a solution, given that certain assumptions and conditions are met. The optimal WTP that solves the equation above is known as the option price (OP), and this OP can be compared to the $1000 cost for the meter.[2] Graham (1981) provides the framework for the derivation of the OP, using a more general case of contingent payments that are not state-dependent. Assuming two states of nature, when the pair of WTP payments in the two states are equal, they are defined as the OP (see Graham, 1981). Obviously above, if the OP is greater than or equal to the $1000 asked of the customers in the household to cover the installation of the meter, they are better off having made the payment, otherwise it is not.

The formal economics conditions that allow such analysis using expected utility functions are known as the axioms of gambles, similar to the axioms of preference that ensure well-behaved utility functions under certainty (see Jehle and Reny, 2001, for a thorough discussion). When these conditions are met, the resulting expected utility functions are often called von Neumann/Morgenstern utility functions. Like most, throughout the rest of this chapter I assume the conditions are met and so one might actually be able to go out and estimate the OP in certain contexts. Next, I very briefly consider uncertainty when water is a factor demanded by a producer rather than when water is demanded by a household. The issues here are not much different from the general water supply decisions, considered in Section 6.2, so a lengthy discussion is postponed until then.

Factor demand under uncertainty

The example of interest here involves the agricultural producer who uses water, that is, the producer demands water as an input in the production of one or more crops. In previous chapters the producer is assumed to maximize profits under certainty. The solution to the problem leads to two or more factor demand equations, or formulas, that economists may use to determine the optimal demand for water. As suggested earlier, however, we can let the agricultural producer, just like a consumer, obtain utility from income. Unlike the simple certainty model, we will let the producer's utility be uncertain because of the random variable influencing the utility. Let this be profit.

Let profit be, as usual, $TR(Q) - TC(Q)$. Let $Q = f(l, k, w)$, again as usual, where l is land, k is capital, and w is water. But now we want to let water be a random variable. We know that any function of a random variable is itself a random variable. Therefore, when w is an r.v. so is Q, and thus, so is profit. Factor demand then actually relates to an overall supply decision involving uncertainty, so we develop this analysis below, and the derivation of factor demands under uncertainty are more carefully and rigorously considered.

6.1.2 Supply under Uncertainty

Uncertain quality and water companies: water treatment

A water supply company faces a good deal of uncertainty in both quantity and quality. As Roseta-Palma and Xepapadeas say in their recent paper: 'Taking into account that surface water flows are often stochastic, there is a role to be played by groundwater or surface reservoirs in protecting users against uncertainty' (2004, p. 21). Water suppliers simply must consider randomness in their decisions to provide for a stable long-run supply to their customers. Chapter 4 illustrated the difficulty of decisions facing the typical municipal water supplier today.

Innes and Cory (2001) also focus on uncertainty, but on water quality rather than quantity aspects. A water supplier that delivers water to households in developed countries cannot deliver raw, untreated water. They must deliver safe water, especially today under many pieces of legislation that regulate water quality standards. However, many water quality problems map onto health, but in a way involving risks rather than certain effects. As noted in Chapter 3, many pollutants cause health problems with a degree of risk, so a wise water supplier must invest in water pollution control and treatment technology to reduce risks, not so as to reduce contaminant levels to zero. Doing the latter would be cost prohibitive for many, many contaminants.

Consider the overall structural model for water supply provided by Innes and Cory. They begin by assuming there is a risk-neutral water company that delivers treated water to N people. They obtain untreated water with quality level X, and can treat it to bring it up to a level u, where $u \geq X$. The raw water quality is random with a probability density function, $g(X)$, indicating that there is inherent randomness in the dispersal of contaminants found there.

Customers may use water for drinking and other, less directly risky purposes (only watering one's lawn with contaminated water probably doesn't lead to health risks), but we assume they drink a fixed amount of the water, $\hat{w}$. The 'other' uses will be a responsive function of the water rate. Total water use is w, and the benefits of w are $B(w)$, which are assumed to decline at the margin, with more use. The households may buy bottled water if desired, with fixed quality $\bar{u}$.

If the consumer uses tap water for everything, she suffers an expected health cost or damage equal to $D_A(u)$, where the first derivative is negative (increasing quality decreases damage) and the second derivative is greater or equal to zero (non-increasing rate).

If the consumer instead buys bottled water to drink, the purchase cost will be C, and an expected health cost will then be $D_B(u)$, where the first derivative is less than or equal to zero (higher tap quality may reduce residual risk) and the second derivative is zero. Figure 6.2 depicts the relationship between health damage functions.

The marginal health benefits of increased tap water quality are higher when household members drink from the tap, but if tap and bottled water have the same high quality, then the expected health damages from either source are the same.

The water company has to decide how much to treat. They can invest in a treatment capacity of y, but they must do so ex ante, that is, before observing X in a given year, and before the outcomes for the random variable X have been realized. Therefore, treatment costs C are given by:

$$C = F(y) + v(u, X, y, W) \qquad (6.9)$$

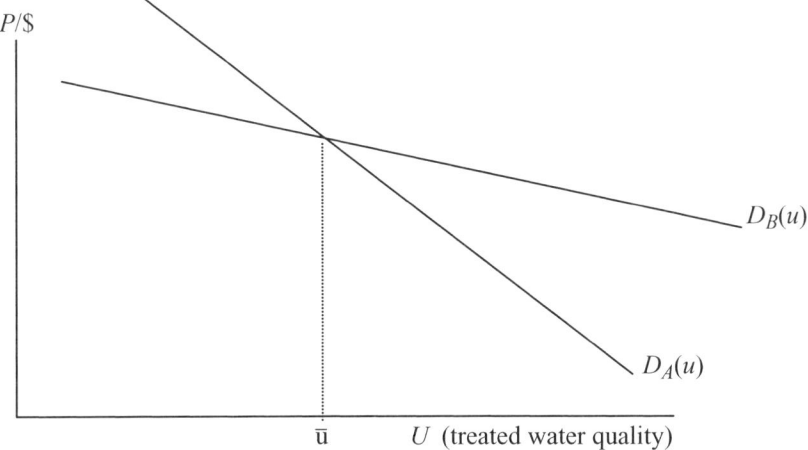

Figure 6.3 Expected damages from tap water (A) versus bottled water (B) consumption

where $W = wN$ is the total amount of water supplied. The first part on the RHS, $F(y)$, is the investment function and the second part, $v(\ )$, is the variable cost portion. Note that if X is random, then variable treatment costs are random. We can say, then, that any optimization problem couched in terms of cost minimization involves risk or uncertainty. Treatment costs have a distribution, and the water supplier must examine their expected costs from this distribution, as well as the costs in the tails of the distribution. A new and more sophisticated look at water supply under uncertainty is called robust control (see Roseta-Palma and Xepapadeas, 2004), but extensive discussion is a bit beyond the scope and level of this book.[3]

Uncertainty and agriculture/farming

Assume that the farmer trades off expected return $E(\pi_{t+1})$ with risk, where risk is measured by the standard deviation around this expected return, or σ. One way of illustrating possible risk preferences is to show three sets of possible indifference curves (aversion (a), risk loving (b), and risk neutral (c)) in Figure 6.4, where the two goods are the expected return or profit and risk (see Helmberger and Chavas, 1996).

Again the standard deviation indicates the spread around the expected return. As we move out along the horizontal axis the spread increases, increasing risk. Moving up along the vertical axis naturally increases the expected return. So, in diagram (a) the upward sloping indifference curves indicate that as the risk increases the farmer will need to obtain an

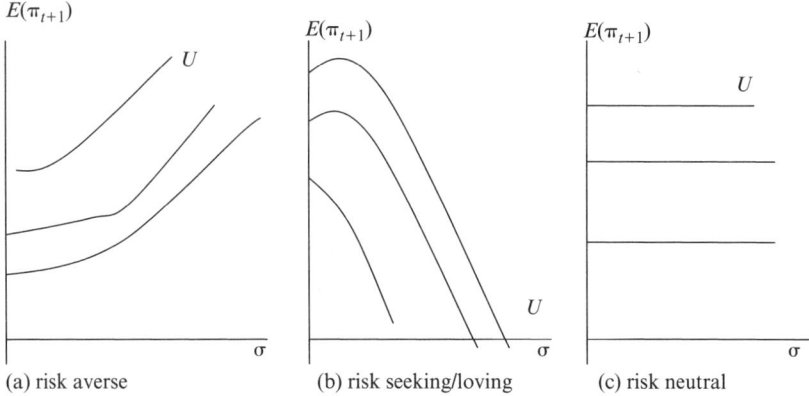

Figure 6.4 Preferences under risk

increasing expected return. Risk is a bad here, and one can glean that a farmer would be willing to pay a positive sum of money to reduce it. Formally, if utility is a function of the standard deviation, diagram (a) of Figure 6.3 indicates that the marginal utility of the spread is negative, or $\partial u/\partial \sigma < 0$.

In all cases above, if utility is a function of this spread and the expected return, then we can take the total differential of $u(\pi, \sigma)$ to obtain:

$$du = \partial u/\partial \pi d\pi + \partial u/\partial \sigma d\sigma \qquad (6.10)$$

The slope of the indifference function is of course $d\pi/d\sigma$, and thus, solving for du and setting this to be equal to zero, we obtain the slope's equivalence to:

$$\frac{d\pi}{d\sigma} = -\frac{\partial u/\partial \sigma}{\partial u/\partial \pi} \qquad (6.11)$$

The left-hand side of equation (6.10) is, of course, the marginal rate of substitution between expected return and risk (the standard deviation), and this makes sense, given that the result flows from examination of the total change in utility being held constant, that is, we are looking at what happens when moving along one indifference curve.

The negative sign on the right-hand side indicates that the numerator has to be negative for the slope to be positive, as we always assume that utility is increasing in profits. Similarly, we can derive the conditions for risk loving and show that there is a positively signed numerator, and for risk neutrality, the numerator is zero.

Note that risk neutrality is assumed whenever the partial derivative vanishes. This obviously will be the case in situations where the standard deviation is absent in the utility function: the farmer simply does not consider the standard deviation to influence utility one way or the other. This indicates that functional forms must be carefully considered when modeling risk.

Risk premiums
We can define the risk premium as the maximum amount of money the farmer is willing to pay to eliminate risk or the spread, driving σ to zero. Formally, this is:

$$u(\pi, \sigma) = u[\pi - WTP, 0] \qquad (6.12)$$

where here, the term on the right-hand side, $\pi - WTP$, is called the certainty equivalent. Naturally, this means that there is an amount of certain income that one would be willing to exchange for risky income. The intuition is simple here and reinforces concepts about risk preferences above. If a person is risk averse, we would of course expect that the certainty equivalent is less than the expected income. As the two sides of equation (6.12) are equal, the certainty equivalent income with no risk on the right-hand side provides the same utility to the farmer as he gets from the mix of profit with a positive spread on the left-hand side. Let's consider some specific utility functions and what they imply:

$$u_t = 4 + 8\pi - 2\sigma^2 \qquad (6.13a)$$

$$u_t = 4 + 8\pi - 2\sigma \qquad (6.13b)$$

$$u_t = 4 + 8\pi \qquad (6.13c)$$

Let $u_t = 52$, an arbitrary amount of utility chosen here for the purpose of providing a numerical example. Solving for profit on the left-hand side we can write the equation to describe the indifference curve. We are interested in the slope of the indifference curve in each of the three cases and what it says about risk taking. To find these slopes, substitute in the value 52 for u_t, and solve the equation for the return (π) on the left-hand side, then take the derivative with respect to the standard deviation. In the first equation we obtain a slope $d\pi/d\sigma = 1/2\sigma$, which is positive.[4] This result corresponds to those who are risk averse: as the graph in Figure 6.4(a) shows, an increase in the spread leads to an increase in expected return at one-half the level of the spread. As risk increases the necessary expected return must increase proportionally.

In the second functional form case the slope is a constant, in this case equal to 1/4. This implies that no matter what the risk, the expected return is just equal to some constant number. In the last case the expected profits obviously do not even depend on the level of the spread or risk in the equation in the first place, so there is no slope to analyse.

Choosing functional forms that allow for different risk preferences is thus important. How do we know what assumptions about risk preferences fit best? The answer is that we need to rely on a combination of intuition, observable characteristics of markets and economic activities, and empirical work. It is probably not wise to assume everyone in a sample of data is risk neutral, but it may be equally incorrect to assume all farmers are risk averse. After all, one may easily guess the opposite is true. An econometric or statistical model may allow estimation of key parameters to reveal whether, on average, a sample of individuals are risk neutral or risk-averse. One set of parameters may best describe a data set collected for a particular setting (location or type of person). For example, in his study Antle (1987) estimates risk attitudes for agricultural producers in a village in India, but such a characterization may not apply to all producers in India or in some other country, and vice versa. In another recent example of modeling the farm's decisions under risk, Randhir and Lee (1997) apply a regional risk programming model to evaluate the impacts of environmental policies on input use and examine how risk and non-point source pollution influence the results. Again, they use a von Neumann-Morgenstern utility function as their objective function (see Lambert, 1990; Lambert and McCarl, 1985, for other examples).

Similarly, Archer and Shogren (1994) consider the role that weeds play in reducing profits, while at the same time considering the application of herbicides to reduce weed infestation, which unfortunately may also increase non-point source pollution. In their simple model, the farmer selects fertilizer (X) and herbicide (H) to maximize expected profits (π), with two states each with probability denoted 'prob':

$$\text{Max } E\pi = prob\{PY_0(X)[1 - D(W)] - rX - cH\} + \\ (1 - prob)\{PY_0(X)[1 - D(W_0)] - rX - \rho cH\} \quad (6.14)$$

The two states denote a failure (the second term) or no failure of the herbicide treatment. The damage function $D(W)$ is in both states, but W_0 is the pre-treatment weed density. P is the crop price, r is the unit price of fertilizer, c is the price of herbicide, and Archer and Shogren let ρ be equal to one when there is a herbicide cost, and zero when the producer incurs no herbicide cost. The post-treatment density can be specified as $W = W_0 e^{-kH}$. The authors then let herbicide be integrated into the model as a type of self-insurance. The idea is that farmers do control the risk of damage from invasive weeds to a degree by using the herbicide, hence, the risk is endogenous to the farmer.

One could easily extend this type of model to the risk of droughts and the damage to crops that occurs, perhaps treating additional investments in stored water as the self-insurance that reduces the risk. I do not know of any economist who has done so yet, so a few further thoughts on the matter are in the appendix to this chapter. However, to really understand farmers and the types of people who regularly engage in business with high risks, we first need to understand futures markets, which are related to the concept of forward contracting. I realize this is an aside from water resource issues, but again the tie is between farmers who face fluctuations in the water supply available to them for growing crops, and a way for them to hedge against risks.

6.2 FUTURES MARKETS AND FORWARD CONTRACTING[5]

I will begin here by talking about futures markets in general, but below the reader will see that it is quite possible that futures in water contracts will evolve over time, at least in the United States. A *forward contract* is a basic type of derivative security, whose value depends on underlying variables. This is an agreement between two parties to transact a specified asset at a specific time in the future at a predetermined price. The specific time is the 'maturity' and the predetermined price is called the delivery price.

One party 'goes short' – assumes a short position, and agrees to *sell* the asset at the specified time at the specified price. The other party 'goes long' – assumes a long position, and agrees to *buy* it. The spot price is the cash price at maturity, C_T. Let the delivery price be K. The payoff to the holder of the long position is $C_T - K$, and the payoff to the holder of the short position is the reverse. Can you see why?

The 'long' agent gains if $C_T > K$ because on the maturity date if the delivery price is lower than the spot price he buys the contract from the seller at K and can immediately turn around and sell it himself that day at C_T. Alternatively, if the spot price is below K then the seller gains.

Such financial instruments are at work today for many agricultural and resource (oil, natural gas, gold) commodities that are traded at the Chicago Board of Trade. This type of contracting may also work in water transactions. Indeed it has been mentioned several times in this book that the absence of water markets causes problems and this is reiterated below in a discussion of risk sharing and efficiency. Today several states throughout the United States have attempted to introduce market features into water resource allocation, and some are even trying to develop futures markets for water contracts. A prominent example is found in the state of California.

In response to the California drought from 1987 to 1992, the state created a Governor's Drought Action Team, which in turn created a drought water bank. We take up the topic of water banks more completely in Chapter 9, but in spirit a water bank is like any other: it exists to make loans to people who wish to borrow water at certain times. Such a water bank came into existence in about 1995 in California, allowing for trading in options. As with the above futures markets for commodities, this market sought the potential for increases in efficiency by reallocating water using annual spot markets in times of scarcity, and also for the purchase of options and other long-term contracts.

An option is just a type of long-term future contract. A water buyer might agree to purchase a given quantity of water rights at future time T at price E. The proper way to assign a value to an option comes from work done by the financial economists Fisher Black and Myron Scholes (1973), along with Robert Merton (1973), and we'll come back to this below.

An option is a contract which gives the holder the right to buy or sell an asset at some predetermined price within a specified period of time. Here is an example. Suppose one owned 100 shares of IBM stock, and on March 22, 1993 these shares sold for $53.50 per share. The owner could give (or sell) to someone else the right to buy the 100 shares at any time during the next four months at a price of, say, $55 per share. The $55 is called the striking or exercise price. This option is called a 'call' option because the purchaser has a call on the 100 shares of stock. The seller is called the option writer.

One can also buy an option which gives the holder the right to sell a stock at a specified price within some future period, called a put option. Suppose you think that IBM's stock price is likely to decline from its current level of $53.50 sometime during the next four months. For $218.75 you could buy a four month option giving you the right to sell 100 shares (which you may not necessarily own) at a price of $50 per share. Here $50 is the exercise price, which is lower than the original price. If the stock actually falls to $45 per share and you pay your $218.75 then your put option is worth $500 = (\$50 - \$45) \times 100$ shares. After paying your contract price your profit is $500 - \$218.75 = \$281.25$.

Here, the financial deal is simply centered on the fact that one party is willing to bet that the price will fall to something at or below $50. On the day the contract is carried out a buyer agrees to buy the shares at $50, but the seller can purchase them for $45 each, and sell them to the contracted buyer for $5 each in profit, less the contract option price.

The way you might see this type of options shares opportunity listed in the newspaper is as follows for March 23, which is giving results for the day before (March 22).

		Calls – last quote			Puts – last quote		
NYSE Close	Strike price	April	May	July	April	May	July
IBM							
53½	50	4¼	4¾	5½	5/8	1⅜	2³/₁₆

The above information indicates that on March 22, an IBM April (one month) $50 call option sold for $4.25. For a given stock price, the higher the stock market's price relative to the strike price, the higher will be the call option price.

All three economists mentioned above (Black, Scholes, and Merton) shared the Nobel prize in economics for their work on pricing stock options. This chapter is not the place to review the complicated theory and solutions for determining options pricing, but the important point to note here is that allowing transfers within a futures market is hoped to reduce the problems of uncertainty by allowing demanders to hedge against uncertainty.

Prior to establishing the California operation, several others had supported the notion that futures markets might alleviate problems of droughts (for example, Michelson and Young, 1993), but to my knowledge no one had put these concepts into practice before 1994. Applying the Black and Scholes formula to water options, University of California-Davis economist Richard Howitt shows that the movement in the price of the option over time is continuous, following a Brownian motion. Specifically, the rate of change in the price of the option over time will follow:

$$\frac{\partial p}{\partial t} = rp - rS\frac{\partial f(\cdot)}{\partial S} - 0.5\sigma^2 S^2 \frac{\partial^2 f(\cdot)}{\partial S^2} \tag{6.15}$$

where r is the real interest rate, σ is the standard deviation of the Brownian process, S is the value of the water right and $f(\cdot)$ is the functional relationship for the option price of the water, which Howitt assumes is equal to $f(S, E, T, t)$, with E the price of the water right at future time T. The first derivative of $f(\ )$ is assumed positive and the second negative, so we can see that the rate of change in the option price for water will increase with a higher variance in the value of water, ceteris paribus, and lower for water stocks that have a higher initial price. Higher real rates of interest also generally increase the option price over time.

In 1991 the California Bank agreed to buy water from farmers at $125 per acre foot. They offered buyers an opportunity to purchase water for an initial cost of $175 per acre foot, telling potential customers that the 30 percent increase over their own cost was to cover the costs of carriage water (used for conveyance), a form of a transactions cost. Initially there was a spot market for water, but no functioning options market. By 1992, much of the water deposited in the bank in 1991 was left over, and so the sale price to purchases was lowered. By 1994 the price was down to $62 per acre foot. Other details about the water bank are found in Howitt (1994), and will be featured in Chapter 9.

While at the beginning of 1991 there was really no options market in California water, the 1994 California program, also tied to the water bank, allowed demanders to purchase an option for water at $3.50 per acre foot, plus a deposit of $10 per acre foot, in the event of a drought. The exercise prices for supply of options ranged from about $36 to $41.50 per acre foot.

In summarizing the results of the California water bank and options market program, Howitt concludes that (i) the water bank was a big success and (ii) when there is a structural shift in demand it may be best to allow for permanent sales and transfers of water, but when changes in demand are driven by events such as a drought, the demander really is just seeking increased reliability and, therefore, a spot market might be ideal in terms of efficiency. Put very simply, short-term reliability may be due to supply shifts that cause movements along the demand curve, and hence, changes in price, while long-term movement in a water market may in fact be due to a shift in the demand function, say because tastes for use of water have changed. In either case the role that transactions costs play is important, but reducing these transactions costs might be more critical for a spot market to function properly.

6.3 WATER'S ALLOCATIVE EFFICIENCY UNDER RISK

In this section water resource efficiency is examined again, allowing for risk. In one of the classic papers written about water resource economics, Burness and Quirk (1979) put several of the above risk and resource allocation concepts together and explored whether the doctrine of appropriation might in fact reach an efficient allocation of water resources. Even before introducing risk or randomness into any model, we already know that the doctrine of prior appropriation can lead to inefficient water allocation practices, such as when an individual diverts water in an effort simply to demonstrate use and avoid claims of abandonment.[6]

In their model Burness and Quirk show that by introducing risk, the very fact that senior and junior water rights holders in the appropriative scheme do not share equally in the burden of risk leads to inefficiency. Note from above that the formula for the cumulative density function $F(x)$ for a continuous random variable such as the flow of water (x) is:

$$F(x) = \int_0^x f(c)dc \qquad (6.16)$$

Let A_i be the aggregate amount of claims to water senior to claims of firm $i+1$. Equivalently, this is the total amount of diversion capacity owned or leased by firms 1 through i. Let $\hat{a}_i$ be the appropriative water rights for firm i, which in turn gives the diversion capacity of firm i. Label the N firms with firm 1 being the most senior, firm 2 the next most senior, and so on. Expected profits (π) for firm i using the CDF for x are:

$$E^i\pi = F(A_{i-1})\pi(0, \hat{a}) + \int_{A_{i-1}}^{A_i} \pi(x - A_{i-1}, \hat{a}_i) f(x)dx + [1 - F(A_i)]\pi(\hat{a}_i, \hat{a}_i)$$
$$(6.17)$$

Assume all firms are identical. Firm i receives zero units of water if the streamflow x is no more than enough to satisfy the claimants senior to firm i.

We can interpret equation (6.17) as follows. The first term on the right-hand side gives the probability that river flows do not exceed A_{i-1}, and the profits for the firm i are then $\pi(0, \hat{a}_i)$. The combined first term yields expected value if flows do not exceed senior claims at all. If flows do exceed such senior claims and can be handled by firm i's diversion capacity, then the second term applies. The last term on the right-hand side gives the probability that the river flow exceeds the capacity of all claimants 1 through i, and then the ith firm gets its entire appropriation. So, one can see from equation (6.17) that it is possible to incorporate water's randomness into a determination of profits, and hence efficiency.

Burness and Quirk (1979) use the expected profit function above to derive a number of interesting propositions, and the mathematics is skipped here. The most important of these propositions is:

> Assume that N firms exploit a waterway, with each firm having an identical separable profit function strictly concave in water usage. If the marginal cost of adding diversion capacity is increasing, then equal sharing is the efficient allocation of diversion capacity and water usage; allocation under the appropriative system is inefficient. (p. 31)

Proving this proposition leads to strong implications for the doctrine of appropriation: for long-run efficiency at equilibrium, equal sharing in risks is a necessary condition for Pareto optimality. The existing appropriative system simply does not accomplish this because when there are risks of unfulfilled water supplies, the greatest burden of risk falls on the junior parties.

Appropriation, uncertainty and in-stream flow protection
We know from Chapter 1 and the above discussion that the doctrine of prior appropriation does have a scheme for allocating water under shortages. It is simply that the least senior, or most junior, party gets their water right unfulfilled first, then the next most junior, and so on up the line to the most senior appropriator. Whoever arrived 'first' may get the entire water right allocated, while all others must do without. A problem left out of most originally formulated water law was how to adjudicate instream flows. As Chapter 8 will show, recognition of instream flows is evolving under current modifications to many states' water laws.

Assume that the key benefit of instream flow is in protecting some species that society cares about. What is the correct economic model of water resource allocation that would incorporate society's preference for protecting aquatic species using instream flows, especially when the species' ability to survive is uncertain? There is a possibility that instream flow can enhance survival of certain species, but the relationship is not a certainty. Ideally again, one wants to incorporate risk. Let the stock size or biomass of the species at time t be $Stock_t$. Suppose that the stock is a function of some initial stock size, S_0, the number taken by predators, SP_t, the level of flow, F_t, and the harvest rate in the previous period, HR_{t-1}. We can write in general terms that:

$$S_t = f(S_0, F_t, HR_{t-1}, SP_t) \qquad (6.18)$$

We might assume that $\partial S_t/\partial F_t > 0$, but to know the direction of any influence requires modeling biological relationships between all influences on the stock and instream flow. To my knowledge (see Chapter 8) this research is ongoing and is generally inconclusive.

Next, there are several possible economic models that one could develop, but suppose society is interested in finding the optimal stock size, which in turn has implications for the optimal level of flows in the river. To begin, what motives and preferences drive society's demand for, say, the species salmon?

There are in fact several possible motives for demanding a positive stock size of salmon, and also a positive harvest rate. People who eat the harvested salmon enjoy direct use, while suppliers of salmon may be commercial anglers who obtain monetary benefits from bringing the salmon to market for sale. Recreational anglers enjoy trying to catch, and also possibly to eat the salmon, and so their utility is a function of the catch rate (CR). Finally, some people in society may simply take satisfaction from knowing that wild salmon are healthy in our rivers, and their utility is a function of the stock size itself. This last motive has no connection with direct use. On the social benefits side of the equation then, we have three components so that benefits at time t are:

$$B_t = U(S_t, HR_t) + U(CR_t) \qquad (6.19)$$

Usually market demand is used to quantify the benefits for the consumer, so that for direct consumers of salmon this portion of benefits can be simply written as $HRD_t(P_t)$, where P is the price of fish and HRD is the harvest demanded. The benefits function could then include this term for those who consume fish in their diet, but it would still need to allow for those who don't consume fish but get utility from knowing they exist, and also for people who have both motives.

Suppliers of the salmon enjoy the benefit of harvested and sold salmon, expressed as the profit function (where PR = the usual total revenue less costs). Assume that revenue is given by a fixed competitive price per pound of salmon at time t, P_t, and that costs are a simple function of the angler's effort, E_t. Therefore, the profits at time t are:

$$PR_t = P_t HR_t - E_t \qquad (6.20)$$

In long-run planning, the objective is typically to maximize the present value of the stream of net benefits over time. Let the social discount rate (see Chapter 2) below be equal to r. Assume continuous rather than discrete discounting over time. This assumption leads to use of integrals rather than summing discrete units over the periods. The unconstrained problem, with no uncertainty, can be expressed as maximizing the following:

$$Max\ NB = \int_{t_o}^{T} \{[HRD_t(P_t) + U(S_t, HR_t) + U(S_t)] + P_t HR_t - E_t\}e^{-rt} \qquad (6.21)$$

This expression in 6.21 already looks a bit messy, but still ignores several important things. First, it ignores constraints, such as the above equation of motion, or the growth function, for the stock size. It also ignores constraints in each period, such as the fact that commercial anglers may not harvest more fish than the current stock size. In addition, it ignores uncertainty.

Where would uncertainty enter in this problem? It could do so at several points.

First, the relationship between the stock at any point in time and the variables that explain that stock, such as predators and flow, is likely to be uncertain. At any point in time flow is most definitely a random variable, as noted in the introduction to this chapter. In reality, the commercial angler also has to lease a boat or choose to maintain the upkeep on a vessel in advance of knowing the market price of fish at the time of harvest.

The above discussion conveniently allows a return to Howitt's discussion of water markets for California. Howitt derives situations where spot markets and the associated trades in that realm are the most efficient arrangements, while in other situations permanent transfers or sales may be efficient. In all of these situations his analysis depends on the assumption that both parties share equally in the risk of a drought, which is precisely what is recommended by Burness and Quirk!

6.4 MORE ON RISK AND WATER QUALITY ISSUES

Water quality research and its connections to health risks could easily fill several books by itself, but I will try to offer at least a better glimpse here than was offered in Chapter 3. The reason is that virtually every contaminant discussed in this book involves a health risk, not a certain outcome. There is no deterministic, exact relationship between MCLs and responses in animals, plants, and human beings. Instead, mortality and morbidity (toxic effects) are most often characterized with risk estimates, for example, expressed as a one in a million chance of dying of lung cancer.

Consider Carson and Mitchell's (forthcoming) study on trihalomethanes in drinking water (see Chapter 3). There the chance of dying from exposure to this contaminant was estimated to be about 420 deaths per million people exposed. If you know you are one of the 420 people who will die, you will certainly support policies to eliminate the risks. But the statistical indicator is supposed to convey the information that we never know it is our own death being contemplated, only that policies need to be considered that may reduce the chance of 420 anonymous people out of a million (0.00042) to say, 419 out of a million. What is the cost of a policy that achieves this risk reduction of one in 1 million? One estimate is that it would cost $200 000 (Council on Environmental Quality, 21st annual report (1990)). If it were your own life, you would probably gladly pay $200 000, but if you were asked to pay $200 000 (or a share of that) to save one anonymous person out of a million, would you do so?

Generally, policies that reduce the risk of mortality are formulated by examining the costs and benefits of saving a life. The costs are related to programs to reduce contaminant levels, presuming that we have a reasonable level of understanding regarding the exposure (dose) and response relationship for particular contaminants. In one empirical example I know of, Smith et al. (1982) found option prices for preventing a deterioration in water quality in the Monongahela River from 'boatable' to unusable. These ranged from about $27 to $95 per year, in 1982 dollars.

The benefits from reducing the risk of contaminants in water again typically relate to the option price (OP) formula examined earlier in the chapter. Social policy depends on assessing the benefit of saving a life, or in the jargon of this literature, on the value of a statistical life (VSL). Rosen (1988) derives an expression for the value of risk reduction for a person between two ages, age1 and age2. Let $S(age1)$ and $S(age2)$ be the probabilities of survival to ages age1 and age2, respectively. Below again let r be the discount rate, δ be the change in risk in the year corresponding to age1, and $V(age1)$ be the value of saving a life in that same year. Then, the value of a risk reduction at the first age, age1, valued at age2 is:

$$Wtp(age1, age2) = S(age1)/S(age2)\ e^{-r(age1-age2)}\delta V(age1) \quad (6.22)$$

This can be converted to an expenditure that alters the life table over multiple years. This yields:

$$V(age1) = \frac{wtp(age1)}{\sum_{age2} S(age1, age2)\delta(age2)(1+r)^{age2-age1}} \quad (6.23)$$

One can then use such formulas coupled with estimates for survival at various ages and arrive at an expenditure to alter one's expected lifespan, corresponding to a risk reduction (see, for example, Åkerman et al., 1991). The VSL literature is in turn vast and controversial because few want to say they know what a life is worth, but a recent central estimate of VSL is around $4 million. Despite the controversy, this sort of value is used nearly every day in formulating drinking water risk reduction policies in the United States.

6.5 RISK PERCEPTIONS AND COMMUNICATION

Thus far we have completely glossed over the actual measurement of risk and how individuals perceive it. When one puts the concepts above into practice the measurement of risks cannot be ignored. First, we have alluded to several measures of risk above, but will individuals in the public understand these? For example, suppose we try to communicate to the public that the risk of dying from cancer from prolonged exposure to arsenic in drinking water is one in 100 000. What does this really mean, that is, is this a 'big' or a 'small' risk? What does 'prolonged' mean? And, what do we make of it when the Mayor of Albuquerque, New Mexico boasts 'I've been drinking [the water] for 56 years and I feel just fine' (see Egan, 2001). In the same article that reported this quote, the Iselta Pueblo Indians, who live downstream of Albuquerque, say that they do not trust the current estimates of arsenic and worry that they are in fact higher than reported. Who is correct in their perception, if either?

Clearly, these perception issues suggest that risks need to be assessed, but then convincingly portrayed and communicated to the public. For purposes of developing a risk management strategy, it may not matter what experts think risk is, only what the public truly believes. A good example of this are the risks associated with transportation of the nation's high level radioactive wastes to one national site, Yucca Mountain, Nevada. At present, President Bush has authorized the Department of Energy (DOE) to go ahead with this plan, hoping for completion of the Yucca Mountain Nuclear Waste Repository by about 2010. Riddel and Shaw (2003) show that despite the DOE's 20 or more years of storage site investigation and the public's awareness of this program, many members of the public still perceive the risks of storage and transportation far differently than the DOE's experts do.

Using a device known as a 'risk ladder', where risks that occur in activities familiar to most people are visualized as a rung or high rung on a ladder, Riddel and Shaw (2003) asked individuals to locate the DOE's estimate of nuclear transportation and storage risk on the ladder. Following this positioning of DOE's risks, the authors asked the respondent to a survey to mark where he or she thought the risks would be. The average level of risk for transportation indicated by the respondents is orders of magnitude higher than the scientists working with and for DOE estimate. This indicates, at the very least, that a huge problem in risk communication looms ahead of DOE in their nuclear waste repository program.

Similarly, another project focused on arsenic in drinking water and the health risks associated with it (see Walker et al., forthcoming, and case study 6.1 below). Again the researchers found large discrepancies between objective measures of water quality and likely health risks, and those perceived by the public. In this case it appears that the public believes risks to be much lower than the scientists do.

CASE STUDY 6.1 ARSENIC IN CHURCHILL COUNTY, NEVADA PRIVATE WELLS

In 2002 several researchers investigated potential health risks from arsenic concentrations in private wells in this rural area of Nevada. The area received national attention because of several incidences of childhood leukemia, though there is no known link between arsenic and this particular disease. However, it is an example of a rural area with a potential serious problem ahead: how to meet the new standard set by the US EPA for arsenic in drinking water. The Bush administration, in a surprise to environmentalists, reversed its initial position and supported a lower standard of 10 parts per billion (ppb) proposed under the Clinton administration, down from the previous standard of 50 ppb. At stake are water treatment costs for thousands of small, rural water suppliers. To complicate matters further in Churchill County, a significant portion of its 23 000 residents (nearly half) are on private wells, which are not regulated by the US EPA in any case.

Walker and his colleagues measured the levels of concentration in the tap water from the private wells and found a high percentage of those in the sample not only violate the new standard of 10 ppb (76 percent), but even the older standard; in many cases private wells had arsenic levels of over 100 ppb and one well had a level of 2100 ppb. Despite these high concentrations many households appear to consume water from their wells for drinking and cooking food. A sample of household members (about 350 completed) were asked in a survey whether they treated their water and whether they drank water from their tap and many in fact did so, using no other water source. A simple model of whether a household treated water or not showed that the cost of treatment, relative to the household's income, played a negative role in the decision (the higher the cost of treatment relative to income, the less likely the household was to treat). So, economics does matter.

Do people understand the health risks they face? The authors concluded that often they did. But if so, why do households at risk continue to drink contaminated water? The reasons for this are complicated, but include the fact that many households do not actually know the arsenic concentration in their wells (only 8 percent did), and some do know, but choose to believe that the

> federal government warnings about health risks do not pertain to their own consumption habits. Of those who completed the survey, about 15 percent said their water would meet the new arsenic standard, but of these, 61 percent were wrong. The role of information in determining behavior is evident, heightening the need for better communication of health risks and water quality problems to the public.
>
> *Sources:* Walker et al. (forthcoming); Shaw et al. (2004).

This finding supports a general finding in empirical work: risk perceptions may be more important than the experts' assessment of risk in explaining individuals' behavior in response to risk management programs. Therefore, the traditional models such as the EUM described above need to be modified to allow for risk perceptions to be integrated into the empirical model. Unfortunately, this complicates the modeling a great deal, and efforts to do this convincingly are difficult.

6.6 SUMMARY/CONCLUSIONS

This chapter has shown that it is possible to deal with risks that can be categorized and quantified using probability distributions. Utility and profit functions can be modified to accommodate random variables and optimization problems can be developed accordingly. As with most topics in this book, the surface has barely been scratched here. One can spend a lifetime investigating risks and the various types of models that allow for behavior under uncertainty. The main points here are two: first, water is by its very nature going to involve randomness and active water markets may help to sort out allocation problems under uncertainty. Second, futures markets may increase the potential for water markets to allocate water efficiently, but thus far these are not widespread in practice. The California water market seems to have its highest potential benefit during times of drought.

The literature on modeling risk is certainly not confined to models with expected income or profits, or expected utility models. There is a vast and growing literature on alternatives to the expected utility model (EUM) that break away from the conventional model's restrictions. The responding models are because the EUM's assumptions are continually rejected by experimental and empirical evidence (see Starmer, 2000; Machina, 1987; Shaw et al., forthcoming).

PROBLEM

6.1 As an exercise, pick a pair of values for expected profit and the variance for each of the equations (6.13a) through (6.13b). Solve for the risk premium.

APPENDIX ON UNCERTAINTY

The material on risk premiums above uses the simple model where utility is a function of expected income and risk, measured by the standard deviation on that income. Instead we could let utility simply be a function of uncertain income x, or $u(x)$, where $x = \mu + \varepsilon$, with $E[\varepsilon] = 0$, so that $E[x] = \mu$. Hanemann (1999) uses this model to show that the risk premium can be defined as $\pi = \pi(\mu)$, equal to $\mu - x^*$. Here, x^* is the certainty equivalent.

Now we can examine expected utility $E[u(x)]$, and the risk premium in this context is then $E[u(x)] = u(\mu - \pi)$. In words, this says that the risk premium is defined such that expected utility on the left-hand side, which depends on the random variable x, is just equal to utility evaluated at the expected income less the amount corresponding to the risk premium. As we know that the risk premium itself is equal to $\mu - x^*$, then another way of seeing the equation is just that $E[u(x)] = u(x^*)$, that is, the person gets the same utility from the certainty equivalent here as they would get from expected utility when x is a random variable. As simple special cases, the risk premium can be nearly zero for a person whose preferences indicate a love of risk or gambling, but it needs to be quite large when a person has a strong aversion to gambling.

Pratt (1964) established a measure of risk preference called the coefficient of absolute risk aversion (it is equal to $-u''(x)/u'(x)$) and showed that there is constant risk aversion in two cases: when there is risk neutrality, and when the utility function is exponential, so that $u(x) = -\exp(-\lambda x)$, for some arbitrary $\lambda \geq 0$, where $r(x) = \lambda$. There is a whole literature on expected utility and alternatives to the basic expected utility model that needs to be digested before one embarks on models that incorporate risks.

NOTES

1. This relies on the fact that when $Y = a + bX$, and X is an r.v., then $E(Y) = a + bE(X)$, where we know that $E(a) = a$, that is, the expected value of a constant is itself a constant.
2. This option price is related to, but not the same as, the price of options in futures markets.
3. The modeling allows the water manager to be concerned about the 'robustness' of decisions to misspecifications of their supply model, including reservoir storage. Such

concerns can be reflected by a family of stochastic perturbations to the Brownian motion assumed in a dynamic model (see Roseta-Palma and Xepapadeas, 2004).
4. The equation is then $52 = 4 + 8\pi + 2\sigma^2$.
5. This material relies to an extent on Lee Ziegler, 'Tests of distributional assumptions and the informational content of agricultural futures options', MS thesis, Montana State University, May 1997.
6. I recall one of the post-doctoral students working at Nevada's Desert Research Institute around the year 2000 telling me that using satellite imagery, they discovered that some farmers on a Nevada River were dumping water on barren fields in the winter. We guessed the farmers were either trying to show use, or were trying to influence storage levels on a reservoir.

REFERENCES

Åkerman, J., F.R. Johnson and L. Bergman (1991), 'Paying for safety: voluntary reduction of residential radon risks', *Land Economics*, **67**(4) (November), 435–46.
Antle, John (1987), 'Econometric estimation of producer's risk attitudes', *American Journal of Agricultural Economics*, **69** (August), 509–22.
Archer, David W. and J.F. Shogren (1994), 'Nonpoint pollution, weeds and risk', *Journal of Agricultural Economics*, **45**(1), 38–51.
Black, Fisher and Myron Scholes (1973), 'The pricing of options and corporate liabilities', *Journal of Political Economy*, **81**(3), 637–59.
Burness, H. Stuart and James P. Quirk (1979), 'Appropriative water rights and the efficient allocation of resources', *American Economic Review*, **69**(1) (March), 25–37.
Carson, R.T. and R.C. Mitchell (forthcoming), 'Public Preferences toward environmental risks: the case of trihalomethanes' in A. Alberini, D. Bjornstad and J. Kahn (eds), *Handbook of Contingent Valuation*, Cheltenham, UK and Northampton, MA: Edward Elgar.
Egan, T. (2001), 'In New Mexico, debate over arsenic strikes home', *New York Times*, 14 April, A-1 and A-7.
Graham, Daniel (1981), 'Cost benefit analysis under uncertainty', *American Economic Review*, **71** (December), 715–25.
Hanemann, W.M. (1999), 'Neo-classical theory and contingent valuation', in Ian Bateman and K.G. Willis (eds), *Valuing Environmental Preferences*, Oxford: Oxford University Press.
Helmberger, Peter G. and Jean-Paul Chavas (1996), *The Economics of Agricultural Prices*, Upper Saddle River, NJ: Prentice Hall.
Howitt, R.E. (1994), 'Empirical analysis of water market institutions: the 1991 California water market', *Resource and Energy Economics*, **16**, 357–71.
Howitt, R.E. (1998), 'Spot prices, option prices, and water markets: an analysis of emerging markets in California', in K.W. Easter, M.W. Rosegrant and A. Dinar (eds), *Markets for Water: Potential and Performance*, Boston, MA: Kluwer Academic Publishers Chapter 8.
Innes, R. and D. Cory (2001), 'The economics of safe drinking water', *Land Economics*, **77**(1) (February), 94–117.
Jehle, G. and P. Reny (2001), *Advanced Microeconomic Theory*, Boston, MA: Addison Wesley Longman.
Knight, Frank H. (1921), *Risk, Uncertainty and Profit*, Boston, MA: Haughton Mifflin Press.

Lambert, D.K. (1990), 'Risk considerations in the reduction of nitrogen fertilizer in agricultural production', *Western Journal of Agricultural Economics*, **15**(2) (December), 234–44.

Lambert, D.K. and B.A. McCarl (1985), 'Risk modeling using direct solutions of nonlinear approximations of the utility function', *American Journal of Agricultural Economics*, **67**(4) (November), 846–52.

Machina, Mark J. (1987), 'Choice under uncertainty: problems solved and unsolved', *Journal of Economic Perspectives*, **1**(1) (Summer), 121–54.

Markowitz, H.M. (1952), 'Portfolio selection', *Journal of Finance*, **7**, 77–91.

Merton, Robert (1973), 'The theory of rational option pricing', *Bell Journal of Economics and Management Science*, **4**(1), 141–83.

Michelson, Ari and Robert Young (1993), 'Optioning agricultural water rights for urban water supplies during drought', *American Journal of Agricultural Economics*, **75**(4), 1010–20.

Ng, Wan Sin and George Kuczera (1993), 'Incorporating demand uncertainty in water supply headworks simulation', *Water Resources Research*, **29**(2) (February), 469–77.

Pratt, J.W. (1964), 'Risk aversion in the small and the large', *Econometrica*, **32**, 122–36.

Randhir, T.O. and J.G. Lee (1997), 'Economic and water quality impacts of reducing nitrogen and pesticide use in agriculture', *Agricultural and Resource Economics Review*, **26**(1) (April), 39–51.

Riddel, M. and W.D. Shaw (2003), 'Option wealth and bequest values: the value of protecting future generations from health risks of nuclear waste storage', *Land Economics*, **79**(4), 537–48.

Rosen, Sherwin (1988), 'The value of changes in life expectancy', *Journal of Risk and Uncertainty*, **1** (June), 285–304.

Roseta-Palma, Caterina and Anastosios Xepapadeas (2004), 'Robust control in water management', *Journal of Risk and Uncertainty*, **29**(1), 21–34.

Shaw, W.D., M. Riddel and P. Jakus (forthcoming), 'Valuing environmental changes in the presence of risk: an update and discussion of some empirical issues', in Henk Folmer and Tom Tietenberg (eds), *International Yearbook of Environmental and Resource Economics: A Survey of Current Issues 2005/2006*, Cheltenham, UK and Northampton, MA: Edward Elgar.

Shaw, W.D., M. Walker and M. Benson (2004), 'Treating and drinking water from private wells in the presence of health risks from arsenic contamination', draft manuscript (unpublished), Texas A&M University.

Smith, V.K., W. Desvouges and M. McGivney (1982), in 'A comparison of alternative approaches for estimating recreation and related benefits of water quality improvement', Chapter 5, draft report prepared for the US Environmental Protection Agency, Economic Analysis Division, Washington, DC.

Starmer, Chris (2000), 'Developments in non-expected utility theory: the hunt for a descriptive theory of choice under risk', *Journal of Economic Literature*, **38** (June), 332–82.

Von Neumann, J. and O. Morgenstern. (1944), *Theory of Games and Economic Behavior*. Princeton, NJ: Princeton University Press.

Walker, M., M. Benson and W.D. Shaw (in press, 2005), 'Significance of private wells in a rural area of Nevada as a route of exposure to aqueous arsenic', *Journal of Water and Health*.

Woodward, R. and R. Bishop (1997), 'How to decide when experts disagree: uncertainty-based choice rules in environmental policy', *Land Economics*, **73**, 492–507.

7. Groundwater[1]

7.0 INTRODUCTION

Groundwater is typically a poorly understood source of water as compared to easily seen lakes and river. It constitutes the vast majority of the world's available freshwater supply (about 98 percent), excluding that found in icecaps and glaciers. In 1985 about 40 percent of all irrigation water used in the US was from groundwater, and today over half (about 53 percent) of the United States uses groundwater for its sole drinking water source.

Data on groundwater use for other countries are often not available, but such high use is similar in countries where inferences can be made (see Chapter 10). For example, consider groundwater use in Indonesia. In his analysis of drinking and wastewater in Jakarta, Indonesia, University of Michigan economist Richard Porter (1996) estimates that over half of all households in Jakarta rely on groundwater found in shallow wells (at depths of 15 meters or less). Porter had to make educated guesses to arrive at any estimated groundwater use because little was known about this resource at the time of his study. Because of the population size and the fact that many households had at least some basic water availability, he calculated that there had to be a million or so of these shallow wells with output of several hundred million cubic meters per year. Guesswork such as this is important, because it highlights the need for better groundwater hydrology in many areas. Quantifying just how much groundwater there is and who uses it, is a remaining problem in many parts of the world.

The chapter begins with a very simple introduction to the physical aspects of groundwater. There are many ways to view groundwater economically, but as always these are subject to laws governing the extraction of this resource (see Tarlock, 1986). An economist thinks of groundwater as something that can be treated as a potentially valuable resource, like many others such as gold or silver. There are economic models for the optimal extraction of groundwater (how much of a resource to take out of the ground and when) and this chapter will look at the optimal management of a groundwater supply as a potentially scarce resource to be managed accordingly. Such extraction depends on a careful accounting of the physical characteristics of the aquifer, including how much water there is, at what depths and in what types of soils or rock. Following a presentation of the basic model there is a brief discussion of the economics of groundwater quality issues and contamination problems.

7.1 WHAT IS GROUNDWATER?

Groundwater lies beneath the ground, but it can form and be collected or concentrated in a variety of ways. Water beneath the surface is called an aquifer. It is often thought of as a distinct 'pool' of water, but it is not any such simple thing. An aquifer is simply water found in dirt, porous rock, or sand. It can be found in very small spaces and the properties of the soil or rock that characterize the aquifer determine a great deal about its extraction. Imagine that you have two jars of soil, one half full of very fine silt and the other containing rougher gravel and larger chunks of sand.[2] Now pour some water in the jars. Will the water travel to the bottom of the jar at the same rate in each? No, not generally.

Once the water has settled, imagine sinking a straw into each jar. First, note that it may be harder to find spaces in the dirt to insert the straw within the fine silt jar. Second, suppose you now wish to suck the water in the jar up into the straw. Again, will it be equally difficult to suck the water up into the straw in each jar? No, and if you try this yourself you will likely find that the fine silt jar requires a good deal more work to lift the water up than the sand jar.

Groundwater flows downward or downhill because of the law of gravity, as does surface water. In 1855 Henry Philibert Gaspard Darcy conducted experiments relating the velocity (V) of groundwater to the permeability of the medium (also known as *hydrologic conductivity*), which we denote K, and the hydraulic gradient (i). His results led to what is now known as Darcy's Law:

$$V = Ki \qquad (7.1)$$

The hydraulic gradient (i) may in turn be defined as *dh/dl*, where h is the change in head between two points at the top of a groundwater table, and l is the distance between those two points (see Cech, 2003). The units of the above formula can be specified as the number of feet of movement per day, or can be translated into feet per year.

While the above indicates that groundwater may move, it may or may not be intimately interconnected to a surface water supply, that is, a river or stream or lake. Precipitation from surface water can infiltrate below ground, limited essentially by being blocked by clay or shale, or absorbed by plant roots. The flow from surface water is called groundwater *recharge*.

Lateral movement in the aquifer relates to hydrologic conductivity. A layer of rock, sand, or soil near the surface may have some water in it, but is unsaturated and so the top surface layer is called the unsaturated, or *vadose*, zone. The layer where the rock, sand, or soil is full of water is the saturated zone. Here there is virtually no air in the spaces in the rock and soil, only water.

Hydrologists care about the rate of movement in groundwater for a variety of reasons, including those connected to groundwater contamination. As an example, hydrologists involved in the choice of Yucca Mountain, Nevada as the sole high level nuclear waste storage site in the United States modeled the flow of groundwater beneath the mountain. They did so to determine what would happen if one or more storage canisters leaked waste into the groundwater. Recent evidence shows that the initial models of flow were out by a factor of 10000 and that groundwater from beneath the mountain makes its way into Death Valley National Park much faster than they had initially calculated.[3]

Aquifers can be classified as either consolidated or unconsolidated (Cech, 2003). Consolidated rock includes sandstone, limestone, granite, and generally, rock that yields a small amount of water. Unconsolidated rock is likely granular sand or gravel, and yields larger amounts of water. Aquifers are also grouped by type, depending on geological features where they are found, and can be *confined* by a bed of material that lies over the aquifer, or *unconfined*. In unconfined aquifers there is no bed of material between the saturated zone and the land surface.

Some readers may have heard of artesian wells. When confined aquifers are under sufficient pressure, water can be forced into a well or other opening that allows water to rise about the water table. In extreme cases water can rise to the recharge zone, creating an artesian spring.

Many aquifers have no good mechanism allowing renewal or recharge, and in this situation they are an *exhaustible* stock, as would be a fixed stock of gold or copper. Other aquifers may get renewed through a connection to a river or stream or at least by precipitation above the ground that eventually percolates down into the aquifer, and in this case we might deem the aquifer a *renewable* resource. For example, the Ogallala aquifer is in part under Texas, but extends north all the way to South Dakota. It is in fact the largest groundwater aquifer in North America (Cech, 2003). In 1997 about 6.2 million acre feet of water were removed from the aquifer, while a recharge of only 438910 acre feet was estimated (the source of this information was the Texas Water Development Board, as cited in Yardley, 2001). This compares quite unfavorably to the Edwards aquifer, also in the same state of Texas, which in 1997 had 430000 af removed, but was recharged with 650000 acre feet. (I should add that because of rapid growth in west and central Texas, the Edwards aquifer is now not without its own problems.)

The examples show that recharge may take quite a long time. For example, Table 7.1 shows the time period in years for groundwater pumping to be balanced at least partly by surface water sources, based on predictions for three-dimensional groundwater models for New Mexico (Balleau, 1988). Table 7.1 omits the well-field drawdown, which is another factor that explains connections between surface and groundwater, but indicates the ability of groundwater modeling to predict flow-duration curves and integrate these into models of both surface and groundwater flow.

Flow-duration curves show the percentage of time that flows of given magnitudes are available from water sources, usually streams or rivers. Because surface water flows are potentially impacted by groundwater depletion, the relationship between these two must be considered. Note that in Table 7.1, when groundwater storage is very high as a percentage of withdrawal, this comes at the expense of surface water depletion (for example, 96.8 percent groundwater and 3.2 percent surface water depletion).

An aquifer can be pumped at a certain rate and, as with extraction of any other resource, pumping can exceed recharge rates, drawing it down. Like the straw in our little experiment above, the pump's ability to bring water up from deep in the ground depends on the characteristics of the soil. A borehole is dug and a pipe (often made of PVC) is used to encase the

Table 7.1 Sources of water (surface water depletion and groundwater storage) supporting groundwater withdrawals, predicted by 3-D groundwater models in New Mexico

Distance to surface water (miles)	Geologic units	Time period (years) groundwater	Percent of withdrawal, surface water storage	Percent of withdrawal, depletion
1 to 7	P Limestone	11	37.6	62.4
4 to 20	T volcanics	34	54.3	45.7
1 to 10	T sediments	50	88.8	11.2
15 to 20	J sediments	30	98.4	1.6
12	P sediments	50	96.8	3.2
40	J/C sediments	47	99.2	0.8
12	T sediments	100	49.6	50.4
1 to 8	T sediments	72	25.0	75.0

Note: P is Permian, T is Tertiary, J is Jurassic, C is Cretaceous.

Source: Adapted from Balleau (1988).

hole. In practice, a screen is placed at the bottom of the pipe in the well shaft (and sometimes on the sides also) to keep dirt from being pumped up along with the water. Energy is required to lift the groundwater up, and more energy is required for this task, the deeper the well. This will be quite important in practical economic analysis.

Once its level is lowered, an aquifer is subject to subsidence (collapse of the surface above it), and, if near the ocean, saltwater intrusion. In addition, a cone of depression can form around a well casing, changing the shape of the aquifer, which also can affect pumping. Also, as with surface water, groundwater can be contaminated by natural and manmade pollutants that seep into the aquifer. Treating the groundwater supply for certain pollutants can be costly or infeasible.

As the above notes, groundwater very often flows, like a river or stream, but typically at a much slower rate, perhaps moving only a few feet per year. Its movement is important in determining connections to other water sources and in tracking the effects of contamination. In many states in the United States, groundwater is by far the largest and most important potential source of supply of freshwater: about 86 percent of freshwater supplied in the US comes from groundwater. However, in some states, freshwater is only now becoming scarce relative to the population's demands and therefore knowledge of groundwater supplies and the dynamics of these supplies is quite limited. As relative scarcity increases, more resources will almost certainly be spent on investigating the local and regional groundwater supply.

7.2 ECONOMICS: MANAGING GROUNDWATER, OR GROUNDWATER 'MINING'

For purposes of economic modeling groundwater recharge rates are quite important. The cost of extracting groundwater relative to the benefits more or less determines the extraction rate for groundwater. It is safe to assume that it is more costly to extract groundwater than it is to use easily accessible surface water supplies and so in some geographical areas groundwater is present, but not used at all. As mentioned above, energy is required to lift the groundwater up and use it for whatever purpose it is to be put. The energy source used to run pumps varies (electricity costs also vary depending on the source of electric power) and the cost of energy fluctuates through time and space, and so estimates of the cost of pumping groundwater also vary greatly.

Economists who wish to explain groundwater withdrawals in an area where the hydrologic science has not revealed much about the nature of the aquifer are forced to make several assumptions or they cannot proceed with any modeling at all. To keep modeling simple, let the aquifer be a pool with a simple shape that allows for assumptions regarding pumping rates and property rights to be made and models to be constructed. The next section adapts a basic resource extraction problem to groundwater and draws on parts of Charles Howe's (1979) chapter (unfortunately out of print) on water resources.

7.2.1 Optimal Extraction Models

Groundwater, like any resource, can be managed so that we can examine the rate of extraction at virtually any point in time. Students uncomfortable with the concept of continuous time and the related mathematics might wish to start with a simple example (see the simple example in the appendix) before reading the continuous time derivation of the model.

When groundwater is substantially recharged in a relatively short amount of time one can treat it as a renewable resource, and consider 'extracting' this in an efficient manner. This is then like a resource that 'grows' (for example, trees), which makes it different from a resource that does not (oil or gold). Economists have several terms for resources that do not grow: depletable, exhaustible, or non-renewable, For resources that can grow or be renewed, the terms are undepletable, renewable, or inexhaustible. Note that some economists and other scholars consider 'mining' only that situation where the aquifer is pumped and has no sufficient recharge (an example is Gisser, 1983). Groundwater mining is defined less rigidly as simply the pumping of groundwater at a rate faster than the rate of recharge (for example, Holland and Moore, 2003).

In simple terms, optimal extraction pricing models follow the general principle in Chapter 2: price is equal to marginal cost. In resource management the MC is the marginal cost of extraction. However, instead of $P = MC$, the general rule is modified to also incorporates what is called the 'scarcity rent', which will become an additional term in the equation. The scarcity rent is the future-related opportunity cost associated with drawing down any resource and this concept can be applied to water (Moncur and Pollack, 1988). Turvey (1976) noted that in the case of water supply, the scarcity rent can be thought of as the savings that result from postponing capacity expansion. Assume there is a constant marginal cost of extraction for water (C_1), up until the point in time, T, where the water supplier must use desalination for its raw water supply, leading to a much higher marginal cost (C_2), again assumed constant. Then the combined costs look as they do in Figure 7.1.

It remains to be seen whether the supplier pays attention to the true nature of the cost function and will try to make a smooth transition up to b, or is forced to respond to a large jump in costs at time T.

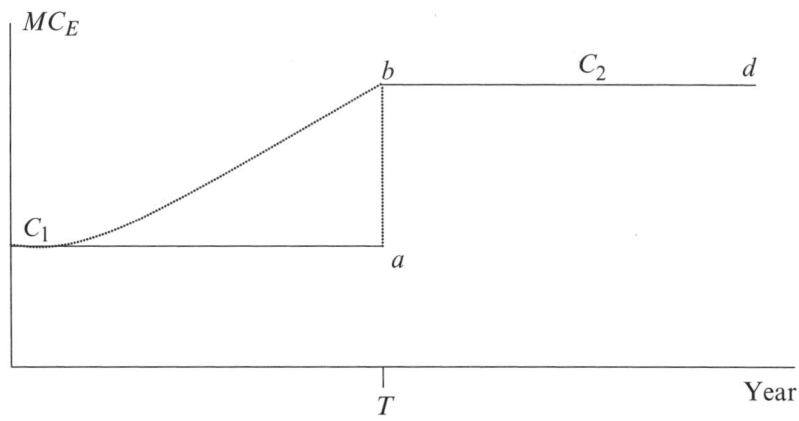

Figure 7.1 Extraction cost path

The proper economics rule of course can be made more complex, but in this simple form one can already see that a wise water resource manager would need to know what the scarcity rent is to set prices efficiently. Moncur and Pollack say that scarcity rent can be thought of as the decrease in the present value of future costs that would result from delaying the year (T in Figure 7.1) when the system must move to much higher costs. The key question for the economist is what the price path based on the costs above looks like.

With some assumptions, one can ascertain that the smooth price path starts at a point near C_1, follows the dotted curved upward sloping line up to point b, and then follows the horizontal line from b out to point d in perpetuity. In other words, an optimal transition in pricing is smooth, not jumpy. Intuitively, this is ideal because smooth operations and transitions in society are thought to be better than rapid shocks. In other words, if you have a chance to adapt gradually to what is coming that is better than suddenly waking up some morning and finding out the price of your water has tripled since the night before.

As Chapter 4 demonstrates, it is unlikely that most water agencies know this, and set rates using any such sophisticated rule, but the formal modeling results are nevertheless very informative. One may well predict that by not following the rule, a water agency is going to get itself in trouble by pricing water too low. For example, Moncur and Pollack (1988) show that it is indeed possible to measure the scarcity rent and determine the optimal price path using data related to the Honolulu (Hawaii) aquifer. Assuming that desalination is the backstop technology for water supply, the authors show that the scarcity rent was about $1.45 per 1000 gallons in about 1988, rising to $2.17 per 1000 gallons some 20 years into the future. They concluded that the water supplier in Honolulu was charging too little, and recommended that rates should be raised from $0.84 per 1000 gallons to about $2.29 per 1000 gallons.

Let's begin with the most simple formal problem in dynamic optimization. The word dynamic implies that there is movement over time that needs to be considered in optimizing the decision. We take a two-period discrete model with the key constraint being a growth function. There are two distinct periods, and in such models we do not worry about what is happening at infinitesimally small points in time during these periods. We can maximize benefits in the first and second periods, and here we let $t=0$, and 1. The problem is then to maximize net benefits, $B(S_t, R_t)$, where S_t and R_t are the stock size and pumping levels in each period, respectively, subject to a simple growth model:

$$Max B(S_o, R_o) + \frac{1}{(1+r)} B(S_1, R_1) + \frac{1}{(1+r)^2} Sal(S_2) \quad (7.2)$$

subject to:
$$S_1 - S_o = f(S_o, R_o)$$
$$S_2 - S_1 = f(S_1, R_1)$$

where here the variable Sal is known as the 'salvage' value, or the value of the resource after the end of the second period. The associated Lagrangian problem can be written as:

$$B(S_o, R_o) + \frac{1}{(1+r)} B(S_1, R_1) + \frac{1}{(1+r)^2} Sal(S_2)$$
$$+ \lambda_1 [F(S_o, R_o) - S_1 + S_o] + \lambda_2 [F(S_1, R_1) - S_2 + S_1] \quad (7.3)$$

Note that there are no explicit costs in (7.3) because net benefits, $B(S_o, R_o)$ are assumed to take costs into consideration: they are benefits net of costs. Taking the derivatives and setting them equal to zero, the first-order conditions yield the following equations:

$$\partial L/\partial S_o = \partial B/\partial S_o + \lambda_1 \partial F(\ )/\partial S_o + \lambda_1 = 0 \quad (7.4\text{i})$$

$$\partial L/\partial S_1 = [1/(1+r)]\partial B/\partial S_1 - \lambda_1 + \lambda_2 \partial F(\ )/\partial S_1 = 0 \quad (7.4\text{ii})$$

$$\partial L/\partial S_2 = [1/(1+r)^2]\partial Sal/\partial S_2 - \lambda_2 = 0 \quad (7.4\text{iii})$$

$$\partial L/\partial R_o = \partial B/\partial R_o + \lambda_1 \partial F(\ )/\partial R_o = 0 \quad (7.4\text{iv})$$

$$\partial L/\partial R_1 = [1/(1+r)]\partial B/\partial R_1 + \lambda_2 \partial F(\ )/\partial R_1 = 0 \quad (7.4\text{v})$$

I will not present the second-order conditions, but remember that they ensure a global maximum for the solution. Before diving into each equation's interpretation, simply recall what optimal conditions in static models often tell you: usually, they just say that the agent should optimize by setting marginal benefits to marginal costs. The above equations are just a generalization of this principle.

The first condition above (7.4.i) immediately shows how these simple dynamic problems are different from the usual simple static ones. The condition states that extraction should be done so that the marginal benefit of the stock in the first period, plus the contribution of that stock to growth, should be equal to the shadow value of the resource in the second period, here indicated by the period 1 subscript. This may be better seen by re-arranging (i) and doing so, we have:

$$\frac{\partial L}{\partial S_o} : \frac{\partial B/\partial S_o}{\lambda_1} = -\left[1 + \frac{\partial F()}{\partial S_o}\right] \qquad (7.4\text{i}')$$

This version of (7.4.i) should look a little more familiar. The left-hand-side term gives the net marginal benefit divided by the shadow price and the term on the right-hand side is the negative of a term involving the contribution of the stock to growth. This rearranged version of the equation recognizes that if a resource manager leaves a resource in the ground (in situ) in the first period, there may well be an additional benefit from that in the second period. Looked at in another way, there is an opportunity cost of withdrawing the stock in any period in terms of the forgone benefits that could be obtained later. The shadow price in dynamic resource extraction models is called the royalty, or is often called the 'marginal user cost' or MUC.

Again, the optimization rules recognize that, in any period, one doesn't ignore the future possible marginal benefit by letting the stock contribute or detract from growth. If the resource manager does ignore this contribution, then he or she is operating in a fashion that is not optimal, unless there truly is no contribution to a change in growth from the stock size. A general rule in resource management problems can generally be stated as follows: extract the resource so that the marginal benefit from doing so in period t is equal to the marginal benefit of leaving the resource in the ground for later.

Note that (7.4.iii) implies that a condition in period 3 holds. It tells us that the shadow value after the end of period 2 should be equal to the discounted value of the marginal contribution of the stock to the salvage value, again all evaluated after the end of period two. Because the world ends after period 2 there is really no period 3, but the conditions inform us of what would be optimal after the world has ended. This may sound silly, but a way of thinking about this is literally to imagine whether society will want resources left over after the end of the world. It is somewhat morbid to think this way, but assuming no one is left alive, why would society leave something for no one?

Equations (7.4.iv) and (7.4.v) provide the conditions on pumping (R), and again just state mathematically that pumping is conducted such that the marginal benefit from pumping in period 0, for example, is equal to the marginal benefit to later period users (period 1) from not pumping it in the earlier period. This benefit is expressed in terms of the marginal effect on the growth or recharge function.

Steady state solutions

It is possible in many resource contexts to define steady state solutions. The steady state is defined by a dynamic equilibrium that results in no further changes. For example, in the above problem we are interested in how pumping rates and the stock's size change over time. If we arrive at optimal steady state pumping rates and a stock size, then further change in them is zero. In other words, society is where it wants to be in terms of pumping rates and thus, without further unanticipated changes in conditions that affect decisions, there is no need to change behavior. This type of solution is but one of many possible dynamic solutions and will be re-examined below.

Application to groundwater

Now, let's make the whole thing more realistic and practical for the purpose of this chapter, couching the model in terms of groundwater. One of the first simple economic models of optimal extraction of groundwater that I know of is found in Brown and Deacon (1972). Their version is still more complicated than what is immediately below, so the more advanced reader is encouraged to see their seminal work on the topic. I raised the point about what the aquifer 'looks' like in models above; it may be helpful to see that many economists like Gardner Brown, Robert Deacon, or Micha Gisser model the aquifer as 'one cell' or like a bathtub. This one cell model is depicted in Figure 7.2 below.

In the above figure WT_o is the initial water table level, R is natural recharge, α is the return-flow coefficient, W is water pumped, S_L is the irrigation elevation, and natural discharge is W_n. Over time, depletion is determined by $W - \alpha W$. Assume here that W_n is zero. Then, the effect on the aquifer is simple to model, as the level at WT dynamically changes over time corresponding to the simple equation of motion: $dWT/dt = R + (\alpha - 1)W$.

Economics is formulated around this simple model for the aquifer's drawdown by introducing costs and monetary benefits (value of marginal product) from pumping. For example, if WT_o decreases in Figure 7.2 then one sees that the 'lift' increases at the left side of the diagram. If cost is

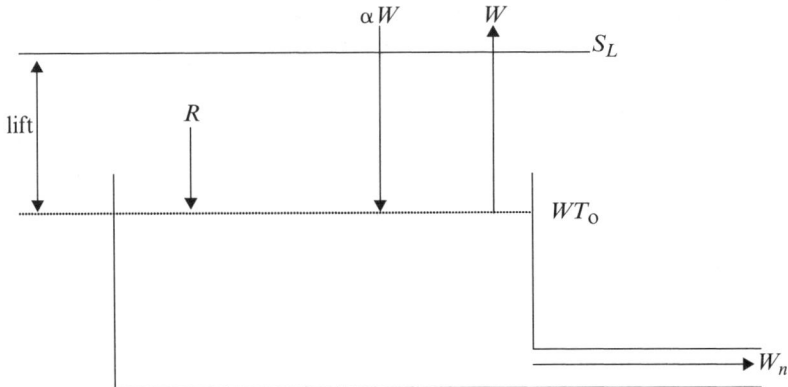

Source: Adapted from Gisser (1983).

Figure 7.2 A 'one cell' aquifer model

proportional to lift, then of course the marginal cost of pumping rises over time. Gisser (1983) incorporates this idea, letting marginal cost per acre foot of lift be c, so the marginal cost of pumping is $c(S_L - WT_t)$. The components and ideas of this model can be recast in the framework of a more formal, but still simple dynamic economic model.

Let there be two stocks of groundwater that are relevant, S_1 and S_2, in each of the periods in the model. The 'growth' equation is provided in equation (7.5). This is the recharge relationship. The stock in period 2 can still grow from the initial level in S_1 after some recharge $h(S)$, and fall with pumping levels in period 1, R_1. Again recharge depends on the stock, and per unit pumping cost is a function of the stock in that period, $w[S_t]$. It is assumed in most groundwater modeling that the lower the stock, the more the recharge, so in a perverse way if users pump the aquifer and draw it down, it speeds up its renewal.

$$H = h(S_1) \qquad [\partial H/\partial S_1 < 0] \qquad (7.5)$$

$$S_2 - S_1 = h(S_1) - R_1 \qquad (7.5b)$$

Next, let demand for pumped groundwater in period 1 be $P(R_1)$, and demand for pumped groundwater in period 2 be $P(R_2)$. We write these as simple inverse demand functions (Price = f(Quantity)) and that is consistent with how they are typically graphed. Per unit pumping costs are again w, assumed to be a function of the stock size (the volume/depth of the aquifer in that period). The problem is again to maximize net benefits over both periods. As before, we recognize that the net benefits in the second period should be discounted at a rate, r.

Formally, maximize net benefits in period 1, as defined by $P(R_1) - w(S_1)R_1$ plus the discounted net benefits in period 2, as defined by $P(R_2) - w(S_2)R_2/(1+r)$. Period 1's net benefits are not discounted, consistent with the assumption that $r=0$ in that period, or when we assume r is equal in all periods, that $t=0$.

The optimization problem described above still has to consider constraints, but to keep it simple we just consider one constraint: the growth equation, which says that the stock in period 1 is equal to the initial stock plus recharge less any pumping in that period. The optimization problem may now be written as the dynamic equivalent of a Lagrangian:

$$L: P(R_1) - w(S_1)R_1 + \{P(R_2) - w(S_2)R_2\}(1+r)^{-1} + (1+r)^{-1}\lambda[S_1 + h(S_1) + h(S_1) - R_1 - S_2] \quad (7.6)$$

where $(1+r)^{-1}$ is $1/(1+r)$. Note that the marginal value after period 2 is assumed to be equal to zero. The term λ is the shadow price, that is, the marginal value of S_2 in period 2. The shadow price is the value of having an additional unit of the stock in that period. This additional value is discounted to convert it to the same present value units as the net benefits in period 1. In resource optimization problems this shadow price is equivalent to the opportunity cost of extracting in a period, versus leaving the resource for the next period.

As noted, the discount factor in period 1 is equal to one $(1/(1+r)^0 = 1)$. Because recharge or 'growth' is higher the lower the stock, the assumption is that $\partial h(S_1)/\partial S_1 < 0$. This is the opposite from the usual assumption in models with biological growth, that growth in the stock is higher, the higher the initial stock. The optimization problem in (7.6) can be solved using the usual rules of differentiation (take the first-order partials and set them equal to zero) to get the first-order conditions with respect to choice variables. Again, the second-order conditions must be fulfilled, but we omit these here.

The framework assumes that the groundwater extractors are price-takers, but they can choose the level to pump in each period, thereby influencing the levels of the stocks. In other words, unlike a monopolist water supplier, the firm here cannot influence the price of water. The key choices then pertain to pumping rates in each period. The necessary first-order conditions yield:

$$\partial L/\partial R_1 = P_1 - w(S_1) - \lambda/(1+r) = 0 \quad (7.6\text{i})$$

$$\partial L/\partial R_2 = P_2 - w(S_2)/(1+r) = 0 \quad (7.6\text{ii})$$

$$\partial L/\partial S_1 = P_1 - w(S_1) + \lambda/(1+r)\{1 + \partial h(S_1)\,\partial/S_1\} = 0 \quad (7.6\text{iii})$$

$$\{\partial L/\partial S_2 = [P_2 - w(S_2)]/(1+r) - \lambda_{t+1}/(1+r) = 0\} \qquad (7.6\text{iv})$$
$$\partial L/\partial \lambda = (1+r)^{-1}[S_1 + h(S_1) - R_1 - S_2] = 0 \qquad (7.6\text{v})$$

The reader may want to move the last left-hand term in (7.6i) through (7.6v) to the right-hand side. The first condition says that, in this period, the discounted net benefit should be equal to the discounted shadow value of the resource. Remember that P_1 is just $\partial P(R_1)/\partial R_1$. So, in (7.6i) the first two terms are the net benefit because w yields pumping cost in the period. The second condition (7.6ii) is somewhat trivial, showing that the discounted net benefit at the end of the second period should be driven to zero. This is only true because we assumed the shadow value at the end of the second period to be zero; generally all first-order conditions will appear as the first one above, but here we have assumed there is no future that matters after period 2, that is, during period 2 the manager will operate as one would in static optimization (that is, without dynamic considerations).

Yet another way to write (7.6i) is to move both the marginal cost and royalty over to the right-hand side. The condition then says that the necessary condition for optimal extraction is when the marginal benefit equals both a current marginal cost, and a discounted marginal user cost (another name for the royalty). In introductory textbooks that cover resource economics, the condition is just written as $MB = MC + MUC$, where MUC is the marginal user cost.

Equation (7.6iii) is probably the trickiest of the group of conditions to interpret, especially for those with no background in resource economics. This necessary condition says that the net marginal benefit from stock size S_1 in the first period should be set equal to the negative of the discounted term of the MUC or royalty plus the marginal decrease in recharge that arises from leaving more stock in this first period. Hence, there is a benefit of having more stock left over from period 1, but also a penalty because recharge will be less than it would have been if the stock had been drawn down by pumping.

To continue, equation (7.6iv) is implied, but because of the assumptions we have made about any value in a 'third' period, we can ignore it; as in the simpler model in equations (7.4) and (7.3), this equation is really just stating that it is assumed to be efficient to end up with nothing at the end of the world.

The manner in which prices and quantities move over time is of most interest in interpreting the results from dynamic resource extraction problems and formulating the practical implications. In the above we can also look at how the royalty changes over time. Often, we examine such movements relating to a steady-state optimum: when at the steady state, the optimal values are unchanging. We won't go through all the mathematics here (the curious reader is directed to Conrad, 1999, again), but the fundamental equation in resource management is the result:

$$\frac{d\lambda_t}{\lambda_t} = r \qquad (7.7)$$

This equation states that the percentage rate of change in the royalty should be equal to the discount rate. This is a generalization of what is called Hotelling's rule. Hotelling ignored marginal costs and simply suggested that optimal extraction leads to the result that the percentage change in the price of a resource over time should rise at the social discount rate. Equation (7.7) recognizes that the royalty, not just the price, should rise in this fashion. It is perhaps the key result in natural resource economics.

In the above groundwater model the royalty, or marginal user cost, is equal to the net benefit, or $P - w(S_t)$ from pumping groundwater. To say more than this we need to consider more than just equations (7.6i) and (7.6ii), so that we can more carefully break down changes in the royalty. In fact by rearranging terms one can see that in general in such resource extraction models the following is true: the growth effect plus the marginal stock effect equals r.

Such models can inform the managers of the resource regarding the quantity path of optimal extraction over time. In other words, the solution to the problem tells a resource manager how much to extract over time, and when. If a steady state solution is possible, it is found by setting the rates of change in the stock and the royalty over time to zero: assuming a positive pumping rate, the resource manager examines results from setting $dS/dt = 0$, and $d\lambda_t/dt = 0$. For example, Roseta-Palma (2002) derives a steady state solution corresponding to M competitive small firms drawing from the same groundwater stock. The solution is to set their pumping rate equal to the recharge rate divided by the number of such firms or, in my notation, $R^* = H/M$, assuming the recharge rate H is a constant over time.

So, how will a quantity of groundwater be extracted as time goes on? The answer is best expressed graphically. With assumptions and an underlying model such as the above a figure such as Figure 7.3 emerges. The shape of the curve in Figure 7.3 depends on specific functional forms being assigned to problems like the one above. With these forms given we can trace out such paths (more on these below). Examples of papers in the literature that offer this can be found in the seminal work by Micha Gisser (1983) and in the paper by Kim et al. (1989). In fact the figure below is adapted from Kim et al.

Kim et al. show two paths of extraction over time involving two circumstances that determine equilibrium and this is depicted above. The top path results in a steeper path of descent. In other words, at the beginning of the time horizon the higher path indicated by $\hat{W}$ suggests that more acre feet of

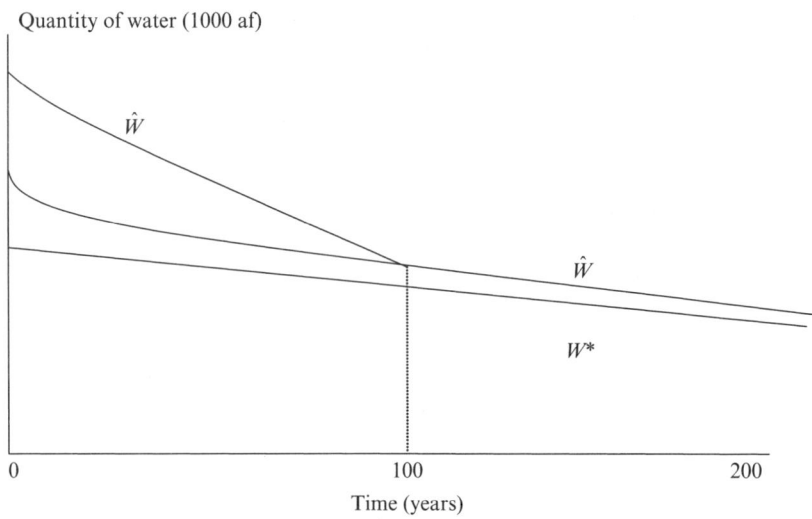

Source: Adapted from Kim et al. (1989).

Figure 7.3 Groundwater mining paths and water allocation patterns

water are being extracted in the initial periods than in the lower path. Current generations then optimally extract more water under the top path than they would if the optimal path were the bottom path, where current generations leave more groundwater unpumped.

The framework associated with equations (7.6) and leading to (7.7) could be expanded, enriched, or modified in many ways. For example, pumping costs could be more carefully developed to be a function of energy requirements for certain lifts (specifics were given in Chapter 5) and prices paid for units of energy used. In addition, the model may be modified to allow the resource manager to adapt to the groundwater resource being depleted over time (see Kim et al., 1989). Or, one might measure the decline in the aquifer using the exact known height of the water table, say as feet above or below sea level.

Clearly the framework above also informs us a great deal about how to manage a groundwater aquifer optimally. As noted in the first section of this chapter hydrologists need to know much about the aquifer: its shape, size, connection to surface water supplies, soil conditions, connections to oceans (if any). These are but a few important details required in the development of a useful economic model. Knowledge of all of the above details may not be enough. Another very important concern arises when groundwater is a common property, or a shared resource with other parties.

Groundwater as common property
Unfortunately, if lateral movement does occur, or if an aquifer has properties that cause impacts from one user's pumping on another user, any aquifer may exhibit features of a common property resource. A common property resource, as it sounds, is just a resource without single and well-defined property ownership rights. Unlike a partnership, a common property resource can be used by all parties who care to do so. An easy example is the ocean fishery.

It is well known that in a common property resource situation a temporal allocation problem occurs. The problem in groundwater is that if Party A's pumping rate negatively influences the stock of groundwater available for Party B, then each has an incentive to pump the water as fast as possible. Each party assumes that if they do not pump quickly, there will be less available to them in the future because A assumes B is going to pump as fast as he can. This leads to over-extraction as compared to optimal withdrawal rates. The problem is exacerbated by some groundwater laws. For example, the state of Texas has laws allowing the 'rule of capture'. Under it a landowner may pump groundwater without regard to his or her neighbor's use. Texas is now paying the price for having this law on the books, with rapid declines in many of its aquifers (Kim et al., 1989; Nieswiadomy, 1985).

This issue of common property and the problems that are generated when it exists are briefly considered by Boggess et al., 1993. The same issues are considered more extensively by Nieswiadomy and by Kim et al. (1989). Nieswiadomy analyzes common property issues as a potential explanation for depletion of the Ogallala aquifer: he appears to conclude that because of soil properties the competitive depletion characterizing the commons is not an issue.

Kim et al. (1989) actually estimate the demand equations that irrigators of cotton and grain sorghum in the southern portion of the Texas High Plains have for groundwater. They go on to investigate the effects of the common property problem in demand. An interesting feature of the dynamic model the authors develop is their hydrological equation, which provides a relationship between the way that the height of the water table (h) changes over time (dh/dt), and several key variables, such as the return flow coefficient of percolation (k) and the storativity coefficient (SC), which indicates the saturation of water in the aquifer deposit. Using their terms more or less, this is written:

$$\frac{dh}{dt} = \frac{R + (k-1)\sum_{i=1}^{n} W_i(t)}{A \cdot SC} \tag{7.8}$$

where R is the average aquifer recharge rate (acre feet per year), A is the size of the aquifer in acres, and W_i measures acre feet of groundwater pumping for crop i. This expression for the change in the height of the aquifer is almost identical to the one suggested by Gisser in his earlier (1983) study.

Using this framework coupled with a modified dynamic model they show two interesting things: first, their optimal dynamic groundwater model is like the above model in (7.6), but also allows for resource managers to adapt to depletion. In this model the optimal allocation of groundwater to irrigating sorghum leads to switching from sorghum to another crop almost 50 years sooner than under the common property equilibrium. In Figure 7.3 the two optimal extraction paths shown are actually as follows: the top path indicated by $\hat{W}$ is a path under a common property equilibrium, and the lower, dashed line the path under a planning equilibrium (W^*). Second, adherence to the optimal modeling rules the authors develop would add about $0.36 million in present value profits relative to the common property strategy.

If competitive depletion holds, as it would under a common property aquifer, then the optimal strategy for mining an aquifer described in Section 7.1 breaks down. A way of characterizing the failure is simply to note that each resource user of a common property aquifer will behave as if the future is worth zero. One can model this by setting the private discount rate that each water user exhibits equal to infinity (see Chapter 2), or, in practice, at least setting private rates very high. This wedge between high private and moderate social discount rates causes market failure because the social and private rates of discount are likely to be sufficiently far apart that the optimal rate of extraction under private resource managers is much higher than socially desired. This is precisely what has happened with certain fisheries around the world, including several species found in the North Atlantic Ocean. Social goals suggest managing the stocks so as to allow long-term harvest goals to be pursued, but the commons lead to the fastest harvest rates that technology allows.

Such a situation might prevail in mining a larger common groundwater aquifer, though likely not nearly to the extremes seen in the world's fisheries. There are several solutions offered in the event that over-extraction or overdepletion is caused by the common property resource situation. As with pollutants and environmental and resource policy in the United States, a typical solution to the groundwater over-pumping problem is to establish federal or state regulations. I do not know of any existing federal regulations, but several states now have regulations put in place to slow down over-pumping. For example, see mention of Arizona's water duties in Kim et al. (1989).

A potential market-based incentive solution rests in putting a tax on the amount that each groundwater user extracts. This increases a user's marginal costs of extraction and, if all else remains the same, should slow down the rate of extraction. Other solutions include introducing tradable permits: this type of solution has been examined in the ocean fishery context, but I know of no consideration in the groundwater context. Still others recommend quotas or limits being placed on the amount of annual withdrawal, but these regulatory actions are generally viewed as being inefficient as compared to the tax or tradable permit schemes.

Finally, note that Gisser shows that conventional solutions of establishing property rights in groundwater management schemes may only lead to a 'second-best' solution, but such property rights schemes are often overlooked and they may come close to levels corresponding to the optimal allocation solution. Gisser specifically recommends that potential new users of groundwater, who are left out in such laws as New Mexico's, be allowed to bargain with incumbent users, and that by doing so a second-best solution might be promoted to a Pareto-optimal solution.

Up to this point I have assumed little direct connection between ground and surface water, but the modern management strategy today likely considers joint management of these two sources of water, known as conjunctive use.

7.3 CONJUNCTIVE USE OF SURFACE AND GROUNDWATER

Surface water commonly percolates down to the aquifer, but it may also be possible for an aquifer to let some groundwater flow back to a stream or river. Pumping groundwater can obviously also deplete water from a river or stream that feeds it. In fact, a stream depletion factor can be calculated using the following formula.

$$sdf = \frac{a^2 S}{T} \tag{7.9}$$

where a is the distance from a well to a stream, S is the specific yield of an aquifer and T is a measure of the aquifer's transmissivity.

This relationship points out the possibility that water from the ground and the stream can be conjunctively used, and interesting economic issues arise. The interested reader is referred to the survey by Provencher (1995). Boggess et al. (1993) consider three possible connections between surface and groundwater:

(i) The stream and aquifer are directly linked: withdrawals from one affect the other.

220   Water resource economics and policy

(ii)   The aquifer is confined and has limited recharge, so surface water is imported to meet demands.
(iii) Surface water is limited and unreliable, but inexpensive. Groundwater is used conjunctively to increase supplies, especially at times of low precipitation and surface water supply conditions.

The first of these connections (i) is very complicated, meaning that hydrologists should develop models that explain the interactions and management strategies developed to accommodate the quantified relationships. In (ii) one needs to consider the timing and issues associated with importing water, and in (iii) one can develop an optimal groundwater pumping scheme to supplement random surface water supply. Following Boggess et al. we consider a model for the last proposed connection (iii), because it is fairly straightforward.

Typically the situation related to the proposed connection in (iii) entails an inexpensive cost of a surface water supply, say $v/af versus a more expensive cost of $c/af associated with pumping from a larger groundwater supply. Assume that within a single region pumping does not much affect the groundwater supply. Let annual surface water be R, a random variable with density function $g(R)$. Let annual water consumption be Y and the annual benefit from consuming the water $B(Y)$, or the consumer's surplus. Consumers can use groundwater (Z) and surface water X. The optimal choice of water can be determined using the constrained optimization problem:

$$L: \text{Max}_{x,z,\lambda} B(X+Z) - vX - cZ + \lambda[R-X] \qquad (7.10)$$

Assuming X, Z are greater than or equal to 0, the term in brackets on the right-hand side is the only other constraint here: X cannot exceed annual surface water (rain or snowfall). Because the constraints involve inequalities rather than strict equalities, the first-order conditions are the Kuhn-Tucker conditions:

$$L_Z = B_Z(X+Z) - c \leq 0; \qquad L_Z Z = [B_Z(X+Z) - c]Z = 0 \qquad (7.10a)$$
$$L_X = B_X(X+Z) - v - \lambda \leq 0; \qquad L_X X = [B_X(X+Z) - v - \lambda]X = 0 \qquad (7.10b)$$
$$L_\lambda = R - X \geq 0; \qquad L_\lambda Z = (R - X)\lambda]Z = 0 \qquad (7.10c)$$

What each pair of equations implies (by a pair, I mean the one to the left and the one to the right of the semi-colon sign) is that if the constraint on the left-hand side is not binding as an equality, then either the term in brackets on the right-hand side or the chosen variable must be zero. This allows for the possibility, for example, that the optimal choice may not lead to so much groundwater (Z) being demanded that the marginal benefit is exactly equal to the marginal cost of groundwater. The left-hand side of equation (7.10a) could hold with <0, so that the marginal benefit is less than the marginal cost, or the marginal net benefits (benefits less costs) are negative. However, if this is true, then the right-hand side part of equation (7.10a) says that Z will not be used at all: in other words, Z will be optimally chosen so that $Z=0$.

Given the way that the Kuhn-Tucker constraints combine there are three possible outcomes for solutions to this problem, depicted as in Figure 7.4.

Let Y_c be the water use level where the marginal benefit of all water used equals the marginal groundwater pumping cost, c. Similarly, let Y_v be the analog when marginal benefit equals the surface water cost, v. The three situations pertaining to the possible outcomes are:

1. In dry years with $R < Y_c$, all the surface water gets used, some groundwater will be pumped, and water use will be at that level where demand equals the pumping cost, as above (point (c, Y_c)). We have $Y = Y_c$, $X = R$ (the total surface water is exhausted by X), and $Z = Y_c - R$.
2. In medium surface water supply years R will fall between Y_c and Y_v, or $Y_c < R < Y_v$: all the surface water will be used but no groundwater will be pumped, and water's price will fall somewhere between c and v, as in u above.
3. In wet years we can easily imagine that not all of the surface water will be used, $R > Y$. Water use will be at the level where the marginal benefits of all water equal the surface water cost, and $Y = X$, $Z = 0$.

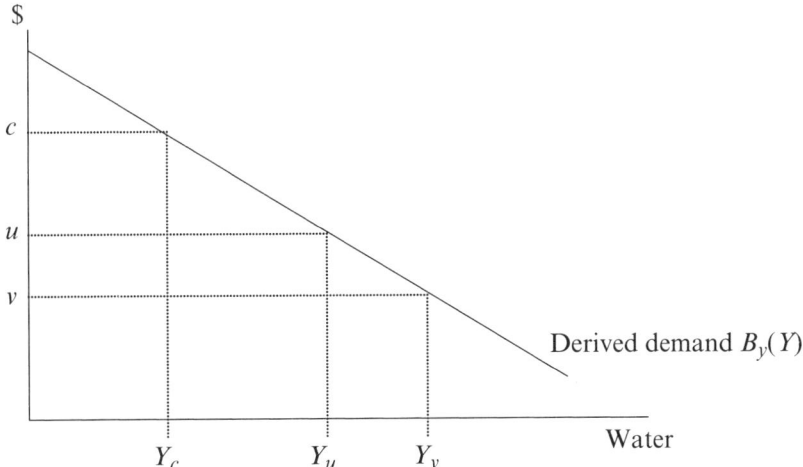

Figure 7.4   Solutions to conjunctive use management

This Kuhn-Tucker analysis is presented here because it is among the most simple of several possible models one could develop, but Boggess et al. show that despite its simplicity, there are some very useful practical observations that one can make. First, consider regions where the groundwater pumping cost (c) is small, as when aquifers are nearer the surface and pumping costs are likely to be lower because less energy is needed for lift. The results from (7.10) suggest that in this case groundwater will be more heavily relied upon than it might be in other regions (situation 1 results in $Z = Y_c - R$, and of course Y_c depends on what the marginal pumping cost is). The authors also note that as surface water is increasingly random or unreliable, conjunctive use is more likely to be used. The above problem can be made more realistic by allowing pumping to reduce the level of the aquifer rather substantially. The curious reader is referred to Boggess et al. (1993) for another, more thorough example of this type of problem.

A real world example

Though useful, all of the above modeling and discussion may leave some readers wondering how the elegant mathematics and diagrams can be used for any real-world analysis. The theoretical framework and results may leave one still begging for several questions to be answered:

(i)   What is the value of groundwater, in monetary terms?
(ii) When should a groundwater aquifer be exhausted, if ever?
(iii) How does the value of groundwater change over time?

One very recent example, from an assessment of an enormous project in the state of Arizona, sheds some light on the answers to these questions. The project combines elements of groundwater and surface water use, so fits under the heading of 'real world' conjunctive use.

After almost 30 years of legal wrangling, Arizona began construction of the Central Arizona Project (CAP) in 1973. Over 1 million acre feet of water is transported by aqueduct approximately 300 miles from the Colorado River, and pumps lift that water over 1000 feet in elevation in the course of its journey. Subsidies by the US federal government helped fund about $5 billion in construction costs, leading to completion of the project in 1987. Operating costs of course continue for the life of the project, and are estimated at about $275 per acre foot. In return for the subsidies, Arizona agreed to revamp its groundwater law, supposedly eliminating groundwater mining by the start of the year 2025. The law, passed in 1980 as the Arizona Groundwater Management Act, also created transferable property rights in groundwater. The CAP was envisioned to alleviate the problem of depletion of groundwater in Arizona. The connection between surface water use and groundwater use thus becomes clear: the supply imported from the Colorado River into the state of Arizona is used as a substitute for the groundwater supply.

In their analysis of this huge project Holland and Moore (2003) analyse the tradeoff between groundwater extraction and surface water use using a model that assesses the net benefits of groundwater extraction, with the surface-water supply as a constrained back-up source of water. This is much like the one in (7.10) above. The authors lay out their optimization problem in the usual dynamic framework, where a 'social planner' chooses water usage and the optimal time to build the CAP so as to maximize the present value of gross surplus minus costs. As is the norm, pumping costs are assumed to increase over time, with depletion of the aquifer. The costs of supplying the surface water to local areas in Arizona also enter the problem. The model extends the usual nonrenewable resource model by allowing a 'backstop' technology or resource, in this case the surface water supply from CAP, which has a setup cost and a flow constraint.

Given their assumptions, the authors find water usage (total water usage is $Q(t) = L + I + q(t)$, where L is local water usage, I is imported water, and $q(t)$ is groundwater pumped at time t and extraction paths. They find that groundwater pumping and surface water imports occur simultaneously to smooth consumption, up until groundwater mining ceases at a defined period in the future. A result from their theoretical modeling is that the efficient time to construct a project like the CAP is when the marginal benefit of water usage plus recharge exceeds the marginal importation costs by the per unit interest payment on the setup cost (the infrastructure and delivery costs) for the project. The reader interested in the theoretical framework should obtain the article by Holland and Moore (2003), but some details regarding how to obtain 'real-world' estimates from such a model are provided here.

A mathematical model like the ones presented above, and the one developed by Holland and Moore, can be parameterized and solved using numerical or programming methods to yield estimates that are useful for policy analysis. Holland and Moore begin by arbitrarily fixing a project construction date. Then a price path is defined by choosing an initial shadow value for the water and finding the equation of motion. Playing with the specific initial shadow value can be done so that the extraction path just exactly leads to pumping groundwater until the cumulative overdraft satisfies the terminal condition for the model.[4] In this way the social net benefits are computed, and then the authors can go back and reset the construction date until the highest social welfare can be obtained. The overall scheme for solving the problem is iterative (meaning one iterates many times until finding the solutions, perhaps as one would engage in a trial and error approach to finding a destination when one is a little bit lost, but close).

Unlike many analyses that remain quite abstract, Holland and Moore provide some description of the important parameter values, and explain to a degree how they obtain them. The authors first provide an equation for aggregate demand. They assume that demand by the agricultural sector is very simply $q = -9108.90p + 4565925$, where q is demand and p is price. Municipal and industrial demand is similarly simple in specification, but the parameters change between the start year of 1950 and the end year of 2100 (see Holland and Moore's table 1). The market value of imported water, assuming a well-functioning interstate market in this water, is about $37 per acre foot, and is assumed to be $0.00 in the absence of such a market. The long-run pumping cost for the Central Arizona aquifer is assumed to be $0.179 per acre foot of lift, and the aquifer is assumed to have a natural recharge rate of 126 000 acre feet per year. The key numbers used above come from existing data provided by the US Bureau of Reclamation in their analysis of repayment obligations, as well as from studies of water demand for the region by several other authors.

Using these numbers and several more (for operating costs, construction costs, annual deliveries, and so on), the authors can use their model to simulate equilibrium conditions under a variety of situations they wish to assess. Note that any results will likely be sensitive to the assumed parameter values and one is wise to assess the sensitivity of results to key values. However, if little existing data is available to characterize the features of the project, as well as the demand for water, one has little hope of doing any numerical analysis that will yield actual policy results. Because such data were available, Holland and Moore are able to arrive at a very interesting conclusion: the CAP was built far too early as compared to the optimal timing for the project – more than 80 years too early. More startling, the authors also conclude that building and finishing the CAP in 1987 was worse in terms of net social benefits than never building the CAP at all. The deadweight loss of about $2.6 billion (the net loss in benefits) stems from the following. Forcing the completion of the CAP by 1987 using federal subsidies resulted in the use of expensive surface water in lieu of what was still, during the period, cheaper groundwater.

Think about these conclusions like this. If you were the social planner in charge of the project, you would want to balance the value and true costs of the water. However, if you are getting a subsidy, the costs you face are lower than the true costs, and you can thus balance the artificially low cost with a lower value of water. The implied construction time thus comes much earlier than it would if you had to face the true costs of the project. In addition, the ban on groundwater mining has a perverse effect: it causes an incentive to mine the groundwater too quickly up to the point where the ban becomes effective.

Water resource economists are skeptics and may not be especially surprised by these negative results,[5] but the public would perhaps be stunned by the conclusions, if they knew of them. Unfortunately for society, the Holland and Moore study is of course an 'ex post' analysis; had we known in the 1970s what these economists have shown now, perhaps the CAP never would have been built, or at least completed. Holland and Moore note that in the late 1970s, then President Jimmy Carter put the CAP on his 'hit list' of federal water projects to be killed. However, political and legal maneuvering led to the green light for the project, subject to groundwater law reforms. Next I turn to groundwater quality issues.

7.4 GROUNDWATER CONTAMINATION AND QUALITY ISSUES

The literature on groundwater contamination has recently expanded, but still is heavily dominated by reports on the effects of agricultural chemicals in groundwater, specifically nitrates found in fertilizers commonly used by irrigators. The renewed and broader interest is due in part to clean up of areas that have subsurface contamination from toxic and other materials in several regions of the United States. The legislation passed in 1980, the Comprehensive Environmental Response, Compensation, and Liability Act, also known as CERCLA or the 'superfund' bill, has led to remediation of groundwater contamination under court-ordered clean up (see Agapoff et al., 2000). It isn't possible to cover all of the newest articles on groundwater contamination and clean up, but the reader is referred to reviews by Gorelick (1990) and Ahlfeld and Heidari (1994), and interesting new work integrating water quantity and quality issues by Roseta-Palma (2002).

A host of contaminants can get into aquifers in several ways. For example, wastes may be dumped or buried in soils and these may contaminate an aquifer, or similarly, an underground storage tank may leak. Wastes may be disposed of in surface waters which in turn recharge aquifers, contaminating them with the same wastes. A spill of some chemicals may result in an underground plume and this may or may not get into drinking-water wells used by humans. Even if the plume does not contaminate a well used for drinking, it may lead to ecological problems. Typical sources of contamination include waste disposal sites (landfills), direct injection of liquid wastes, mining wastes, radioactive wastes, and applications of fertilizers, pesticides, and herbicides to agricultural lands and crops. It is worth remembering that some contaminants are found in nature, so an aquifer may be contaminated without interference of humans.

Innes and Cory (2001) report some statistics on data from groundwater wells in Arizona, a state where 60 percent of drinking water is dependent on this source. On average, 68 percent of the wells sampled between 1990 and 1993 showed levels of nitrates, and about 22 percent showed levels of heavy metals of some concern. Nitrates pose minor health risks, but heavy metals can be toxic at high enough levels (see Chapter 3). The mean sulfate level across ten groundwater basins in Arizona exceeded the secondary MCL of 250 mg/liter.

The severity of the contamination in groundwater depends on several factors (see Reichard et al., 1990) including the fate and transport of the chemicals, what the chemicals are, and what organisms are exposed in the process. The receptor medium concerns whether the contaminant was released in the unsaturated or saturated zone of the aquifer. Some contaminants are extremely difficult, if not impossible, to rid the aquifer of; clean up may take 50 years or more. Other types of contaminants may be reduced or eliminated using a pump and treat process, or even using bioremediation technology.[6]

There are innovations under way to model the remediation more carefully, starting with how the wastes underground flow to a remediation trap or well. One way to model this is via advective control models that simulate flows using particle movement and dynamics (for example, Mulligan and Ahlfeld, 1999). As remediation of contamination in aquifers may be expensive, it is important again for economists to assess what the benefits of such exercises may be to society.

Valuing groundwater and groundwater protection
Most of the economics literature focuses on optimal extraction patterns relating to models such as the ones provided in Section 7.2: these generally offer only what theory has to say about extraction paths. Far fewer studies offer actual empirical estimates of groundwater's quantity value, and somewhat more offer estimates of the value for groundwater quality protection.

A quantity value study
A study of the market value for Ogallala aquifer water is by Torell et al. (1990). The aquifer underlies parts of Colorado, Kansas, Nebraska, New Mexico, Oklahoma, Texas, South Dakota, and Wyoming. In that study the authors use farmland values in irrigated versus dryland states to assess the value of the aquifer, which had been declining steadily from heavy pumping rates. The price differential between dryland and irrigated

farmland is used as a dependent variable in a regression on characteristics of the land that might explain this variation. The model indicates that a decrease of $0.14 per acre of land results with each additional foot of depth for the aquifer, reflecting the additional cost that a farmer would incur with increasing depths. The results can also be used to estimate the value of water in storage for various states, and the highest value per acre foot of water obtained is about $9.50 per acre foot, for New Mexico. While the authors cannot claim to have a definitive estimate of the value of groundwater, their values can be compared to other studies that produce estimates of the value of stored water, allowing some sense of the range to be obtained for such values.

Groundwater quality values

Groundwater can be lost to users, permanently or at least temporarily, because contamination makes it unusable, at least for some intended uses. Even if not deemed useless, poor quality can lead to a lower value for it. For example, some contaminants may not impose a human health or ecological risk, but they may introduce an unpleasant smell or taste that makes groundwater less attractive as a drinking water source (see Chapter 3). Also, as we saw in Chapter 6, estimates of risk may change over time, as knowledge is gained regarding the exact relationship between toxicity and doses during exposure.

Because there is no market for groundwater quality, we must rely on 'non-market' methods of economic valuation to assess the value of protection for this resource. It is a mistake to suggest that the market price or rate paid by the household who obtains delivered water from groundwater tells us the benefit of groundwater quality. If there is such a market rate, all that it likely tells us is the equilibrium water rate (determined by the intersection of supply and demand), which is possibly influenced by a regulatory agency. This rate almost certainly incorporates pumping costs, and it may reflect the cost of the supplier's water treatment, but it does not necessarily have much of a relationship to the value of groundwater quality. Still, if a well-functioning market for groundwater did exist, one could use some information to provide the value of groundwater quality improvements.

As an example, consider Figure 7.5, which simply shows a Marshallian, or typical demand function for a good with units T on the horizontal axis (acre feet, or cubic meters) and the price P on the vertical axis. The graph shows that demand for groundwater can shift upward with an improvement in environmental quality (q). The assumption is that purer groundwater may taste better or be more attractive as a drinking-water source than groundwater that is somehow tainted. (As always, because we can most

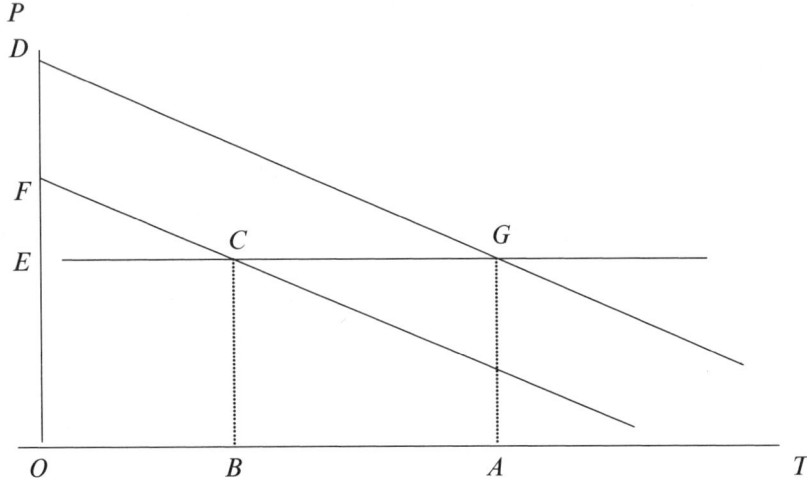

Figure 7.5 The Marshallian demand for groundwater

easily depict a graph in two dimensions, $D = D(P, Y, q)$, but Y and q can be illustrated as demand shifters.)

This graph is useful for analysis of either groundwater valuation, but there are other issues that must be considered if non-use values enter the realm of possibility. We return to the meaning of non-use values below.

Let the original number of units consumed (gallons of water or some other water quantity) be OB, and the increased or new units consumed after the quality change be BA. Marshallian consumer's surplus in the original state is the triangle defined by FEC. What is desired is the benefit measure given by the trapezoid $DFCG$, which is the difference in consumer's surplus in the two states (before and after the quality change). Geometrically or graphically, this area can be found by taking the difference between the areas within two triangles: DEG minus the triangle area FEC.

In the absence of an existing and well-functioning market in groundwater (for example when there are distortions in a public supply system or when households are on private wells), we must identify the CS some other way than the above. Recall that if a demand function can be identified, each point on this curve tells us the maximum willingness to pay (WTP) rather than do without the resource. When prices are effectively zero, the entire area under a non-market demand function tells us the consumer's surplus, or net benefit. In contrast, those on private wells pay a pumping cost and, in theory, one could trace out the individual's demand function for private well water using a variety of energy costs.

Passive use or 'non-use' values

There is nothing in economics that always forces the restriction of actual use for there to be a value for a resource. This is an assumption that may be made, known as weak complementarity. Let actual use of a groundwater be denoted Y, groundwater quality be q, x be a vector of all goods, and the utility function is $U = u(x, y, \text{income}, q)$. Weak complementarity is a property of the utility function such that:

$$\text{If } Y = 0, \; \partial U/\partial q = 0 \qquad (7.11)$$

In words (7.11) states the marginal utility of groundwater quality will be zero if the actual use of groundwater is zero. There is no effect of the change in q unless a person actually uses the groundwater. This assumption about the utility function is often useful in theory because it allows economists to clearly assess the theoretical properties of certain consumer's surplus or welfare measures, and it is a plausible assumption in many contexts. However, the assumption rules out passive use values and there may be no such restriction on the utility function. If, for example, a household has no current groundwater use, but hopes that groundwater quality is good for future generations, this household can have a positive marginal utility, and hence a value, for groundwater protection in the absence of current use. If not convinced, ask yourself this: can you think of a resource that you would pay some small amount to protect annually, but which you never plan to use? Values that are associated with future generations are often called bequest values, and values associated with resource protection for its own sake are deemed preservation or existence values (see, for example, Stevens et al., 1991).

Non-use or passive use values may be substantial, but in general, economists have few good ways of sorting out total values that include those values associated with current use and non-use from either distinct use or passive use values. The reasons are many, but at a practical level one always obtains passive use values from surveys, and it is often difficult to ask questions in such a way as to obtain only a use or a non-use, as opposed to a total, value. Because society does often have both types of value, many believe that the only thing that really matters is obtaining an accurate estimate of total value.

The majority of the economics valuation studies related to groundwater protection or quality at present obtain values for protection from nitrate contamination, a common pollutant that arises because of agricultural activities. If a household gets their water from a public supplier who in turn uses groundwater, we can observe the rate the household pays. If that rate changes because the supplier passes on the costs of added treatment for increased quality, then there is some market data that could be used to value improvements in groundwater quality. Similarly, private well owners may engage in behaviors in response to quality changes that could be used in valuation. However, in either case observed behavior or market rate changes may miss part or all of the total benefit from groundwater quality improvement.

In most studies I know of, non-market valuation techniques are applied to obtain groundwater quality values. Agapoff et al. (2000) reviewed the literature and found a huge range of values in their survey of the groundwater valuation literature, so it is difficult to identify any one value for groundwater or its protection. Table 7.2 indicates the variation in, and complexity of, reported values. The most frequently applied primary method in the collection of studies reviewed in the table is likely the contingent valuation method (CVM), which uses surveys to ask individuals their values under hypothetical conditions.

The CVM typically elicits a stated value for a program to protect a resource or improve groundwater quality. Values are typically for the household, and are stated as a monthly or annual maximum willingness to pay. Agapoff et al. (2000) report estimates of WTP that range from the low tens of dollars all the way up to the high hundreds of dollars annually. This range is not very helpful if one is trying to narrow down the value of groundwater protection.[7]

Of the non-CVM studies considered by Agapoff et al. many of the researchers attempt to use the cost of averting behavior as an estimate for the benefit of reducing contamination in groundwater. Averting behavior is an action taken to avoid a health risk. For example, a home with a private well that becomes contaminated may switch, if it can, to a public water supply system, or it may purchase bottled water, or it may simply boil all of the water it uses for drinking and cooking purposes. The idea in using the costs of averting behavior is that they may provide some information on the true underlying, but unobservable benefit for groundwater quality. However, averting costs and the related benefits are not identical.

For example, suppose a household finds out their well is contaminated with arsenic, and that members of the household are at risk of getting lung cancer. They decide to switch to bottled water for drinking and cooking, but continue to take showers using their well water. The observed cost of buying bottled water likely is not an accurate estimate of the household's WTP to reduce risks from the contaminated well water. The literature on averting behavior strongly suggests that averting or mitigating costs are, at best, a lower bound estimate of the benefits associated with a risk reduction.

Skim the many estimates of value in Table 7.2. Several factors cause the value estimates to be different. Authors of different studies often use

Table 7.2 *Midpoint values for groundwater quality for various scenarios, ordered from lowest to highest WTP*

Authors/dates	Contaminant	Scenario difference	Midpoint value (2000 $, hh/yr) WTP
Randall and de Zoysa	Nitrates	Groundwater nitrate levels reduced from 0.5–3 mg/liter to 0.5 to 1 mg/liter with protection program	$4.26
Carson and Mitchell, forthcoming	Trihalomethanes	THM reduction from 0.11 ppm to 0.10 ppm, decrease from 0.61 to 0.57 deaths/100 000, change of 0.04 deaths/100 000, public treatment	$4.54
Randall and de Zoysa	Nitrates	Groundwater nitrate levels reduced from 0.5–3 mg/liter to 0.5 to 1 mg/liter plus surface water and wetland improvement	$7.37
Powell, 1991; Powell et al., 1994	Unspecified (TCE, diesel fuel)	No experience with contamination and already feel 'very safe', will remain 'very safe' with program	$14.34
Carson and Mitchell, forthcoming	Trihalomethanes	THM reduction from 0.55 ppm to 0.10 ppm, decrease from 3 to 0.57 deaths/100 000 (change of 2.43 deaths/100 000), public treatment	$18.71
Kohlhase, 1991	Varies according to site	Average housing market WTP for an additional mile away from EPA Superfund site if located 6 miles from site	$20.87
Carson and Mitchell, forthcoming	Trihalomethanes	THM reduction from 0.33 ppm to 0.10 ppm, decrease from 1.9 to 0.57 deaths/100 000, change of 1.33 deaths/100 000, public treatment	$32.53
Delavan, 1997	Nitrates	Increase in probability of uncontaminated well from 50% (real baseline) to 75% (hypothetical baseline after 10 yrs, payment for 10 yrs)	$51.34

Table 7.2 (continued)

Authors/dates	Contaminant	Scenario difference	Midpoint value (2000 $, hh/yr) WTP
Abraham et al., 2000	Unspecified	Averting costs adjusted for joint production (current expenditures on filters and bottled water minus an adjustment factor for joint production of aesthetic properties of the water)	$53.00
McClelland et al., 1992	Unspecified hypothetical leakage from landfill	Non-use values of complete clean up of plume 700 feet long, 390 feet wide, 25 feet deep affects 40% of water supply, would cause 1/100 000 more cancer deaths per year if used	$53.27
Schulz and Lindsay, 1990	Unspecified (benzene, toxic wastes)	(All water from groundwater sources) median value for protection program which will reduce risk (unspecified) of groundwater contamination, will not guarantee prevention of pollution	$57.75
Cho, 1996	Hardness, sulfates, copper and iron	Sulfate, baseline currently above recommended levels, will be under level with program	$58.23
Caudill, 1992	Unspecified (nitrates, pesticide)	Rural respondent modeled value for scientific information program about groundwater contamination	$58.81
Cho, 1996	Hardness, sulfates, copper and iron	Copper, baseline currently above recommended levels, will be under level with program	$58.91
McClelland et al., 1992	Unspecified hypothetical leakage from landfill	Containment of 700 feet by 390 feet by 25 feet plume affecting 40% of water supply and causing 1/100 000 more cancer deaths per year if used	$59.44

Reference	Contaminant	Description	Value
McClelland et al., 1992	Unspecified hypothetical leakage from landfill	Public treatment of water from contaminated aquifer with 700 feet by 390 feet by 25 feet plume affecting 40% of water supply and causing 1/100 000 more cancer deaths per year if used without treatment	$60.49
Poe and Bishop, 1999; Poe, 1998	Nitrates	Subjective probability of participant well contamination in 5 yrs = 25% without program, hypothetically 0% with program	$65.49
Carson and Mitchell, forthcoming	Trihalomethanes	THM reduction from 1.65 ppm to 0.10 ppm or a decrease from 9.5 to 0.57 deaths/100 000 (change of 8.93 deaths/100 000), public treatment	$67.75
Walker and Hoehn, 1990	Nitrates	Average hh income = 15 000 (1983 $ about $26 000 in 2000 $), community size = 2000, rainfall = 30 ins per year reduction of 10 mg/liter (baseline not specified)	$68.59
Cho, 1996	Hardness, sulfates, copper and iron	Iron, baseline currently above recommended levels, will be under level with program	$70.61
Cho, 1996	Hardness, sulfates, copper and iron	Hardness, baseline currently above recommended levels, will be under level with program	$71.68
Laughland et al., 1993, 1996	Giardia	Averting costs, operating costs only (zero time costs)	$92.00
Caudill, 1992	Unspecified (nitrates, pesticide)	Urban respondent modeled value for scientific information program	$92.78
Caudill, 1992	Unspecified (nitrates, pesticide)	Urban respondent modeled value for scientific information, prevention and well-protection program	$98.01
McClelland et al., 1992	Unspecified hypothetical leakage from landfill	Complete clean up of plume 700 feet long, 390 feet wide, 25 feet deep affects 40% of water supply, would cause 1/100 000 more cancer deaths per year if used	$105.34
Poe and Bishop, 1999; Poe, 1998	Nitrates	Current nitrate exposure = 2 mg/liter, with program will stay below 10 mg/liter	$105.43

Table 7.2 (continued)

Authors/dates	Contaminant	Scenario difference	Midpoint value (2000 $, hh/yr) WTP
Michaels and Smith, 1990	Not specified	Average housing market WTP for removal of closest waste site (0.8 miles more to next nearest site)	$107.10
Walker, and Hoehn, 1990	Nitrates	Average hh income = 15 000 (1983 $ about $26 000 in 2000 $), community size = 500, rainfall = 30 ins per year, 10 mg/liter reduction, baseline level not specified	$111.47
Walker and Hoehn, 1990	Nitrates	Average hh income = 30 000 (1983 $ about $51 400 in 2000 $), community size = 500, rainfall = 30 ins per year, 10 mg/liter reduction, baseline level not specified	$144.05
Powell, 1991; Powell et al., 1994.	Unspecified (TCE, diesel fuel)	Experienced contamination incident and change from 'unsafe' to 'very safe' (subjective) with program	$149.01
Jordan and Elnagheeb, 1993	Nitrates	City users' value for treating water and making sure water safe to drink; water currently mostly safe with nitrates increasing	$151.54
Smith and Desvousges, 1987	Unspecified hazardous waste	Reduction in risk of dying in 30 years from exposure to HW from 0.01 to 0.004 (1000/100 000 to 400/100 000)	$157.81
Kiel, 1995	TCE	One mile increase in distance from hazardous waste site post-EPA announcement	$165.30
Schulz and Lindsay, 1990	Unspecified (benzene, toxic wastes)	(All water from groundwater sources) mean value for protection program which will reduce risk (unspecified) of groundwater contamination, will not guarantee prevention of pollution	$186.25
Jordan and Elnagheeb, 1993	Nitrates	Well users' value for installing and maintaining nitrate removal system if water currently exceeded safe levels	$186.30

Study	Contaminant	Description	Value
Smith and Desvousges, 1987	Unspecified hazardous waste	Reduction in risk of dying in 30 years from exposure to HW from 1/120 000 to 1/300 000 (closer to actual risk reduction) or 0.83/100 000 to 0.33/100 000	$199.44
McClelland et al., 1992	Unspecified hypothetical leakage from landfill	Complete clean up of plume 700 feet long, 390 feet wide, 25 feet deep effects 70% of water supply, would cause 1/100 000 more cancer deaths per year if used	$200.75
Laughland et al., 1993, 1996	Giardia	Averting costs and minimum wage assumed for time costs	$216.00
Abdalla, 1990	PCE	Averting costs of average household (including non-averters) assuming minimum wage for time costs	$258.61
Abdalla, 1990	PCE	Average household (including non-averters) assuming average wage for time costs	$300.70
Kiel, 1995	TCE	One mile increase in distance from hazardous waste site post community awareness pre EPA announcement	$306.00
Edwards, 1988	Nitrates	Average income and decrease in probability of contamination of 0.25	$311.31
Poe and Bishop, 1999; Poe, 1998	Nitrates	Ex-post complete information	$315.39
Poe and Bishop, 1999; Poe, 1998	Nitrates	Ex-ante no information	$337.71
Michaels and Smith, 1990	Not specified	Full sample WTP for removal of closest waste site (1.08 miles or more to next nearest site)	$349.49
Poe and Bishop, 1999; Poe, 1998	Nitrates	Current nitrate exposure = 20 mg/liter; with program will be less than 10 mg/liter	$466.78
Harrington et al., 1989, 1991	Giardia	Actual cost of substituted water (lower bound), time costs assumed zero for non-employed individuals	$482.00
Poe and Bishop, 1999; Poe, 1998	Nitrates	Ex-ante with information	$503.12

Table 7.2 (continued)

Authors/dates	Contaminant	Scenario difference	Midpoint value (2000 $, hh/yr) WTP
Poe and Bishop, 1999; Poe, 1998	Nitrates	25% reduction in nitrate levels given initial level of ~15 mg/liter	$516.66
Kohlhase, 1991	Varies according to site	Average housing market WTP for an additional mile away from EPA Superfund site if located 3 miles from site	$543.86
Kiel, 1995	TCE	One mile increase in distance from hazardous waste site early cleaning stages after EPA announcement	$551.19
Laughland et al., 1993, 1996	Giardia	Averting costs with sample average wage for time costs	$554.00
Abdalla, 1990	PCE	Upper bound estimate (perfect substitute: cost of POE granular activated carbon treatment system)	$576.00
Poe and Bishop, 1999; Poe, 1998	Nitrates	Subjective probability participant well contamination in 5 yrs = 100% without program, 0% with hypothetical program	$646.80
Crutchfield et al., 1997	Nitrates	Indiana, adjusted to average demographics, hypothetical reduction of 15 to 10 mg/liter	$695.79
Smith and Desvousges, 1987	Unspecified hazardous waste	Reduction in risk of dying in 30 years from exposure to HW from 0.005 to 0.0025 (from 500/100 000 to 250/100 000)	$703.65
Crutchfield et al., 1997	Nitrates	Washington state, adjusted to average demographics, hypothetical reduction of 15 to 10 mg/liter	$842.66

Source	Contaminant	Description	Value
Smith and Desvousges, 1987	Unspecified hazardous waste	Avoid increase in risk of dying in 30 years from exposure to HW from 0.001 to 0.005 (from 100/100 000 to 500/100 000)	$936.42
Kohlhase, 1991	Varies according to site	Average housing market WTP for additional mile away from EPA Superfund site if located at the site	$1030.96
Crutchfield et al., 1997	Nitrates	Washington state, adjusted to average demographics, hypothetical reduction of 15 to 0 mg/liter	$1031.30
Edwards, 1988	Nitrates	Average income for 1986 ($30 759), 84% reduction in probability of contamination	$1034.30
Smith and Desvousges, 1987	Unspecified hazardous waste	Reduction in risk of dying in 30 years from exposure to HW from 0.005 to 0.001 (from 500/100 000 to 100/100 000)	$1043.54
Harrington et al., 1989, 1991	Giardia	Best estimate (average of upper and lower bounds) with after-tax minimum wage assumed for time costs	$1453.00
Edwards, 1988	Nitrates	Mean income $55 000 (180% of national average income for 1986) and 0.84 decrease in probability of contamination	$1863.32
Michaels and Smith, 1990	Not specified	Premier housing market WTP for removal of closest waste site (3.9 miles more to next site)	$5,070.45
Harrington et al., 1989, 1991	Giardia	Cost of replacing amount of water that would have been consumed before contamination assuming average after-tax wage rate of sample = time cost for non-employed (upper bound)	$6,446.00

Source: Agapoff et al. (2000).

Table 7.3   Cost of selected substitutes for household water supply

Type	Annual maintenance	Initial investment	Life expectancy	Annual cost
Under sink reverse osmosis system for nitrate removal	$100	$500–$1100	10 years	$194–279hh/yr
Whole house reverse osmosis system or other POE system	$230 yearly plus $250 every 5 years	$2000–$3000	10 years	$643–786hh/yr
Delivery of treated drinking water (urban area)	NA	NA	$525/hh/yr	$525/hh/yr

Note: Annual costs were found using method in Abdalla (1990, p. 461) with his same assumptions of a 5 per cent inflation and a 7 per cent discount rate.

different resource changes (quantities) in their valuation exercise, or use different levels of risk and exposure. Some of the contaminants being studied are quite different from others, leading perhaps to changes in odor or taste versus more severe health risks such as cancers and mortality. Values can also be influenced by the sample population's characteristics, that is, their income, education levels, the availability of substitute water supplies, and other factors.

It is interesting to note that many groundwater quality studies acknowledge the presence of risk and uncertainty in health effects and therefore attempt to find a value that incorporates this uncertainty. Recall that the option price (OP – see Chapter 6) is the preferred measure. Bergstrom et al. (2001) use surveys and a variation on the CVM to assess the option price for groundwater quality improvements in Georgia and Maine. Their model assumes all parties are risk neutral, which may be a bit tenuous as an assumption, but they estimate option prices for preventing nitrate contamination from rising above federal standards (10 mg/L of NO_3-N). Their reported estimates range from about $225 to $320 per year, depending on several assumptions made about the sample of respondents. These estimates appear large given that in both states most people had access to drinking water from groundwater sources that were well within the safety range for compliance with the MCL.

In another approach to handling risk and uncertainty, the authors do not seek any risk-related values or welfare measures for groundwater contamination risks. Lichtenberg et al. (1989) assess how regulatory approaches may change when one changes the margin of safety and preferences for risk

Table 7.4 Damage estimates from McClelland et al. under varying assumptions about non-respondents (2000 dollars, annual payment for 10 years)

Scenario	Non-respondents same as respondents	Non-respondents have one-half WTP of respondents	Non-respondents have zero WTP
Total damages (before clean up and containment), 40% of drinking water supplies contaminated	$105/hh/yr	$86/hh/yr	$66/hh/yr
Total damages with 70% of drinking water supplies contaminated	$201/hh/yr	$164/hh/yr	$127/hh/yr
Total damages with 10% of drinking water contaminated	$58/hh/yr	$47/hh/yr	$37/hh/yr
Damages if containment zone instead of complete clean up if 40% of drinking water supplies contaminated	$46/hh/yr	$37/hh/yr	$29/hh/yr

associated with groundwater contaminated by a pesticide, 1,2-dibromo-3-chloropropane or 'DBCP'. The case study was for groundwater near Fresno County, California. The authors assume the effective dose of groundwater is the product of four parameters, and excess cancer risk R is then:

$$R = GUAFQ$$

where G = the lifetime time-weighted average concentration of DBCP in drinking water; U = the sampling error involved in estimating G from available monitoring data; A = the lifetime time-weighted average consumption of drinking water; F = a factor transforming animal doses into human equivalents; and Q = a dose/response potency parameter.

Using this dose-response model Lichtenberg et al. assess two programs to reduce contamination risks. One involves drilling new wells, and the other involves installing a filtration system on individual wells. They estimate a cost function for risk reduction and show that, as expected, meeting a risk standard with a higher margin of safety entails higher costs. However, what is surprising is that when using a uniform approach to regulation, which is thought to be inefficient, allowing for uncertainty leads to relatively small social losses when compared to the 'least cost' regulatory approach. This suggests that when risks are involved, some of the standard criticism of inefficient regulatory approaches may be overstated.

In another recent study Stevens et al. (1997) examine household's rankings of choices for groundwater quality protection. The choices included paying for an aquifer protection district, a proposed town-wide treatment facility, a private pollution control device, and the purchase of bottled water. The 'price' of each program is given to individuals and they may chose to purchase the program, or not, or in another scheme they may rank the programs. Their estimates for annual willingness to pay, on average, are in Table 7.5.

Their empirical results show that various schemes to handle the data result in quite different estimates of value. It should be noted that for the construction of the water treatment plant the household must make payments for ten years, and similarly, to have bottled water delivered, they must also make the payments for ten years. To purchase the groundwater protection district they make payments of $88 per year for five years.

Most of the above studies focus on human health risks from urban and naturally found contaminants. Van Kooten et al. (1998) elicit groundwater values for reducing pollution associated with composting livestock wastes. Their study is conducted in rural Canada, in the District of Abbotsford, a town of about 25 000 people. Almost half the population drink groundwater. The largest household WTP they find for eliminating these wastes from groundwater is about $248 per year (US). Another study integrates both groundwater quality and quantity considerations for Kern County,

Table 7.5   Conjoint value estimates (average, $/household/year)

Type of protection program	Binary choice	Traditional ratings model	Ratings difference model
Aquifer protection district	$35.00	$340.70	$242.70
Treatment plant	$15.92	$191.78	$106.00
Private water filter	$24.04	$317.62	$214.00
Bottled water	$9.05	$75.75	$2.70

Source: Stevens et al. (1997).

California (see Dinar and Xepapadeas, 1998). Whatever the source of contamination, it is clear that groundwater protection does have a social value that is positive and nonzero. The values seen in the literature are substantially higher than the cost of piping water into a home and may even be higher than the cost of providing bottled water. When groundwater quality is threatened or harmed, an economist may well intervene with estimates of value to help obtain clean up (see case study 7.1).

CASE STUDY 7.1 GROUNDWATER CONTAMINATION IN MICHIGAN

Under CERCLA those who are perhaps responsible for contaminant release are called the potentially responsible party, or PRP. In the early 1990s I was asked by the state of Michigan to assist in responding to a report written on behalf of PRPs to address contamination involving a groundwater aquifer (Cicchetti, 1992). The report related to a 100 acre superfund site known as the G&H landfill, located northwest of the city of Utica, Michigan, about 20 miles north of Detroit. The G&H landfill was listed as the most contaminated superfund site in the state of Michigan in 1983, no small feat in a state with scores of superfund sites and large amounts of industrial pollution. Groundwater near the site had concentrations of PCBs of up to 9.5 parts per billion (ppb), up to almost 20 times the maximum concentration level (MCL) for PCBs set by the US EPA (0.5 ppb).

The state had prepared a claim for damages on the basis of the value of water that was lost in contamination of the aquifer. Engineers for the state had calculated damages using the cost of providing water from another source than the contaminated aquifer. The PRP's groundwater analysis assumed that five industrial facilities had injured groundwater and they recognized that aquifer users would likely have to switch to the municipal water supply system in the future. The water rate the system charged was about $1.09 per 100 cubic feet. Estimated consumption was about 1.4 million gallons or 190 000 cubic feet annually (there are 7.48 gallons in a cubic foot of water), and thus the expected water bill to obtain the municipal supply water was calculated to be about $4000 per year. Discounting and aggregating over 35 years, the total estimated groundwater loss from contamination of the aquifer was about $170 000.

The consultants for the PRPs argued that damages associated with the aquifer were in fact quite small, and offered an alternative estimate of damages based on a small amount of recreational opportunity lost in conjunction with impairment of the Rochester-Utica State Recreation Area (RUSRA). RUSRA was located along the banks of the Clinton River, adjacent to the landfill site and the injuries to the landfill area were acknowledged to have spilled over to this site.

I had to determine whether the consultants' claim was valid or invalid, but in fact first argued with the state that their own estimate of 'damages' using the cost of replacement was not sound to begin with. Damages are based on the benefits that are lost when the releases of hazardous substances occurred. They are not simply the cost of replacement. As costs are not equal to benefits, I considered what benefits of the aquifer existed before releases of the PCBs. The benefits relate to the values of the water, which in turn relate to the availability of substitutes. Benefits can be found, as I showed above, using estimates of individuals' WTP for groundwater. There were other nearby aquifers that could constitute an easy substitute resource, thereby diminishing the benefits of the aquifer relative to what might be true in a case where there is no good substitute drinking water supply that is easily accessible.

In this situation I had to agree somewhat with the PRPs' consultants that groundwater damages were small, though for different reasons than they gave. The PRP consultants also claimed that there was no basis for inclusion of passive use values, and I do not think their claim was supportable, as total remediation of an aquifer's PCB contamination is debatable (Curtis and Doty, 1990); one cannot know with certainty what future conditions may be and how these might affect relative scarcity.

The case reached a conclusion by concentrating on the recreation damages, as the PRP consultants had suggested. After an interesting settlement meeting that had aspects of David (the state of Michigan) against Goliath (several huge corporate polluters in Michigan), the PRPs and the state of Michigan settled out of court for a mutually agreed sum of money covering compensable damages. The settlement decree also stipulated that the PRPs would agree to monitor, and pump and treat the aquifer for many years into the future. As often happens in such situations, the PRPs publicly advertised the clean up as a benefit that they were providing to the state – to make Michigan a better place to live.

7.5 GROUNDWATER'S FUTURE

What is groundwater's future in the United States and elsewhere? I suspect that it will be used more and more, all over the world, and prices or rates based on this source will also rise. As I write this, yet another example of groundwater over-depletion has made the news. In Arkansas rice farmers in the Grand Prairie region are draining their aquifer dry. In past decades farmers there increased their pumping rates by a factor of ten, while at the same time decreasing the level of the Alluvia Aquifer there by more than one foot per year (Jehl, 2002) It is estimated that by 2015 there will not be enough water in the aquifer to sustain the area's 1000 farms. These farms produce about 5 percent of the nation's rice. At stake is a federal bailout of farmers and the current administration (under President Bush) is seriously considering helping them out to the tune of hundreds of millions of dollars.

Generally economists believe that scarce resources, ceteris paribus, should command higher prices. Naturally we are unable to predict how much higher or when prices will rise, but it may be that groundwater (and water in general) will command a higher price than it does currently, if relative scarcity of water increases. Today some states allow private ownership of groundwater (Texas), while others have laws that suggest groundwater is the property of all of the state's citizens (Nevada). Recently a Texas oil tycoon proposed pumping billions of gallons of groundwater for sale to the highest bidder, anticipating that the deal could be worth $1 billion (Yardley, 2001). This speculation in the value of groundwater may be a sign of things to come.

Naturally, the conjunctive use model shows that switching to groundwater, even with its already higher extraction cost, makes sense under certain conditions. It is indeed optimal to use groundwater at times of scarcity in surface water supplies. A consistent theme in this book is that relative scarcity is the concept that matters: what is demand relative to supply?

The State of Nevada is another interesting case study in the western United States because it is a very large state geographically, it has a small total population, it is the most arid state in the US, and yet in the areas around Las Vegas (within Clark County), the population has been one of the fastest growing in the entire United States. Clark County has depended on allocations from the state's right to withdrawals from the Colorado River, but several agencies have estimated that if this area's population continues to grow at rates of 3 to 5 percent annually, the supply from the Colorado will be inadequate. At that point, what do we think will happen?

Some scholars have suggested that scarce water supplies will be an impediment to future population growth, but there is relatively little evidence to support this hypothesis. Instead, the economics of long-term supplies such as groundwater has showed thus far that populations shift to using more expensive sources like this. Still, the groundwater quality problem mentioned above seems to be growing. Very recently economists have called for the management of both groundwater quality and quantity to be modeled simultaneously in recognition that the value of water as a resource 'depends as much on the quantity available as on its quality' (Roseta-Palma, 2002, p. 93).

APPENDIX

A7.1 Simple Dynamic Optimization Models

Instead of assuming that the equation of motion is continuous, it is often easier to begin to understand dynamic models by simply examining two periods, 1 and 2, in a discrete time model. Here I more or less adapt Jon Conrad's (1999) excellent discussion of these kinds of models. Surprisingly, a two-period model can often provide results consistent with a multi-period continuous model, so that is all one may need. It may help provide credibility by considering the second period to be the 'last' period, or the one where, effectively, no choices matter by the end of that period. There is always a tiny problem in two-period discrete models with sorting out whether something is happening at the 'beginning' or 'end' of the period. Below, assume that recharge in period 2 happens at the beginning so that period 2 users can benefit from this recharge for the entire period.

In a two-period model it is typically assumed that, by the end of the second period, society has got all the benefits from the resource that it can. This precludes leaving the resource for 'future' generations, as there is no future generation. I will begin with Conrad's notation and framework. He simply lets the net benefit of a stock X_t be denoted by π, and the harvest at time t be Y_t. Net benefits are then written $\pi(X_t, Y_t)$. Let the discount factor in any period be $\rho^t = [1/(1+r)^t]$, so that $\rho^0 = 1$, and $\rho = 1/(1+r)$. The resource manager's problem is to:

$$\text{Maximize } \pi = \Sigma_{t=0} \rho^t \pi(X_t, Y_t)$$

subject to:

$$X_{t+1} - X_t = F(X_t) - Y_t$$

And we assume X_0 is given.

Groundwater

Conrad writes the dynamic equivalent of the Lagrangian we discussed in Chapter 2 as:

$$L = \Sigma_{t=0} \rho^t \{\pi(X_t, Y_t) + \rho \lambda_{t+1} [X_t + F(X_t) - Y_t - X_{t-1}]\}$$

Suppose then that we have two periods, $t=0$ and $t=1$. Substitute in the definition for the discount factor above. This Langrangian implies that:

$$L = \pi(X_0, Y_0) + 1/(1+r)\lambda_1 [X_0 + F(X_0) - Y_0 - X_1] + [1/(1+r)]\pi(X_1, Y_1) + 1/(1+r)\lambda_2 [X_1 + F(X_1) - Y_1 - X_2]$$

Now, note that this version of the problem involves X_2, which is the stock in a period after $t=1$. If there is no period $t=2$, then this tells us the stock left over after the last period. Consider the meaning then, of λ_2. It tells us the value of having an additional unit of the stock left over. If we want to impose some positive value for this we can, but alternatively, if we want to say that the value of anything left over after the world has ended is zero, then we can set $\lambda_2 = 0$ and the last term drops out.

A7.2 Continuous Version of the Model

Assume that per unit pumping costs (w) are proportional to the stock of groundwater at time t, $S(t)$, so that we can write these as $w[S(t)]$. The stock can grow with recharge and it falls with pumping, $R_o(t)$. The recharge relation is assumed to be:

$$H(t) = h[S(t)] \qquad (A7.1)$$

The rate of change in the stock of the aquifer is thus:

$$dS(t)/dt = H(t) - R_o(t) \qquad (A7.2)$$

Equation (7.2) defines an equation of motion, which is common in such optimization problems. The manager's problem is to maximize the net benefits of extracting the resource over time. Let the inverse demand function for water be $P(q, t)$. Here we assume that functions are continuous in time, as is often most realistic. Therefore, when considering net benefits over time, the way to examine continuous functions is to evaluate integrals. Let the marginal cost of pumping water be w. Assume that the manager is aware of and considers the social discount rate r so that the discounted present value of net benefits over time is examined.

The manager wants to maximize net benefits by choosing optimal pumping rates, or maximize over $R_o(t)$:

$$\int_0^\infty \left[\int_0^{R(t)} P(q,t)dq - w[S(t)] \cdot R(t) \right] e^{-rt} dt \qquad (A7.3)$$

subject to A7.2 and:

$$S(t) >= 0 \qquad (A7.4)$$

Note that in (A7.3) the term e^{-rt} is the continuous discounting analog to what you have seen before, where we divide each period's discrete net benefits by $(1+r)^t$, or multiply the net benefits by the discount factor $1/(1+r)^t$.

This problem can be solved using the calculus of variations or optimal control theory. The latter yields something like the Lagrangian multiplier method we used at the beginning of the theory sections in Chapter 2, but allowing for some dynamic analysis, the Lagrangian expression is called the 'Hamiltonian'. The Hamiltonian (φ) is the first part to be maximized plus only part of the usual constraint. The constraint is the Lagrangian multiplier for each period (λ_t) times the equation of motion, or:

$$\varphi = \int P(q,t)dq - wS(t) \cdot R_o(t) + \lambda_t[H(S(t)) - R_o(t)] \qquad (A7.5)$$

Howe shows that the first-order conditions are simply:

$$P(t) = w[S(t)] + \lambda_t \qquad (A7.6)$$

and

$$d\lambda_t/dt = r \cdot \lambda_t - \partial\varphi/\partial S(t) \qquad (A7.7)$$

where the second term on the right-hand side is the derivative of the Hamiltonian with respect to $S(t)$. This second condition can be rewritten as:

$$d\lambda_t/dt = [r - dH/dS(t)]\lambda_t + dw/dS(t)R_o, \qquad (A7.7a)$$

or as

$$d\lambda_t/dt/\lambda_t = r - dH/dS(t) + [dw/dS(t) R_o]/\lambda_t \qquad (A7.7b)$$

The first condition simply is to pump water so that the price or marginal value (assumed to be the price here) is equal to the sum of the marginal pumping cost w plus the scarcity rent. The latter is the value of letting another unit of water stay in the ground. This is just marginal benefit equal to marginal cost, supplemented by a connection to the future because there is a value to not pumping now.

The second condition (see equation (A7.8b)) says that the rate of change in the scarcity rent is related to the discount rate and two stock effects. If you divide both sides by λ you get the percentage change in the royalty, or scarcity rent is equal to the discount rate less a stock effect related to the recharge rate and the change in pumping costs due to different stock sizes. Note that the recharge is lower with more stocks in the current period, but pumping costs are lower with more stock in the current period. The second condition is quite intuitive, but does the reader know why the first condition is true? Thinking about this will help us to really understand what is going on in these dynamic models, and it will help a great deal if one thinks back to the simple rule in static models: price equals marginal cost. Hint: How is equation (A7.7) different from that?

The interested reader who wishes to see this model put into practice should see the article applied to Texas High Plains groundwater extraction by Kim et al. (1989).

NOTES

1. I hope the material in this chapter has benefited from my discussions about resource extraction with my former Nevada colleague, Kees van Kooten, who now sees much greener grass in Victoria, British Columbia. I also appreciate comments from Gene O'Donnell, a former student.
2. I thank a student, Ron Peterson, who has an MS degree in hydrogeology, for showing the economists this easy little experiment during a class meeting.
3. This is unlikely to deter the federal government from sending the wastes there (see Riddel and Shaw, 2004).
4. The terminal conditions pertain to constraints that must hold at the end of all periods and relate to total available resources.
5. Perhaps with the exception of the result that the reform on groundwater law did not produce much in the way of net benefits to society.
6. As an example of the latter, the 2002 Darcy lecturer, David Hyndman, described efforts by Michigan State, Stanford University, and a host of other university researchers to use bioremediation methods to reduce a certain type of contaminant in a Michigan aquifer (the Schoolcraft Bioaugmentation Experiment).
7. Poe et al. (2001) also survey the CVM papers in groundwater and provide a range of values relating to different issues. They use a method known as 'meta analysis', mentioned in Chapter 4, wherein the reported study values are regressed on all of the factors that are present across studies that are hypothesized to explain the variation in the values.

REFERENCES

Abdall, Charles W., Brian Roach and Donald J. Epp (1992), 'Valuing Environmental Quality Changes Using Averting Expenditures: an Application on Groundwater Contamination', *Land Economics*, **68**(2) (May), 163–9.
Agapoff, Jean, Elizabeth Fadali and W. Douglass Shaw (2000), 'Summary of the literature on groundwater valuation', a draft report to the California State Water Quality Control Board, Sacramento, CA.
Ahlfeld, D.P. and M. Heidari (1994), 'Applications of optimal hydraulic control to groundwater systems', *Journal of Water Resources Planning and Management*, **120**(3), 350–65.
Balleau, W.P. (1988), 'Water appropriation and transfer in a general hydrogeologic system', *Natural Resources Journal*, **28** (Spring), 269–91.
Bergstrom, J.C., K.J. Boyle and M. Yabe (2001), 'Determinants of groundwater quality values: Georgia and Maine case studies', in J.C. Bergrstom, K.J. Boyle and G.L. Poe (eds), *The Economic Value of Water Quality*, Cheltenham, UK and Northampton, MA: Edward Elgar, chapter 2.
Boggess, W. et al. (1993), 'Economics of water use in agriculture', in G. Carlson, D. Zilberman and J. Miranowski (eds), *Agricultural and Environmental Resource Economics*, Boston, MA: Oxford University Press, chapter 8.
Brown Jr, G. and R. Deacon (1972), 'Economic optimization of a single-cell aquifer', *Water Resources Research*, **8** (June), 557–64.
Cech, Thomas V. (2003), *Principles of Water Resources: History, Development, Management, and Policy*, New York: John Wiley and Sons.
Cicchetti, Charles J. (1992), report by managing director of Arthur Anderson Economic Consulting, Arthur Anderson & Company, submitted to the state of Michigan.
Conrad, Jon (1999), *Resource Economics*, Cambridge: Cambridge University Press.
Curtis, T. and C. Doty (1990), 'Can contaminated aquifers at superfund sites be remediated?', *Environmental Science and Technology*, **24**(10), 1464.
Dinar, A. and A. Xepapadeas (1998), 'Regulating water quantity and quality in irrigated agriculture', *Journal of Environmental Management*, **54**, 273–89.
Gisser, Micha (1983), 'Groundwater: focusing on the real issue', *Journal of Political Economy*, **91**(6), 1001–27.
Gorelick, S.M. (1990), 'Large scale nonlinear deterministic and stochastic optimization: tormulations involving simulation of subsurface contamination', *Mathematical Programming*, **48**, 19–39.
Holland, Stephen P. and Michael R. Moore (2003), 'Cadillac desert revisited: property rights, public policy and water-resource depletion', *Journal of Environmental Economics and Manage*, **46**, 131–55.
Howe, C.W. (1979), 'Water resource system', in *Natural Resource Economics*, Baltimore, MD: John Wiley and Sons, chapter 14 (out of print)
Innes, Robert and Dennis Cory (2001), 'The economics of safe drinking water', *Land Economics*, **77**(1), 94–117.
Jehl, Douglas (2002), 'Arkansas rice farmers run dry, and US remedy sets off debate', *New York Times*, national edn, 11 November, p. 1.
Kim, C.S., M.R. Moore, J.J. Hanchar and M. Nieswiadomy (1989), 'A dynamic model of adaptation to resource depletion: theory and application to groundwater mining', *Journal of Environmental Economics and Management*, **17**(1) (July), 66–82.

Lichtenberg, E., D. Zilberman and K.T. Bogen (1989), 'Regulating environmental health risks under uncertainty: groundwater contamination in California', *Journal of Environmental Economics and Management*, **17**(1) (July), 22–34.
Moncur, James E.T. and R.L. Pollack (1988), 'Scarcity rents for water: a valuation and pricing model', *Land Economics*, **64**(1) (February), 62–73.
Mulligan, A.E. and D.P. Ahlfeld (1999), 'Advective control of groundwater contaminant plumes: model development and comparison to hydraulic control', *Water Resources Research*, **35**(8), 2285–94.
Nieswiadomy, M. (1985), 'The demand for irrigation water in the High Plains of Texas', *American Journal of Agricultural Economics*, **67**(3), 619–26.
Poe, Greg, Kevin Boyle and John Bergstrom (2001), 'A preliminary meta-analysis of contingent values for groundwater quality revisited', in J.C. Bergstrom, K.J. Boyle and G.L. Poe (eds), *The Economic Value of Water Quality*, Cheltenham, UK and Northampton, MA: Edward Elgar.
Porter, Richard C. (1996), 'The economics of water and waste: a case study of Jakarta, Indonesia', Brookfield, VT: Avebury Press.
Provencher, B. (1995), 'Issues in the conjunctive use of surface water and groundwater', in D.B. Bromley (ed.), *The Handbook of Environmental Economics*, Oxford: Blackwell.
Reichard, E. et al. (The International Commission on Groundwater Working Group on Groundwater Contamination Risk Assessment) (1990), *Groundwater Contamination Risk Assessment: A Guide to Understanding and Managing Uncertainties*, International Hydrological Programme of UNESCO, IAHS publication no. 196.
Riddel, M. and W.D. Shaw (2004), 'An update on nuclear waste storage and perceived risks', draft manuscript, University of Nevada, Reno.
Roseta-Palma, C. (2002), 'Groundwater management when water quality is endogenous', *Journal of Environmental Economics and Manage*ment, **44** (July), 93–105.
Stevens, T. et al. (1991), 'Measuring the existence value of wildife: what do CVM estimates really show?', *Land Economics*, **67**(4), 390–400.
Stevens, T.H., C. Barrett and C.E. Willis (1997), 'Conjoint analysis of groundwater protection programs', *Agricultural and Resource Economics Review*, **26**(1) (October), 229–36.
Tarlock, A.D. (1986), 'An overview of the law of groundwater management', *Water Resources Research*, **21**, 1751–76.
Torell, L.A., J.D. Libbin and M.D. Miller (1990), 'The market value of water in the Ogallala aquifer', *Land Economics*, **66**(2) (May), 163–75.
Turvey, R. (1976), 'Analyzing the marginal cost of water supply', *Land Economics*, **52**, 158–68.
Van Kooten, G.C., R. Athwal and L.M. Arthur (1998), 'Use of public perceptions of groundwater quality benefits in developing livestock management options', *Canadian Journal of Agricultural Economics*, **46** (November), 273–85.
Yardley, Jim (2001), 'For Texas water, not oil is liquid gold', *New York Times*, 16 April, A-1, A-14.

SUGGESTED FURTHER READING

Bergstrom, J.C. et al. (eds) (2001), *The Economic Value of Water Quality*, Cheltenham, UK and Northampton, MA: Edward Elgar.

Bredehoeft, John D. and Robert A. Young (1970), 'The temporal allocation of groundwater – a simulation approach', *Water Resources Research*, **6**(1) (February).

WEBSITE

http://www.Water.usugs.gov/nwis. Data on 1.5 million sites, about 80 percent of which are wells.

8. In situ uses of water: environmental and recreational values

8.0 INTRODUCTION

In this chapter values associated with in situ uses of water are explored. The intent is to demonstrate that water may have value even if it is not withdrawn for consumptive purposes. Considered below are the several types of values that relate to keeping stream flow at some flow rate, groundwater at a level, or a lake at some level. Maintaining these quantities supports water-based recreation, supports a fishery or the habitat for certain species, and provides ecosystem services. The connection to environment is a fundamental one, though different from Chapter 3's focus on water quality tied to health risks. One of the most important human uses of in situ water in the United States is for recreational purposes.

Water-based recreation
Water-based recreation takes many forms, as noted in Chapter 3. There is no withdrawal or consumption of the water from the water course or water body, but volumes of water left in place may be an important determinant contributing to the pleasure or satisfaction of the experience. Recreational activities are often thought to be in the domain of the wealthy, but many types of water-based recreation do not require boats or other expensive equipment, allowing people with middle and even low incomes to engage in them. Cities and towns that are located near lakes and rivers may provide easy and inexpensive access to river banks and lake shores. In many states in the US today it is estimated that more than half the population engages in some form of outdoor recreation, and a good portion of this relates to opportunities connected to surface waters.

Some forms of recreation are seen as coming into conflict with other water uses such as agriculture, hydropower production, or for drinking water, and this is true, though there are few studies that accurately assess or quantify the conflicts. It is also true today that some specific recreational activities may come into conflict with one another. For example, Naeser and Smith (1995) show that anglers and rafters on the upper Arkansas River of Colorado are often in conflict in this area where commercial rafting provides some $30 million in revenue. The anglers do not, apparently, like the rafters to get in the way of their fishing.

Water quantity changes and recreation

Recreational activities may be impaired by an undesirable water level, so that utility or satisfaction is impaired, much in the same way as water quality changes are (see Chapter 3). The water level in the river or lake may be too high (flooding) or too low (corresponding with droughts, or human intervention). There are several mechanisms by which recreational use and values may be impacted, likely depending on whether activities are consumptive or non-consumptive. Assume that a recreational angler desires to catch a fish. Water quantity changes may affect fish or other aquatic species populations, in turn affecting anglers' ability to catch the fish. At one extreme, lakes will have a critical minimum level of water and rivers may have a critical or minimum instream flow quantity, below which fish populations are not viable. At the other extreme, too high flows, perhaps corresponding to flood levels, can also adversely impact fish and aquatic habitat.

There are hundreds of studies in the literature that examine the relationship between the use of and value for recreational resources and water quality or quantity, but most of the literature examines the effect of water quality changes. Probably the majority of the economics literature focuses on marine environments; most of the other studies provide information relating to lakes or reservoirs. A very small portion of the literature examines river-based recreation. This literature is much too vast to summarize here, but the importance of water-based recreation has led to modifications of water laws.

Types of in situ use and the associated values for water are increasingly viewed as being very important, along with irrigation and municipal uses that involve withdrawals. For example, very recently, the Colorado State Supreme Court gave the cities of Golden, Vail, and Breckenridge permission to use state-governed rivers to fill their whitewater kayaking courses; the actual court member vote resulted in a three to three tie, but recreation and environmental (in-situ) use groups viewed this as a victory (Pankratz, 2003).

As another example, the Oregon Water Resources Department today recommends a flow of 250 cubic feet per second (cfs) on the stretch of the Deschutes River that is designated as wild and scenic, in order to meet the needs of fish, wildlife, and recreational users (Turner and Perry, 1997).[1]

Historically, as Chapter 1 points out, water laws in the western US did not recognize 'instream' flow as a beneficial use. But this has changed and many western states now do formally recognize instream flow as a beneficial use, and may even grant water rights to this purpose. The legal implications are controversial and more complicated than can be resolved in this chapter. However, the gist of the fundamental legal issue is whether appropriated rights, especially on 'fully' appropriated rivers and streams, supersede or are junior to instream flow rights that might have been granted at much later dates.

Very recently (January 2004) a federal US judge ruled that the US government owed a group of California irrigators $14 million in damages because the US Fish and Wildlife Service cut back water supplies to protect fish in another endangered species situation. The group, including Kern County irrigators, had filed a law suit to recover damages they felt they had incurred by not having water. Clearly the only such irrigators harmed would ordinarily have been relatively junior ones. The judge's rule is the first such order for compensation that has received widespread media coverage and attention in the United States, and fears are running high that this type of compensatory payment will hamper the federal government's use of the Endangered Species Act (see Boxall, 2004). Despite common use of instream flow protection rights as described above, many groups who feel they have been harmed, or at least could be, have filed law suits just like this one.

One of the themes in this book is the appropriate role, and effectiveness of, a market for water. I offer a very brief account of a legal case involving water rights and instream flows below (Section 8.3). As a preview, a complete market for water would allow parties that have a positive willingness to pay to maintain stream flow to purchase water rights. These rights could be used to maintain a volume of water in a reservoir, and agents would factor these rights into long-run planning. Some parties and government agencies currently demand water rights to secure environmental protection or maintain recreational services at a particular desirable level. Short and long-term leases for these flows are developing in the US, though often the 'agent' that acts on behalf of those who demand them is the government.

Chapter 3 dealt with the issue of water quality and briefly illustrated the application of economic techniques that can be used to value clean up of, better quality of, and reduced health risks from water resources, such as the contingent valuation method (for example, Carson and Mitchell, 1993). Many of these same techniques may be applied in the valuation of water quantities, though the valuation literature in this area only blossomed recently. After a brief review of non-market methods the growing literature in water-based recreation that addresses the water quantity issue is featured. Following this, I offer a few case studies from research done in the Pacific Northwest and in Nevada: I consider endangered species issues on the Columbia, a dying Nevada lake, the infamous dispute over the Truckee River and the Newlands project withdrawals, and a newer study on the impacts of dewatering gold mines in Nevada's Humboldt River Basin.

8.1 BACKGROUND ON NON-MARKET VALUATION APPLIED TO WATER

Three primary valuation methods that can be applied to valuing water quantity and quality changes are reviewed. The primary valuation methods are those that incorporate the use of direct survey or other data, and the reader will see that a secondary method known as benefits transfer is also frequently used in policy making. The primary valuation methods are:

- the contingent valuation method (CVM) or contingent behavior method (CBM),
- the travel cost or recreation demand model (TCM), and
- the hedonic property valuation approach or method (HPM).

The CVM has already been mentioned in the book (see Chapters 3 and 7). The CVM directly asks an individual to state his or her value for a resource change and is called a 'stated preference' approach. It is still presumed to be the only method that allows the recovery of non-use values. Stated preference methods are probably the most common approaches taken in non-market valuation,[2] but they are somewhat controversial among economists and other interested parties, particularly when the purpose is to obtain non-use or passive use values. The credibility of the CVM has held up under attacks from such esteemed economists as were hired by the Exxon Corporation in their efforts to discredit the method. Exxon's effort was related to the law suit over the 1989 Exxon Valdez oil spill. After legal negotiations the Exxon Corporation settled compensatory damages out of court for approximately $1 billion. Naturally one would not want to assume that the sole reason for the settlement was the threat of application of the CVM to recover damages, but it no doubt played a role.

The contingent behavior method (CBM) is a variation on the CVM. It asks a person what he or she would do in response to a hypothetical set of conditions. For example, one might propose a change in a lake level (higher or lower) and ask how many more or fewer trips a person might take there as a consequence. Is has the advantage of allowing responses to changes that are well outside the normal range of water conditions observed over some past period.

The travel cost method (TCM) uses individual's costs to and from a recreation destination to proxy the price for a unit of the non-market good, a 'trip' to a destination. By tracing out the demand for the good, which in water-based recreation is a lake, river, or ocean, one can then recover estimates of consumer's surplus for resource changes. The intuition is that a rational individual would not take a trip to a destination unless the total value of doing so exceeded the cost. The TCM approach is known as a 'revealed preference' approach because rather than directly ask a person his or her value for a lake, we get a revelation of the value of the resource by observing trip-taking behavior. There are so many existing travel cost studies now that it would be impossible to list them, but the interested reader is referred to one of several books on the subject of travel cost or recreation demand modeling (for example, the fairly new book by Hanley et al., 2003).

The HPM uses observed differences over time or spatially, across properties, in the value of property (lake shorefront homes versus homes inset from the lake's shoreline) to reveal values for the resource. For example, in their study of lakefront property in central Texas, Lansford and Jones found a premium of $60 000 to $100 000 for being on the waterfront, as opposed to elsewhere in the region. In their analysis of 4000 homes sold in the county of New Haven, Connecticut, Acharya and Bennett (2001) examine the influence of both the distance to the nearest lake, and distance to the Long Island Sound on property values. They find negative and significant influences in their modeling, but do not report the marginal value of closer proximity in their paper. Along the same lines, another HPM study focuses specifically on water quality in 34 Maine lakes. Boyle and Taylor (2001) use water clarity data, as measured by a secchi disk (see Chapter 3), specifically measuring the minimum summer month water clarity (in meters). They also include a lake view variable in their model. They do calculate the marginal value of water clarity on property values and find high ones, ranging from $2000 to $8000 per meter of increased clarity.

One key point is that when the home is near the water, the water can probably be easily seen by looking out the window of the house, and this adds to the value of the home. It is debatable as to whether a view of a water body provides only use value (an easy access to boating or swimming or the enjoyment of the view), or something more. Therefore, it is not clear whether the HPM only provides an estimate of the use value of a lake or river, or incorporates some non use values as well.

All the above methods have been used to value water, in situ. In the next section I consider some of the estimates.

8.2 WATER-BASED VALUES AND RECREATION

8.2.1 Water Quality Changes

I begin with discussion of a water quality study that uses the CVM to examine issues in California's San Joaquin Valley (Jones & Stokes, 1990).

Because Chapter 3 covered water quality issues, the discussion here will be brief. To review, remember that any value can be expressed as a maximum willingness to pay (WTP) or minimum willingness to accept compensation (WTA) for a change in water quality. In the San Joaquin study two researchers, Michael Hanemann and John Loomis, thought that fish and wildlife and wetlands were three important non-market goods in the San Joaquin Valley. They calculated that the best way to identify and measure values for them was by applying the CVM. Working with an environmental consulting firm, Jones & Stokes, they designed and implemented a survey of households to assess their sense of importance of and value for regional fish and wildlife.

As always in the western US, the study was controversial because resource protection in the San Joaquin Valley was viewed by some as in conflict with agricultural use of water and land in this same valley. The study's valuation (WTP) results can be summarized as follows (Table 8.1).

The values in Table 8.1 are clearly substantial. They are also important because California is a state that is typical of regions with rapidly growing populations and conflicts over water. The results suggest that there is a cost to development of water resources used for municipal and agricultural purposes that may be in the form of diminished water quality values. Such values would be ignored, as there is no market for such a loss. The non-market values for wetlands in Table 8.1 point out that wetlands may indeed be a key

Table 8.1 Summary of willingness to pay estimates for the San Joaquin Valley study

Category or Program	Annual WTP per household
Maintain wetlands	$92 NC, $174 residents*
Improve wetlands	$161 NC, $286 residents
Avoid contamination of wildlife at evaporation ponds	$93 NC, $197 residents (prevent increase)
Improve salmon fishery in San Joaquin River	$103 NC, $202 residents
Combined programs	$1448 package of three** – residents
Total WTP	$1.76 billion: entire California population of 9 842 000 households

Notes:
* NC = out of state (Oregon, Washington, and Nevada) residents are from the San Joaquin Valley.
** package of three includes wetlands, evaporation ponds, and river salmon.

Source: Jones & Stokes (1990).

part of water quality improvement programs: households state that they are willing to pay substantial sums of money each year for their protection.

On a larger scale, the state of California embarked on major changes in water quality via two pieces of legislation in the 1990s. The Central Valley Project Improvement Act of 1992 transferred substantial quantities of water from farmer to environmental uses, and the Bay-Delta Accord of 1995 further relocates water from both urban and agricultural uses to restoration of the environment. These transfers resulted in an 8.6 percent reduction in aggregate surface water supplies normally given to farmers and urban uses (in normal precipitation years), and a 21.8 percent reduction in dry years (Howitt and Lund, 1999). Howitt and Lund highlight the importance of the California Drought Water Banks in facilitating some short-term transactions. But a first step in establishing the demand on the part of environmental interests is to do some sort of study such as done by Hanemann and Loomis.

In another regional water quality study Whitehead and Blomquist (1991) estimate the WTP for preservation of the Clear Creek wetland in western Kentucky. In this study households have an opportunity to buy into a program to purchase wetlands, including lakes, ponds, marshes, swamps, sloughs for their preservation. This stated contribution toward the purchase price reveals consumer's surplus (WTP), and the results indicate values in the range of $4 to $17 per household, depending on details provided in the surveys. Here again, households demonstrate a value associated with water quality, specifically here, wetlands that provide ecosystem services (fish habitat, wildlife, plants).

One of the best known large-scale examples of a water quality study is the Mitchell and Carson CVM study of improvements tied to the Clean Water Act (Carson and Mitchell, 1993). This was discussed in Chapter 3, and while such studies may be complicated by the presence of risk and uncertainty (see Chapter 6), households do seem to understand the important issues surrounding water quality improvements. Next I consider valuing changes in water quantity.

8.2.2 Water Quantity Changes

Consider the value of changes in the quantity of water, and, of particular interest, the value of instream flow. The theory here needs a bit more consideration, as the units being valued (a change in a quantity of water) are different from water quality. Chapters 1 and 2 mentioned the importance of the marginal unit. Suppose the unit is one acre foot, to be kept in a river. Clearly, the value of an acre foot of water will depend on how much water one already has, regardless of the type of in situ use from it.

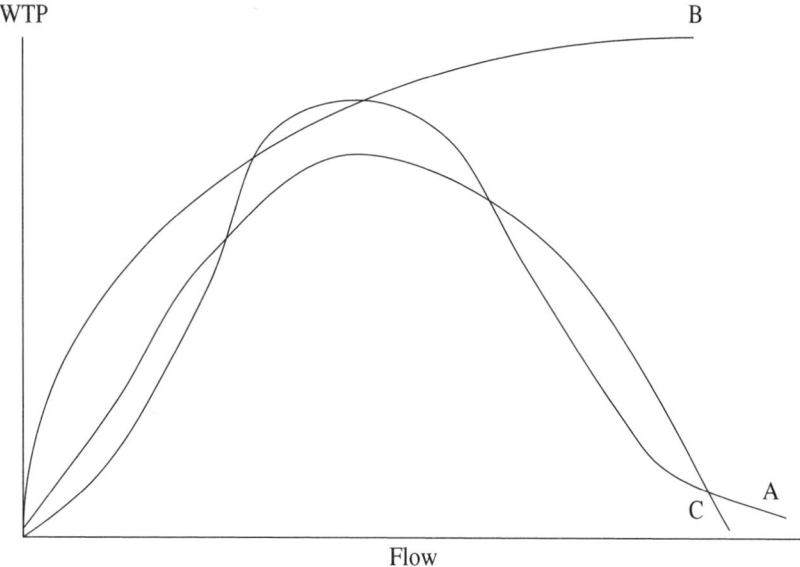

Figure 8.1   Total benefit function (WTP and flow levels)

Let a total benefit function relate a recreational user's WTP to particular flow levels (see Figure 8.1). Suppose total benefit is small at very low instream flow levels, then it rises, and at some relatively high level it might fall, or at least flatten out. A story could be told that the very low flows lead to low total benefit because they are too low to support aquatic life, then at some critical level of flow a high value accrues, and so on. The marginal benefit function maps the slope of the total benefit function to these flow levels (see Figure 8.2). The total or marginal benefit function might take shape A, B, or C in Figure 8.1 for any particular type of in situ use or any particular situation. Then, the associated marginal benefit function might be constant or might be expected to be initially high and fall with increases in flows (see MB_1 and MB_2).

The theory points out that whether the first, middle, or the last unit of flow is being valued will likely lead to large differences in estimated values for water quantity changes. Scarcity is the key in most cases. In other words, the marginal unit is probably quite important, and one must be careful in valuing water based on the average unit. Though the Daubert and Young (1981) study precedes it, one of the more careful discussions of the theory about instream flow can be found in Frank Ward's paper (1987).

Underlying the concept that humans place value on leaving water in a river or stream are the ecological and biological relationships between

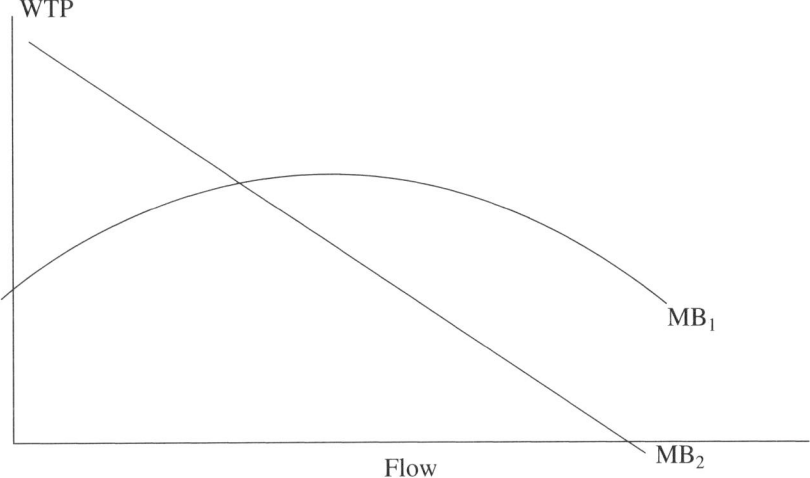

Figure 8.2   Marginal benefit function (slope of total benefit function)

water quantities and aquatic health. Ward (1987) assumes that water is used to produce fish or recreational experiences.[3] Ward first collects data to estimate a travel cost model for visits to New Mexico's Rio Chama, a tributary of the Rio Grande in the northern part of the state used for angling and whitewater boating; the model lets visits and value be a function of flow levels. The results are used to construct a total and marginal benefit function associated with upstream reservoir releases which can be used to augment downstream natural flows in the river.

Ward lets utility for the ith recreational user be $U_i = U(Y, x_i, h_i, f)$ where Y is a vector of non-recreation goods, x are trips to the river per season, h is the expected catch of fish for anglers, and f is the streamflow for either anglers or boaters. Maximizing a budget constraint yields a demand function for trips, $x_i = x_i(c_i, M_i, h_i, f)$ where c is travel cost per trip and M is the person's income.

Ordinary consumer's surplus for a change in flow levels from f^0 to f^* can be found as the area between shifted trip demand functions. Ward aggregates across all I users:

$$CS = \sum_{i=1}^{I} \int_{C_{i0}}^{C_{i**}} x_i(c_i, M_i, h_i, f^*) - \sum_{i=1}^{I} \int_{C_{i0}}^{C_{i*}} x_i(c_i, M_i, h_i, f^0) \qquad (8.1)$$

Graphically, this is simply the usual trapezoid between two straight-lined demand functions, where the one farther to the right reflects the higher flow levels.

Ward (1987) goes further than most economists had up to that point and considers the optimal timing of releases [$w(t)$] from an upstream reservoir that would augment natural stream flow [$z(t)$]. The model is a continuous dynamic optimization model, such as we considered in the groundwater chapter (Chapter 7). He maximizes the present value of seasonal net benefits (NB):

$$NB = \int_0^T e^{-rt}\{cs[w(t) + z(t)] - \Gamma[w(t), t]\}dt \quad (8.2)$$

where Γ is the cost of managing the river in light of upstream releases. Note that equation (8.2) directly incorporates the consumer's surplus (CS) from equation (8.1).

To implement the model, Ward (1987) may have developed one of the very first contingent behavior studies in the literature.[4] This is because visitors at the site are actually presented with seven photographs that correspond to various average daily flow levels (50, 100, 250, 500, 1000, 2000, and 4000 cfs) and then asked how many visits they would take to the Rio Chama at those flow rates. Ward (1987) is then able to uncover a relationship between CS and flow, one of the first people I know of to do this:

$$CS = 261{,}689 + 961.9f + 0.321f^2 + 0.00011f^3 \quad (8.3)$$

With this function Ward (1987) can approximate total seasonable benefits per cfs for any flow level. Marginal benefits (such as in Figure 8.2) are a quadratic function of his total benefits function in 1.3. He says that for his sample, marginal benefits peak at 2900 cfs. His estimates of the value per cfs are shown in Table 8.2, and again, it appears that Ward's integration of equation (8.3) and the optimal control model may be the first of its kind in the literature.

8.2.3 In Situ or Instream Flow Value Estimates

Below I consider some estimates of the value of water. The variation in estimates is substantial. Average values are quite common in the literature, as opposed to a carefully defined marginal value. An average value of an acre foot of water may be found by converting the total value an individual has for protecting an entire lake from drying up to a per unit value. There may often be some key threshold level of river flow or lake volume, after which, if the lake falls or river flows are lower, the recreational activity there may be worth little. For example, there are ideal flows (cubic feet per second) for white-water rafting and the relevant value per flow would be that last unit below which the experience rapidly diminishes or becomes impossible.

Table 8.2   Literature estimates of value of water quantity**

Berrens, et al. (1996) (Contingent valuation, New Mexico)	$28.73 annual WTP for protection of silvery minnow, Middle Rio Grande
	$89.68 annual WTP for protection of minimum instream flow, all major New Mexico rivers
Brown and Duffield (Contingent valuation, Montana)	$3 to $23 annual WTP for Montana instream flow protection (1994)
Creel and Loomis (1992); Loomis and Creel (1992) (Travel cost, California)	$300 to $350 per acre foot for San Joaquin River water; also $70 per acre foot for San Joaquin and Stanislaus for recreational use only
Colby (1993) (Literature review study)	$40 to $80 annual WTP per household for 'western' instream flows
Eiswerth et al. (2000) (Travel cost plus contingent behavior, Nevada)	$240 to $360 annual WTP for a 20 foot increase (50 000 af) at Walker Lake
Loomis (1987) (Contingent valuation, California)	$154 to $350 annual WTP to protect Mono Lake from decline
Loomis and Cooper (1990) (Travel cost, Feather River California)	$1458 per season for fishing benefits from increase in 20 cubic feet per second (average of $72.90 per cfs)
Cordell and Bergstrom (1993) (Contingent valuation, Tennessee)	$33 annual WTP to increase Fall Tennessee Reservoir levels
Ward (1987) (Travel cost and dynamic programming models)	$900 to $1100 per acre foot 'gross shadow value', Rio Chama/Rio Grande Basin
Ward (1989) (Travel cost, New Mexico)	$133 per acre foot for New Mexico lakes
Ward et al. (1997) (Travel cost demand system, New Mexico)	$1 to $11 per acre foot for New Mexico reservoirs
Lansford and Jones (1995) (Hedonic property valuation)	$110 to $136 per acre foot for homes on Lake Travis, central Texas
Jakus et al. (2000) (Travel cost model, Tennessee)	$1.82 seasonal WTP to obtain 'full pool' at Tennessee Reservoirs

Note: *All dollar estimates in study year dollars.

Sources: Various studies cited, and appendix to the Walker River Draft EIS, by Shaw (2002).

Similarly, as seen in the Walker Lake case study below, a minimum volume of a lake might support a fishery, while even one less acre foot than this minimum may not. Unfortunately, few studies actually provide this kind of information.

Table 8.2 reports estimates of the value of water put to in situ, and most often specific recreational uses. As seen there, these values are converted as best as possible to similar compatible units, but still vary. The two main ways to report such values are in annual maximum willingness to pay or in dollars per acre foot. The WTP is an estimated consumer's surplus (see Chapter 2), typically based on application of the contingent valuation method. The estimates in dollar per acre foot terms presumably imply the maximum willingness to pay rather than do without that acre foot of water. These units are a standard way of expressing the value of the acre foot quantity of water, but how the authors arrived at this per unit value is not always clear.

Caution should be used when examining the estimates in Table 8.2. For example, instream flow may be valued because of the fact that it protects a species. Is a reported value for maintaining flow, as in the studies by Bob Berrens and his colleagues (1996), then really a value for protecting a species of fish? The question is hard to answer, but the answer might be found using statistical analyses that pin the source of value down to characteristics that are associated with the program to maintain flow.

Similarly, why do the values per acre foot vary all the way from the low tens of dollars to hundreds of dollars in Table 8.2? It is known that some types of recreation are more highly valued than others, and there may be reasons why one regional population has higher values for water related to recreation than others, but these reasons alone do not explain the large variation. I do know that in some cases a consumer's surplus estimate that was for a season or year was artificially converted to a per unit (acre foot) estimate and this may be one cause of discrepancy. A legitimate calculation may be as follows:

$$\frac{CS}{af} = \frac{CS}{day} \times \frac{\Delta day}{af} \tag{8.4}$$

The idea is to take an estimate of the CS per day and convert it to CS per acre foot using an estimate of how many more/fewer days will be spent recreating per acre foot of water. However, some reported CS per acre foot values may not be calculated this way.

Eiswerth et al. (2000) obtain a mixture of various types of specific consumer's surplus (CS) estimates. Some CS estimates are elicited in a survey where the individual was asked how many more or fewer trips would be taken under changed water level conditions (the contingent behavior approach).

Combining the information from the CBM, the authors can get an average CS per acre foot. In that same study, though, the authors obtained estimates of total consumer's surplus for the season or year to prevent elimination/loss of the lake. This total CS was converted to a per-unit measure for comparability to other study values in the same terms. To convert the latter to CS per acre foot requires many more assumptions.

Is there any way to reach a consensus regarding the value of instream flow? In one of the few studies I know of that tries to assess the national benefits of enhanced in-stream flow on recreational fishing, Hansen and Hallam (1991) link a hydrologic model to a fishing demand or supply model. Their idea was to consider the effect of increased flow in a river on a downstream fishery. They consider the household production framework, wherein an angler 'produces' a day of fishing using various inputs, including flow in a river. Across all the regions they examined in the United States, the change in fishing days for a one acre foot change in stream flow is in the range of 0.03 days to about 0.7 days; in 81 of the 99 regions studied, the estimated response is less than one day per acre foot increase in flow. Some of the modeling they do is not clear, and these estimates of the marginal effect of flow on the 'production' of a fishing day sound small, but in fact it is significant that the numbers are as large as they are, because, as they say, a change in flow of one acre foot might not be noticeable at all on some rivers.

Hansen and Hallam's table (1991, table 2, p. 172) reports 'marginal values per acre-foot, in 1980 dollars' that range from $0.26 (trout), to values in the tens of dollars ($11.90 for trout, $17.91 for bass), to hundreds of dollars ($140.97 trout, $105.70 bass), all the way up to $288.08 (trout) and $302.01 (bass). The huge divergence in values per acre foot is perhaps because of numbers generated for different 'aggregated subareas' (based on the US Water Resources Council designations), and the fact that several ASAs connect to other ASAs via cross-region flow effects. For example, the $288 trout value seems to come from ASA 1603, which surprisingly (from their map) looks as though it is in Northern Nevada. And they state that the change of one acre foot in ASA 1010 (whish appears to be in Iowa) changes the total days fished not only in that ASA, but in several others, though the impact is small. The authors conclude that their marginal values of water for recreational bass fishing exceed water's net marginal value in irrigation in 51 of the 67 ASAs where irrigation takes place.

Hansen and Hallam appear to cull estimates of the value of an acre foot of water in fishing from studies by Michael Hay (Hay, 1988; Brown and Hay, 1987). The details they provide do not make it possible to know how they converted Hay's values, which I am sure are originally in terms of values per day of fishing, to their per acre foot fishing values. It may be that they take the value of a fishing day in each ASA from Hay's reports, and then multiply this value per fishing 'day' times the marginal change of a day attributable to a unit (acre foot) change in flow, yielding the marginal fishing value per acre foot, which is much like the process in equation (8.4) above. Next I turn to some case studies.

8.3 CASE STUDIES

8.3.1 Instream Flows: The Columbia River and Endangered Species

In the United States one of the most controversial environmental laws is the Endangered Species Act. It allows species to be listed as threatened or endangered and, once this is done, for habitat to be protected to enhance the chance of the species' survival. As I write this there are several calls for a review of the status of listed species of fish in the Columbia River Basin, and growing, vocal opposition to the Endangered Species Act. The opposition is from a fairly small, but powerful minority in the United States, the agricultural producers (ranchers and farmers) and other irrigators. This small group of individuals has political clout and they are angry about their economic losses when water is maintained at certain levels that protect species, but prevent them from obtaining their water. There is therefore a possible conflict between long-run management of the species, and existing claims and needs for immediate withdrawals. Below I report on a fairly recent legal case involving these issues.

In the Fall of 2002 I was engaged to assist the Department of Ecology in the State of Washington (hereafter WADOE) in their efforts to defend themselves against a law suit by the Columbia/Snake River Irrigators Association.[5] The suit involved various claims for withdrawals, totaling somewhere between about 300 cfs and 1000 cfs, with point of withdrawal in the Tri-Cities area (Kennewick, Pasco, Richland) of Washington. The prosecuting team, representing irrigators and some municipal interests, maintained that such withdrawals, as compared to annual average flows in the range of 200 million acre feet per year, would go unnoticed in any hydrologic sense. Further, they claimed that to deny such claims would result in a loss of economic benefits, as the parties petitioning for new water would lose their opportunity to put the water to beneficial use. They argued that the value of water per unit (say, an acre foot) was clearly higher than the value of water put to another use, for example, for non-consumptive or instream purposes.

The plaintiffs fairly easily argued that if water were put to beneficial use then being denied this opportunity for use resulted in forgone economic benefits. However, issues in the case are not nearly as simple as they might first seem. The state (the defendant) had concerns that were they to grant new permits, they would be liable in another law suit against them for violating the spirit of the Endangered Species Act, probably brought by environmental interests, or even the federal government.

The Snake River (a tributary of the Columbia River) sockeye salmon (*Oncorhynchus nerka*), was listed as endangered in 1991 under the Endangered Species Act, and other species listed as threatened or endangered in the Columbia River System are the chinook salmon (*Oncorhynchus tshawytscha*), chum salmon (*Oncorhynchus keta*), and steelhead (*Oncorhynchus mykiss*)]. These species are an anadromous species, living in freshwater and saltwater. After birth in freshwater reaches the juveniles attempt to migrate out to the ocean, and then migrate upstream again as adults, in order to spawn. Annual production of adult salmonids within the US portion of the Columbia River Basin (south of the Canadian border) is estimated to have dropped 75 to 85 percent in the past 150 years or so (see Northwest Power Planning Council, 1987).

The exact causes of the decline are controversial, but include the simple fact that many dams make passage for the fish quite difficult. Concerns about this issue led to the passage of the Northwest Power Planning Act's Fish and Wildlife Program, designed to reduce salmon mortality. As part of this program salmon that cannot pass dams during their migration are put on barges and taken around impassable sections.

Flow conditions were also suspected of causing the decline. The National Marine Fisheries Service (NMFS) found that adequate instream flows were critical to the successful downstream migration of juvenile salmonids and NMFS (Olsen, 2002) identified Columbia River flow objectives as part of a salmon recovery program: in Spring, 135 kcfs (thousand cubic feet per second) at Priest Rapids Dam and 220–60 kcfs at McNary Dam; in Summer, the flow targets by location are 200 kcfs at McNary Dam (WADOE, 2002). Revisions in 1997 to the state of Washington's Administrative Code (WAC 173–563) required WADOE to consult with appropriate agencies including the Washington Department of Fish and Wildlife (WDFD) when reviewing water right applications.

Around 1980 both state and federal agencies had tried to establish the best available estimates of minimum stream flow levels (referred to as the NMFS BIOP flows).[6] The levels, as compared to existing annual average flows, are difficult to obtain via water resource management schemes, and are essentially impossible to obtain in low water years. However, the problem was that if these minimum flow levels pertained, then the appropriate policy to pursue for any agency granting new water allocation permits would be to deny all new claims. It was to this perceived policy that the plaintiffs filed their suit.

The prosecution maintained that the listings for species were unnecessary and that there was no scientific basis for flow augmentation programs because the best available biology and hydrology indicates no relationship between flow and species survival. My interpretation was that the physical science was such that it was not possible to ascertain with certainty whether there is a quantifiable relationship between flows and species survival. Based on that, any economic analysis should incorporate uncertainty analysis. In a world free from legal restrictions, the option value or option price for instream flows should be estimated and compared to the values for water in other uses. Recall from Chapter 6 that the option price (OP) is the appropriate value measure under uncertainty.

Because there is no estimate of the option price for salmon protection in the economics literature I concluded that the state had too little information to make a sound economic decision, presuming they had the legal obligation to make one at all. I testified to this sentiment during a trial.

After two and one-half days of trial, the judge wisely asked the parties to attempt to settle the case. The parties did in fact settle. The settlement terms are in two parts. First, Ecology agreed to grant permits to the seven applicants at issue in one of two ways. The permits will be conditioned either on the NMFS BIOP flows or on an obligation to pay $10 per acre foot of water used each year. Ecology would then use the payments to mitigate the water use. Ecology believes the amount of money they get will be more than sufficient to mitigate for these water uses, thereby essentially producing a 'no net loss' scenario.

The other part of the settlement is focusing more on the long term. In that part Ecology agrees to make some rule proposals that would allow approximately 300 water rights that are currently subject to interruption during low flow times the ability to take other actions (either mitigation or long-term payment of money) to eliminate the interruptability of their rights. Ecology agreed only to propose this concept in rule, not to adopt it. The rulemaking process could result in Ecology adopting some other approach. Finally, in exchange for these actions, the plaintiffs dismissed their case.

This case highlights the failure of existing laws in incorporating instream flow values. Recall from Chapter 1 that the Doctrine of Prior Appropriation has rules largely inconsistent with achieving an economically efficient allocation of water. Consider the likely implications if existing appropriators in Washington are given rights that are senior to instream flow rights, or vice versa.[7] If appropriators are given the senior right, during any time that flows are low, as in a drought situation, the instream flow rights will be secondary to the appropriated ones, and minimum conditions for survival may not be met, exacerbating the situation for the fish. While the science is inconclusive, very low flows at least appear to contribute to mortality for the juvenile fish, so during extreme conditions there could be a serious problem. Granting existing appropriators the senior right will ignore the possibility that protecting fish from possible extinction may have a higher value than the value of the water going to existing appropriators.

In contrast, assume that new small claims are junior to instream flow rights. It would then be up to the agency preserving the instream flow rights to determine if and when new claimants would be allowed to obtain water on the river. Such a determination would be quite difficult because the protection of the species is a long-run dynamic problem. Considered in the absence of laws, the correct economic modeling would lead to the optimal harvest of salmon, if any positive nonzero harvest can be supported. A bio-economist should define the harvest path between now and the harvest point which corresponds to some optimal stock of salmon.[8]

8.3.2 Study of Walker Lake

This next case study concerns Nevada's Walker Lake, which is threatened with drying up, or at least becoming unusable for many recreational purposes, and again pits agricultural against recreational and ecological interests. Nevada is the driest state in the United States and much of the state is in the geologic formation known as the Great Basin. The Great Basin is unusual in that water within the basin stays there – unlike most western rivers, the rivers do not flow to the Pacific Ocean. What is not unusual is that even in this most arid of all states, one can observe irrigated agriculture.

The Walker River of Nevada terminates at Walker Lake in the desert near the town of Hawthorne. Its headwaters are in two forks (West and East) in California. The Walker River Basin is diverse in several aspects, with precipitation in its 4050 square miles ranging from 6 inches to 40 inches per year. Upstream, near the headwaters, there is a blue-ribbon (excellent) trout fishery, and slightly further downstream irrigators grow some highly valued crops such as onions and garlic. Still further downstream, irrigators grow the predominant crop in Nevada, alfalfa or hay. Gross income to farmers in 1992 for the areas of Antelope, Smith, Mason, Brideport, Schurz, and Hawthorne was estimated to be about $187 million.

Walker Lake has provided habitat for migrating birds (loons), and the several sport fish, including the Lahonton cutthroat trout (LCT), which is also listed by the US Fish and Wildlife Service as a threatened species. Since the late 1800s there has been a severe decline in the lake's volume and level. Estimates are that the lake has declined by about 140 feet and current volume is around 2 million acre feet. Headwater discharge is about 305 000 acre feet per year (acre feet per year – af/yr), and consumptive use is over

200000 af/yr. Walker Lake has a total dissolved solids (TDS) problem. TDS are basically salts. A 'normal' body of water might have a TDS level less than 1000 mg/L. TDS in Walker Lake has increased in connection with diminished volume, increasing the likelihood that several species of fish will be unable to survive. Estimates are that TDS is increasing by about 170 mg/L per year at Walker Lake, and has gone from 2500 mg/L in 1882 to about 13 000 mg/L in 1994. Agricultural withdrawals are generally blamed for the decrease in water levels. However, if all TDS loads from agriculture were eliminated, the lake might still exhibit increasing TDS levels because of its natural hydrologic balance (Humberstone, 1999).

Some formal physical science on the relationship between the LCT and TDS in the lake has been conducted. Dickerson and Vinyard (1999) determined that exposing trout to water with a TDS concentration of 16 000 mg/L results in a 100 percent mortality rate within 48 hours. The long-term TDS level must, however, be lower than 16 000 mg/L to create a buffer, and the US Department of Interior (DOI) has selected 10 000 mg/L for purposes of planning for sustainability.

These TDS concentrations are important, as are upstream impacts, but cannot be used in formal biological or economic models at this time. Instead, a rough correlation between the necessary volume of water at Walker Lake and the key TDS level is used below. To maintain the TDS levels at the 1994 concentrations of about 13 000 mg/L would require adding 33 000 more acre feet annually to Walker Lake than the current estimate of long-run average inflow allows. However, to support the LCT fishery it has been suggested that the volume of Walker Lake increase by about 700 000 acre feet, or that the lake's level rise by about 20 feet.

In an effort to save Walker Lake researchers and policy makers began to explore the possibility of transferring water from upper reaches downstream, even considering developing what would be Nevada's first water bank to support and facilitate this effort. Many of the public gave the agencies a small chance of succeeding (Wilson, 2001). Before the workings of a water bank could be developed, researchers analysed the potential 'market', or demand and supply for this water. The key players constituting the demand and supply sides are the states of California and Nevada, several US federal agencies, agriculture (the local irrigation districts), county and local governments, environmentalists and recreational users, and the Washoe Native American Indian tribe.

The Walker River Basin is in a very rural area. It is some 90 miles to the closest city with a population greater than about 50 000 to 100 000 people (Carson City or Reno, Nevada). There is no hydropower production and there are no large cities that would want the water at this time. Therefore, the demand side of the market accompanying a water bank in this region would have to be the anglers or environmental interests wanting to save the lake. The supply side would be the upstream irrigators.

To see if a market for transactions could function, one desires information on the value of water to local irrigators (literally, the clearing price) and the value of water from the viewpoint of environmental and downstream recreation interests. The idea is to see if the WTP on the demand side is near the market supply price. At the start of the project in 1995 researchers found that few studies in the literature existed on the value that recreational users would have for lake levels or river flow.[9] Ward (1989) found values for water of up to $133 per acre foot, Ward et al. (1997) found values at New Mexico reservoirs to be in the range of $1 to $11 per acre foot; and Creel and Loomis (1992) found values between $300 and $350 per acre foot for the San Joaquin Valley. Other than these studies, there was little economic analysis of in situ water quantities at all, though the aesthetic importance of river flow had been considered by Brown and Daniel (1991).[10] The paucity of existing literature led to several primary valuation studies.

To begin, in 1996 and 1997 a survey team went to several regional waters including Walker Lake to intercept recreational users and give them a short survey questionnaire. A numerical scale was used to let respondents indicate the importance of water levels to them. A survey question asked respondents to circle the number below that best reflected the importance of water levels to their experiences:

Not at all important   1   2   3   4   5   Very important

Few existing studies had ever even considered whether and how water levels might matter to recreational users of waters, so the researchers did not really have a feel for how respondents would answer, on average.

Responding to this survey question, 35 percent of the sample said that water levels were 'very important', which corresponds to scale 5 in choosing a water at which to recreate, and similarly 22 percent said it was 'quite important', or scale level 4. Over 80 percent of the sample rated the water level as level 3 or higher.

Using this and other data on recreational visits to waters as recreation demand, two versions of the travel cost model were developed. In addition to obtaining basic data on recreational trips, the survey incorporated contingent behavior scenarios. In these the respondents were asked how many more or fewer trips they would take to Walker Lake if conditions were either better (higher levels) or worse (lower lake levels). The first travel cost model did not use the contingent behavior scenarios, but revealed that a sample of recreational users of Walker Lake might be willing to pay $2 per choice occasion (a trip) to prevent the lake's decline from a maximum pool level, to a level about 4.5 feet lower. Similarly, members of the sample were willing to pay about $11 per trip to prevent the lake from being lost altogether (see Fadali and Shaw, 1998).

In the second version of the travel cost model the researchers used the CBM to assess the value of a 20 foot increase in Walker Lake's level (see Eiswerth et al., 2000). Estimates for the 20 foot rise range from about $240 to $360 per year, per recreational user, depending on the specific scenario evaluated. Combining the two approaches, the authors conclude that a total aggregate value of about $4 million for recreation water at Walker Lake (Fadali and Shaw, 1998) holds. Next, the values which irrigators had for the water had to be explored.

Would the regions' 221 farms and ranches be potential sellers? That depended on their supply price. Water in a water bank is typically rented during a season, but it could also be permanently sold. For compatibility of the prices or values, the market values for water need to be in terms of the WTP per acre foot. Farmers do not think in terms of WTP per year. Agricultural producers in the region mainly produce hay or alfalfa, but about seven farms in an area near the Walker River also produce higher valued crops of onion and garlic (MacDiarmid et al., 2000). Typical crop rotation for alfalfa has land taken out of production for two years, following two or three years of production. An estimated 10 725 acres are taken out of production in the Basin each year. Determining the value of an acre foot to upstream Walker River irrigators would require that one of several agricultural valuation methods be applied, as explained in Chapter 5. None had been applied at the time of the study, but preliminary approximation methods yield an irrigation value for water of about $12 to $45 per acre foot (see MacDiarmid et al., 2000).[11]

Based on comparing the aggregate estimates for the supply and demand sides, Fadali and Shaw (1998) concluded that a water bank had the potential to succeed in establishing and promoting a market that could then be used to save the lake. This was confirmed by Eiswerth et al. (2000). The agricultural side of the equation is still not fully calculated or understood, so the conclusion is subject to this caveat.

At the time of writing, the US Federal agencies involved in the conflict (the US Bureau of Reclamation, the US Fish and Wildlife Service, and the Bureau of Land Management) made the decision that, if possible, they would save Walker Lake. A draft environmental impact statement (EIS) is being prepared to consider which of the alternatives of purchasing agricultural water or using technological water-saving methods is the best strategy for saving the Lake. The options to be analysed include (i) do nothing; (ii) technological solutions such as cloud seeding; (iii) purchases from agricultural producers and farm retirement; and (iv) some combination of

(ii) and (iii). Under the do nothing or 'No Action' alternative, Walker Lake will dry up, but the timing depends on random weather patterns. The project boiled down to the feasible alternatives or 'Action Alternatives' resulting in 50 000 more acre feet of water per year getting to Walker Lake, with an option also of purchasing 50 000 af of additional water for use in settling disputes.

I helped on a small part of the EIS, assessing only the non-market values involved in potential transactions and flow changes. I determined that there were three important aspects of any program to try to save Walker Lake: the social losses if Walker Lake is not saved; upstream and downstream gains from in situ use if less water is diverted upstream for eventual distribution to Walker Lake; and the potential social loss of lost agricultural land from reduced withdrawals.

The last aspect is relatively new, but the idea is that society benefits from having agricultural land in existence. If agricultural land is converted to housing developments, non-farmers may experience a loss. This value is not the lost producer's surplus from a reduction in agricultural output. Some economists have already considered the value of agricultural land to the public, who enjoy seeing it as open space, especially when irrigated (for example, Rosenberger and Walsh, 1997).

Hydrologists at the Desert Research Institute in Nevada estimated the impact of changes in various hydrological alternatives, including diversions that would correspond to water rights purchases in the Antelope, Upper and Lower Eastern parts of the Walker River Basin, and in the East and West Mason Valleys. There were eight possible hydrologic scenarios to be considered, including the 'do nothing' alternative. Some alternatives had no impact on wildlife and fish habitat, and others did.

The economic analysis had to consider the impacts of these potential physical changes. With a quick analysis that does not involve primary economic research, one must conduct a benefits transfer exercise. The key is to determine baseline activity levels and values, then determine potential changes in these for the alternatives being considered. For example, for recreation analysis one must start with the activity levels under current conditions, that is, baseline recreational trips to Walker Lake and River. The river trips were difficult to assess, but some information on Walker Lake trips could be obtained from the Nevada Division of State Parks and more was obtained in the surveys done by Fadali and Shaw, and Eiswerth et al. Trip data are reported in Table 8.3. However, these estimates include only those visits recorded at the state park facilities at the lake.

It is interesting to note the low visit rates in the years 1991 to 1994. One must be cautious in reading too much into the numbers, but these were years of drought, which could be a possible contributing factor to the

Table 8.3 Baseline Lake Walker trips

Year	Annual visit
1982	46 777
1983	53 270
1984	63 887
1985	71 222
1986	57 483
1987	80 552
1988	66 944
1989	64 783
1990	52 848
1991	37 709
1992	37 475
1993	51 025
1994	31 053

Source: Nevada Division of State Parks.

reduced number of visits. For the EIS one has to predict the number of new visits that would occur with increased lake levels, which is more difficult than looking at simple past estimates of visits.

Using some back of the envelope estimates and common sense analysis, my conclusions are as follows:

1. With the No Action Alternative there will be substantial social, non-market, economic losses associated with the loss of the Walker Lake freshwater ecosystem and fishery. Using Benefits Transfer (secondary methods) I estimated that almost $20 million per year would be lost if Walker Lake is allowed to dry up.
2. With the Action Alternatives there will be some non-market economic gains at Walker Lake, but possibly diminished public values for impacted agricultural lands.
3. The Action Alternatives all provide for increased river flow, and thus, upriver stream flow is enhanced as compared to the No Action Alternative, resulting in an additional non-market benefit to users of in-stream flows. These make some of the Action Alternatives more socially beneficial, but are difficult to quantify at this time.
4. All of the Action Alternatives result in a loss of agricultural land. There is potential public, social value for open space, and agricultural land, suggesting that these Action Alternatives result in losses related to public values for agricultural land. However, the most likely future

outcome for this land is either that it remains open, but 'brown', or that it gets developed. Either outcome suggests that public values to obtain this state would be low.[12]

At the time I write this the Walker Lake draft EIS is under review for comments and is being revised. The issues are contentious and emotions run high. Farmers and residents of rural areas see efforts to 'take' farmer's water ending their way of life, whether it be farming alfalfa or grazing cattle on a ranch (see DeLong, 2000). Attorneys for the parties opposing redistribution of water to Walker Lake are busily working to discredit the EIS, a standard tactic to use in such situations. However, it remains to be seen how many agricultural water rights holders will voluntarily step forward and sell some of their water if the Federal agencies act as buyers on behalf of that portion of society that values saving Walker Lake.

8.3.3 Case Study on the Truckee-Carson River[13]

The Truckee River is small, but infamous in that it has been the subject of one of the most litigated river disputes in US history (Egan, 1997). There have been legal challenges for almost 100 years (Branson, 1997a) and this dispute is an example of the newfound power that Native American Indian tribes have in such situations. The US government brought suit against parties in the Orr Ditch Decree in 1973 (see *Nevada* v. *US* 463 US 110, 113, 1983). In 1981 the Paiute Indian Tribe brought suit against California water purveyors. All of this litigation culminated in the Truckee-Carson-Pyramid Lake Water Settlement Act, Title II of PL 101–618 (NRC, 1992) and the Truckee River Operating Agreement (TROA – see Branson, 1997a and 1997b).

Lake Tahoe is the eleventh deepest lake in the world, and is internationally known for its beauty and clarity. With a total capacity of about 122 million acre feet, it is the source of the Truckee River, which winds its way out of California and into Nevada, ending at Pyramid Lake after a 105 mile journey. About 500 000 acre feet of water flow through the system each year, but flow has varied in the river from 1.8 million af (1983) to a low of about 0.13 af in 1931. Lake Tahoe is regulated to have a maximum fluctuation of about 6 feet, so its usable storage capacity is much less than its total, at about 744 000 acre feet.

The lower Truckee-Carson basin is arid, receiving about 9 inches of precipitation per year. The Truckee River, like all others in Nevada, is fully adjudicated. The river must serve the needs of an Indian tribe at the terminus point, the fast-growing metropolitan area around Reno known as the Truckee Meadows, the Newlands agricultural project, and the needs in the Lahontan Valley wetlands. Groundwater in the Truckee meadows is estimated to provide about 20 percent of urban supply. Amazingly, though this region is sparsely populated and has little industry to speak of, the conflicts between these sources of demand have been profound. They are emblematic of the conflicts over water that exist today.

In 1888 Senator Francis G. Newlands of Nevada, then a private citizen, privately financed the Truckee-Carson projection, which failed. When he became a senator, he drafted the Reclamation Act of 1902, and the Newlands Project was one of the first projects authorized after its passage. In 1905 the Derby Dam was constructed on the Truckee River near the town of Fernley, and the Truckee Canal diverted more than one-half of the flow into the Carson River Basin. The original goal of the project was for 300 000 acres of farmland to be created.

The Truckee-Carson Irrigation District (TCID) became the Bureau of Reclamation's contract operator for the Newlands Project. As of 1985 it was estimated that only about 63 100 acres of agricultural land were irrigated under this project, mostly alfalfa grown by about 4000 farmers. The cost of delivered water today is about $34 per acre. This is a far cry from the originally planned acreage (Egan, 1997). Today some of the alfalfa grown in the region is actually exported to countries in Asia. A little under half of the farms in the area are small, with fewer than 50 acres. But these farmers hold fairly senior water rights, with most of them having been established in the early 1900s. About $66 per ton is the break-even price of alfalfa for a farmer with a larger farm, or one with over 300 acres of land. In 2001 the market price per ton was about $95, so farmers with these larger farms were perhaps earning a reasonable profit. However, if alfalfa is the farmer's sole source of income, then a farmer might be tempted to sell some water to a willing purchaser, should one be found.

It is estimated that the Newlands Project diversions caused an 80 foot drop in Pyramid Lake, the terminus point of the Truckee River. Before the project, an average of about 600 000 acre feet flowed into Pyramid Lake each year. Inflows were reduced by about one-half after the project (NRC, 1992). At Pyramid Lake, the cui-ui, a large sucker fish, was found to be an endangered species. Also there were huge American cutthroat trout, with some weighing in at 42 pounds (Egan, 1997), and these are now threatened. Because of their status, the trout and the cui-ui's viability fall under the jurisdiction of the federal government. Diversions also resulted in the loss of Winnemucca Lake.

Truckee River rights
The highest priority rights in the Truckee River system now in fact belong to the tribe at Pyramid Lake, who hold the cui-ui to be a sacred species.

Migration that promoted spawning of the species was blocked by a delta formed by the reduced flow into the lake. The tribe's rights were granted in 1859, upon creation of the reservation there, and so they claimed that flow had to be increased to protect their tribal rights. Eventually they used the Endangered Species Act to change allocation of water on the Truckee River.

The states of Nevada and California also have rights. Truckee River water use is controlled by the Orr Ditch decree (*US* v. *Orr Water Ditch Company*, 1944). It is the federal water master's job to maintain a minimum flow at the California–Nevada border as part of this decree. However, it was felt that the Orr Ditch decree conflicted with the Alpine decree (1980) for Carson River allocation, and that the decree favored the Newlands Project over the rights of the Pyramid Lake Tribe.

The Pyramid Paiute Tribe began their challenge to the Orr decree in the 1960s, mainly objecting to the lack of their ability to provide water tied to subsistence fishing and cultural needs. The US Department of Interior was ordered to modify operations of the Newlands Project (*Pyramid Lake Paiute Tribe of Indians* v. *Morton*, 1973), but reductions in diversions accompanying this modification did not drastically improve the situation at Pyramid Lake.

The cities of Reno and Sparks and the water company that provides service for the municipalities' roughly 200 000 people also have rights. This metropolitan area (known as the Truckee Meadows) has been growing quickly. Prior to the settlement, satisfying the demands of water customers was a concern. In October of 1996 the cities and county agreed to purchase water rights from agricultural users on the Truckee with about $24 million. In the late 1990s water rights could be purchased by developers for about $2000 per acre foot, and that price seems to hold today.

Several years ago, the Sierra Pacific Power Company, based in Reno, Nevada, also had rights, related to the production of hydropower. Sierra Pacific, now operating under management of the Nevada Power Company after a recent merger, also had storage rights in upstream reservoirs built in the 1960s. In the past two years the power company sold off its water division, so now the Truckee Meadows water is provided and managed by a county government agency, the Truckee Meadows Water Authority.

The next player, the Stillwater Wildlife Management Area, is part of the basin and comprises a waterfowl sanctuary of over 24 000 acres. It is the largest primary wetlands area within the Lahontan Valley and it supports numerous species of birds during their migrations north and south. By the 1970s, inflows into the area were diminished and became polluted, and the marshes were reduced to between 4000 and 6000 acres (NRC, 1992). Because the US Bureau of Reclamation's policies to promote irrigation nearby were having an adverse effect on this area, two federal government agencies were pitted against one another, and people began to worry that the area would become devastated, much like the Kesterson Wildlife Refuge in California (see Harris, 1991). Section 206 of TROA allows US Fish and Wildlife to transfer the 'consumptive portion' of water purchased (about 22 000 acre feet) to protect these wetlands. The consumptive portion is estimated to be about 2.99 of 3.5 af of water applied to each acre of land.

Under PL 101-618 the Pyramid Tribe, the DOI, the state of Nevada and the city of Reno-Sparks reached an agreement (Section 205, Title II under PL 101-618 is the TROA) involving complicated arrangements. Legislation was passed on November 16, 1990. Key flow features of the agreement are summarized in Table 8.4.

Signatories to TROA include the DOI, Sierra Pacific Power, the states of Nevada and California, and the Pyramid Lake Paiute Tribe. The major shift is that while agriculture originally received over half of the water in the Truckee, it now receives about one-fifth. One particular arrangement lets upstream reservoirs be used to maintain spawning flows. Another is that the Paiute Tribe agreed to drop its law suit against the city of Reno, challenging

Table 8.4 Key environmental and hydrologic features of the Truckee River operating agreement

---

Goals and Institutional Changes

Conserve the endangered and threatened fishes at Pyramid Lake: the cui-ui and the Lahontan cutthroat trout

Achieve wetlands protection (section 206)

Initiate water rights purchase program from willing sellers (Alpine Decree dictates that only the consumptive portion of the water right may be transferred)

Change Nevada state water law regarding the use of water meters

Legislate approval of an inverted Block-Rate Water Rate Structure

Flow Changes

Lake Tahoe releases: must meet minimum flow of 75 cfs 72 percent of the time

Donner Lake releases: must meet minimum flow of 8 cfs 85 percent of the time

Stampede Reservoir releases: must meet minimum flow of 45 cfs 84 percent of the time. Sierra Pacific Power company to pay $225 000 to store 5000 cubic acre feet of water here

Truckee River at Floriston: must meet flow rates of 500 cfs from April through September, and 400 cfs from October through March

---

Source: Lecture by Tom Crawford, US Department of Interior, Director of the Truckee-River Operating Agreement, Environmental Impact Analysis, Carson City, Nevada.

expansion of its sewage treatment plant. During the interim period Sierra Pacific Power Company was paying $ 225 000 to store 5000 cubic feet of water upstream in California reservoirs just below Lake Tahoe. In order to secure this right SPPC gave up its top priority right for 40 cfs in the river, for a small hydroelectric power facility. As another part of the agreement, SPPC agreed to let excess municipal water be released rather than stored: in wet years downstream parties can get a windfall, for which SPPC gets a credit that can be used to enhance the fishery (Branson, 1997b). Finally, at the end of this settlement process the Pyramid Tribe received about $40 million in direct benefits, but under its provisions, cannot touch the principal amount.

The politics of the TROA and related settlement negotiations are described by O'Leary (1994), who suggests that the old operating agreement was confusing, out of date, and violated the rights of some downstream parties. Under the old agreement, the federal water master was required to maintain flows between California and Nevada. The river must meet the Floriston rates of 500 cfs from April through September, and 400 cfs in other months.[14] In the event that these rates cannot be met, the Federal water master can cease releases to the lowest priority users on the river. Under the new TROA, the rates will hold, but downstream flows can be reduced if an equal amount is going into upstream storage.

From 1990 to 2000 the average price of water rights purchased was about $394 per acre foot, with a range of $255 to $520 per acre foot. Of great interest would be what effect the purchases of agricultural water rights by the US Fish and Wildlife service have had on efficiency in the basin. It may be too early to tell. To my knowledge the only ex post investigation of some of the features of this dispute are in Colby et al. (1991). Colby et al. note that transactions costs were large in settling the Truckee River disputes and led to extensive, long, and drawn-out litigation. Property rights had to be defined, and information made available; buyers and sellers have to find each other. The county and cities in the late 1990s in fact hired a firm to search for water rights. Eventually, the Nevada state legislature had to make about $9 million available in 1989 to settle water rights disputes in the Truckee Basin. (See Nevada SB 189 (1989): Nev. Rev. Stat § 538.600 (1987).)

8.3.4 Total Water Values: Case Study of Mine Dewatering

This section describes a case study on another arid river basin. The Humboldt River Basin (HRB), located in northern Nevada, is the home of some of the largest gold mines in North America. While some deep underground mines are still in operation throughout the world, a standard gold mining practice today involves extraction of microscopic particles of gold from enormous quantities of rock. The rock is dug from huge open pits. A chemical process known as heap leaching was developed in recent years and it uses a cyanide solution to dissolve out the gold from the rock or ore. Large trucks continuously drive to the bottom of huge pits and load up the rock that will be processed, then drive back to the top of the pit.

Nevada produces enough gold to make it among the top three or four gold producers in the world. Though gold prices fell afterward, revenue from gold mining in Nevada in 1998 was $2.6 billion (see Carlton, 2000), up from $200 million in 1980. This case study focuses on one small aspect of gold mining, known as dewatering. Dewatering refers to the process of removing groundwater from around the pits. If this were not done, groundwater would seep into the pit, making passage of the trucks carrying the ore impossible. When mining stops, the mines will turn off the huge pumps, and it is expected that the pits will eventually fill with water, reducing surface flows in the river to levels *below* the pre-mining historical levels. Dewatering areas around the huge pits have caused considerable controversy in Nevada (Carlton, 2000).

Open pit mine in Northern Nevada

Pitted against the mines in their concerns relating to water resources are the agricultural and environmental interests and recreational users. Agriculture is the fourth biggest industry in Nevada, well behind gaming, manufacturing, and mining, but a small group of ranchers has some political clout. Three separate studies were pursued in the dewatering valuation exercise considered, and these are reviewed below. In the final subsection of this section an attempt is made to synthesize and possibly integrate the values from each separate approach.

Applying the usual theoretical framework to the gold mining context, consumers derive consumer's surplus from consumption of gold and producers derive producer's surplus from the profits generated by supplying gold. But non-market environmental goods and resources are also involved in the gold mining operation. There may be lost consumer's surplus associated with terrestrial, aquatic, groundwater, surface water, and wildlife impacts associated with mining. There are also producers of agricultural goods in the HRB who may gain or lose producer's surplus from the use of surface water for irrigation purposes. This use is connected to dewatering activities, especially when the pumped groundwater is deposited in the Humboldt River. A farmer downstream from the mines may benefit from enhanced downstream flows, leading to an increase in profits. On the opposite side of the ledger, if dewatering decreases the services from aquifers in areas near the gold mines, then these lost services may adversely affect either agricultural users or consumers who use groundwater for drinking water or other purposes.

In 1997 several research economists received a small portion of a grant from the Watersheds Grants program of the US Environmental Protection Agency and the National Science Foundation to analyse some of the ecosystem impacts from gold mining. Because of the scope of the project and the availability of information at that time, the focus of the economists was only on downstream dewatering impacts.

Valuation approaches taken
The researchers initially had to decide whether to pursue a 'top-down' ecosystem valuation strategy or a 'bottom-up' partial analysis. The latter strategy was chosen after conducting focus groups in the HRB as well as a pre-test mail survey contingent valuation study (Netusil et al., 1998). Pre-test mail survey results made it clear that it would be impossible to do a complex contingent valuation study of all possible gold mining impacts, or even a rigorous analysis of mine dewatering impacts using a mail survey (see Netusil et al., 1998). Recreational use of water resources was initially thought to be important, but turned out to be less important than either agricultural impacts or total impacts from dewatering. A decision was made to do (i) a travel cost analysis using existing county-level data to assess recreational impacts (Huszar et al., 1999); (ii) a programming analysis to try to obtain the shadow values of water in agricultural production (see Chapter 5 and Lambert and Shaw); and (iii) a telephone contingent valuation survey (see Huszar et al., 2001). Each of these is summarized below.

Travel cost analysis The travel cost analysis focused on use of a small reservoir on the Humboldt River, Rye Patch Reservoir, which has a total storage capacity of 220 886 000 cubic meters. State data indicated about 70 000 visits per year occur at Rye Patch, which demonstrates a potentially small total use value. However, this reservoir has been the source of contention because agricultural users drained the reservoir in 1992, killing thousands of fish. The event caused some to state that Nevada had failed the public trust doctrine, which has its US origins in the case of *Illinois Central Railroad* v. *State of Illinois* [146 US 387 (1892)].[15] One of the biggest legal decisions supporting this doctrine is the Mono Lake case (*National Audubon Society* v. *Superior Court of Alpine County* (89 Cal. Rptr. 346 (1983))).

With this idea in mind, Huszar et al. (1999) examined the damages corresponding to the draining in 1992, and also estimated the gain in total consumer's surplus that would be likely from dewatering, as downstream flows are stabilized. This is a positive externality to recreational users. A county-level aggregate count data model was used and produced estimates of the order of $100 000 per year for stable flows consistent with dewatering. Once dewatering stops, which would happen as the mines close and shut off the pumps, this consumer's surplus would be lost to downstream users. It is expected that mines will close around the year 2020, but future use was not projected, which could change the estimate of the total loss of the initial 'windfall' gain that downstream recreational users get from the mine's dewatering.

Linear programming model of recreational and agricultural impact
Lambert and Shaw (2000) focus on the recreation at Rye Patch also, but use a dynamic stochastic programming model to analyse both these impacts and the gains and losses of downstream agricultural users. The model allows changes in planting/harvest for what are primarily arid lands agricultural producers (alfalfa), but does not allow rescheduling of irrigation patterns. The impacts of several different scenarios are assessed, but I report only a few here. Under dewatering, the shadow price of agricultural land is $192 per acre in the first year being modeled, roughly five times the value under historical pre-dewatering flows. Values for recreational users are typically small because property rights for reservoir water are assumed to be held by agricultural users. Qualitatively, it is not surprising that the total agricultural values of the additional supplies of water downstream are larger in given years than the total recreational benefits. This is at least partially due to the small regular use of Rye Patch Reservoir.

Total valuation (CVM) The third study attempted to elicit a maximum willingness to pay for two programs related to dewatering (Huszar et al., 2001). A pre-test survey suggested that the 'extent of the market' was small (Netusil et al., 1998). In other words, few Nevadans in total would care about impacts in the Basin, especially since most Nevadans live around the city of Las Vegas, hundreds of miles away from the HRB.

Two programs were evaluated by survey respondents. In the first respondents are asked if they would support a pumping program to continue to enjoy downstream benefits consistent with those that are being realized with the mine's dewatering. Respondents are then told that if this program fails the pit lakes will fill up with water, creating pit lakes, and are asked their willingness to pay to support a program ensuring access to the pit lakes for purposes of recreation. The standard double-bounded referendum approach was used for the first program bid, resulting in a mean one-time bid of about $60. Aggregation to a relevant population (excluding Clark County, where Las Vegas is located) yields a total value of about $14 million.

The single-bounded referendum bid in the second program is elicited in the form of a per-day entry fee, and the mean for this program is about $14, or in present value terms, about $7 per day visit. This $7 per day value is almost exactly the cost of entry to Rye Patch Reservoir currently, and provides some support for the validity of this CVM program. Aggregation depends on expected future use of the pit lake, which involves guesswork, but assuming the same average annual use as Rye Patch gets at present, this results in about $0.5 million per year in recreational values.

Conclusions about HRB impacts When compared to total revenue from gold mining, the sum of the dewatering impacts is small. The analysis indicated that passive use (no-use) values may be quite a bit larger than use values as a portion of total value. A more complete partial analysis would identify all the sources of overlap in the values above. For example, it might be possible to sort out the potential double-counting in values or benefits that arise from doing both a contingent valuation study and a travel cost study for Rye Patch recreation. Probably the simplest approach to sorting values would have been to ask respondents in the telephone CVM whether they used Rye Patch Reservoir for the purpose of recreation, and if so, to try to break apart use and total values. The relationship between mining and water frequently arises and while the study only scratches the surface, it shows that some water quantity values can be estimated using non-market valuation and other methods.

8.4 CONCLUSIONS

Environmental, in-situ, and recreational values are going to remain important considerations in water allocation and water quality programs in the United States and Europe. As Chapter 10 will indicate, they may also be of growing importance in other, less developed countries. It is still safe to say that the number one issue relates to protecting human health in drinking water (Chapter 3), but as average household incomes grow, more leisure time allows experiencing lakes and rivers firsthand, and the importance that society places on protecting these resources for these experiences will also increase.

NOTES

1. The Deschutes River drains into the Columbia River, which eventually flows to the Pacific Ocean.
2. In their bibliography of such studies Richard Carson and his colleagues mention over 1000 unpublished and published CVM studies.
3. In a later paper Loomis and Cooper (1990) actually estimate a relationship between an angler's kept fish (creel) and flow (cfs) finding that flow is positively and significantly related to the total number of fish caught at time t in a section of the Feather River.

4. Ward's use of pictures and collection of data on hypothesized trips certainly appear to be the first contingent behavior experiment in the environmental or resource economics literature. At least it appears to be the first such experiment applied in the water quantity arena.
5. The case was *Columbia/Snake River Irrigators* v. *Department of Ecology, Benton County Superior Court, Kennewick, Washington*. I thank Mary Sue Wilson, the state's attorney and Shannon Ragland of Science Applications Incorporated for their essential, beneficial discussions with me on the issues in the case.
6. These are the flows established in biological opinions of the National Marine Fisheries Service group assigned to study this problem.
7. The reader interested in broader issues is referred to Turner and Perry (1997), or Thompson (1982).
8. See the groundwater chapter – Chapter 7 – for a discussion of optimal dynamic modeling of this nature.
9. The study by Trudy Cameron et al. (1996) was one existing exception, but researchers were not aware of it. John Bergstrom in Georgia and Frank Ward in New Mexico had provided others, and since then there have been several other studies, including Jakus et al.'s study for Tennessee reservoirs.
10. Brown and Daniel (1991) measured the relationship between flow quantity and scenic beauty perceptions or judgements for the Poudre River in Colorado. Their study suggests that flow increases scenic beauty up to about 100 to 1500 cubic feet per second (cfs), but then reduces scenic beauty with increases beyond that. More recently, economic studies have emerged (for example, Berrens et al., 1996).
11. Estimating the willingness to sell on the part of irrigators can be quite difficult; researchers must try to implement a survey, or in the absence of observable market data, develop a mathematical programming model to determine farmers' willingness to lease or sell water (see, for example, Turner and Perry, 1997).
12. Interestingly, in nearby Douglas County (just south of the Nevada state capital of Carson City) voters rejected a quarter-cent increase in sales tax which was to be used to help preserve Carson Valley open space (Anderson, 2000). Proceeds from a 7 percent sales tax would have been used to purchase and retire development rights from willing sellers of agricultural land.
13. I thank Tom Crawford, who was the special appointed administrator for the US DOI on the Truckee River Operating Agreement and who gave a talk in my class on this topic in about 2000. Some of the thoughts below are excerpted from his lecture.
14. Floriston is just a spot about one-half of the distance between the mountain town of Truckee, California and Reno, Nevada.
15. Nevada law declares that water supplies within state boundaries, whether above or beneath the surface of the ground, belong to the public (NRS. 533.025).

REFERENCES

Acharya, G. and L.L. Bennett (2001), 'Valuing open space and land-use patterns in urban watersheds', *Journal of Real Estate Finance and Economics*, **22**(2/3) (March–May – special double issue on real estate and the environment), 221–37.
Anderson, Tim (2000), 'Douglas rejects open space', *Reno Gazette-Journal* (November 8).
Bergstrom, J.C., J.R. Stoll, J.P. Titre and V.L. Wright (1990), 'Economic value of wetlands-based recreation', *Ecological Economics,* **2**, 129–47.
Berrens, R.P., P. Ganderton and C.L. Silva (1996), 'Valuing the protection of minimum instream flows in New Mexico.' *Journal of Agricultural and Resource Economics*, **21**(2) (December), 294–309.

Bingham, G. et al. (1995), 'Issues in ecosystem valuation: improving information for decision making', *Ecological Economics*, **14**, 73–90.

Bockstael, N., R. Costanza, I. Strand, W. Boynton, K. Bell and L. Wainger (1995), 'Ecological economic modeling and valuation of ecosystems', *Ecological Economics*, **14**, 143–59.

Boxall, Bettina (2004), 'US billed for lost water', *Los Angeles Times* (January 26).

Boyle, K.E. and L. Taylor (2001), 'Does the measurement of property and structural characteristics affect estimated implicit prices for environmental amenities in a hedonic model', *Journal of Real Estate Finance and Economics*, **22**(2/3) (March–May – special double issue on real estate and the environment), 303–18.

Branson, Tanya (1997a), 'River users seek agreement', *Tahoe World* (August 21).

Branson, Tanya (1997b), 'Better water management goal of operating agreement', *Sierra Sun* (August 28).

Brown, G. and M.J. Hay (1987), 'Net economic recreation values for deer, water fowl hunting, and trout fishing (1980)', working paper 23, US Fish and Wildlife Service, Washington, DC.

Brown, T.C. and T.C. Daniel (1991), 'Landscape aesthetics of riparian environments: relationship of flow quantity to scenic quality along a wild and scenic river', *Water Resources Research*, **27**(8), 1787–95.

Brussard, P.F., J.M. Reed and G. Vinyard (1995), 'The Walker River Basin and Walker Lake dilemma', discussion paper, Biological Resources Research Center, University of Nevada, Reno.

Cameron, T.A., W.D. Shaw, S. Ragland, J.M. Callaway and S. Keefe (1996), 'Using actual, contingent, and time-varying trip data in recreation demand modeling', *Journal of Agricultural and Resource Economics*, **21**(1) (June), 130–49.

Carlton, Jim (2000), 'Gold is pitted against a vital resource: in Nevada, factions decry mines' diversion of big amounts of water', *Wall Street Journal* (February 16), A2–A6.

Carson, R.T. and R.C. Mitchell (1993), 'The value of clean water: the public's willingness to pay for boatable, fishable, and swimmable quality water', *Water Resources Research*, **29**(7), 2445–54.

Colby, B. et al. (1991), 'Mitigating environmental externalities through voluntary and involuntary water reallocation: Nevada's Truckee-Carson River Basin', *Natural Resources Journal*, **31** (Fall), 758–83.

Constanza, R., R. d'Arge, R. de Groot, S. Farber, M. Grasso, B. Hannon, K. Limburg, S. Naeem, R. O'Neill, J. Paruelo, R. Raskin, P. Sutton and M. van den Belt (1997), 'The value of the world's ecosystem services and natural capital', *Nature*, **387** (May), 253–60.

Costanza, R. and H.E. Daly (1987), 'Toward an ecological economics', *Ecological Modeling*, **38** (September), 1–7.

Creel, Michael and John Loomis (1992), 'Recreational value of water to wetlands in the San Joaquin Valley: linked multinomial logit and count data trip frequency models', *Water Resources Research*, **28**(10) (October), 2597–606.

Crouter, Jan (2000), 'A water bank game with fishy externalities', discussion paper, Department of Economics, Whitman College, Walla Walla, WA 99362. Presented at the annual meeting of the Western Economics Association, Vancouver, BC (June).

Cummings, R.C. and G. Harrison (1995), 'The measurement and decomposition of nonuse values: a critical review', *Environmental and Resource Economics*, **5**, 225–47.

Daubert, John T. and Robert A. Young (1981), 'Recreational demands for maintaining instream flows: a contingent valuation approach', *American Journal of Agricultural Economics*, **63**(4) (November), 666–76.

DeLong, J. (2000), 'Ranches disappearing', *Reno Gazette-Journal* (November 3), 9c.

Egan, Timothy (1997), 'Where water is power, the balance shifts', *New York Times* (November 30), 1 and 16.

Eiswerth, M.E. et al. (2000), 'The value of water levels in water-based recreation: a pooled revealed preference/contingent behavior mode', *Water Resources Research*, **36**(4) (April), 1079–86.

Fadali, Elizabeth and W. Douglass Shaw (1998), 'Can recreation values for a lake constitute a market for banked agricultural water?', *Contemporary Economic Policy*, **16** (October), 433–41.

Hamilton, J., N.K. Whittlesey and P. Halverson (1989), 'Interruptible water markets in the Pacific Northwest', *American Journal of Agricultural Economics*, **71** (February), 63–75.

Hanley, N.D., W.D. Shaw and R. Wright (eds) (2003), *The New Economics of Outdoor Recreation*, Cheltenham, UK and Northampton, MA: Edward Elgar.

Hansen, L.T. and A. Hallam (1991), 'National estimates of the recreational value of streamflow', *Water Resources Research*, **27**(2) (February), 167–75.

Harris, Tom (1991), *Death in the Marsh*, Washington, DC: Island Press.

Hay, M.J. (1988), 'Net economic recreation values for deer, elk, water fowl hunting, and bass fishing (1985)', working paper 85-1, US Fish and Wildlife Service, Washington, DC.

Howitt, Richard E. and Jay R. Lund (1999), 'Measuring the economic impacts of environmental reallocations of water in California', *American Journal of Agricultural Economics*, **81**(5) (December – Papers and Proceedings), 1268–72.

Humberstone, Julie (1999), 'Walker river basin water quality modeling', unpublished MS thesis, Department of Hydrologic Sciences, University of Nevada, Reno.

Huszar, E., J. Englin, W.D. Shaw and N. Netusil (1999), 'Recreational damages from reservoir storage level changes', *Water Resources Research*, **35**(11) (November), 3489–94.

Huszar, E., N. Netusil and W.D. Shaw (2001), 'Contingent valuation of some mining externalities', *Journal of Water Resources Planning and Management*, **127**(6) (November), 393–401.

Jakus, Paul M., M. Downing, M. Bevelhimer and J. Fly (1997), 'Do sportfish consumption advisories affect reservoir anglers' site choice?', *Agricultural and Resource Economics Review*, **26**(2), 196–204.

Jones & Stokes Associates Inc. (1990), 'Environmental benefits study of San Joaquin Valley's fish and wildlife resources', (JSA 87-150), Sacramento, CA. Prepared by J.B. Loomis, W.M. Hanemann and T.C. Wegge under contract for the Federal-State San Joaquin Valley Drainage Program (September, Final Report – US Bureau of Reclamation Cooperative Agreement No. 9-FC-20-07420).

Lambert, D.K. and W.D. Shaw (2000), 'Agricultural and recreational impacts from surface flow changes due to gold mining operations', *Journal of Agricultural and Resource Economics* (December).

Lansford Jr, N.H. and L.L. Jones (1995), 'Recreational and aesthetic value of water using hedonic price analysis', *Journal of Agricultural and Resource Economics*, **20**(2) (December), 341–55.

Loomis, J. and J. Cooper (1990), 'Economic benefits of instream flow to fisheries: a case study of California's Feather River', *Rivers*, **1**(1), 23–30.

Lynne, G.D., J.S. Shonkwiler and L.R. Rola (1988), 'Attitudes and farmer conservation behavior', *American Journal of Agricultural Economics*, **70**, 12–19.

MacDiarmid, T.R., E.B. Miller and R. Narayanan (2000), 'A preliminary study of the potential for water banking within the Walker River Basin of Nevada and California', Draft report prepared for the US Bureau of Reclamation, contract no. 6-FC-20-14090.

MacDonnell, Lawrence J. with Charles W. Howe, Kathleen Miller, Teresa Rice and Sarah Bates (1994), 'Water Banks in the West', report of the Natural Resources Law Center, University of Colorado, School of Law, Boulder, Colo. (August 31).

Miller, Kathleen (1996), 'Water banking to manage supply variability', in D.C. Hall (ed.), *Advances in the Economics of Environmental Resources*, vol 1, Baltimore, MD: JAI Press, pp. 185–210.

Morrison, M., J. Bennett and R. Blamey (1999) 'Valuing improved wetland quality using choice modeling', *Water Resources Research*, **35**(9), 2805–14.

Naeser, R.B. and M.G. Smith (1995), 'Playing with borrowed water: conflicts over instream flows on the upper Arkansas River', *Natural Resources Journal*, **35** (winter), 93–110.

National Research Council (1992), 'The Truckee-Carson Basins in Nevada: Indian tribes and wildlife concerns shape a reallocation strategy', Chapter 5 in Committee on Western Water Management, *Water Transfers in the West: Efficiency, Equity, and the Environment*, Washington, DC: National Academy Press.

Netusil, N., E. Huszar, C. Leversee and W.D. Shaw (1998), 'Potential economic impacts of mine dewatering in the Humboldt River Basin of Nevada: preliminary survey results', *Proceedings of the Annual Meetings of the University Council on Water Resources*, Hood River, OR: University Council on Water.

New York Times Staff (1996), 'Novel use of clean-water loans brightens outlook for a river', *New York Times* (October 31), C20.

Northwest Power Planning Councils (NPPC) (1987), '1987 Columbia River Basin fish and wildlife program', Portland, OR:NPPC.

O'Leary, R. (1994), 'The bureaucratic politics paradox: the case of wetlands legislation in Nevada', *Journal of Public Administration Research and Theory*, **4** (October), 443–67.

Olsen, Darryll (2002), Pacific Northwest Project technical memorandum/declaration to hearings review under Benton County Superior Court Judge Dennis Yule, 21 August.

Panktratz, H. (2003), 'Recreational water use buoyed.' *Denver Post* (May 20), 1, 10a.

Ranquist, H.A. (1980), 'Res judicata – will it stop instream flows from being the wave of the future?', *Natural Resources Journal*, **20**(1), 121–47.

Rosenberger, R. and R.G. Walsh (1997) 'Non-market value of Western Valley ranchland using contingent valuation', *Journal of Agricultural and Resource Economics*, **22**(2) (December), 296–309.

Savic, Misha (2000), 'Cyanide spill alarms Europe', *Reno Gazette Journal* (February 13), Associate Press, 1.

Shaw, W. Douglass (2002), 'Non-market impacts', appendix to the Draft EIS for Walker Lake, prepared for the Desert Research Institute and the US Bureau of Land Management, Carson City, NV.

Shaw, W. Douglass, Mark Eiswerth and Eric Huszar (2000), 'Environmental damages from gold mining', special issue of the journal *Environmental Economics*, Colegio de Economistas de Catalunya, Spain.
Swallow, S.K. (1996), 'Economic issues in ecosystem management: an introduction and overview', *Agricultural and Resource Economics Review* (October), 86–100.
Thompson, R.A. (1982), 'Statutory recognition of instream flow preservation: a proposed solution for Wyoming', *Land and Water Law Review,* **17**, 139–54.
Turner, B. and G. Perry (1997), 'Agriculture to instream water transfers under uncertain water availability: a case study of the Deschutes River, Oregon', *Journal of Agricultural and Resource Economics*, **22**(2) (December), 208–21.
Washington Department of Ecology (2002), draft of report of examination to appropriate public waters of the state of Washington, 8 February, Olympia, WA.
Ward, Frank A. (1987), 'Economics of water allocation to instream uses in a fully appropriated river basin: evidence from a New Mexico wild river', *Water Resources Research*, **23**(3), 381–92.
Ward, Frank (1989), 'Efficiently managing spatially competing water uses: new evidence from a regional recreation demand model,' *Journal of Regional Science,* **29**(2) (May), 229–46.
Ward, Frank et al. (1997), 'Limiting environmental program contradictions: a demand systems application to fishery management', *American Journal of Agricultural Economics*, **79**, 803–13.
Whitehead, J.C. and G.C. Blomquist (1991), 'Measuring contingent values for wetlands: effects of information about related environmental goods', *Water Resources Research*, **27**(10) (October), 2523–31.
Wilson, T. (2001), 'A slim chance remains to save Walker Lake', *Nevada Appeal* (July 11), 42.
Zhang, X. and V.K. Smith (1997), 'An integrated model of use and nonuse values', discussion paper, Center for Environmental and Resource Economics, Duke University, Durham, NC.

9. Floods and droughts and the role of dams

> In the first three decades after World War II, major dams were completed in the Columbia Basin at a pace faster than one per year. It is a river so transformed as seemingly invented. If you want to see how America dreamed at the height of the American Century, come to the Columbia.
> (William Dietrich, *Northwest Passage*, 1995)

This chapter focuses on two naturally occurring events that are typically thought of as quite negative in their effects on mankind, floods and droughts. The two topics at first may appear to have little relationship to one another as they represent extremely 'wet' and extremely 'dry' conditions, but they are in fact linked together as extremes in precipitation. Floods and droughts are natural, random events that are often characterized as to the magnitude of their negative impacts for society. Floods and droughts can kill people, animals, and plants. Floods do have some positive impacts, and one of the more beneficial stems from the deposit of rich sediments on land that can then be used for growing crops. An excellent example of this was the Nile River before it was dammed. In fact damming the river effectively reduced this benefit.

The severity of flood and drought impacts can also be affected by human behavior. Building a good dam provides flood protection and also provides upstream storage that can be used to offset the impacts during a drought. Negative flood effects may be diminished when one or more protective actions are taken. Dredging, building inferior dams, and changing the natural course of a river can increase a flood's consequences. As so aptly depicted in many books, choices frequently made by people make a drought's consequences far worse than they otherwise might be.

Early in this chapter floods and the dams that can control them are discussed. Following this is a brief examination of droughts, and in addition to storage in reservoirs behind dams, we consider more carefully whether water banks can alleviate droughts. As will be seen, water banks may require physical mechanisms of redistributing water, and are a relatively new feature in water management in the western United States.

288   *Water resource economics and policy*

9.0 INTRODUCTION TO FLOODS AND DROUGHTS

While writing this chapter, I looked to see if there was a very recent and important flood or drought, figuring that these are common enough events for this to be possible. There were several small floods that occurred throughout the US, and in fact the National Oceanic and Atmospheric Administration (NOAA) has a National Weather Service (NWS) website that updates flood statements and warnings every five minutes. Flood warnings exist for many rivers, including the Mississippi River.[1]

In late May of 2004 nature wrought havoc in Haiti and the Dominican Republic. Two weeks of heavy rain, with as much as 5 feet falling in a 36 hour period in Haiti, led to a possible 2000 deaths, displacement of over 10 000 families, and destruction of thousands of homes (Wiener and Polgreen, 2004). Haiti is the poorest nation in the Western Hemisphere, with an annual per-capita income of about $400, and a large portion of the population lives in rural areas in the floodplain. The Dominican Republic is only slightly better off than Haiti (annual per-capita income of $2000) and the town of Jimani there was devastated: one poor neighborhood was literally built in a previously dry riverbed. Unlike in many Western developed nations, there was simply no preparedness for a major flood in this region.

There was also an easily identifiable drought. The Northeastern United States was undergoing a drought in 2002, and it appears that this drought continues in part of the Great Lakes region today (2004), and several parts of the West, including Colorado. I will provide more on this recent drought in Section 9.3, below.

Causes of floods and droughts

Floods and droughts may happen at any time with some positive, non-zero probability. As Chapter 6 explained, probabilities are an essential part of uncertainty or randomness. The actual precipitation that causes a flood may be of long or very short duration, such as the cloud burst that resulted in the 1976 flood of Colorado's Big Thompson River, or there may be a long period of accumulated snowfall, followed by warm weather that rapidly melts the snow. Flooding on big rivers in the US (for example, the Mississippi River) is not at all uncommon and gets national attention because of the river's size and the magnitude of potential impacts. Smaller rivers may flood, but this goes largely unnoticed. Areas where the risks are known to be high may be protected by dams or dikes or levees.

In Reno, Nevada, a large flood occurred in early January 1997. The Truckee River has its headwaters in the famous Lake Tahoe, and flows right through the middle of downtown Reno. This flood did not kill any human beings, and is often forgotten about by people living in the region. In fact, after the flood, the city government of Reno encouraged and allowed development of a new, multiplex cinema in downtown Reno, just a few feet from the banks of the Truckee River.

Droughts have many similarities to floods, but with opposite causes: too little rain or snow over some period of time. The period during which a lack of rain or snow is of little or no concern is probably longer than one might expect in the United States today, because many steps have been taken to secure adequate supplies of drinking water and more long-term storage. For example, while the northeastern drought was a real concern in 2002, some states did not predict dire consequences during that spring unless the drought continued for another year. This was because several cities and communities had adequate storage to get them through the year. Problems are greatly exacerbated when drought conditions continue for many years, as happened in the west and northwest in the late 1980s and early 1990s, because stored supplies may run very low.

Another feature of floods and droughts that causes me to devote a whole chapter to them is that their randomness causes human beings to understand them poorly. For many months after the January 1997 Reno flood, floods were a major topic of conversation among people in the area. As mentioned, this flood has now been largely forgotten. Similarly, Colorado experienced a drought of considerable concern in 2002, and this has been forgotten today. This mental attitude and short-run focus is typical of risky events: they get attention during an event and immediately afterward, then later, protecting against them takes a back seat to other priorities. Psychologists have shown that human beings will generally tend to over-estimate the risks of their occurrence just after such events, but as time passes, people tend to under-estimate the risks.

In reality of course, the actual long-term risks (probabilities) of flooding and droughts, as predicted by very long time trends exhibited by data, do not often change. However, the consequences of a certain magnitude of flood or drought may change greatly over time because of human behaviors. Because society's perceptions of the events change, the public needs to be reminded of risks when they have forgotten them. All of this is fundamentally tied to economics, because public projects that mitigate against drought or flood are expensive. When given a choice, the public may well vote against spending on flood or drought protection programs once concern about such events lessens.

9.1 FLOODS/DAMS

Exactly what is a flood? Simply defined, a flood is when water normally confined within the banks of a river or stream overflows them. A lake can also rise above its shores, as can the sea.[2] Floods can be small or large, but it is difficult to measure them without introducing their likelihood of occurring. In fact, floods are typically measured or defined in terms of the probability of a flood of similar magnitude occurring over the course of a long period of time. For example, a 100 year flood is a flood of the scale such that we expect it to happen once every 100 years. All this means is that the magnitude of the flood is such that the expected frequency of occurrence is once every 100 years. There are 50 year floods, 200 year floods, and so on. As in all probabilistic estimates, this does not mean that if a 100 year flood happens in a given year, say, in 1997, that it cannot happen again until the year 2097. Any size flood can happen with a non-zero probability in any year. The public probably does not understand this concept of randomness, which may help explain illogical behavior.[3]

Floods are also measured in terms of their flow levels at specific geographical locations, or in terms of the number of inches or feet the water has risen above the banks or shore. Floods are of most concern near populations and property, for the obvious reason that humans likely care most about the loss of human and animal life. The loss of property and other economic losses of materials and structures is the next concern. The physical area that may be impacted by a flood of some magnitude is called the floodplain. What happens in the floodplain and when can be modeled by a hydrologist, allowing extensive plans to be developed for coping with floods of certain magnitudes (for example, see Bhavnagri and Bugliarello, 1965).

It is a reasonable hypothesis to assume that the larger the flow, the higher the potential for loss of life and property. The same will be true, the closer the flood is to urban and rural populations. In Chapter 3 I spoke briefly about valuing a statistical life (VSL), and this same method of valuing lives saved is used in estimating the value of extreme damages from flooding. Agencies such as the US Army Corps of Engineers (COE) use the VSL and additional estimates of the cost of lost buildings, property, and productivity to assess the damages of floods in urban and rural areas. Flooding in unpopulated areas leads to ecological damage, and this topic remains relatively unexplored.

9.1.1 Economic Damages of Floods

One of the most famous floods in US history was the Johnstown, Pennsylvania flood on May 31, 1889. The South Fork Dam above the town broke and sent 20 million tons of water and debris down the valley, killing over 2000 people. In another relatively well-known flood event, in a very short period on one day in July 1976 eight inches of rain fell in Colorado's Big Thompson Canyon, near Rocky Mountain National Park (above and to the west of the town of Loveland, Colorado). In two hours the resulting flood destroyed 316 homes, 45 mobile homes, wiped out 52 businesses, and killed many people. Seventy-three mobile homes suffered major damage and scores of people were injured.

Though it was a small flood and no lives were lost, let's revisit the Reno flood mentioned earlier, because details on economic damages for it are easily accessible. In January 1997 the Truckee River swelled beyond its banks, running right through the heart of downtown Reno and its neighboring town of Sparks. A warm rain melted much of the snow pack that had accumulated in the Sierras (the nearby mountain range), flooding Squaw Creek, a tributary to the Truckee River. An estimated 25 inches of rain and snowmelt occurred between December 30, 1996 and January 6, 1997. This same warm rain resulted in flooding of the Carson and Walker Rivers as well, which are considerably to the south of the city of Reno.

The Truckee River flood was originally designated as a less than 50-year flood event, though that now seems debatable. Property damage was reported to be $540 million (Bremner, 1997). Though the benefits in terms of reduced damages have not been estimated, a study suggests that regulatory dams diminished the effects of this flood in the Reno metropolitan area, also known as the Truckee Meadows (NDWP, 1997). In 1986, well before the 1997 flood, the US Army Corps of Engineers submitted a $90 million plan to control floods on the Truckee River, including five miles of flood walls, and seven miles of levees. For a variety of reasons the plan was never implemented and so the Reno area suffered from the flood's impacts. Compared to over $500 million in damages, the $90 million sounds like a bargain.

Following the flood event the US Army Corps recommended that $101 million worth of flood-control projects should be instigated. Nothing has been done to date. The city of Reno and parties in the Truckee Meadows struggle today with difficult planning issues relating to the risks of the next flood (Pike, 2001). Again, such projects are costly, and few builders in a rapidly growing urban area want to hear that they are prohibited from building in the floodplain. What's more, the probability of the next flood probably seems very low to such builders and to city managers who have to foot the bill for additional flood protection. This is the dilemma for those who manage dams on rivers and streams for flood control, and attempt to persuade the public to live in areas outside the floodplain.

Costs and benefits of flood control

The costs of flood control are mainly estimated using engineering and management costs. Other than providing upstream flood storage protection, possible downstream solutions include levees and walls like the ones discussed above, and 'channel benching'. This has become known as the 'living river' concept (Pike, 2001, p. 13). Unfortunately, channel benching, where a series of elevated benches along the banks allows the river to climb, can cause worse downstream damage. This in turn can cause downstream parties to object to flood control. For example, on the Truckee River, the last stop (105 miles from its headwaters) is Pyramid Lake, and the Pyramid Lake Paiute Tribe (see Chapter 8) does not wish to bear the consequences of additional damages from channel benching near the Truckee Meadows.

As with many such engineering and construction costs (for example, the costs of constructing levees or dams, manipulating stream courses, and so on), they are not terribly difficult to estimate, but it may be difficult to predict future costs accurately, especially in times of inflation. It is well known, for example, that the actual cost of completing dams built in the 1960s in the United States were often under-estimated in advance of their construction. Despite this potential shortcoming, the cost of flood control is not very difficult to estimate in many regions within the United States. Estimates for particular small regions might be more difficult to find.

The Federal Interagency Floodplain Management Task Force estimated that the nation spent approximately $35–$40 billion on flood control between 1960 and 1987 (Devine, 1995). Once a flood has occurred, the taxpayer often bears the major burden in paying for damages, via disaster relief funds and subsidized insurance from the federal government. Private insurance companies generally offer no flood protection, inserting an exemption from their coverage for 'acts of God'. So, in 1973 the US Congress passed legislation creating the National Flood Insurance Program. This program allows coverage for damage from floods. In densely populated areas in the US most local governments are supposed to have developed assessments of the area of the floodplain and the National Flood Insurance Program stipulates that provisions for insurance are to be tied to management of property within these floodplains. Some flood researchers have called for a rather strict form of flood control: a ban on building within the floodplain. These recommendations are often ignored, or at least builders claim that they can build structures that can withstand floods of certain magnitudes.

The benefits of flood control may simply be viewed as averted or avoided flood damages. There are many models of flood damages, and some relate the depth of the flood to the amount of structural damage (damage to buildings and other structures). These are known as depth-damage curves, and one example is the curve used by the Federal Insurance Administration (FIA). The FIA uses data collected from past flood surveys conducted by the US Army Corps of Engineers, and their model includes both structural damage and contents (things like appliances, clothing, books, furniture, etc. that are damaged when a dwelling or office is flooded). Most depth-damage curves show considerable difference in the estimated percentage of a structure and its contents that are damaged, depending on whether the building has a basement, only one floor, or two or more floors, and the type of building: residential, multi-family dwelling, mobile home, etc. (see EEQ International, 2000). For example, the percentage of a mobile home structure that is damaged by a particular flood might be 64 percent, while this is only 3.3 percent if the structure is a school or library (see EEQ International, 2000).

Predicting flood damages is more difficult than doing an ex ante cost calculation for flood control, but it is certainly possible and it is done on a regular basis by several agencies in the United States. One could use past damage estimates in conjunction with the size of the floods that caused them, along with estimates of property values in the floodplain. Then hydrologists and economists should work together to determine how much particular flood control programs will reduce the predicted damages, arriving at 'avoided costs'.

One of the first lessons in economics is that costs and benefits are not identical. There may be omissions in the estimation of benefits using this avoided cost calculation because it typically focuses on structural damages such as mentioned above, much in the same way that health economists miss significant benefits when they use the avoided costs of doctor bills as the health-related benefits of environmental improvements. Pain and suffering, and emotional losses from fear and anxiety would likely not be captured in an estimate of avoided damages or costs of a flood.

There are few published studies of the benefits of flood control. In one, Ramirez et al. (1988) considered the benefits of flood control for a region of Minnesota. At that time they estimated that the United States experienced damages of about $1 billion per year from floods. They focused efforts on an analysis of flood protection for one small region so that the items that needed to be considered in such an analysis could be examined carefully.

Their ex-ante benefit cost analysis suggested that the benefit-cost ratio for flood protection on the Root River and Rush Creek Minnesota was about 2:1, that is, that benefits exceeded the costs by just over a 2 to 1 margin. The authors, however, used information obtained much later to reassess the benefits and costs of the project. Total federal costs by 1968 were approximately $2.8 million, depending on the discount rate used.

To estimate the benefits of flood protection requires that one consider the damages to property when a flood occurs. For a particular area, the houses, industrial and commercial properties must be catalogued and identified, along with their values. Losses may not be total, depending on where the properties are located, so the authors apply a unit damage function that shows the percentage of the market value of the property that is lost given the number of feet of inundation. This function differs for houses with basements and those without in that those houses with a basement experience a loss even with small amounts of water from the flood. Using this approach the authors estimate that the benefits of flood protection were about $36 million, in undiscounted terms. Table 9.1 shows the present value benefits for various discount rates for these areas in Minnesota.

The above scenario by Ramirez et al. (1988) doesn't appear to account for the benefits of averting deaths. In 1976 the Teton Dam in Fremont County, Idaho broke, sending about 80 billion gallons of water downstream and wiping out the town of Wilford. The tragedy resulted in the deaths of 11 people. In a mere two hours the Big Thompson flood killed at least 139 people. And as mentioned at the beginning of the chapter, thousands of people died in the Haiti flood.

The usual estimates of the benefits of flood control should include estimates of avoided mortality over the life of the flood control project.

Table 9.1   An ex post benefit-cost analysis of flood protection for Root River, Rush Creek Minnesota

1967 Present values	Discount rate			
	8 7/8 %	7 %	5%	3 1/8 %
Past benefits	$4.18 million	$4.95 million	$5.96 million	$7.16 million
Future benefits	$2.03 million	$3.51 million	$6.80 million	$14.1 million
Total benefits	$6.21 million	$8.46 million	$12.77 million	$21.2 million
Annualized benefits	$551 033	$593 011	$642 555	$696 866
Annualized cost	$352 829	$278 769	$200 405	$127 292
Additional repairs	$24 225	$21 505	$18 430	$14 212
Total annualized cost	$377 054	$300 274	$218 835	$141 504
Benefit-cost ratio	1.5	2.0	2.9	4.9

Note: One hundred-year project life and 1967 price level. Analysis for Minnesota region.

Source: Ramirez et al. (1988, p. 1402).

Though it may offend some readers to think so, an analysis of flood control benefits from preventing a Wilford-sized flood should include an additional $11 to $55 million in benefits. The offense may come from the realization that the implied value of a life is $1 to $5 million (11 lives times $1 to $5 million per life equals $11 to $55 million). Policy analysts argue, however, that if there is a true risk of 11 lives being lost, then the benefit of flood control includes the value of expected lives saved. As stated recently in an article that involved the use of VSL in assessing flood control benefits, 'Simplistic quantifications in terms of actuarial values have proven to be unsatisfactory and in many cases have been overruled by sympathetic juries' (Agthe et al., 2000, p. 247). The US government's attempt to compensate the families of victims of the September 11, 2001 terrorist attack highlights the controversy and emotions that relate to such calculations. Still, such calculations should factor into an assessment of the optimal level of flood control.

Market failure and the optimal provision of flood control

The federal government recently ordered that a study be done of a flooding event for Reno corresponding to one that would be considerably worse than the 1997 flood. This worst-case scenario involves leakage from upstream reservoirs. It is predicted under this scenario that a 67 foot wall of water would hit the Chalk Bluffs Water Treatment plant, on the west edge of the city of Reno. Maybe it would unduly scare some members of the public to learn of this risk, but it highlights the importance of doing such studies of extremes. The extreme consequences must then be considered along with the use of state-of-the-art science to predict the probability of occurrence of such events. Planning the socially optimal level of flood control must certainly involve an assessment of risk.

Agthe, Billings and Ince (ABI) considered the problem with allocating flood control. Remember that, in Chapter 2, a basic theme is that private goods are allocated efficiently when the marginal costs of supplying the good are equal to the marginal benefits. Flood control, however, is not a pure, private good. It is either a public good, or, as argued by ABI, an impure public good. In such cases, free riders get flood protection at the producer's desired level of flood control (Q) (Hirshleifer, 1983). A simple graph shows the problem (Figure 9.1), adapted from Agthe et al. (2000).

A key problem in allocation of flood control can be explained using Figure 9.1. Suppose there are two downstream users that would benefit from flood control, with benefits represented by the first user's demand (AB in the above graph), and the second further downstream party (CD). To arrive at the 'market' demand for a public good, vertically sum the demand functions (see Chapter 2), to get the line segment EFD.

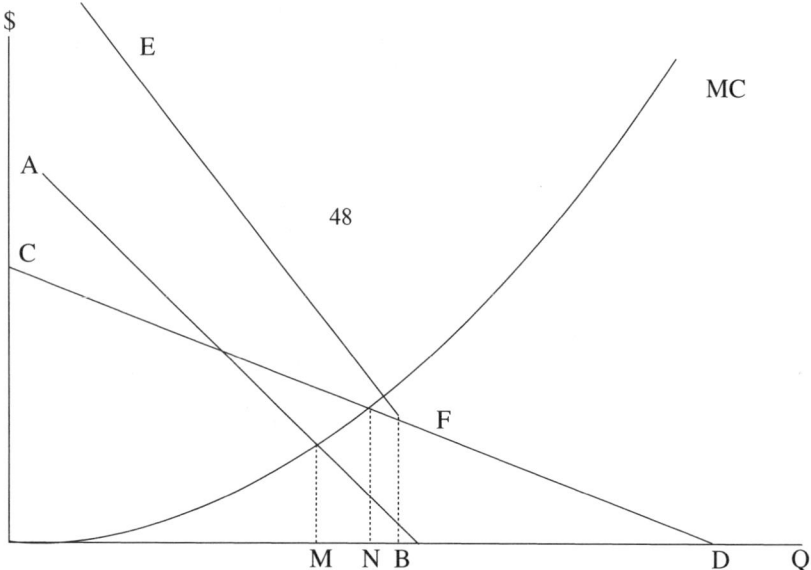

Figure 9.1 Provision of flood control (Q), a public good

If party 1 decides to purchase flood control, he seeks the amount up to M. Party 2 now can get flood control up to M as a free rider, but ideally wants a level corresponding to quantity N. Party 2 may possibly try to enter the market for flood control after party 1 does, in order to bid to get the incremental amount MN. All will depend on the mechanism, if any is provided, for determining who bids first to obtain the desired level of flood control. Unfortunately, however, the optimal market amount is where the MC curve intersects the market curve (EFD), which is a point in between N and B, and regardless of the strategy to purchase flood control, there is unlikely to be such a solution. Hence, the 'efficient' level of flood control is not usually going to be reached.

Because of this market failure Agthe et al. (2000) prescribe a mix of responsibility on the part of private and government agents in providing flood control, echoing the recommendation by the Interagency Floodplain Management Review Committee in 1994. As noted above, planning for such extreme events must be done using uncertainty analysis, for the risks of such a flood make it uncertain that this will happen at all, and it should be noted that the above graphical analysis does not allow this. Still, it provides a nice starting point and enables policy makers to see the public goods aspects of flood control, which will make it difficult to determine the optimal amount.

9.2 DAMS IN THE TWENTY-FIRST CENTURY

Because dams have been such an important part of water management throughout the world, it is worth giving their current status some special attention here. A tremendous amount of dam-building occurred in the US from the late 1930s to the 1960s. Part of this was because of federally funded public projects that were initiated to put people back to work after the depression. The Reclamation Act of 1902 sent the United States Bureau of Reclamation on its way to constructing dams and irrigation projects. Part of the impetus was to promote further development in the western United States, which was still largely unsettled at that time. This era of building dams and water projects lasted, some say, all the way up until President Carter vetoed nine Bureau of Reclamation projects in 1977. Economics strongly contributed to this outcome: President Carter vetoed these projects because they had low benefit-cost ratios (Holland and Moore, 2003; Worster, 1985).

Today there are more than 100 000 dams on rivers and creeks in the United States, making it second only to China in this regard (Devine, 1995). Most dams were built in the 1950s, and were in the western half of the United States (on the Missouri and Columbia, for example). But there were also many Tennessee Valley Authority (TVA project) dams built in the southeastern US to provide hydroelectric power. Only 3 percent of the 75 000 or so dams were built to provide hydroelectric power – most were built for multipurpose goals, or they were built with the understanding (at least eventually) that human beings could benefit from many different possible purposes of the dams.[4]

In contrast, today the US Army Corps of Engineers reports in their national inventory that the largest percentage of dams have, as their primary purpose, the provision of water-based recreation. This represents an interesting shift in priorities, especially when one considers that water-based recreation was hardly mentioned as a benefit of some dams built early on.

The US Bureau of Reclamation was so heavily involved in the activity of building dams that for a time they changed their name to the Bureau of Water and Power. They went about damming every major river in the West: examples are the Columbia River, its tributaries of the Snake and Kootenai (see the map on p. 27 of Butcher et al., 1986); the Colorado River (Hoover Dam and Glen Canyon Dam for Lakes Meade and Powell respectively); and the Missouri River, with several large dams in Montana. The first big (still the biggest) dam to be constructed on the Columbia was Grand Coulee (at Lake Roosevelt), which began producing power in 1941, and the last dam added for hydropower on the Columbia was completed in about 1975. Grand Coulee has a generation capacity of 6494 megawatts, enough to provide power for the people of the city of Seattle several times over.

As other notorious examples of huge dams, Glen Canyon is 710 feet high and impounds 27 million acre feet of water, with an installed generating capacity of greater than 1000 megawatts, and Hoover Dam is 726 feet high, with a reservoir capacity of 9.6 trillion gallons.

Why were these dams really built? As mentioned, dams provide several benefits to people. For some dams, flood control is, or was, the obvious benefit. For others, the first and foremost of these benefits might be to provide storage for irrigation purposes. There are several purposes for dams including:

- irrigation/storage
- hydroelectric power production
- flood protection
- reservoir recreation
- municipal storage supply
- navigation

Many dams provide two or more of these services. Unfortunately, many of these purposes directly conflict with each other in shaping how the dam is to be managed and operated. Flood protection is at its highest capability when the reservoir is low, or at least not so full that additional flow can be safely stored behind the dam. Navigation likely requires a higher flow downstream, requiring liberal releases from the dam. If a river doesn't freeze, and large ones typically do not, navigational needs may be substantial at any time during the year.

Irrigators likely want releases during the time of most need, in the middle and late summer, when temperatures are very high and crops demand a good deal of water. Irrigators may also change their planting and land use decisions in response to flood control programs (Theiler, 1969), perhaps increasing croplands in low-lying areas that benefit from increased protection from floods that might otherwise ruin them.

Hydroelectric power generation requires a high level of water behind the dam, and humans need electricity for heating and cooling, often indicating a seasonal need for large releases. Hydropower production is determined by the 'developed head', which is the height of the retained body of water above generating turbines, and the volume of water that flows through the turbines. Power generation is expressed in kilowatt hours that can be provided, or kWh. For example, Bonneville Dam has 59 feet in gross head, and has a capability of generating 51 kWh per acre foot. Compare this to the

Snake River dam at Brownlee, which has a gross head of 272 feet, and had a generating capability in 1980 of 1141 kWh per af. The latter figures show how much electricity can be generated by letting 1 acre foot of water flow downstream. Put into perspective, a large house in a city might use around 4200 kWh (this equals 4 megawatts because 4000 kW = 4 megawatts) of electricity per year.

Butcher et al. (1986) discuss the fact that irrigators account for 95 percent of the consumptive use of the Columbia (about 20 million af), but that dams even in low-flow conditions provide about 110 billion kilowatt hours (kWh) of electricity per year. The cost of energy generated using hydroelectric power is only about $0.003 per kWh. In nominal terms, and without consideration of environmental externalities, hydropower is the cheapest electric power in the US today. Retail rates passed to consumers are still only about $0.015 per kWh, which is about one-half of the national average cost of electricity. Note, however, that if the negative environmental externalities were included with appropriate values assigned to them, this might not be the true cost of hydropower.

Finally, recreational boaters desire a reasonable level of water at a reservoir to facilitate the launching of their boats and to avoid hitting rocks beneath the surface. Shore users may not want water levels too high because beach areas may be unusable. There is an entire body of literature in economics devoted to estimating the benefits of recreational users, but most of it focuses on the benefits that anglers get from fishing. Some new studies examine the benefits to recreational users of having additional flows or higher water levels (see Chapter 8).

Consider the potential for conflict among all these different users of a dam's services. Suppose that the climate and geography in a region is such that freshwater comes from snows in the mountains. A city is located downstream, and has built a dam in the foothills of the mountains. In the dam there are some turbines that generate hydropower. Downstream users, perhaps below the city, also include irrigators. If the dam managers or operators want to maximize the potential for downstream flood protection, then they should empty the reservoir behind the dam just before the snow melts in the late spring, thereby allowing storage of newly created freshwater. This action will help to prevent streams and rivers from overflowing.

Alas, releases of water behind the dam in the winter may not be of much economic benefit to irrigators who could use it at other times. As long as storage is increased during snow melt and releases are ample during the hot summer, this may not cause great conflict. However, if a later period of very small releases occurs, this could adversely affect hydroelectric power generation. The irrigators' wants and needs for surface water for their crops can definitely influence hydropower production because of their seasonal demands. At the same time, other irrigators may require electricity, especially when their main source is pumped groundwater, which requires electricity to lift the water out of the ground.

Irrigators have another connection to dams. The US government has frequently provided an economic subsidy to irrigators in the form of building and operating many dams that provide irrigation storage (see Chapter 5). Some irrigation districts are supposed to repay the federal government the cost of building and operating a dam, but most irrigators pay no interest on this repayment. Former US Bureau of Reclamation (USBR) economist Richard Wahl estimates that irrigators benefiting from USBR's water projects typically end up paying only about 12 to 15 percent of the construction costs for their facilities (Devine, 1995).

Construction and operation of dams also lead to damages, not just benefits. Dams prevent fish migrations, important for anadromous species like salmon. They result in impairment of river-based recreation. They may change the downstream ecosystem and the temperature of the water. They flood canyons of scenic beauty. They may displace residents, which is especially significant in flat areas with large dams and in developing countries.

Finally, another interesting conflict is described by Devine (1995) that relates to their operation in the twenty-first century. He notes that dams on the Columbia and Snake Rivers have caused shipping, mainly on large barges, to rely on locks for navigation and transportation. The burden of funding for such systems falls on the general taxpayer, not on the barge companies: in 1995 the COE budgeted $786 million for inland waterways. Next, I consider impacts on the ecosystem from building dams. An educated guess is that the primary reason fewer dams are built today, is because of their huge potential environmental impacts.

Environmental and ecosystem impacts from releases from dams
Today dams are increasingly being used in another manner than described above. They can be used to manipulate seasonal flows, trying to reproduce what would have been natural fluctuations in flow during seasons in the absence of mankind's interference. In particular, a rise in spring flows and an ebb in summer flow may better enhance the ability of fish, birds, and plants to cope with the environment (Harden, 2002b). This is also controversial and a good example is debate over the 2341 mile Missouri River. The Missouri River was once a meandering river, and the US Army Corps of Engineers (COE), with its mission of enhancing navigation, straightened it, causing environmental degradation. Today issues of endangered species may pit the US Fish and Wildlife Service against the COE.

At stake in the debate on the Missouri are several issues, including planting in the floodplain during the spring, maintaining summer flows for shipping on barges, and cooling thermal and nuclear power plants in Missouri. Economic conflicts occur between states, as upstream reservoirs in North and South Dakota are typically drawn down in the summer. During droughts economic losses in these upstream states may be larger than downstream gains to the barge industry (Harden, 2002a).

Changes in flow have many impacts including changing the natural sediment load. Downstream of a dam the riverbed may be eroded, deepening the bed, which in turn can lower the groundwater table. Gravels in the riverbed are reduced, changing fish and plant habitat. The impacts of flow changes are not confined within the banks of the river.

Downstream soils can change because of reduced sediment deposited there. This can lower agricultural productivity in these regions. Also, the mouth of the river is often where there are estuaries, creating a rich habitat for aquatic life and these can be negatively impacted. For example, the Akasombo Dam has led to the disappearance of the clam industry in Ghana.

Resolving the conflicts
How does society regulate the flows and resolve this enormous number of conflicts? Clearly, many different parties are involved, including private irrigators, irrigation ditch companies, the US Bureau of Reclamation, the COE (with authority over navigation and flood control and – in the Pacific NW – the major producer of power), the power producers in the region, which may include the Bonneville Power Authority (they market the power for COE in the Pacific NW). Part of any operation scheme for a dam leads to two things: a dam project must be evaluated, and in the US today, virtually any changes then dictate that an environmental impact statement or regulatory impact analysis be conducted.

The Federal Energy Regulatory Commission (FERC)
FERC was formerly the agency called the Federal Power Commission. This is the main federal regulatory authority over non-federal hydropower plants and projects. They can license water rights to private parties for the purpose of power production. FERC licenses cannot be overruled by states and local governments.

FERC has considerable real power to affect changes on water courses. For example, it recently denied a license for the Edwards Dam on the Kennebec River in Maine and ordered the owner of the dam to remove it to enhance fish passage on the river (salmon, striped bass, and shad run). Another timely example involves tearing out or breaching dams, discussed below. The FERC re-licensing process may well involve what is deemed to be project evaluation.

9.2.1 Project Evaluation of Dams and Other Water Projects

As the above shows dams and other water projects may involve many social objectives and operators and managers need a way to try to evaluate and balance more than one of these objectives (see Loughlin, 1977). Water projects today are typically evaluated using a variety of criteria, but the standard economic measure is akin to the benefit-cost ratio. Benefits and costs were discussed in Chapter 2, and the ratio of them yields a number less than, equal to, or greater than one.

Because projects have benefits and costs that accrue to future generations, society often discounts these future impacts. To review,[5] let the discount rate that society uses to evaluate public projects be r. The discount factor then is equal to $1/(1+r)$. This factor decreases over time. Let t indicate the year of the project, $t=0,1,\ldots,T$. In each year then, the discount factor is $1(1+r)^t$. To evaluate the net benefits for a project, the present value of all benefits and costs in each year should be summed. Mathematically, this is equivalent to:

$$PVNB = \Sigma\ (B_t - C_t)/(1+r)^t \qquad (9.1)$$

Projects with a present value $B-C$ ratio of less than one have a negative present value of net benefits, and should almost certainly be rejected. However, this simple rule is not necessarily consistent with the economist's goal of maximizing the discounted net benefits of a project. That goal dictates that a different set of operating conditions should be pursued. In addition, as discussed earlier, many projects in the United States and throughout the world were probably built with no regard to their benefit–cost ratio.

To evaluate a water project, there is an accounting stance for assessing benefits and costs that must be assumed. This stance defines the area for which the evaluation is being done. For example, net benefits can be evaluated for one region, or for several regions, or for the nation. Some regional benefits (for example, gains in regional employment) may come at the expense of other regions, so these wash out. For example, as a dam is being built in region A, workers may migrate in from region B, resulting in a loss in employment in region B. From a national perspective many of the gains and losses in particular regions offset one another, and therefore are typically ignored.

Howe (1986) suggests that few water projects are ever evaluated ex-post, that is, after the project has been completed and has been going on for several years. Most projects are evaluated by the federal government as part of a regulatory impact analysis (RIA) ex ante, or before a project is begun.

In a rare study of the Colorado–Big Thompson Project of Northern Colorado that draws on Howe et al. (1982), Howe examines the ex-post benefits of the project. He concludes that from a national perspective, the Colorado–Big Thompson Project is a loser (with a B−C ratio either equal to 0.38 or 0.60, depending on assumptions about the life of the project). From a regional perspective however, the project was of considerable benefit to the region of Colorado, with a B−C ratio of either 8.11 or 11.11, again depending on assumptions.

It would be interesting to do such ex-post analysis on a host of dams across the West and in other parts of the United States to see if they have been of overall positive benefit to society. No matter what the outcome, however, it is safe to say that the era of building huge dams in the United States is over. That era continues in some other countries, such as China.

9.2.2 Dams in Developing and other Countries

Across the world there are some 40 000 dams, with reservoirs encompassing about 400 000 square kilometers. Currently the largest impoundment in the world is the Volta Reservoir (8500 sq. km.) behind Ghana's Akasombo Dam. Several dams outside the US are notorious, or even infamous. Egypt's High Aswan Dam immediately comes to mind, one of the largest dams in the world, damming the Nile, which in turn is the longest river in the world. The High Aswan Dam is the second major dam built on the Nile, at 364 feet high. It cost about $1 billion to build and was completed in 1970.

Dams were recently, and are currently, being built in Egypt, India, and China, and on a massive scale. It is important to remember that while we take having electricity in our homes for granted, there are still very large concentrations of people in the world who have none. Dams are a potential solution to bringing power and electricity to areas with inadequate supplies of other fuels (natural gas or coal), but with plenty of water. Egypt's High Aswan Dam provides about 10 billion kwH annually, using 12 175-megawatt turbines.[6] Up to the time of its completion it was the largest dam ever built.

Building both the original and new (High) Aswan Dams resulted in lost archeological treasures and relocation of 150 000 residents of Nubia. The government's engineers had to confront relocating some of the oldest artifacts and archeological objects on the earth. Some famous statues and other structures were 3000 years old and surely of nearly astronomical historical value. The cost of relocating many archeological monuments was about $40 million. As of 1997 about 110 million tons of silt had accumulated at the reservoir and there had been important changes in the ecological balance before that, leading to the need for increased water treatment (White, 1988).

The largest, most expensive dam ever built for hydroelectric power and flood control is the Three Gorges Dam in China's Yangtze River Valley, with an expected completion date of 2009. Discussion of it highlights some modern problems encountered when building dams. The Yangtze River Basin is home to 380 million people, a third of the Chinese population. The dam is proposed to be 1.3 miles long and 610 feet high. The reservoir created by the dam is to be 385 miles long. Twenty-six sets of 700 megawatt turbines are proposed. The plan is for 18 000 megawatts of electricity to be produced every year, supplying 10 percent of China's energy. This is equivalent to power produced by 18 nuclear power plants. The dam is also to provide flood control protection. More than 300 000 people died from floods in the region during the twentieth century. The current estimate of the dam's cost is $75 billion. This has been financed via bonds issued by China's Development Bank, underwritten by firms in the United States. The World Bank has been involved only in supervising a feasibility study.

About 1.4 million people will have to be resettled as a result of this project, and there is great concern over the flooding of cultural artifacts, some dating back about 10 000 years (Topping, 1995). The Chinese government has promised to spend $4.8 billion on resettlement alone. The project is so controversial that the Minister of Water Resources, Qian Zhengying, banned a publication that was in opposition to Three Gorges in 1992.

Presuming Three Gorges Dam is completed, 12 711 archeological sites will be submerged. The US government is reported to have set aside $37.5 million for excavation of these sites. Whitefin dolphins and the Chinese sturgeon are found in the Yangtze, but face extinction with completion of the project. No one seems to know what the quality of the reservoir water will be in coming years, and there is concern that the reservoir will be on top of an active fault line.

9.2.3 Removing Dams in the Twenty-first Century

Today there is a new issue: not building dams, but removing them. Over 100 of the members of the US House of Representatives wrote a letter to then President Clinton, urging him to consider dam removal in some river or another (Paulson, 1999). The motivation for this is typically because the river's environmental conditions will improve in the absence of the dam, or because anadromous species of fish (see Chapter 8) will be able to migrate. The Pacific Northwest is full of examples: the Elwha and Glines Canyon dams, and four of the lower Snake River dams including Ice Harbor,

Little Goose, Lower Monumental, and Lower Granite. The Elwah River is on the Olympic Peninsula, and the dams have a combined capacity of 24 megawatts, with annual output of 140 000 hours. One estimate is that the cost of removal is greater than $200 million, but an April 1998 press release said the cost would be $113 million. Slade Gorton, then a US senator from Washington, wanted to block the removal of dams in his state, and introduced legislation limiting the powers of the federal agencies to promote salmon migration and remove dams (see Westneat, 1998). The issue remains politically charged.

Economists view this debate in cost-benefit terms. Economist John Loomis (1996) used a dichotomous choice contingent valuation survey to obtain the WTP to remove the Elwah Dam. The survey scenarios depicted provide the survey respondent with estimates in bar chart form for how many more pink salmon there would be with removal of the dam. The survey suggests that dam removal would result in 200 000 more salmon than in a situation requiring the use of fish ladders. The sample mean estimates are about $59 per household in Clallam County, and $73 per household elsewhere in Washington. When aggregated, Loomis' benefit estimates translate to about $138 million annually for about ten years to all residents of the State of Washington. If the one-time cost of removing the Elwah is around $100 million, then even if discounted, the present value of benefits should exceed the costs for removing this dam.

In Loomis' study there is no mention of the loss in flood protection benefits, if any existed. There are also other costs to consider when removing dams, including a loss in hydroelectric power production leading to an increase in the costs of electricity generated by using some alternative source. One needs to consider the cost of electricity using the next best alternative supply, typically coal. Each person in the region would face a higher utility bill using coal plant generation rather than hydroelectric power generation. Ideally, a survey would be designed to mention this possibility to the respondent, allowing them to factor this into their decision to support dam removal.

9.3 DROUGHTS AND WATER BANKS

When the well runs dry we know the true value of water.

Benjamin Franklin

Franklin's quote is all too true during a drought. The word drought does not only apply when the well is dry, or when there is no water at all. Reservoirs in spring 2002 were half full in the northeastern United States, but the public and the public agencies were calling the conditions there a 'record setting' drought. In 2004 the western United States was so dry that water managers had come to revise their assessment of 'normal' precipitation for their region. Runoff projections for the Colorado River were down by 55 percent on average by early May, and predictions were for the demise of a famous lake (Lake Powell in Utah) if trends continued (see Johnson and Murphy, 2004). Some water scientists in fact raised the question of the duration of the region's drought. Dr John Dohrenwend, retired from the US Geological Survey, said 'If we are only in the middle of the drought, then Lake Powell might be very close to some very dramatic problems' (Johnson and Murphy, 2004).

A drought can, like a flood, vary in severity, from an extreme drought to a milder one, so the lack of precipitation is a matter of degree. A drought is simply any prolonged occasion of abnormally low precipitation. Some droughts may last for more than five years, while others consist of one year of low precipitation that results in drawing down of surface water supplies. For example, precipitation in 2001 in Maine was the lowest in 108 years of record keeping. Predicting droughts, or even knowing when they are serious, is complicated, but fundamentally dependent on recorded measurements. In the western United States records of stream flow date back about 60 to 80 years.

Hydrologists have just ascertained that the period since 1999 is now officially the driest period of recorded history in the Colorado River Basin, in 98 years of keeping records (Johnson and Murphy, 2004). More sophisticated methods allow reconstruction of flows much farther back in time than 1000 years. Tree-ring studies at Lee's Ferry on the Colorado River allow measurement of the river's flows from the year 1520 to the 1800s. Recent interpretation of this data suggests that an annual average flow of about 13 million acre feet is reasonable for the Colorado River, much lower than the 15 million acre feet implied by the conventional records from 1906 to 1985 (Dracup and Kendall, 1990). Unfortunately, legal allocations between the upper and lower Colorado River Basin states were based on the 1906–85 data. The Colorado River Compact (see Chapter 1) probably needs to be revised in light of the new data. Prior to 1999 hydrologists probably measured drought cycles or average precipitation in the basin incorrectly, and scientists studying tree rings and ocean temperatures see the settlement and development of the arid West in the United States as a 'colossal miscalculation' (ibid., p. A1).

Measuring droughts
There are in fact several formal definitions of droughts (see Hayes, 2002).[7] For example, farmers may be most interested in a crop soil moisture index,

but this may be less useful for those interested in predicting impacts on municipal supplies from reductions in reservoir storage than other drought indices or indicators. A problem is that soils, reservoirs, snow pack, and groundwater all react to drought conditions differently. Soils react to changes in precipitation relatively quickly, while reservoirs and snow pack may reflect changes much more slowly. Groundwater aquifers may be extremely slow in their reaction to changes in surface conditions.

A severe drought was indicated when the Palmer Hydrological Drought Indices (PHDI or simply the 'Palmer') was ≤ -3 (see Riebsame et al., 1991). The Palmer is a soil moisture algorithm calibrated for fairly homogeneous regions. Many state and federal agencies still use the Palmer today to trigger drought relief programs. It appears to be less suitable for mountainous land and areas with frequent climatic extremes, and may lag behind emerging droughts (Hayes, 2002). In fact, Hayes states that it is probably best used for uniform topography. The US National Drought Mitigation Center uses a new index today, the Standardized Precipitation Index (SPI) (see McKee et al., 1995; Edwards and McKee, 1997). This index is based on the probability of precipitation for any time scale and values over 2 indicate extremely 'wet', while those at -1.5 to -1.99 are 'severely dry' and those at -2 and less are 'extremely dry'. As suggested, the SPI is not as sensitive to time scales as some other indices.

9.3.1 Drought Impacts

What are the impacts of a drought? Of course these again depend on the severity of the drought and on the amount of precautionary activity that has been taken by any community to mitigate or alleviate drought conditions. However, potential negative impacts may include all of the following:

- environmental/ecological
- human health (death, illness)
- agriculture (prices, quantities, more insects)
- transportation (shipping activity down, but airlines have fewer weather delays)
- power generation (brownouts, less hydro, higher revenue to power companies for air conditioning)
- commerce and industry (recreation/tourist industry down)
- urban areas (lawn irrigation, sanitation, drinking)
- water resources
- education (reduced school hours)
- governmental operations (conflicts between states)

Some of these impacts may not have occurred to the reader, but should be considered when evaluating drought's impacts, though perhaps on a region-specific basis. For example, in 2002 the impacts of the drought in the state of Maine were not evenly distributed. Households on wells that were deep enough were barely affected. The city of Portland's water supply came from a lake unlikely to be affected (Harden, 2002a).

Most people impacted by a drought are losers and this loss leads to economic damages. Consider the impact of the 1988 drought in the United States. Grain production fell by 31 percent. The price of corn increased 50 percent because of scarcity, which may have temporarily made some corn producers better off. But the price of cattle fell because of the need to send the cattle to market quickly, with livestock watering supplies scarce. The average loss per farm in Illinois was $48 000 during this time. The Mississippi River shipping industry lost over $200 million, or 20 percent of their usual annual income. National hydropower production was down 13 percent in 1988 from 1987.

Droughts also occurred from 2000 to 2002 in the midwestern and northeastern United States. Great Lakes shipping was impacted, though economic damages have not yet been estimated. In Maine in 2002 households on shallow wells ended up paying $5000 to $10 000 to have new or improved wells dug (Harden, 2002a).

9.3.2 Preparing for Droughts

There are several actions that society may take to prepare against the worst consequences of a drought. Society, represented by government agencies, might:

1. provide reliable storage/emergency supplies (build new reservoirs, drill new groundwater wells);
2. dredge rivers;
3. build facilities that allow access to low level waters;
4. provide subsidies to power producers to allow peak power production for air conditioning;
5. increase emergency medical response;
6. provide drought assistance to farmers;
7. create a government-sponsored water bank.

Note that some of these actions conflict with preparation to cope with floods or may be impractical today. For example, (1) suggests the building of new dams, but discussion above strongly suggests that building a new dam in many countries today is not feasible. In the next section I consider the role that water banks may play in alleviating a drought. Water banks were introduced in earlier chapters, but they are directly related to actions that society may take to cope with, or prepare against, a drought, so they receive special attention below.

9.4 WATER BANKS

What is a water bank and how could it help alleviate drought's impacts? A water bank is, as it sounds, a bank to save water in, which can be loaned out, just as any other resource like money. The main idea is to be able to provide water to those who need it on a short-term basis, or, in other words, to establish a functioning rental market. The idea of renting water is not novel in many states. For example, in the Upper Snake River Basin of Idaho, there was a recent temporary transfer of 14 700 acre feet of water at a price of $0.17 per acre foot (MacDonnell et al., 1994). The thought is that a bank can cut through a lot of the transactions costs associated with a rental market (willing renters or sellers finding willing buyers) and that reallocation of water supplies can be accomplished to promote efficiency.

Rental schemes are much more flexible than permanent purchases and sales, which may be daunting to the buyer and prevent short-term reallocation. The party wishing to rent water hopes to get water through the bank for a short period, and less expensively than he could have done in some other way. The party agreeing to rent their water in turn hopes to temporarily part with some water they don't need and make some money on this excess water, while retaining the permanent right to the water so that they can use it when they do need it.

Such rental markets are already at work. The State of Idaho created three regional water banks in the past 25 years. The Upper Snake River Water Bank was created in about 1979 (see Crouter, 2000; MacDonnell et al., 1994). There, common trades would involve irrigators depositing water in the bank, and the Idaho Power Company leasing that water. The state of California has an emergency drought water bank, discussed in detail below. Texas, Washington, and Kansas also had proposed water banks, or at least something similar to the bank concept, as of 1994. The operations of these institutions vary, and are carefully described in MacDonnell et al. (1994).

Each state's bank must operate within the confines of state water law. For example, Idaho allows an irrigator to hold both storage and flow rights, and the storage rights are important because they give an irrigator the possibility of carrying over a right when they do not use the water in a given year. In contrast, flow rights not used in a given year pass to the next appropriator in line. As in most western states, the party not using the water had best be careful; failure to use water for the original purpose for a period of five years results in loss of the appropriated right. With this in mind the Idaho bank program had to decide whether to also allow rental of both kinds of rights. They decided to make only storage rights available.

9.4.1 Water Bank Rules and Setting Prices

The legal issues have to be very carefully considered so that parties volunteering to deposit water in the bank on a temporary basis are not in jeopardy of losing their water in a law suit. Laws must give assurances that depositors do not forfeit their water right in perpetuity. In addition, the actions of those who deposit must be protected against law suits related to claims of injury.

There are many restrictions and priorities and rules accompanying water banks. These can be complicated, and unfortunately, they may limit the potential to achieve economic efficiency through transfers. Idaho gives first preference to irrigation and agriculture as the primary beneficiaries of the water bank, subject to any rights granted in the local public interest (MacDonnell et al. 1994, pp. 2–9). However, priorities given to renters even vary by district in Idaho, and by dates of withdrawals. In addition, the governing board must determine if water on the Columbia River tributaries (for example, the Snake River) is to be rented for the benefit of salmon migration, and if so, whether this use will injure other water rights. In California's bank, the rules are much looser: first, priority for rights granted is to those needs that are deemed 'critical'.

One type of contract in the California bank was a fallowing contract, requiring growers to fallow their land or withhold the application of any irrigation water to crops normally irrigated. Agreement to fallow land was checked using aerial surveys by the Department of Water Resources. The fallowing contracts amounted to about one-half of water acquired in 1991 by the bank. Other contracts allowed farmers to sell surface water, substituting groundwater in their continued irrigation. The difference is that the fallowing contract is attractive to those willing to sell or rent water at the selling price and forgo expected income from crop production under irrigation, while the groundwater contract allows continued farming, but likely with higher costs associated with pumping groundwater.

Most banks have the responsibility of setting trading prices. The governing board of the water bank in Idaho set rates that vary by water district, ranging from $2.70 per acre foot (Payette River region) to $6.50 per acre foot (Boise River region). In California those who deposit water do have an input into the price. Membership in the emergency drought bank entitles the member to representation (one vote) on the water purchase

Floods and droughts and the role of dams   311

committee, which establishes the price at which water may be purchased. The 1991 price of water in the California water bank was set at a single 'melded rate' reflecting all costs incurred to acquire water, resulting in a $175 per acre foot of consumptive use purchase price (plus delivery charges below a pumping plant). Of the $175 per acre foot, $125 would be given to the sellers.

Prices can fluctuate depending on flow conditions. In both Idaho and California the water banks seem to be most desirable in low flow, or drought years. In such years it may well be that instream flow is more valuable at the margin to hydroelectric power producers than to agricultural producers (Hamilton et al., 1989). However, in these same years many agricultural producers may be reluctant to offer the water up for lease. It appears that changes in drought conditions led to different selling and purchase prices for the California Water Bank in 1992. MacDonnell et al. (1994) mention a purchase price for 1992 of $50 per acre foot and a selling price net of delivery charges of $72, both lower than the 1991 price. Then, after a wet year in 1993, 1994 was dry again and the California Bank offered water for purchase again at $50 per acre foot. The mechanism for trading can be seen by playing a water bank game.

9.4.2 The Water Bank Game

Professor Jan Crouter (at Whitman College) developed a game that students can play that helps them understand how a water bank might work. Here is how the game works. There are three participants:

1. Irrigators: divert water from tributary streams to irrigate crops and have 100 acre feet available to them that can be leased or sold. The value of the irrigation water is given to them. Irrigators are told to maximize the surplus they get from the sale of the right (the price minus the value of the diversion right if applied to irrigation).
2. Electric Utilities: sell hydropower generated from turbines. This group is told the value of flow in electricity production, and it is told to maximize its surplus (the value of the acquired diversion right in power production minus its price).
3. Anglers who fly fish: enjoy benefits from instream flows relating to catching brook, cutthroat, or rainbow trout. These benefits are assumed to increase when the electric utilities purchase water rights from irrigators because instream flows upstream increase, enhancing habitat. This group is also told to maximize surplus, assumed to be the value of the diversion right times the number of diversion rights sold, minus any contribution the angler pays to encourage a transaction.

Table 9.2 Assigned marginal values in the water bank game with 19 players

Irrigators	Utilities	Fly-fishing anglers
V(A) $680	V(1) 710	V(brook) 60
V(B) 730	V(2) 620	V(cutthroat) 40
V(C) 560	V(3) 720	V(rainbow) 20
V(D) 710	V(4) 690	
V(E) 780	V(5) 750	
V(F) 620	V(6) 660	
V(G) 800	V(7) 580	
V(H) 840	V(8) 600	

Note: V = Value.

Source: Crouter (2000) and personal communication.

It is suggested by Professor Crouter and others who have had their students play this game that the number of irrigators should be ≥ 4, the number of utilities should be in the same range, and the number of fly-fishing anglers ≥ 2.

Values for the contracts suggested by Professor Crouter are in Table 9.2.

The game begins with a few trading periods. The leader should establish a 'trading area' where trades will occur. During trading, irrigators may yell out offer or selling prices, and utilities can offer their bids in whole dollar units. This is consistent with what is called a double-oral auction. Fly-fishing anglers stay out of the game and only observe the first rounds. Irrigators may only sell one diversion right per period, and each utility can purchase one, at most. Partial rights cannot be sold. Upon completion of a transaction, the party leaves the trading area. If the game is played for about three trading periods one examines what appears to be an 'equilibrium' price for the contracted right.

In Phase II of the game, let the fly-fishing anglers enter the game. They may collaborate with each other, or with any other market participant. This is the only information given. I ran this game in my class in 2002 and Table 9.3 illustrates the results based on the students' responses and trades.

While this game helps one learn how a water bank could work in theory, MacDonnell et al. (1994) note that there may be an actual difference in the way transactions are actually determined in a real setting, depending on the reliability of the water. Storage rights might be highly secure and could therefore be traded prior to the irrigation season beginning. The authors

Table 9.3   Experimental results of the game for fourteen students

Round 1: Irrigator C sold 100 af for $600 to Utility 5, and Irrigator A sold 100 af to Utility 1 for $700. No other action.
Round 2: Irrigator C sold 100 af to Utility 3 for $700. Irrigator F sold 100 af to Utility 5 for $700. Irrigator A sold 100 af to Utility 1 for $708. No other action.
Round 3: Irrigator C sold 100 af to Utility 3 *and* cut-throat trout angler (joint cooperation) for $720; Irrigator B sold 100 af to Utility 5 for $740; and Irrigator F sold to utility 4 for $720.
Round 4: Irrigator D sold to Utility D and brook angler (joint/cooperation) for $725; Irrigator C sold to Utility 5 and cut-throat trout angler (joint) for $720; and Irrigator F sold to Utility 3 for $720.

Notes: Rounds 1 and 2 are in Phase I with anglers sitting out. N = 14 students: six irrigators, six utilities, two anglers.

also mention the possibility of making forward trades, akin to a futures market. Here a price is fixed and the water can be taken at any time. As the season unfolds, and weather and market conditions become known, participants can change their initial positions and attempt to engage in spot market transactions. For example, if a buyer locks in prior to the beginning of the season for, say, $30 for an acre foot, but then the market conditions result in higher spot market prices for water, he might sell his locked-in acre foot at $35, making a profit to offset any potential loss in production owed to higher water prices. Next, I consider a few case studies of water banks.

9.5   CASE STUDIES: EXISTING WATER BANKS IN CALIFORNIA, IDAHO

As you recall from Chapter 8, Walker Lake and the Walker River Basin were the topics of a possible water bank setting. At this point it appears that the draft Environmental Impact Statement suggests favorable benefits for taking actions to promote voluntary transfers between farmers who hold the water rights and federal agencies acting on behalf of the public to save Walker Lake. However, I have seen no concrete language pertaining to the creation of a water bank for Nevada. So, it might be helpful to examine the workings of two existing water banks and see what the obstacles to creating such a bank are.

9.5.1 Idaho's Water Bank

One indication of whether a bank is a 'success' is the amount of water transferred. Since the inception of the Idaho–Upper Snake River water bank in 1979, over 4 million acre feet have been transferred. However, Green and O'Connor (2001) suggest that inflexibilities regarding the water price have resulted in operations that are inefficient in an economic sense. They distinguish between a 'fixed price' and 'flexible price' water bank and conclude that a water bank with a flexible price structure better reflects higher valued uses and promotes transfer to these from lower valued uses. Idaho's bank may work better under such a scheme. There may be real importance in allowing different types of water banks, especially when the goals are environmentally oriented.

Green and O'Connor (2001) examine various types of water banking policies on the Snake River that relate to restoring habitat for endangered species. Huppert (1999) examines the costs of meeting recovery goals for the Snake River salmon and estimates these to be in the range of $246 to $359 million per year. This is a substantial commitment to an environmental program involving the management of flows, and a water bank can help meet it. Green and O'Connor use a spatial optimization model to compare and contrast which policies work best to augment instream flows. They show that the Idaho water bank may best help restore fish habitat by providing water supplies for instream flow, but note that water prices were probably too low at the outset of the trading program. For example, the price of water during peak demand corresponding to the 1993 drought was $6.05 per acre foot, which the authors say was well below the marginal value of water for most water uses in the Snake River region. Their flexible price model shows that prices must differ when flow targets vary, with a range for the average, more efficient water bank price of between $20.52 and $99.14 per acre foot.

9.5.2 California's Water Bank

Richard Howitt (at University of California at Davis) has now written extensively about his experiences with the California drought bank (see Howitt, 1994, 1998). California's bank has been deemed a success, but it was not so immediately following its creation. There was much hard work in setting it up and convincing both sides (supply and demand) to participate. Several unexpected transactions costs and a general initial unwillingness to rent water on the part of agricultural users plagued the bank in the beginning (Howitt, 1994). To alleviate some of these problems there is a need for both spot and options markets (discussed in Chapter 6) to allow for hedging against risk (Howitt, 1998). This type of price flexibility is supported by the research of Green and O'Connor (2001).

9.6 CONCLUSIONS

Floods remain a serious problem today, with the most devastating consequences being in developing countries like Haiti, where little has been done to prepare for them. There is a tradeoff between providing flood control and the negative consequences of building dams. Many believe that droughts and their impacts are going to get worse, not better. Part of this has to do with the predicted impacts of global warming, and part of it has to do with population growth in arid regions. There is some hope that society is learning to cope with all these problems better than it has in the past, but there is a need for additional adjustment in behaviors, including managing growth in arid areas.

It appears that water banks do have the potential to smooth out the effects of drought in the future. However, their creation and operation remain difficult issues. An interesting analysis would compare the net social benefits from creating and running a water bank to the net social benefits of using a new, increased water supply (a reservoir or tapping an aquifer) to mitigate against uncertain drought events.

NOTES

1. The curious can see http://www.nws.noaa.com.
2. A special topic not covered here is sea level rise and ocean floods. Sea level rise is frequently discussed as a likely consequence of global warming.
3. A scene in the movie *The World According to Garp* communicates this sentiment very well. Robin Williams' character is thinking of buying a home. He walks up to the home with the real estate agent and just then a small airplane hits the house. Williams says something like this immediately after the crash, Wow! I'll buy it. That could never happen again! Similarly, it is common to observe people rebuilding their home on the same spot, just after it has been destroyed by a flood.
4. In his account of his travels across America by boat, an author and adventurer notes about the Missouri River: 'Small by Missouri River standards, the first [hydroelectric dam] was completed in 1890 and the last in 1958; it's hard to believe a power company could persuade the public today to allow, for the sake of a few megawatts, so massive an impairment of one of the most magnificent riverscapes in America' (Heat-Moon, 1999).
5. For those who have not had discounting, see Chapter 2. For a more in-depth discussion, virtually any principles of economics textbook covers this topic.
6. See http://www.gps.caltech.edu/~ge148/1997C/Reports/148niled.html.
7. See also http://enso.unl.ndmc/enigma/indices.htm.

REFERENCES

Agthe, D.E., R. Bruce Billings and S. Ince (2000), 'Integrating market solutions into government flood control policies', *Water Resources Management*, **14**, 247–56.

Bhavnagri, V.S. and G. Bugliarello (1965), 'Mathematical representation of an urban flood plain', *Proceedings of the American Society of Civil Engineers*, **91**(HY1).

Bremner, Faith (1997), 'Corps seeking $101 million in control efforts', *Reno Gazette Journal*.

Butcher, Walter et al. (1986), 'Competition between irrigation and hydropower in the Pacific Northwest', chapter 2 in K.D. Frederick (ed.), *Scarce Water and Institutional Change*, Washington, DC: Resources for the Future.

Crouter, Jan (2000), 'A water bank game with fishy externalities', discussion paper, Department of Economics, Whitman College, Walla Walla, WA 99362. Presented at the annual meeting of the Western Economics Association, Vancouver, BC (June).

Devine, Robert S. (1995), 'The trouble with dams', *The Atlantic Monthly* (August), downloadable at www.theatlantic.com/politics/environ/dams.htm.

Dracup, J.A. and D.R. Kendall (1990), 'Floods and droughts,' a chapter in P.E. Waggoner (ed.), *Climate Change and U.S. Water Resources*, New York: John Wiley, pp. 243–47.

Edwards, D.C. and T.B. McKee (1997), 'Characteristics of 20th century drought in the United States at multiple time scales', climatology report no. 97-2, Colorado State University, Fort Collins, Colorado.

EEQ International (2000), 'Determination of impacts from flood study modifications for the McAlpine Creek Watershed', report (May 2000) prepared for the Mecklenburg County Engineering and Building Standards Division, 700 North Tyron Street, Charlotte, NC 28202.

Green, G.P. and J.P. O'Connor (2001), 'Water banking and restoration of endangered species habitat: an application to the Snake River', *Contemporary Economic Policy*, **19**(2) (April), 225–37.

Hamilton, J., N.K. Whittlesey and P. Halverson (1989), 'Interruptible water markets in the Pacific Northwest', *American Journal of Agricultural Economics*, **71** (February), 63–75.

Harden, Blaine (2002a), 'Drought leaves Maine stoic but struggling', *New York Times* (March 15), A1, A16.

Harden, Blaine (2002b), 'Dams and politics channel mighty river', *New York Times* (May 5), 1, 18.

Hayes, Michael J. (2002), 'Drought indices', http://enso.unl.edu/ndmc/enigma/indices.htm.

Heat-Moon, William Least (1999), *River-Horse: Across America by Boat*, New York: Penguin Putnam, Inc.

Hirshleifer, J. (1983), 'From weakest-link to best shot: the voluntary provision of public goods', *Public Choice*, **41**(3), 371–83.

Holland, Stephen P. and Michael R. Moore (2003), 'Cadillac desert revisited: property rights, public policy, and water-resource depletion', *Journal of Environmental Economics and Management*, **46**, 131–55.

Howe, C.W. (1986), 'Project benefits and costs from national and regional viewpoints: methodolgical issues and case study of the Colorado–Big Thompson project', *Natural Resources Journal*, **26** (Winter), 77–92.

Howe, C.W., D. Schurmeier and W.D. Shaw (1982), 'Innovations in water management: an ex-post analysis of the Colorado Big Thompson project and the Northern Colorado Water Conservancy District', unpublished book manuscript, University of Colorado, Boulder.
Howitt, R.E. (1994), 'Empirical analysis of water market institutions: the 1991 California water market', *Resource and Energy Economics*, **16**, 357–71.
Howitt, R.E. (1998), 'Spot prices, option prices, and water markets: an analysis of emerging markets in California', Chapter 8 in K.W. Easter, M.W. Rosegrant and A. Dinar (eds), *Markets for Water: Potential and Performance*, Boston: Kluwer Academic Publishers.
Huppert, D.P. (1999), 'Snake River salmon recovery: quantifying the costs', *Contemporary Economic Policy*, **17**(4) (October), 476–91.
Johnson, Kirk and Dean E. Murphy (2004), 'Drought settles in, lake shrinks and West's worries grow', *New York Times* (National Edition) (May 2), A1 and A24.
Loomis, John B. (1996), 'Measuring the economic benefits of removing dams and restoring the Elwha River: results of a contingent valuation survey', *Water Resources Research*, **32**(2) (February), 441–7.
Loughlin, J.C. (1977), 'The efficiency and equity of cost allocation methods for multipurpose water projects', *Water Resources Research*, **13**(2) (February), 8–14.
MacDonnell, Lawrence J. with Charles W. Howe, Kathleen Miller, Teresa Rice and Sarah Bates (1994), 'Water banks in the West', report of the Natural Resources Law Center, University of Colorado, School of Law, Boulder, CO (August 31). Research sponsored by the US Geological Survey, DOI, No. 1434-92-G-2253.
McKee, T.B., N.J. Doesken and J. Keist (1995), 'Drought monitoring with multiple time scales', preprints, Ninth Conference on Applied Climatology, January 15–20, Dallas, TX, pp. 233–36.
Nevada Division of Water Planning (1997), 'The flood of 1997', report for the Nevada Department of Conservation and Natural Resources.
Paulson, M. (1999), 'Clinton urged to weigh NW dam removal', *Seattle Post Intelligencer* (August 5).
Pike, D. (2001), 'Dam dangers', *Reno News and Review* (March 1), 13, 14.
Ramirez, J., W.L. Adamowicz, K.W. Easter and T. Graham-Tomasi (1988), 'Ex-post analysis of flood control: benefit-cost analysis and the value of information', *Water Resources Research*, **24**(8) (August), 1397–405.
Riebsame, William, Stanley Changnon and Thomas Karl (1991), *Drought and Natural Resources Management in the United States: Impacts and Implications of the 1987–89 Drought*, Boulder, CO: Westview Press.
Theiler, D.F. (1969), 'Effects of flood protection on land use in the Coon Creek, Wisconsin, Watershed', *Water Resources Research*, **5**(6) (December), 1216–21.
Topping, Audrey (1995), 'Damming the Yangtze', *Foreign Affairs* (September), 132–45.
Westneat, Danny (1998), 'Gorton threatens to block removal of Elwha Dam', *Seattle Times* (April 3).
White, G.F. (1988), 'The environmental effects of the High Dam at Aswan', *Environment*, **30** (7), 5–40.
Weiner, Tim and Lydia Polgreen (2004), 'Struggle as Haitians and Dominicans tally flood losses', *New York Times* (Western Edition) (May 28), A1 and A8.
Worster, D. (1985), *Rivers of the Empire: Water, Aridity, and the Growth of the American West*, New York: Pantheon Books.

SUGGESTED FURTHER READING

McPhee, John (1971), *Encounters with the Archdruid*, New York: Douglas and Mcintyre Press.
National Research Council (1995), *Flood Risk Management and the American River Basin*, Washington, DC: National Academy Press.

WEBPAGES

http://www.usatoday.com/weather/whydro00.htm.
http://enso.unl.edu/ndmc/enigma/watch/watch.htm.
http://www.wrcc.sage.dri.edu/spi/spi.htm.

10. Water issues outside the United States[1]

10.0 INTRODUCTION

This chapter discusses some of the important water-related issues in countries other than the United States. As there are so many, this presentation of ideas only scratches the surface. We are especially interested in, for lack of better words, developing countries (DCs),[2] or those countries that might have low gross domestic products per capita. The list of countries, which excludes the developed countries in North America, Australia, and Europe, also includes the newly industrialized countries (NICs) such as South Korea and Taiwan, but the focus here will be mainly on countries that are clearly less developed than the NICs. These countries are found in Africa, Latin America, and parts of Asia (particularly India and Pakistan). The reader should remember that many countries around the world (for example, in Europe) still have severe water quality problems. However, extensive discussion of these is omitted because many developed countries try to solve their water quality and quantity problems in similar ways to the United States. They use regulations developed, monitored, and enforced by national and local government agencies, coupled with some market-based incentive programs. In contrast, many DCs still do not have well-functioning environmental regulations and natural resource laws.

The material below is basically divided into issues connected to water quality, namely provision of clean water to drink, and, following this section, water quantity or allocation issues. Water quality issues are still near the top of the priority list for less developed countries, As always, it is often difficult or impossible to separate the two issues of quality and quantity. Different geographical regions, even within single continents, can have very different allocations of natural precipitation. For example, Table 10.1 shows precipitation in different geographical areas on the African continent.

Note that Sudan, South Africa, and Swaziland have high rates of use of their internal resources, but benefit from important resources and significant amounts of incoming water. Not only is the annual amount of precipitation important in many countries outside the United States, it is important to consider the distribution of this precipitation over the course

Table 10.1 Regional distribution of water resources within Africa

Region	Area (1000 km²)	Precipitation (km³/yr)	Internal renewable resources			
			(km³/yr)	(mm/yr)	% of total	% of precipitation
Northern	5 753	411	50	8.7	1.2	12.2
Sudano-Sahelian	8 591	2 878	170	19.8	4.3	5.9
Gulf of Guinea	2 106	2 965	952	452.0	23.8	32.1
Central	5 329	7 621	1 946	365.2	48.8	25.5
Eastern	2 916	2 364	259	88.8	6.5	11.0
Islands (I.O.)*	591	1 005	340	575.3	8.5	33.8
Southern	4 739	2 967	274	57.8	6.9	9.2
Total	30 025	20 211	3 991	132.9	100.0	19.7

Note: Km² are square kilometers, km³ are cubic kilometers, and mm are millimeters. I.O. indicates the islands are in the Indian Ocean.

of the year, and as in the US, across the country itself. The timing of rainfall is, in many cases, totally different than in the US because of extremes (monsoons, droughts). For example, in India almost all of the annual precipitation occurs during four or five months, corresponding to two monsoons.

The fundamental water issue in developing countries today involves supplying basic drinking and sanitation needs, and poor health associated with drinking water of poor quality. These issues are in stark contrast to the usual concerns about water in the developed nations (for example, supplying growing urban or rural populations in the arid west of the United States, largely so that they can grow green grass in the desert; non-point source pollution; some groundwater contamination issues from agricultural pollutants and salt water intrusion). One estimate of the number of deaths from water scarcity is 12 million per year.[3] The World Health Organization (WHO) estimates that as many as 10 000 people in the world die every day from diarrhea (WHO, 1998). More than 3 million children die of this every year. Mortality and morbidity, and especially infant mortality, are quite often associated with bacteria being consumed in drinking water. Much of the developing world today still cannot get clean drinking water. Table 10.2 summarizes some statistics for a few countries.

The reader should consider 'access' to drinking water in Table 10.2 carefully, and imagine whether people in developed nations would be happy with a 10 or 15 minute walk to the nearest drinking water source. A pattern repeated in many, but not all developing countries is that safe water access

Table 10.2 Global indicators on access to safe water and adequate sanitation

Country/year	Population with access* to safe water (%)		Population with access to adequate sanitation (%)	
	Urban	Rural	Urban	Rural
Bangladesh, 1995	49	–	41	36
Cambodia, 1995	20	12	–	–
Haiti, 1995	38	39	43	16
Nepal, 1996	61	59	74	18
Romania, 1991–93	70	10	81	03
Uganda, 1995	60	36	60	50
Zambia, 1995	66	37	66	37

Note: * 'Access' defined as in the home, or within 15 minutes walking distance.

Source: WHO (1998).

is better in urban areas than rural ones, and the same goes for access to sanitation. Table 10.2 may surprise some readers used to thinking that all of the numbers above would be close to 100 percent. In fact, one is correct in believing that 100 percent of the population has access to safe water in countries such as the United States, Iceland, Switzerland, or England, but the sample of figures above are representative of many, many developing countries, where the percentages fall well below 75 and even 50 percent. In the countries of India and Niger in 1995, only 4 and 5 percent of the rural population, respectively, had access to adequate sanitation. So, it is reasonable to conclude that rural area problems in developing nations are of special concern.

For example, in urban areas of Kenya today, the primary method for obtaining drinking water still appears to be to buy it from a street vendor.[4] However, about 35 miles from the city of Nairobi, a private household in a rural area invested about $300 (US) to hand-dig a well. The household then sold the water to others in 20 liter plastic containers for about 3 Kenyan shillings (KSh), the equivalent of about $0.04. A young man in the village with entrepreneurial skills carted this water a short distance away and sold it for the equivalent of $0.12 for 20 liters. This is because in Nariobi itself, the going price for street-vendor water appeared to be about six times higher than in the rural area, at about 1 KSh per liter of water. Often villages in rural areas in such countries have a well provided to them by some external foundation, church, or non-governmental organization, but the pump has broken or for other reasons the well is no longer producing water. The villagers frequently have no knowledge or tools enabling them to fix the problem. So, a basic need for clean drinking water fundamentally enters as a problem for many households in developing countries.

A second fundamental water issue in DCs, again often impossible to separate from the above, relates to adequate sanitation. As an example of the problem, piped sewerage is found today in only three cities in the Philippines outside Metropolitan Manila (Lauria et al., 1999). Such a shortage of modern sanitation facilities is common in DCs. It connects to safe drinking water because in villages and towns with no sewer or sanitation system bacteria from human waste easily find their way into the water and food consumed by the people who live there.

10.1 ECONOMIC PROBLEMS IN DCs AND LOW INCOME COUNTRIES

DCs are often characterized by many features and examining these will make it easier to understand why meeting such a basic need as clean water is so hard in a country like Kenya. First and foremost is the fact that average household income in DCs is quite low in comparison to the developed nations, and even as compared to the NICs, and this fact alone helps explain water distribution problems. For example, gross national product (GNP) per capita in 1983 was only $130 in Bangladesh, compared to $14 080 in the United States that same year. Perhaps a more useful characterization than 'less' or 'more' developed is simply to characterize some countries as 'low income', relative to others, but there is more underlying the difficulties DCs have than this. Many developing countries have distributions of income across its people that are bimodal: the very rich and the very poor constitute two groups in the population and there are few people in between. Often, the number of very rich is an extremely small number of people in total, so the vast majority of the population is very poor. One does not want to assume that a country with a relatively high per capita income has no water problems because this ignores the distribution of income.[5]

Many households in DCs and other low income countries are living in abject poverty. In fact, nearly half of the people of the world live on less than $2 per day, and one-fifth survive on less than $1 per day (Kahn and Weiner, 2002). Impoverished people such as this simply cannot afford to have plumbing and sanitation if they must finance such infrastructure themselves, nor can they really afford to pay exorbitant prices for water on the street, as it leaves them little remaining income for other goods and services. It is a common assumption that impoverished people, or those on subsistence income, care little about anything aside from food and water. One further assumption is that these same people will not care about the 'environment', but this may be an error. Rural poor people may be beginning to understand the connection between environmental quality, health, and protecting water resources. For example, poor groups in some countries such as India have rallied behind the cause of environmental protection. They have done so because it may help them gain in their own struggle for a share of resources that would otherwise go to the very rich (see Bandyopadhyay and Shiva, 1989).

There are several more common themes or perceptions about developing countries. After or before low income, a second common perception is that DCs can be characterized as having high population growth rates as compared to the developed world, and a third perception is that DCs have comparatively less 'clean' economic activity: industrial and service sectors that do not pollute are absent in DCs. A fourth perception relates to poor health and related issues, and a fifth is that DCs often have accumulated enormous debts to other nations and non-governmental organizations (NGOs).

Consider the population issue. Many environmental scholars suggest that every single environmental problem in developing countries can in some way be related to overpopulation. For example, a common population growth rate in DCs is between 2 and 3 percent per year or even higher (the urban population in the Philippines has been growing recently at about 5 percent per year), as compared to less than 1 percent or even zero population growth in developed nations. These DC growth rates may not sound high to those unfamiliar with population statistics, but they translate into a doubling of the population in 14 to 23 years.[6]

As an aside, despite much research on the topic, there is still no universally accepted and clear relationship between population growth and economic, or productivity, growth. In 1801 Thomas Malthus wrote an essay in which he essentially formulated a theory that said that the long-run equilibrium standard of living was at the subsistence level, as populations would always grow to offset increases in GNP. Malthus was looking at agrarian societies. In those societies all labor went into producing more agricultural output. As income per household grew there was enough to enable the parents in the household to have more children who could eventually work the fields. But, as population grew, Malthus predicted that it would outpace the available income and food supply, leading to starvation and eventually, a reversal of the initially favorable situation. These predictions added to the perception that the moniker of the 'dismal science' which was given to economics was appropriate. Of course Malthus' dire predictions have not been borne out for many developed nations for a variety of reasons, including technological change and innovation, and education of the population regarding the benefits of smaller family sizes. Clearly, in many countries food supply has grown much faster than Malthus would have thought possible, culminating in the huge, corporate farm. Still, one does not see corporate farming much in developing countries.

The simple economics of most countries can be laid out in national income accounting equations. Gross national product, or GNP, is a way to measure the entire income of a nation. It is a monetary measure of all goods and services produced within a country. As in all accounting, there are two sides to the ledger, a plus side, which in macroeconomics is called the injections, and a minus side, called withdrawals. The injections into the economy for a country are composed of consumption (C), investment (I), government spending (G), and income from exports (X), and we write:

$$Y = C + I + G + X \qquad (10.1)$$

The withdrawals again include consumption, but we add savings (S), tax revenue (T), and spending on imports (M), which is money that flows to other countries. For reasons that I won't go into here, consumption, or consumer spending, is, for accounting purposes, both a withdrawal and an injection. We can write $Y = C + S + T + M$ on the withdrawals side. If an economy is in balance, injections are equal to withdrawals. The consumption on both sides cancels out, and we are left with:

$$I + G + X = S + T + M \qquad (10.2)$$

This is the fundamental equation for determining whether a balanced equilibrium holds for an economy. I cannot resist the temptation to note that a 'balanced budget', where $G = T$, is only one part of this equation because there is so much talk about it in the United States at this time. To balance the economy is what is most important, and it remains unbalanced even if $G = T$, as long as there is no balance with other components.

The role that exports and imports might play in a country is also clear. If imports are large the nation's economy is likely out of balance (withdrawals exceed injections) unless something on the left-hand side offsets them. One possibility for a remedy is to expand the export sector, which may help the economy grow and put the economy back into balance, but another is to run a 'trade deficit', where imports exceed exports, while trying to push up injections in another sector, perhaps domestic investment. With a trade deficit more money goes overseas than comes in from abroad, and this can affect a country's currency value and internal finance.

Some developing countries have been able to raise the standard of living considerably, following the prescriptions of 'export-led' growth, or 'import substitution' or some combination of these and other policies. It is probably a given that rapid population growth is a negative phenomenon; that overpopulation is a major cause of many environmental problems is undisputed by most environmental scientists. Even optimists who hypothesize that innovation is positively related to population size, such as the pop economist Julian Simon, might agree that 'moderate' rather than rapid population growth is desirable (for a representative sample of his popular work see Simon, 1981).

Evidence suggests that health problems tend to be more pronounced in poorer countries. Infant mortality may be correlated with the availability of clean drinking water, though it is affected by other factors such as poverty and the availability of food. In some developing countries infant mortality rates today are over twice what they are on average, in the world, at over 80 deaths per 1000 births.

Low average household incomes lead to the fact that governments and regulatory agencies in DCs may have a very small budget tied to a low national income. Thus, they are unlikely to be able to deal with water pollution problems, and hence, their enforceable environmental protection programs may be virtually non-existent. Governments of course vary in their methods of financing government expenditures, but no matter what schemes are used, all governments in the world eventually have to carefully consider sources of revenue versus desired outlays. In times of budget shortfall and with changing priorities, even the United States cuts expenditures on environmental programs, at least in terms of the percentage of the overall budget, or as a percentage of gross domestic product (GDP).

Environmental programs such as those found in Europe and North America are funded by tax revenue collected via a national income tax, or at least via regional or state income, or other kinds of taxes (sales, property, import, or excise taxes). The ability of a government to collect tax revenue is naturally a function of both income per household and politics. Governments in DCs may have little political resistance to taxation policies, but face low average income per household. Poor households are thought, on average, to save little of their income, meaning that a government would be taxing consumption. So, an additional problem in many macroeconomic situations is that taxing private consumption may lead to reduced, not increased economic growth.

The relevant point here is that, with low tax receipts, agencies in DCs that seek water quality protection likely must rely on funding from countries other than their own. Often, water quality improvement programs are funded from loans through non-governmental organizations (NGOs) such as the World and Asian Development Banks. Like any bank, virtually all NGOs are in business to make money from interest and payback of loans, but in their case, they lend money to governments and private industry in other countries. Naturally an NGO wants to lend money to a country with a reasonable expectation that the government of that country will pay the loan back. So, an NGO like the World Bank evaluates the expected rate of return on the loan, meaning that they scrutinize the country's source of expected future income and derive terms of repayment that are both feasible and profitable to the NGO.

In many DCs the NGO will see that an agency or firm's revenue and income are tied to one or more natural resources such as oil, gold or another metal, or agricultural goods, including timber. For such resource-rich countries, the goal is to produce these materials for export to other countries, with sales resulting in higher national income and the influx of foreign currency. Therefore, in such a country an NGO will likely evaluate a project, such as lending a country money for a sewer or new drinking water system, factoring in whether profits for that country's resource base will flourish.

Unfortunately, the late twentieth century is full of examples where countries have been unable to pay back loans, borrowing ever more, and racking up mountains of debt. As an example, from 1972 to 1981 a group of 15 developing countries ran deficits (years where expenditures exceeded income) of more than 18 percent of their exports of goods and services, mostly by borrowing from commercial banks in the US, Japan, and Europe. Part of the cause for this borrowing had been the oil shocks of 1979–80, which shifted income from those countries with little oil to the oil-rich nations. By 1986 these countries' outstanding debt exceeded 60 percent of their combined annual GDPs (Abel and Bernanke, 2001).

The 1980s were an era of collapse for many natural resource markets, and income from the export of oil, tin, or copper just did not lead to the national income many countries had expected. By 1982 many private banks refused to make new loans to many DCs. In 1986 a sharp drop in oil prices led to problems for some DCs with oil to export, such as Mexico. The loss of confidence in many DCs such as Mexico led to intervention by the International Monetary Fund and the World Bank. This vicious cycle leads to the need for even more aid from developed nations.

Today aid to other countries from Japan, the United States, France, Germany, and Britain, which contribute the most foreign aid, is down considerably (Kahn and Weiner, 2002) as compared to past years. This makes matters even worse for those countries needing basic water supply and sanitation. The alternative for an LDC, with no funding from outside or tax revenue, is to sell the water quality improvement and environmental protection services in their country to someone else. This selling of services is essentially the privatization movement, which extends worldwide and includes selling the service of supplying water to communities to private companies. I return to privatization below.

Finally, climate and environmental conditions in DCs are often markedly different than in the developed nations. The United States essentially has very little rainforest (there is some on Washington's Olympic Peninsula), or areas that experience anything like southeast Asia's monsoons. Other countries have more definite and distinct dry and wet seasons, and soil conditions and vegetation may be quite different from that found in developed nations. Coastal forests such as mangroves have many important connections to water quality, and these connections, as well as other geographical and ecological features, must be understood by western scholars and NGOs before pronouncing water quality and quantity programs in DCs worthwhile or recommending particular policies. These features make it unlikely that adopting the western world's prescriptions for solving water problems will lead to effective solutions.

In the remainder of this chapter, I will discuss special water quality issues and their relationship to sanitation in DCs. Next I highlight some special water quantity issues, after first connecting these to water quality issues.

10.2 COUNTRY-SPECIFIC CASE STUDIES

Chapter 3 provides the bulk of the material one needs to get an introduction to basic water quality issues, including a description of contaminants of concern in the United States. However, as the above introduction notes, water contamination problems in DCs may be quite different. A basic and simple water quality problem that is much more common in DCs than elsewhere relates to bacteria from human wastes. This does not mean that surface water supplies in major Asian cities are absent more modern industrial wastes, but inadequate sanitation and water treatment almost certainly ensure that health problems related to ingesting bacteria are pervasive. Various problems in several geographical regions around the world are briefly examined next.

Eastern Europe
As the Soviet Union collapsed in the late 1980s the world learned a great deal about countries that were part of the Soviet bloc. For example, Hungary established a constitution in 1989 and information about its poor environmental quality began to emerge quickly afterward. Water quality in Hungary's rivers was in steady decline from 1975 to 1995, with industrial and sewerage discharge the primary causes (*European Environmental Almanac*, 1995). Only one-third of discharged industrial waste was treated biologically or chemically, and less than half the population was connected to the sewer

system as of 1995. The Sajo valley is one of the most industrial parts of the country, and the Sajo River is contaminated with heavy metals. Nitrate levels above 200 mg/l have been recorded in groundwater in the south and east of the country. It is hoped that the newly formed Ministry of Environment and Regional Policy (1990) will help improve water quality over time.

Romania, which is similar to Hungary in that it adopted a new constitution in 1991, also shares water quality problems. It is estimated that approximately 85 percent of Romania's rivers provide water unfit for drinking. Groundwater pollution is also rampant, with contaminants from industrial wastes, agriculture, and mining. In 1991, Romania's capital, Bucharest, had no wastewater treatment plant. This was the situation for a city of over 2 million people.

There are also a growing number of studies on Asian and Pacific Rim countries and their water pollution problems. I will feature studies done in the Philippines, Nigeria, Haiti, and Pakistan here, as they are especially informative and were the subject of some good recent studies. Following these, a brief review of two studies, one in Korea and one in China, is given.

Calamba, the Philippines

The following is excerpted from Lauria et al.'s (1999) discussion of their Philippines research, funded by the World Bank. Unsanitary conditions in Philippine cities have contributed to a deterioration in groundwater and surface water supplies. Sources of urban pollution have caused problems in lakes and rivers affecting aquatic species that might be eaten to supplement a meager food budget. In this study the authors sought to predict how different households might react to programs offering improved sanitation services, at different prices that were offered to them.[7] Their study developed and implemented one of the largest contingent valuation studies ever done in a developing country. The part of this work considered here focuses on sanitation in the city of Calamba, located about 60 km south of Manila, with an estimated population of 175 000. Calamba's residents are middle and high income households, relative to the general population in the Philippines, but some in the study sample earned the equivalent of less than $120 (US) per month.

Oddly, water quantity does not seem to be a primary issue in this region. The Calamba Water District operates a piped distribution system from two groundwater sources and one ground-level reservoir. Only 40 percent of the water the CWD produces is sold, so that only 20 percent of the city's households are serviced. It is estimated that average consumption is 40 liters per capita, per day (190 per household, or about 50 gallons per day per household[8]). About 48 percent of households in the city use a private well, and the remainder of households get their water from neighbors or from public hand-pumped wells.

Now, imagine your own city, how many households have a private flush toilet? Would it be all of them? While public toilets are more common in European multiple dwelling residences, private toilets are the norm in the United States. Compare that to the 86 percent of households who have a private flush toilet in Calamba, which at first appears to be a very high proportion as compared to some cities in other developing countries. While it sounds high, the problem here is that very few private toilets are connected to proper septic systems, so much of the actual human waste goes into ditches, and eventually into Laguna de Bay, creating pollution there. Of the remaining 14 percent of Calamba residents who do not have private flush toilets, most have some type of public toilet, but many of these also empty directly into streams, ditches, or lakes. So, while toilets are available to remove wastes directly from the household, there are few connections to any sewer line.

A sample of households in the study were surveyed, and asked whether they would be willing to support programs for several possible types of improved sanitation. These included (i) a sewer system only, (ii) a sewer system plus wastewater treatment plant, and (iii) a program like (ii), but with a larger/better water treatment system that would allow the lake's quality to improve. In the approach taken by the researchers, the household member answers yes or no to support for these programs, and for each program, a range of prices is specified.

At a price of 25 pesos per month (about US$1) 57 percent of households who responded to the survey agreed to purchase option (i), 71 percent agreed to pay for (ii), and again 71 percent agreed to purchase option (iii). This reflects the fact that the household understood, and preferred, options (ii) and (iii), which provide higher environmental services. At a price of 200 pesos per month ($8) these percentages fell to 8, 11, and 6 percent respectively.

I should note that in contrast to the study above, Lee et al. (1997) also consider similar water quality and quantity issues in the Phillippines, but do not arrive at the same conclusions. They do not find significant effects of water supply sources on children's health in the countries of Bangladesh and the Philippines. However, their data do show that about 20 percent of those surveyed in Bangladesh get their water from a pond, river, or canal. Their sophisticated statistical analysis examines the various effects on children's weight and survival, concluding that the most important variable is the household's wealth.

Nigeria

In a similar study Whittington et al. (1991) provide a good example of problems relating to adequate supplies of safe water in Nigeria. Though one could view their study as about water quantity, it is clear that in many rural villages getting 'enough' water is not sufficient. Obtaining water safe for domestic uses is the key goal, so water quantity studies are still of interest in exploring water quality issues, because of the strong overlap between the two in Nigeria. The authors' analysis again uses a contingent valuation survey to estimate the household's maximum willingness to pay for water in the city of Onitsha, a city of about 100 000 households. At the time of the study (1987) one-third to one-half of the population lived in conditions with no piped water or indoor toilets. Such a situation is not at all uncommon in the developing world.

Piped water in the city was provided by the local water authority, subsidized by the government, but insufficient resources existed to expand the service. Instead, mobile water vendors took up the slack, and household members could either go to them, or if time were important, they could have the water delivered to their dwelling. Data suggested that households in Onitsha were paying about N120 000 (N is the abbreviation used for the Nigerian currency, the Naira) per day to private water vendors in the dry season. At August 1987 exchange rates of $1.00 per N4.3, this meant an average payment of about $2800 per day for all households during the dry season going to these private vendors.

Two hundred and thirty-five households completed a survey wherein they were asked if they would like to be connected to a new water supply service for a price of N1 per drum (one drum = 45 gallons). If they said yes, they were asked the same question at a higher price and if they said yes again another bid was given, and so on, resulting in a 'bidding game' to arrive at maximum willingness to pay. About 44 percent of households were willing to pay between N0.50 and N0.99 for a drum of water. During the dry season poorer households were actually paying up to 18 percent of their income for water, and this was borne out in results of the contingent valuation survey.

The results of the CVM study also showed that 99 percent of respondents would choose to connect to the new system at a price of N3 per 1000 gallons, and with increases in price that this percentage would fall, but not drastically. The study concluded that the local water authority could charge a price of the order of N8–10 per 1000 gallons, which would substantially increase revenue for them, but still be much less than the prices the local private vendors were charging.

Haiti
Whittington et al. (1990) conducted studies in Haiti. The team involved some of the same authors as the Nigerian study. They estimated WTP for water services in southern Haiti, again implementing a CVM. In August 1986 the authors initiated the study in the village of Laurent,

a rural area in southern Haiti. They used the fact that the international agency CARE was funding rural water supply projects in about 40 towns and villages to justify their presence and obtain cooperation for their own study. Haiti's annual per capita income in 1980 was about US$155, roughly one-hundredth of incomes per capita in many developed nations. As a technical exercise, it was interesting to see if a CVM survey could be done convincingly in a setting with extreme poverty and high illiteracy. More than 80 percent of Laurent's 1500 people (mostly farmers) were illiterate. The villagers relied on unreliable springs for water, traveling an average of 3 kilometers to them, and waiting for periods of over an hour to draw water from the source. Women carried most of the water for the household.

The survey asked villagers their monthly WTP for public stand posts in their village or a private water system, presuming they had no private connection. A rule of thumb in DCs is that the maximum WTP for water supplies by a household might be 5 percent of their annual income. The mean WTP obtained for public stand posts was 5.7 gourdes per household, per month. Annual average income in Laurent was assumed to be about 4000 gourdes (which equaled US$800 at that time). This 5.7 gourdes thus translated into about 1.7 percent of household income, lower than the rule of thumb for the maximum. Assuming the household's village already had a public stand post, some households were also asked their monthly maximum WTP for a private connection. For private connections, the mean WTP was about 7.1 gourdes per household, per month, translating to about 2.1 percent of income. Munasinghe (1993) concludes that on the basis of the Haiti study, it is possible to do a CVM survey of households that are very poor and illiterate, and obtain reasonable estimates of the value for improved water supplies. I would agree based on the information that I have reviewed (mainly the reasonable fraction of annual income that the estimated WTPs constitute). However, without any doubt, a CVM survey given to such a sample group must involve a tremendous amount of work and care to make the exercise comprehensible to the respondents.

Pakistan (the Punjab)
In one of the many studies conducted in developing countries involving Dale Whittington and Mir Anjum Altaf, several economists and environmental scientists examined water issues in rural Pakistan (see Altaf et al., 1993). Unlike many other studies in developing countries (such as the Haiti study), the focus of the Pakistan study is on the role that water plays in regions of a developing country with rapid economic development. The authors again apply the CVM to examine households' willingness to pay for improved and more reliable water service.

The first Pakistan study described here involves data collected in interviews conducted with 756 households in 11 villages in 1988. These villages were split between the Sheikhupura and Faisalabad districts of the Punjab. The former is in the 'sweet-water' and the latter in the 'brackish water' zone. Many households were again buying their water from street vendors, as they do in Nigeria. The price of a 20 liter container of water in 1990 was about Rs 1. The authors report that in 1990 $1 = Rs 21, or Rs 1 = about $0.05 in US currency. Other villages used handpumped water, or had a connection to handpumps, and some had electric pumps without or with household connections. Most in the Sheikhupura sweet-water zone had their own wells with connections.

Households in each district, that is, in both the sweet and brackish water zones, were asked questions to determine their WTP for improved water services. The 'improvement' varied between zones, as the sweet-water zone's basic quality of service was already better than the brackish zone. The overall mean monthly WTP for the sweet water zone was Rs 21 (about $1) and, for the brackish zone, about Rs 40. The authors of the study draw several conclusions regarding rural water supply improvements in this part of Pakistan:

(i) Unlike other rural areas of DCs this region's population had little desire for a public stand post, preferring instead metered connections.
(ii) The government wrongly assumed that the villagers were waiting for them to implement improvements. The authors found that the private sector had already moved in to assist in water supply improvement. The government needed to re-evaluate its policies.
(iii) The government was paying too little attention to sanitation and drainage problems. Increased water supply via electric pumps had increased drainage problems.
(iv) Full cost recovery is quite feasible in many areas of the Punjab, but the government should abandon a uniform, centralized water supply focus in favor of a decentralized, demand-driven policy.

Altaf has also conducted other studies in Pakistan. These include a study of about 1000 households in Gujranwala, Pakistan, a 'secondary city' with a population of about one million, but with a rapid annual population growth rate of about 7.3 percent. Just over half of the city's households had access to the public piped water system, and 40 percent had access to the public sewer line, but there was no treatment plant in the city for sewage or wastewater. Wastes were discharged into abandoned irrigation canals near the city, and the city's households contribute about 500 tons of solid waste daily. Those not on the public sewer system discharged effluents into neighborhood sewage ponds. There was actually a good proportion of households in middle and high income groups in the city and those with sufficient income supplemented the poor service of the public delivery and sanitation system using their own investments.

Again using the CVM approach, Altaf (1994) estimates the demand for improved public services for these residents. Surveys were conducted during the Fall of 1990. At this time one dollar (US) exchanged for Rs 19.75, the Pakistan currency. The survey team asked households in the study their maximum willingness to pay per month for various services. Those without piped water were offered a standard service, and those who already had it were offered a higher level of service (this is not carefully detailed in the report of the study). Altaf's results are shown in Table 10.3.

Altaf notes that sample mean WTP is less than existing per household expenditure for water, but this WTP exceeds the per household expenditure for sanitation. He believes that this may be because unreliability and poor performance are more probable in the public water system. The WTPs are favorable for cost recovery, as seen by comparing these to the supply costs reported in the table.

Altaf arrives at several important conclusions. First, it is significant that these problems exist even in fairly large cities, as opposed to only in rural areas such as in the Altaf et al. (1993) study. Second, he believes that there is a strong demand for public services and that a modest tariff could be raised to provide improved public service, in a much more economically efficient manner than having each individual household invest in their own improvements (via motor pumps, pipelines, and so on).

Table 10.3 Comparison of average existing expenditure, supply cost and willingness to pay for improved services (Rs per household, per month)

	Existing expenditure	Willingness to pay	Supply cost*
Water			
Households without piped supply	75	36	30
Households with piped supply	90	44	n.a.
Sanitation			
Households without a sewer	20	26	63
Households with a sewer	18	20	n.a.

Note: * The supply cost of upgraded water and sewer systems was not available.

Source: Altaf (1994).

Korea

Um et al. (2002) consider how a sample of individuals respond to the risks of drinking tap water in South Korea. They allow households to perceive risks in their own particular fashion rather than developing a model based on the assessments of health risks given by expert scientists. As noted earlier, South Korea is a NIC, and not a DC, but in fact the fast pace of development and industrialization have caused deterioration of water quality in key rivers. The Nak-Dong River was traditionally used as a water source for 8 million residents in the Pusan and Kyungnam Province. As of 1999, 93 per cent of Pusan tap water came from this river. In 1998, the Korean Ministry of Environment stated that this water could be drunk only after advanced water treatment with pre-filtration. A 1995 survey reported that only 1.4 percent of Pusan residents were drinking water directly from their tap. Most of the remaining population boiled the water (30 percent), or drew spring or groundwater (63 percent).

The authors sampled from the population to see how they averted or mitigated against risk in 1998. The sample group for the study had a mean household income of approximately US$2300 equivalent (in 1998 US$1 = 900 Korean Won), with monthly average water bills of $13. Using this sample and responses to WTP questions, the authors first estimate the average WTP for a small reduction (10 mg/liter) in the concentration of suspended solids using a conventional averting behavior model. Their results are in the range of $0.70 to $1.70 per month, per household. This reduction is estimated from a baseline of 335 mg/liter, the average concentration of suspended solids in Pusan in 1998. The public drinking water standard is 500 mg/liter, so in this regard the average levels were already below the standard. However, perceptions and the Environment Ministry's assessments of contamination differ. Using the perceptions of households the authors re-estimate the WTP and find a monthly average value that is considerably larger: $4.20 to $6.10 per month, per household.

Zimbabwe

Munasinghe (1993) summarizes several case studies that value resources in other countries, including one done by Fredriksson and Persson in 1989 to evaluate the Manicaland Health, Water and Sanitation Program in Zimbabwe. The objectives of the program were to improve living conditions in the 'communal' areas by improving existing, and constructing new, water supply facilities, as well as improving sanitation conditions by constructing latrines. The project also provided health education to the locals, with attention to hygienic practices. The authors do an assessment of water prices, with and without the project, and calculate the change in consumer's surplus accordingly. The price of water in this case is calculated using the mean kCals of energy used in walking and carrying water and therefore involves the time and energy cost of performing this task. It is interesting to consider their exact approach.

The Maniculand Province is in east Zimbabwe and is at a high altitude, with the highest average rainfall in the country. It is agriculturally rich, with production in forestry, fruit, maize, groundnuts, tea, coffee, dairy, beef, and cotton. Of the 1.27 million who live there (in 1987) 66 percent live on communal lands, and over half are under age 15. About 65 percent are working in the agricultural sector. Rather than perform any sort of non-market valuation calculations the authors rely on the main costs of delivering water in the region to calculate the consumer's surplus change, as well as the possible reduction in the cost of illness and death.

The cost of most interest here is for labor and the authors make some assumptions about the shadow price of labor to calculate this. Typically, in equilibrium labor–leisure choice models indicate that the opportunity cost of an individual's time is the market wage, but this may not be true in DCs and, in any case, getting good information on market wages may be impossible. There is high unemployment during the dry season in Zimbabwe and the authors assume that the shadow price of unskilled laborers during that period is zero. At the peak harvest season there is a labor shortage and the shadow price of unskilled labor is assumed to be equal to, or a fraction of the market wage, which was then Z$0.46 per hour in Zimbabwean dollars.[9] Skilled labor's shadow wage is assumed to be equal to 100 percent of the market wage.

The authors use the above information to assess the change in consumer surplus per year for the reduced 'price' of carrying water home. They also calculate the drop in the cost of illness and the value of lives saved with the project. It is often assumed that the main cost of illness is the cost of forgone production, and for valuing lives, this forgone production is also considered for the rest of the individual's life. The latter is called the 'human capital' approach to valuing lives saved. Costs of illness also involve physician costs and transportation to medical care facilities. These were factored into the calculations. Reduced morbidity was estimated to be worth Z$6.27 million per year, assuming 100 percent of the shadow wage and 100 percent reduction in disease.

As it was hoped that many children would be saved by the project and the remainder of their productive life could be fairly long, this suggests that substantial benefits for the project were possible. At a social discount rate of 4.86, a child's life saved is worth Z$2813, and an 'adult' of age greater than five years saved has a value of Z$1131. Compared to current estimates that range from about $1 to $7 million used today by the US EPA, these values for a life saved are quite low.

Using a discount rate of 4.86 percent (the commercial bank lending rate less the inflation rate of 9.89 percent), a 100 percent improvement in health, and a duration of the project of 40 years, the authors conclude that the project has a positive internal rate of return or IRR. Calculating the IRR is often the way that NGOs such as the World Bank, Asian Development Bank, and IMF make an assessment of the net benefit of a project. So, this project looks beneficial to those in the region of Manicaland. However, when the social discount rate is assumed to be higher, at 7.24 percent, the project is not profitable. The authors note that their calculations do provide a lower bound on the value of a life saved, that they do not consider the benefits of the project to local industry, and that the distribution of income because of the project may change, possibly increasing benefits further.

Russia
Though Russia would not generally be considered a 'developing' country, in yet another study some economists (Larson and Gnedenko, 1999) examine drinking water quality and associated health risks in Moscow. Avoidance behavior is examined for 615 households surveyed, with findings that 88 percent of the sample regularly boil water. Avoidance decisions are related to income and city locations. There are few other details about water quality problems in Russia at this time, suggesting an area ripe for further research. It would be particularly interesting to examine what has happened in a country that used to have centralized government, but now does not.

China
Finally, I end this section on specific countries with discussion of China. This study indicates that there is some hope for the role that economic incentives can play. Water pollution in China is very serious, mainly caused by industry. Oddly, Article 18 of China's Environmental Protection Law specifies that a charge will be levied on industry when their discharges of water pollutants exceed state limits. This may seem somewhat surprising as there are still no well-functioning water emissions charges in the United States. From about 1980, when the levy was introduced, to 1996, Chinese regulators have collected about 30 billion RMB yuan from over 500 000 major polluters (both air and water).[10] About 63 percent of the total pollution charge in 1996 was contributed by water pollution charges. This is the largest application of a market-based regulatory instrument in the developing world (Wang and Wheeler, 2000). In their investigation of industry in China, Wang and Wheeler in fact find that industry has responded significantly to the levy, decreasing the intensity of pollution in the production process, and in the case of water, by treating water pollution at the end of pipe.

Cross-country studies

Torras and Boyce (1998) regress pollution variables across countries to explore the variation in the causes of pollution in several settings. Included in their exploration are two water pollution variables: dissolved oxygen and fecal coliform for various stations in 58 countries. They get these from the Global Environmental Monitoring System (GEMS) data set.

The regressions performed indicate that income does have a positive relationship with the concentrations for these variables, which relates to the idea of an environmental 'Kuznets' curve. Simon Kuznets gave a 1954 presidential address to the American Economic Association and in it he discussed the tendency for there to be an inverted U shape between the level of economic development and the degree of income inequality. The environmental Kuznets curve idea borrows from this and was put forward by Gene Grossman and Alan Krueger, as well as others, exploring per capita income's effect on environmental degradation. The results were for water and air pollutants over a span of 12 years (about 1977 to 1990, depending on which pollutant) and over 66 countries. Data were collected via the Global Environmental Monitoring System (GEMS).[11] For water pollution the authors examined the pollutants or water quality parameters, BOD, coliform, dissolved oxygen, fecal coliform, and arsenic (see Chapter 3). They concluded there was a significant U-shaped relationship: pollution seemed to be highest at intermediate (not low or very high) income levels, while pollution was low at relatively low and high levels of income. However, these results are obtained with exclusion of inequality variables such as a Gini coefficient, which measures the degree of equality of the distribution of income within various countries.

Recognizing the role of income distribution, Torras and Boyce (1998) find that countries with more equitable distributions of income tend to have better environmental quality. However, using exactly the same data as Grossman and Krueger (1995) and a new specification (the fixed effects econometric model, which fixes numbers such as income level and growth cross-sectionally), Bradford et al. (2000) find mixed results: some pollutants support the inverted U shape and others do not.

10.3 WATER SUPPLY AND ALLOCATION IN OTHER COUNTRIES

I turn now to allocating water in other countries. Perhaps the most obvious and prevalent conflict between two countries in people's minds today is over occupation of the West Bank and Gaza Strip (see discussion below). In this region annual water availability is less than 200 cubic meters per person. Review the conversion table in Chapter 1 and put this amount of water into perspective. In 1985 the per capita use of water was 1952 cubic meters. A typical household in the western United States today uses something in the range from a half to an entire acre foot per year, or about 325 000 gallons per year. The West Bank average per person availability is about 52 769 gallons per year, or only about 144 gallons per day. This may sound like an ample amount when one only thinks of water to drink, but this amount of water must cover all needs and wants discussed in Chapter 1, bathing, cleaning, and so on. About 1000 cubic meters per capita is considered the bare minimum amount necessary in industrialized nations (Homer-Dixon et al., 1993).

The Jordan River discharges most of its water into Israel, but in fact most of the recharge for the river occurs in Syria and Lebanon. Nearly every single attempt to negotiate over the Golan Heights involves discussion of allocation of water in the Jordan River. While it is perhaps overstating the case to say that the only cause of the dispute in the region is water, it certainly plays a central role.

10.3.1 Water Supply

Water supply problems remain for many countries around the world (for example, Frankel, 1975). Historically, even communities near large European cities have needed to assess water supply issues, again because of population growth relative to the supply. An example comes from examining the water supply system near Venice, Italy. Surprisingly for this city where people regularly commute on the waters and canals, in the early 1990s the areas around the city suffered from shortages. New canal systems alleviated the problem, but this was possible because finance was available.

Bhattia and Falkernmark (1993) note that many large cities in developing countries still experience frequent water sales by street vendors, even when water from public utilities appears to be available. Here again, the supply price matters. The supply price that vendors charge for water greatly exceeds the price utilities charge. In some cases this is by a factor of as much as 20 to 1, and even 100 to 1 (Port-au-Prince, Haiti).[12] It would seem logical that most such cities would be better off with a different scheme for supplying water. Easter et al. (1999) propose that developing countries might also benefit from consideration and formation of water markets as a means to improve allocation.

10.3.2 Approaches to Management and Allocation

River basin management

Some countries have reorganized water management around entire river basins. For example, in 1973 a new water act in England and Wales created ten regional water authorities. By 1988, the government had decided on a plan to privatize the water industry, and the ten authorities created in 1973 became ten companies. These companies are regulated by the Director General of Water Services (DGWS); much as in the US, public utility commissions provide regulatory oversight to private water utilities. This restructuring of the water supply industry is being examined by other countries around the world (see Spulber and Sabbaghi, 1998, chapter 10), but the biggest trend in past years has been toward privatization.

Privatization of water supply and sanitation

In the introduction to this chapter I mentioned the trend toward privatization. In the US today many cities are turning to private companies to run and operate their water systems. They are in fact late in following a trend around the world. In countries outside the US many urban area governments have turned not only operation, but ownership, of water supply over to private companies. From discussion above, we know that many developing countries are facing huge debts. As world lending agencies such as the World Bank try to help and advise them, their recommendation may be to privatize services typically provided by the government in hopes of cost savings: likely the main goal of privatizing water supply systems. The thought is that governments may operate their own water systems inefficiently, wasting money when they have little to waste. Small urban water supply systems may simply be unable to attract skilled laborers familiar with water quantity and quality issues. Huge foreign or multinational companies, such as France's Vivendi Environnement and Suez Corporations, have been created to provide expertise in this manner. Vivendi merged with Seagram's Universal media business in the 1990s and recently bought US Filter, a national water-services group, for more than $6 billion (Finnegan, 2002). The three largest water management firms in the world now serve a population about the same size as the United States' (Tagliabue, 2002).

In December 1992 a 30 year concession was granted to a private sector consortium to operate the water and sanitation system in Buenos Aires, Argentina. This was again in reaction to dire economic conditions: hyperinflation and a failing economic system. Buenos Aires had about 10 million people in 1992, 2 million of whom were deemed 'poor', presumably below the poverty line of $500 per month, US equivalent. Despite having an ample supply of reasonably clean water, the state-owned water utility, Obras Sanitarias de la Nacion (OSN), was providing a limited water service of poor quality in the city. This situation is now common in many DCs. Losses were estimated at 45 percent of the total volume supplied, and only 70 percent of the population was connected to the water system (unknown author, 2002). The suburban areas, occupied by the poor, were receiving the least public system water, relying instead on wells of poorer quality due to contamination of groundwater by untreated industrial waste. The consortium that bid and won the project is Aguas Argentinas, run by Lyonnaise des Eaux, another French company.

The consortium planned to have its newest customers, the surburban poor, bear the bulk of the cost of the secondary expansion needed to get them water. They assumed that this could be done via financial assistance, a loan to be repaid at 12 percent interest. At this point it appears as though the goal of providing water to 100 percent of Buenos Aires' 10 million residents will not be reached in 30 years. Progress is being made, but access to water by the poor remains low because of their inability to afford service.

In the Tucumán Province of Argentina a similar situation, with Vivendi providing the water, finally led the company to abandon its long-term contract, after local protest over price increases (Tagliabue, 2002). This came after losses of $3 million a month, and bill collection rates fell to 10 percent.

While corporations now own or operate water systems around the world, grossing about $200 billion and functioning for about 7 percent of the world market, it is far from clear that privatization of water systems is working to promote efficiency (Tagliabue, 2002). This is true even in the United States. Recently, the city council of Atlanta, one of the largest cities in the US to privatize operations of their system (Suez runs their system via a subsidiary company in the US), expressed concern over their 20 year contract and the fact that the providing company had asked for more money. Of more concern is whether privatization is working in DCs, or at least in countries outside the US.

Finnegan provides an interesting case study of privatization in Bolivia (2002). The story begins with Bolivian debt, and management and pressure to adjust their economy from the World Bank and International Montary Fund (IMF). Finnegan suggests in fact that the World Bank is 'getting out the dam business and into water privatization' (p. 44). In 1999 the Bolivian government auctioned one area's water system as part of its privatization program to Aguas del Tunari, a consortium controlled by International Water, a British firm in turn owned by the Bechtel Corporation. The story reaches its climax in the Cochabamba riot of April 2000, with the death of a 17-year-old boy, shot in the face by the Bolivian

Army during a protest over local water rates that were controlled by Aguas del Tunari.

Prior to selling the Cochabamban water system, a local cooperative had dug new wells and was providing water to about 210 families at a cost of between $2 and $5 per month. Aguas del Tunari contracted to take over the system for 40 years, at a cost of $2.5 billion. The contract guaranteed the company a minimum rate of annual return on investment of 15 percent, to be annually adjusted to the CPI in the US. After Aguas del Tunari took over and first began billing its customers (January 2000), some people discovered that their bills had doubled. The most important point is that many workers now faced water bills that amounted to one-fourth of their monthly income! The consortium said that price hikes were necessary in order to invest to expand the city's water system to accommodate future growth, and repair old, failing systems. By February 2000 many people had begun to protest.

The day after the funeral of the fallen youth, a leader of the protest movement announced that the water consortium had departed, apparently concerned for their own safety after the people rebelled in reaction to the killing of the boy by the army. Today the operation of the water system for Cochabamba has returned to the old public utility, much to the dismay of the Bolivian government. The saga suggests that privatization has many problems, but Finnegan reports that following all of this Bechtel, through International Water, has included two major new water deals in Ecuador and Estonia. Privatization seems to be failing in many parts of Latin America (Panama, Peru, Brazil, and Argentina) and there have been protests against it in Indonesia, Pakistan, India, South Africa, and Poland. Still, some predict that privatization will expand to serve about 17 percent of the world's population (Tagliabue, 2002).

10.4 DAMS IN DEVELOPING COUNTRIES

Much of Chapter 9 was devoted to dams and issues relating to them in the United States. There are some different issues associated with dams in DCs. Across the world there are some 40 000 dams, with reservoirs encompassing about 400 000 square kilometers. Currently the largest impoundment in the world is the Volta Reservoir (8500 sq. km.) behind Ghana's Akasombo Dam. While the era of building big dams is probably over in the US, dams are still being built today in developing countries such as India and China, and on a massive scale. The following case study adds to what was reported in Chapter 9 on China's Three Gorges Dam.

CASE STUDY: THREE GORGES DAM

The largest, most expensive dam ever built for hydroelectric power and flood control is the Three Gorges Dam (called Sanxia Ba in China) in China's Yangtze River Valley, which produces about one-half of China's food. The Yangtze River, the longest river in China, is home to 380 million people, a third of the Chinese population. The dam is proposed to be 1.3 miles long and 610 feet high. The reservoir created by the dam is to be 385 miles long. Twenty-six sets of 700 megawatt turbines are proposed. The plan is for 18 000 megawatts of electricity to be produced every year, supplying 10 percent of China's energy. This amount of energy is equivalent to the power produced by 18 nuclear power plants. Scheduled completion at this time is June, 2003.

The dam is also to provide flood control protection. More than 300 000 people died from floods in the region during the twentieth century. The current estimate of the dam's cost is $75 billion. This has been financed via bonds issued by China's Development Bank, and much of the financing has been underwritten by US firms. The World Bank has only been involved in supervising a feasibility study.

Negative impacts: resettlement
One of the most difficult aspects of building huge dams is that the people who live in areas that will be inundated must move. The High Aswan caused relocation of about 120 000 Narobi people. This is small in comparison to the Yangtze Valley's 1.4 million people, all of whom will have to be resettled as a result of this project. Many of these are farmers, who must move with the loss of about 74 000 acres of prime agricultural land. It is not clear that they will be able to continue farming, nor what the cost of this will be for the food/farming sector (Flahive, 2003).

The Chinese government has promised to spend $4.8 billion on resettlement alone. Is the mere cost of resettlement the true cost to society? Many would argue not. Sociologists say that the impact of leaving one's home affects the people's sense of culture, their ability to be re-educated, and their ability to fit into their new surroundings and find meaningful work. Transplanted people may never fully adjust. What is the full negative impact on the people who must leave their homes, and could this be cast in economic terms? To find out, one would likely wish to do some sort of valuation exercise to ascertain what an individual's WTP to prevent losing their home would be, or alternatively what minimum compensation would be required to make them indifferent between giving up their home and moving. To my knowledge, this type of study has never been done.

There is also great concern over the flooding of cultural artifacts that date back about 10 000 years (Topping, 1995). If the dam is completed, 12 711 archeological sites will be submerged. The US government supposedly set aside $37.5 million for excavation of these sites. Again, is it really moving the sites that is the true cost to society? Or, is there some additional cost that involves the loss of their original location?

Finally, there are conventional environmental impacts with large dams such as the Three Gorges Dam. In the Amazonian region, where large dam projects are still under way, it has been found that siltation rates have been grossly underpredicted. For example, the Anchicaya Project in the Colombian Amazon experienced a loss of 80 percent of its storage capacity in the first 12 years of operation because of siltation (Allen, 1972, cited in Cummings, 1990). As other examples, whitefin dolphins and the Chinese sturgeon are found in the Yangtze, but face extinction with completion of the project. In addition, however, no one seems to know what the quality of the reservoir water will be in coming years, and there is concern that the reservoir will be on top of an active fault line.

Sources: Topping (1995); Salazar (2000); Cummings (1990).

10.5 VIOLENT CONFLICT AND THE POTENTIAL FOR MORE IN THE FUTURE

It can easily be demonstrated that many existing international political disputes have their roots in, or at least have as an integral part, struggles over natural resources including water. Resources are not a minor variable to consider (see Homer-Dixon et al, 1993). Rival countries took to arms on 37 recorded occasions involving water-related interactions (Wolf, 2004). Most disputes rise to the level of angry words only, but fighting over water is not constrained to the boundaries of the western United States. In the past the problems have manifested themselves as struggles over agricultural land, but if that land is desirable because its productivity is enhanced by access to irrigation water, then the struggles could also be said to have been about water. Though technological innovation in irrigation systems does help make water use more efficient, the problems may get worse, especially in countries with high population growths.

United Nations Secretary Kofi Annan has stated that 'fierce competition for fresh water may well become a source of conflict and wars in the future' (see Postel and Wolf, 2001). Despite this warning it is still true that many countries hostile to one another have managed to negotiate water sharing agreements. These include the Mekong River Basin countries of China, Thailand, Cambodia, and Vietnam (Wolf, 2004). Still, friction remains high and as demands for water increase, tensions are likely to lead to increasing conflict. For example, Wolf (2004) reports that the Israelis allocate one-fourth of the amount they receive in West Bank aquifer water to the Palestinians occupying the West Bank. Conflicts there are well known, but as mentioned elsewhere in this book, it may surprise some to know that water is a key issue in disputes.

10.6 ARE THERE SOLUTIONS TO WATER PROBLEMS IN OTHER COUNTRIES?

As the world shrinks because of innovations in rapid communication networks, much more attention is given to issues such as water scarcity and water pollution problems than was received in different eras, so there may be hope for solving these problems. I do not suggest that all water allocation problems have been solved in developed nations such as the US (the continuing disputes over water in the American West are evidence of this), but most would agree that problems relating to water in the US and Europe likely pale in comparison to those in DCs. For example, plagued by years of water pollution, West Germany embarked on a program of effluents or discharge fees, and this market-based incentive has been credited with bringing about considerable clean up of West German waters. Ironically, it was implemented well before such programs in the United States. One hears little about such programs in DCs.

Many scholars have turned their focus for their water work away from the developed nations and toward issues in DCs. The process of collecting much-needed data for analysis of the causes and potential solutions to the problems is now well under way. Criticism of building dams in the 1960s and 1970s has led the large international lending agencies such as the World Bank to shy away from such projects, or at least to put more emphasis on including environmental analysis in assessment of a project's rate of return. More hope comes via linkages to programs to promote the concept and plans pertaining to economic reform and sustainability. These are addressed in the next two sections, but I again emphasize that the culture and natural setting in many DCs is so vastly different from the western world that it seems likely that each country's water issues may demand specific attention.

Economic reform
As indicated throughout this chapter, major lending and financial institutions such as the World Bank and IMF play a major role in economic policies in DCs. Egypt is a good example for this chapter, because it is almost completely dependent on irrigation, and the connection of water use policy to economic reform is critical (see a discussion of other countries in Bromley et al., 1980). In 1991 Egypt embarked on major economic reform in accordance with a World Bank/IMF-recommended structural adjustment program. The overall goals of the reform relate to price liberalization and liberalizing trade through a reduction of tariffs and other barriers to imports and exports. Since most of Egypt's economy was tied to a fixed agricultural base, it became important to consider whether water was a constraint on achieving the reforms the Bank/IMF had in mind. Robinson and Gehlar (1995) developed a computable general equilibrium model (CGE) of the Egyptian economy to examine the potential for water to impede economic activity, focusing the CGE model on the role that both land and water play in the economy.

The authors found that land, not water, was the binding constraint on farmers from 1986 to 1988, the policy regime they considered. This suggests a low marginal value of water in Egyptian agriculture, which is hard to believe. The reason is that then, and this remains true today, farmers were not charged for water, but received adequate supplies to irrigate their crops. Robinson and Gehlar's modeling suggests that if and when the agricultural sector grows, but the supply of water does not, water's value to farmers will increase greatly. They conclude that, along with the economic reforms suggested by the Bank/IMF, there will likely be structural changes and increasing water scarcity, and Egypt must reform its water allocation system.

In fact, a common theme in DCs is the need for reform of water systems, as even with government promising to provide water, many households in DCs do not believe or trust the government to carry through. This appears to be correlated with the failure of many governments actually to provide a reliable supply (for example, see the Whittington et al. study of Nigeria, 1990).

Sustainable development
The famous Brundtland Report was given to the World Commission on Environment and Development in 1987 and since then there has been a great

deal of interest in how to promote development and growth while maintaining or sustaining current environmental and resource conditions. This relates to water management issues in developing countries. Some interpret the word sustainability to mean that future generations must not be allowed to experience any degradation in resource or environmental amenities as compared to present generations. Under such a strict interpretation a country would not be allowed to mine, cut down tropical rainforests that could not easily be reproduced, or currently extract exhaustible resources, because these resources would not be available for future generations.

A somewhat more flexible interpretation of sustainability would allow some resource use as long as future generations can be given the same opportunity to a standard of living as current generations. I suppose that if a water project results in an irreversible decision, such as flooding a spectacular canyon that future generations can never afterward see or use, then this project would have to be ruled out under even the loosest interpretation of sustainability. Some economists therefore object to that interpretation, and would suggest that future generations can be made as 'well off' from the loss of a natural resource simply by having more income per household. The assumption is that money at some level would adequately compensate an individual for the loss of a resource.

Water pollution remains a huge problem around the world and many forms of water quality degradation could again be interpreted as unsustainable. As the Chinese example above showed, there may be hope that economic incentives, coupled with new, enforceable environmental regulations can bring about efficient environmental improvement. But this will work only if curbing degradation of water quality remains a priority, and if the interface with water quantity allows it. As the reader knows by now, water quantity and quality problems are very often inseparable.

If indeed, as some say, society has already gone beyond the point where freshwater supplies are adequate to meet the needs of current world populations, then increasing those supplies comes into conflict with the goals of sustainability, and there is much work ahead to solve this issue. Again, the role that population growth plays rises to the surface. Even in traditional neoclassical growth models that do not require sustainability goals to be met, rising populations can lead to dire future consequences.

For now, current generations are faced with a large number of difficult tradeoffs. Most would agree that saving lives is important, and to the extent that improving sanitation and securing new and clean supplies of freshwater positively contributes, then society must devote current resources to these activities. At the same time however, society simply must continue to develop means to slow population growth in countries well in excess of zero population growth (ZPG).

Water markets/water pricing
All economists acknowledge that pricing policies may have an effect on the demand for resources such as water, but unlike other resources, it is unacceptable to price ourselves out of this particular good. If water prices do increase, these may make currently expensive strategies such as desalinization practicable. In addition, I would expect that water's 'secondary' uses, such as watering golf courses and household lawns in arid areas, may diminish over time. Water markets have been operating in some DCs for a long time. They seem to have helped allocate water efficiently in several countries, including Pakistan's groundwater (see Meinzen-Dick, 1998), and it appears that water markets are more successful in regions where water is scarce, which mimics the US experience. However, a concern is that in countries with large numbers of extremely poor people, higher water prices resulting from the emergence of functioning water markets will hurt the poor, especially small farmers, more than others. It may be that if water markets lead to worsening income distribution they must be coupled with active programs to address poverty.

Saleth (1999) suggests that social and cultural institutions in developing countries like India help mitigate against the feared consequence where the poor (in her case, farmers) lose out in water markets. This is because the people treat each other quite differently in such countries than is assumed by western economists who believe in competitive behavior. In small irrigation districts in the western US a kinship among water users is also prevalent, at least to a degree. Sometimes one can observe a western farmer or rancher who behaves oddly. Anecdotal evidence suggests that this odd behavior is because the farmer does not want to ruin a neighbor's livelihood by engaging in a radical water transaction, perhaps creating a large, negative third party effect.[13]

Whatever the success of water pricing policies in establishing secure water supplies and more efficient water allocation, the private sector will most certainly continue to explore the developing and newly industrialized countries as potential areas for business activity. Many continue to believe that there is a natural process leading to environmental regulation and expenditure, including better sanitation and water-related technologies. In DCs the government, largely through aid or loans, will continue to fund improved sanitation, water pollution abatement, and water supply improvements. In the early 1990s, for example, the World Bank and several western countries gave the Bangkok (Thailand) government advances to allow conversion from groundwater to piped water systems. Private companies' view is that as countries such as Thailand develop, the burden of water treatment and abatement shifts from government to private industry, and their plan may be to capitalize on this situation by introducing cost-saving technologies to those very industries.

NOTES

1. Thanks to Samantha Goldstein for her comments on this chapter.
2. In the 1970s the initials most often used were LDC, for less developed countries.
3. This estimate is from the Mason Water Yearbook, 2001 and was found in a presentation by Saur International to the World Bank, on the World Bank's website.
4. This information comes from discussions with Ron Petersen, a consulting MS in hydrology, who visited Kenya in early Spring, 2002, and it echoes much of what is found in the study of the Anambra region of Nigeria by Whittington et al. back in 1991.
5. For example, when it comes to water issues it is misleading to lump countries such as Kuwait in with the developed or industrialized nations. Kuwait had a per capita annual income of about $21 000 as compared to about $11 000 in the US in 1981. Nevertheless, Al-Qunaibet and Johnston (1985) found that municipal residents in Kuwait would respond to water price increases. This is because Kuwait has a very small number of wealthy individuals, and a huge number of poor ones.
6. Those unfamiliar with population issues might wish to research the 'rule of 70' which shows that when one wants to know the doubling time for a population, a simple approximation can be found by dividing 70 by the annual percentage growth rate (for example, 70/2 percent yields 35 years).
7. This is the dichotomous choice contingent valuation method approach.
8. There are 3.79 liters in one gallon.
9. The author notes that converting currencies should be done using Harberger's formula to calculate the shadow price of foreign exchange. Assuming Zimbabwe is a price taker, one can substitute the supply and demand elasticities of foreign exchange with the import demand and export supply elasticities. With export supply elasticity set to zero, Harberger's formula is $R' = [nM(1 + T)R]/nM = (1 + T)R$, where R' is the shadow price of foreign exchange, R is the official exchange rate, M = import values in foreign currency terms, T = import duties, n = elasticity of demand for foreign exchange.
10. At the time of their study US$1 = 8.2 RMB yuan.
11. Water data are from http://www.cciw.ca/gems/summary.intro.html.
12. As cited by Rosengrant and Cline (2002).
13. I thank David Zilberman, who shared this observation with me before I saw it myself.

REFERENCES

Abel, A.B. and B.S. Bernanke (2001), *Macroeconomics,* 4th edn, Boston: Addison-Wesley.

Al-Qunaibet, Mohammed H. and Richard S. Johnston (1985), 'Municipal demand for water in Kuwait: methodological issues and empirical results', *Water Resources Research*, **21**(4) (April), 433–8.

Altaf, M.A. (1994), 'Household demand for improved water and sanitation in a large secondary city: findings from a study in Gujranwala, Pakistan', *Habitat International,* **18**(1), 45–55.

Altaf, M.A., D. Whittington, H. Jamal and V.K. Smith (1993), 'Rethinking rural water supply policy in the Punjab, Pakistan', *Water Resources Research*, **29**(7) (July), 1943–54.

Allen, R.N. (1972), 'The Anchicaya Hydroelectric Project in Columbia: design and sedimentation problems', in *The Careless Technology,* New York: Natural History Press, pp. 318–42.

Bandyopadhyay, J. and V. Shiva (1989), 'Development, poverty, and growth of the green movement in India', *The Ecologist*, **19** (May–June), 111–17.

Bhattia, R. and M. Falkernmark (1993), 'Water resource policies and the urban poor: innovative approaches and policy imperatives', Water and Sanitation Current UNDP–World Bank Water and Sanitation Program, World Bank, Washington, DC.

Bradford, D.F., R. Schlieckert and S.H. Shore (2000), 'The environmental Kuznets curve: exploring a fresh specification', National Bureau of Economic Research, Cambridge, MA.

Bromley, D.W., D.C. Taylor and D.E. Parker (1980), 'Water reform and economic development: institutional aspects of water management in the developing countries', *Economic Development and Cultural Change*, **28**(2) (January).

Cummings, Barbara J. (1990), *Dam the Rivers, Damn the People: Development and Resistance in Amazonian Brazil*, London: Earthscan Publications.

Easter, K.William, M.W. Rosengrant and A. Dinar (1999), 'Formal and informal markets for water: institutions, performance, and constraints', *The World Bank Research Observer*, **14**(1) (February), 99–116.

European Environmental Almanac (1995), Jonathan Hewett (principal ed.), Washington, DC: World Wildlife Fund, and London: Earthscan Publications.

Finnegan, William (2002), 'Letter from Bolivia: leasing the rain', *New Yorker* (April 8), 43–53.

Flahive, C. (2003), 'Forced urbanization: the Three Gorges Dam relocation process', in Thomas V. Cech, *Principles of Water Resources: History, Development, Management, and Policy*, New York: John Wiley and Sons.

Frankel, Richard J. (1975), 'Systems evaluation of village water supply and treatment in Thailand', *Water Resources Research*, **11**(3) (June).

Frederiksson, P. and A. Persson (1989), 'The Manicaland Health, Water and Sanitation Program, Zimbabwe – A Social Cost-Benefit Analysis', *Minor Field Study – Series No. 9*, Stockholm: Stockholm School of Economics.

Grossman, G.M. and A.B. Krueger (1995), 'Economic growth and the environment', *Quarterly Journal of Economics*, **110**, 353–77.

Homer-Dixon, T.F., J.H. Boutwell and G.W. Rathjens (1993), 'Environmental change and violent conflict', *Scientific American* (February), 38–45.

Kahn, Joseph and Tim Weiner (2002), 'World leaders rethinking strategy on aid to poor', *New York Times* (March 18), A3.

Larson, B. and E.K. Gnedenko (1999), 'Avoiding health risks from drinking water in Moscow: an empirical analysis', *Environment and Development Economics*, **4**(4) (October), 565–81.

Lauria, D.T., D. Whittington, K. Choe, C. Turinggan and V. Abiad (1999), 'Household demand for improved sanitation services: a case study of Calamba, the Philippines', in Ian Bateman and K.G. Willis (eds), *Valuing Environmental Preferences*, Oxford: Oxford University Press.

Lee, Lung-fei, M.R. Rosenzweig and M.M. Pitt (1997), 'The effects of improved nutrition, sanitation, and water quality on child health in high-mortality populations', *Journal of Econometrics*, **77**, 209–35.

Meinzen-Dick, R.S (1998), 'Groundwater markets in Pakistan: institutional development and productivity impacts', in K.W. Easter, M.W. Rosegrant and A. Dinar (eds), *Markets for Water: Potential and Performance*, Boston: Kluwer Academic Publishers.

Milliman, Jerome W. (1978), 'Village water supply: economics and policy in the developing world: a review', *Land Economics*, **54**(1) (February).

Munasinghe, M. (ed.) (1993), *Environmental Economics and Natural Resource*

Management in Developing Countries, Committee of International Development Institutions on the Environment, Washington, DC: World Bank.

Postel, S. and A. Wolf (2001), 'Dehyrdating conflict', *Foreign Policy* (September 18).

Robinson, S. and C.G. Gehlar (1995), 'Land, water and agriculture in Egypt: the economy-wide impact of policy reform', discussion paper, Trade and Macroeconomics Division, International Food Policy Research Institute (August), Washington, DC.

Rosengrant, Mark W. and Sarah Cline (2002), 'The politics and economics of water pricing in developing countries', *Water Resources Impact*, **4**(1) (January), 6–8.

Salazar, J.G. (2000), 'Damming the child of the ocean: the Three Gorges project', *Journal of Environment and Development*, **9**(2), 160–74.

Saleth, M.R. (1999), 'Water markets in India: economic and institutional aspects', in K.William Easter, Mark W. Rosengrant and Ariel Dinar (eds) (1998), *Markets for Water: Potential and Performance,* Boston, MA: Klumer Academic Publishers.

Simon, Julian (1981), *The Ultimate Resource,* Princeton: Princeton University Press.

Spulber, Nicolas and Asghar Sabbaghi (1998), *Economics of Water Resources: From Regulation to Privatization,* Boston: Kluwer Academic Publishers.

Tagliabue, John (2002), 'As multinationals run the taps, anger rises over water for profit', *New York Times* (New England edition) (August 26), 1.

Topping, Audrey R. (1995), 'Ecological roulette: damming the Yangtze', *Foreign Affairs* (September–October), 132–43.

Torras, M. and J.K. Boyce (1998), 'Income, inequality, and pollution: a reassessment of the environmental Kuznets curve', *Ecological Economics*, **25** (May), 147–60.

Um, M., S. Kwak and T. Kim (2002), 'Estimating willingness to pay for improved drinking water quality using averting behavior method with perception measure', *Environmental and Resource Economics*, **21**, 287–302.

Unknown author (2002), 'Privatization and Argentina: historical and political background', *Water Resources Impact*, **4**(1) (January), 2–4.

Wang, H. and D. Wheeler (2000), 'Endogenous enforcement and effectiveness of China's pollution levy system', presented at the AERE Workshop on Market Based Instruments for Environmental Protection, Harvard University, Boston, July 1999.

Whittington, D., A. Okorafor, A. Okore and A. McPhail (1990), 'Strategy for cost recovery in the rural water sector: a case study of Nsukka District, Anambra State, Nigeria', *Water Resources Research*, **26**(9) (September), 1899–913.

Whittington, D., D. Lauria and X. Mu (1991), 'A study of water vending and willingness to pay for water in Onitsha, Nigeria', *World Development*, **19**(2–3), 179–98.

Wolf, A.T. (2004), 'Transboundary water conflicts and cooperation', Unpublished manuscript.

World Health Organization (1998), 'Monitoring and evaluation of health for all strategy' (database as of March 13, 1998).

SUGGESTED FURTHER READING

Shaw, Daigee, Yu-Lan Chien and Yih-Ming Lin (1999), 'Alternative approach to combining revealed and stated preference data: evaluating water quality of a river system in Taipei', *Environmental Economics and Policy Studies*, **2**(2), 97–112.

WEBSITES

http:/www.irn.org/basics/impacts.shtml International Rivers Network, Berkeley, CA 94703.
http://www.worldbank.org/wbi/B-SPAN/sub_int_water_business.htm Watch a video of Jean-Francois Talbot, Chairman of the international water supply firm, SAUR Intl.
http://www.nrp.org/ramfiles/totn/20020416.totn.0 (NPR's Talk of the Nation, April 16, 2002 show on privatization of water).
http://www.worldbank.org/agadirconference (Irrigation water policies, June 2002, conference topics).
http://www.worldbank.org/wbi\B-SPAN/sub_waterNE.htm Here you can watch a video of a conference on water issues in the Near East broken into several parts. Speakers include Aaron Wolf and John Briscoe.

11. Summary, suggestions for future work, conclusions

11.0 INTRODUCTION

In this final chapter I summarize and offer a few thoughts on what lies on the road ahead for work in water resource economics, or at least suggest a few roads that might be taken by those interested in pursuing research. By this point in the book, the reader may agree with many who deem water 'the ultimate resource', but may also see that water resource allocation is no simple matter. The complexities explain why, after all of these years, water still seems to be 'found' when it is most needed. The previous ten chapters cover a wide range of topics, and each chapter suggests omissions in the literature, and areas that need more attention. I put these into broad categories below: uncertainty, which includes the climate change issue; water transfers, economics, and the evolution of water law; and work in countries outside the United States, especially the developing ones.

A theme that connects all three of these broad categories is growing relative water scarcity. Despite some slowed population growth in a few countries, world population growth remains a concern, especially the rapid growth in China and India. Exacerbating the problem in the water arena, there have been many shifts in population growth from fairly wet regions of some countries to quite arid ones. The huge shift in US population centers, from the midwestern and northeastern region, to the arid southwest, is an example. California is the most populated state in the country, and southern California (host to the cities of Los Angeles and San Diego) is largely arid.

As with all resources, water can be managed in such a way as to allocate water between users and over time. However, unlike every other resource that I can think of, it is difficult to imagine the day when humans can find a substitute for water in its most basic uses: drinking and as a necessary ingredient in growing food. Of course, it may well be that developing new water sources, including seawater and vast areas of currently uncharted groundwater, will become economically feasible in the future when today they are largely not. No doubt the role that energy development and energy prices play will be critical, since tapping groundwater and seawater supplies are energy-intensive prospects.

11.1 UNCERTAINTY

Economists, as Chapter 6 suggests, know something about risk and uncertainty, but this is one of the areas of economics where there needs to be much more empirical work. It may seem to some that if we do not know about something, such as the future, there is little point in doing research on or involving it. But uncertainty analysis can establish extremely helpful boundaries regarding where society may be in the future, or what outcomes may arise as the uncertainty is resolved. Water resources are fraught with uncertainty problems, and thus provide an excellent avenue for uncertainty research.

Though most climate change scientists agree that global warming is happening, there is still some debate about the specifics of climate change, and this includes whether currently wet (dry) areas will become dry (wet) ones as climate regimes may shift in the future (Frederick, 1993). By doing analysis that allows for uncertainty regarding the timing of climate shifts, as well as the magnitude or intensity of changes, society may at least be better prepared to address possible courses of action in response to potential events occurring. Society already does this today, in preparing for droughts and floods that may or may not happen at point X in time, with an unknown degree of severity.

Engineers often build in uncertainty into their deterministic models for water supply projects. What is still missing today are serious empirical or statistical studies of water demand or supply that incorporate uncertainty into the modeling. Agricultural economists interested in production have been interested for many years and have applied dynamic or stochastic programming incorporating uncertainty (see, for example, Turner and Perry, 1997). However, empirical or econometric modeling using observational data is still quite difficult to do and this explains why there is so little actual empirical (data-driven) work in the literature. New ground is being broken in the use of econometric models that incorporate uncertainty and use data on individual's preferences for health or environmental risk (for example, see Riddel et al., 2003) and this type of work may spawn more such studies in other areas of economics. What they may offer are predictions of expected demand or supply functions, which build in probabilities of random variables such as water flows, and even ex ante benefit estimates for provision of desirable, but uncertain water supplies.

11.2 WATER TRANSFERS, MARKETS, AND WATER LAW

Quite some time ago economists began evaluating the potential for water marketing and transfers as a means of resolving local water scarcity. A good example is the classic study by Vaux and Howitt (1984). They concluded that water trades could indeed be a substitute for new supplies, and that developing vast new sources for the state of California could not be justified. The basis for trade involves one party's gain, while making the other party at least no worse off. Ideally there are mutual gains from trade. So, step one is to try to identify potential gains from trade, when two or more parties may be unaware of the possibility, or at least not understand the details.

Water can still be 'found' in the United States. It is found in agriculture's stock of it that exists via the sector's long historical use and established water rights, so it is not 'new' water in any sense of the word. The agricultural sector in the US is finding that it is losing water to other sectors, particularly as urban and environmental demands increase the demand for regional supplies. Things are changing. As water moves from agriculture to other sectors, farmers may benefit from trading more among themselves.

Using California as an important institutional example, Zilberman et al. (1994) show that the doctrine of prior appropriation still hampers the smooth trade and reallocation of water. Under California law, Central Valley Project 'contractors' cannot trade water. The authors argue that at higher water prices farmers are encouraged to use more modern irrigation technologies (drip and sprinkler systems) to increase profits. However, the current system still encourages farmers to use water at a level where the value of its marginal product is close to zero, and this will promote the continued use of older, traditional technology (furrows and shortened runs). If trading is allowed to mimic a true water market, the authors show that it is more likely that modern irrigation technologies will be adopted, thus promoting efficient water use in agriculture. For example, at a price per acre foot of $62 they suggest that irrigated land will be 900 000 acres, while at a price per acre foot of water of $118.40, irrigated land actually increases to 1.05 million acres because of the use of modern technology, with a gain in social welfare of about 24 percent (see Zilberman et al., 1994).

Today a common potential exchange in the United States is from the farmer to either an urban water agency or an industrial entity, including hydroelectric power. Hydropower's importance has certainly not diminished. In fact, in 2001 the California energy crisis was caused to a large extent because normally reliable hydropower production in the Pacific Northwest failed because of the drought conditions that existed at the time. It is therefore important to estimate the benefits of water from hydropower production, as Hamilton et al. (1989) have done. Their estimates show that the benefits of water use in hydropower production are ten times greater than the farm income that would be lost via a trade, suggesting gains from trade.

Economists still do not know enough about the value of water in other uses, including the marginal value of water to urban water agencies. Existing market transactions indicate that the value of water is quite high for municipalities, but this alone does not tell us the actual marginal value. Very exciting steps are being taken to remedy the shortcomings of the existing literature. In one of the most ambitious exercises I know of, Jay Lund and his colleagues at the University of California at Davis have built an enormous model of state water supply and demand for the state (see http://cee.engr.ucdavis.edu/faculty/lund). The model and work are called 'CALVIN'. This linear programming model incorporates hydrology and economics, including all of the major surface water supplies and known groundwater aquifers that act as storage. It can be used to predict water values for urban users, allowing predictions of conditions in future years.

One prediction is that urban water scarcity in California will cost California about $1.6 billion per year by the year 2020 (see Jenkins et al., 2003). The model so far involves calibration of about 1 million parameters and currently does not include transactions costs. These costs can be included, as development of the model progresses, but even in its current state the model shows how water can be transferred from one part of the state of California to another, from agency to party or other agencies within a region, or from one party to another in other contexts.

11.3 ECONOMIC ANALYSIS IN DEVELOPING COUNTRIES

Many of the environmental and natural, and water resource economists I know in the United States seem to think that most of the interesting issues have already been addressed. I am not sure I agree, but it is hard to argue that the big challenges for resource economists are in other countries. Educated people know that developing nations still simply struggle with feeding their people and overcoming basic problems like providing clean drinking water. Chapter 10 makes clear that the reason this is true is because these countries are so poor that the basic services are not provided – but then, if so, one must know how society can solve this problem. Water is connected to growth of food, and here again, there is evidence of diminished water supplies, and some have stated that this is leading to lower agricultural productivity. There is growing alarm that the problems are getting worse, not better, and that the issue of unavailable water has spread enough for this to be called a 'global' problem (Brown, 2003).

Can economists contribute to analysis of the connection between diminished water supplies and food production? Yes, they can – they can start by taking a look at the data from the perspective of a resource economist. In his book Lester Brown presents a list of countries he says are over-pumping their groundwater (Brown attributes the numbers to another source of information). These countries, including the United States because of declining aquifers in Texas, Oklahoma, and Kansas, along with their populations, are reproduced in Table 11.1. (Brown does not provide estimates of the volume of water in each country, but these are available elsewhere, though the accuracy of such estimates for many countries may be worth scrutiny. As examples, note that China's 51 million hectares of irrigated land depends on 9 million hectares (mh) of groundwater, while India's 44 mh of irrigable land depends on 42 mh of groundwater.) Still, many world-problem-oriented agencies seem to share Brown's view that there is cause for concern. For example, the World Bank foresees 'catastrophic

Table 11.1 Countries with extensive over-pumping of aquifers in 2002*

Country	Population (millions)
China	1295
India	1050
United States	291
Pakistan	150
Mexico	102
Iran	68
South Korea	47
Morocco	30
Saudi Arabia	24
Yemen	19
Syria	17
Tunisia	10
Israel	6
Jordon	5

Note: *Yemen's water table is falling at a rate of between 2 and 6 meters or 20 feet per year. Iran's conditions caused a drop of 8 meters in one aquifer in 2001. Mexico's Guanajuato area water table is falling by 1.8 to 3.3 meters a year.

Source: From Brown (2003) and United Nations, *World Population Prospects* (February 2003).

consequences for future generations' from the situation in Northern China (World Bank, 2001).

This is an extensive or at least important list in that it totals about one-half of the planet earth's population, but Brown (2003) draws special attention to Northern China, stating that over-pumping has largely depleted the shallow aquifer in the North China Plain, which produces over one-half of China's wheat and over one-third of its corn. Agricultural interests, he says, have switched to pumping the deep aquifer in the region, which has fallen an average of 2.9 meters, and cannot be replenished. Another report Brown mentions says that some Chinese farmers are pumping from depths of 1000 feet below the surface, and farmers in Saudi Arabia are pumping from depths of 4000 feet. Again, these huge depths are presented as evidence of a growing problem with water scarcity and are connected to land's productivity in agriculture.

Pumping groundwater from greater depths increases the cost of pumping (see Chapter 7), so one can infer from this that the cost to farmers may increase as the required well depth increases. Brown, again citing the US Embassy in China and the World Bank, goes further and states that the wheat and rice crops in China are suffering because of these water shortages and will continue to do so. In making the link between food production and water scarcity, Brown frequently makes use of a ratio of water used per ton of output. For example, he says that it takes 1000 tons of water to produce 1 ton of wheat, implying a constant input–output ratio for water. He correctly notes that farmers around the world are selling their water to other users when the value of the water commands a higher price than it does in agriculture. This also hastens the loss of agricultural production because much of the land used in agriculture is worthless for that purpose without irrigation water.

In a later chapter (2003, chapter 7) Brown raises an interesting concept: an emerging measure of water productivity is in units of kilograms of grain produced, per ton of water. He and others then state that using this measure, one can focus on ways to raise water's productivity. For India, he provides a measure of the gain in productivity by changing from conventional surface irrigation to drip irrigation. Some of the crop-specific results are reproduced in Table 11.2.

Economists think of marginal productivity as the change in output (Q) for a small change in the input (W), or $\partial Q/\partial W$, which typically implies that levels of other inputs are held constant to examine the marginal product. It would be interesting to examine whether the numbers above are consistent with that assumption.

In fact, water resource economists should certainly be interested in all of these issues, but I am reminded of the energy scare in the 1970s. At that

Table 11.2 Productivity gains from shifting from conventional surface to drip irrigation systems in India

Crop	Change in yield	Change in water use (percent)	Water productivity gain (crop yield/units of water)
Bananas	52	−45	173
Potato	46	0	46
Sweet potato	39	−60	243
Tomato	50	−39	145

Source: Adapted by Brown (2003) from Sandra Postel et al., 'Drip Irrigation for Small Farmers', *Water International* (March 2001).

time physicists and other scientists reported that the world would run out of oil, with some projections of the world's end to oil as early as 1986.[1] In response, several prominent energy and environmental and resource economists analysed data using economic models and showed that the projections had largely left out the role that price and other economic variables play in determining the path to exhaustion of a resource. I write this section in 2004 and though again there is much discussion of oil's scarcity, 1986 has of course come and gone. Geologists are quarreling again today, with some of the same players as those involved in the 1970s debates forecasting doom and gloom, and at least two geologists forecasting the peak of global oil production in just six years, in about 2010 (Campbell and Laherrère, 1998).

Similarly, economists can (and I intend to) assess the path to exhaustion of aquifers, develop and analyse models that relate water volumes to food production, and see if Brown's reported concerns are proved. If these are proved, how much time does society (in China or otherwise) have to consider options that might alleviate or prevent food shortages in one or many such countries?

Even if Brown's and others' concerns are not as immediate as they think, there is no escaping the issue of food shortages in impoverished countries. Brown notes that an efficient way of substituting for scarce water is simply to import food, but, at what cost can this be done? An increase in the demand for imported wheat likely drives up its price.[2] Rising prices may help alleviate water being used up too fast, but they will only hurt poor people more. So, more ambitiously, what can water resource economists do to help developing countries obtain the resources needed to supply clean water for drinking and sanitation to its people today?

As mentioned in Chapter 10, some believe that privatization is the answer to the water supply problem in developing countries, but others strongly disagree. If the demand side of the equation is weak because those who need water supply the most are unable to pay for it, then privatization seems doomed. Alternatively, water economists rarely pay attention to the distribution of income, and perhaps this is a topic that needs our attention. Could a redistribution of income lead to better health precisely because impoverished people would have a better chance to purchase clean water? To my knowledge this has not been carefully addressed.

11.3 CONCLUSIONS

As I write this today a radio report documents trouble for the Shell Oil Company, relating to revised predictions of its 'known' stock of oil reserves. The company had to revise its estimate downward by 20 percent. The radio commentator went on to say that this would not matter in the global scheme of oil reserves, because Saudi Arabia, other parts of the Middle East, and Russia held most of the oil anyway, and Shell did not, so 'we' didn't need to worry. Will we ever have such a type of report regarding the amount of freshwater, at least in some regions in the world, and will these reports depend on 'ownership' of water supplies? So far, scarcity of water in the United States has caused temporary discomfort and hardships, but we do not experience the conflict that plagues the West Bank, nor do we see large populations in the arid American West give up and move away during droughts. Still, many wonder if the day will finally come when California's thirst for water will slow, or even stop, the rapid growth experienced there. It will be very interesting to watch the outcome of the recent wrangling over Colorado River rights.

This book has scratched the surface of the possible issues and topics in water resource economics. Each chapter topic could of course become a book in and of itself. In some cases I am guilty of raising more questions than I provide answers to. I hope some reader will be inspired to continue to research issues in water resource economics.

NOTES

1. In fact in his recent book Rifkin (2003) reminds us that the geophysicist M. King Hubbert published a paper in 1956 predicting that US oil production would peak in the 1970s. It did.
2. In fact he says that the world wheat price rose from $1.90 to $4.89 per bushel in 1972 in response to the Soviet Union's increased demand for imported wheat.

REFERENCES

Brown, Lester R. (2003), *Plan B: Rescuing a Planet under Stress and a Civilization in Trouble*, New York: W.W. Norton.
Campbell, Colin J. and Jean H. Laherrère (1998), 'The end of cheap oil', *Scientific American* (March), 80.
Frederick, K.D. (1993), 'Climate change impacts on water resources and possible responses in the Mink region', *Climatic Change*, **10** (June), 83–115.
Hamilton, J.R., N.K. Whittlesey and P. Halverson (1989), 'Interruptible water markets in the Pacific Northwest', *American Journal of Agricultural Economics* (February), 63–75.
Jenkins, M.W., J.R. Lund and R.E. Howitt (2003), 'Economic losses for urban water scarcity in California', *Journal of the American Water Works Association* (February).
Postel, Sandra et al. (2001), 'Drip irrigation for small farmers: a new initiative to alleviate hunger and poverty', *Water International*, (March), 3–13.
Riddel, Mary, C. Dwyer and W.D. Shaw (2003), 'Environmental risk and uncertainty: Insights from Yucca Mountain', *Journal of Regional Science*, **43**(3), 435–57.
Rifkin, Jeremy (2003), *The Hydrogen Economy*, New York: Tarcher/Putnam.
Turner, B. and G.M. Perry (1997), 'Agriculture to instream water transfers under uncertain water availability: a case study of the Deschutes River, Oregon', *Journal of Agricultural and Resource Economics*, **22**(2), 208–21.
United Nations (2003), *World Population Prospects*, Washington, DC, February, accessed at www.un.org.
Vaux Jr, H.J. and R.E. Howitt (1984), 'Managing water scarcity: an evaluation of interregional transfers', *Water Resources Research*, **20**(7) (July), 785–92.
World Bank (2001), 'China: agenda for water sector strategy for North China', Washington, DC (April).
Zilberman, D., N. MacDougall and F. Shah (1994), 'Changes in water allocation mechanisms for California agriculture', *Contemporary Economic Policy*, **12** (January), 122–33.

SUGGESTED FURTHER READING

Gleick, Peter, *The World's Water* (Ongoing series, available in 2002 and other years), Washington, DC: Island Press.
Postel, Sandra (1999), *Pillar of Sand*, New York: W.W. Norton.

WEBSITES

http://www.cgiar.org.iwmi (the International Water Management Institute).
http://www.worldwater.org (The World's Water).
http://www.fao.org/waicent/faoinfo/agricult/agl/aglw/aquastat/main./index.stm (Global information system of water and agriculture from the United Nations Food and Agriculture Organization).

Index

acre foot 8–9, 35–6, 53
agriculture
   production in 45–6, 138–41, 145, 149–50
   profits in (*see* profit)
   and uncertainty 183–5 (*see also* uncertainty, risk)
   value of water in (*see* value of water)
Argentina 339–40
Arizona 12, 13, 28, 100, 123, 152
   Central Arizona Project 222–5
   Tucson 131
arsenic 71
   in drinking water 87, 196
   risk perceptions related to 196–8

Bangladesh 329
banking water (*see* water banks)
Berrens, Robert 261, 262
biochemical oxygen demand (BOD) 71–2
block rate pricing 110–12, 119, 120
   demand and 121–2
Blue Ribbon Committee (*see* California, Los Angeles)
Bolivia 340, 341
Burness, Stuart 57, 190, 191

California 13, 27, 30, 66, 88, 100, 126, 129, 136, 140, 147, 151, 162, 165–6, 352, 354
   Los Angeles 101, 115, 116–17, 129
   San Joaquin Valley 154, 256
   water bank in 156, 190, 314–15
California Doctrine 20
Canada 92
cancer risk (*see* human health)
Carter, President James 297
Cech, Thomas viii, 5, 8, 10, 13, 20, 69, 101, 204
China 304, 336, 341–3, 356, 357
Clean Water Act 85

climate 173, 327, 353
climate change 353
Clinton, President William J. 304
Colby, Bonnie 63, 261, 277
Colorado 122, 125, 126, 161, 303
Colorado doctrine 20
Colorado River 8, 14, 66, 243, 297, 359
   Compact of 1922 27, 166, 306
   salinity in 157–8
Columbia River 8, 9, 264–7, 287, 297, 299, 300
common property resource 16, 217–19
conflicts (*see* international conflicts)
conjunctive use 219–25
contingent behavior model 254, 260
contingent valuation 88, 93, 230, 238, 254–5, 279, 280, 305, 330, 331, 333
correlative rights 18
costs, cost functions 46–9
   average, marginal 47–9, 53, 104–106, 110
   control costs 85–7
   delivered water (cost of) 161–2
   of extraction (of groundwater) 207
   joint 110
   marginal user cost 214
   pumping (groundwater) 206, 207, 212, 214, 220, 221, 224, 245
   total 46–7
   transactions costs 63
   treatment costs (*see* water treatment)
consumer's surplus 51–3, 259, 260, 262
Crouter, Jan 311, 312

dams 104, 287, 297–305
   in developing countries 341–3
   removal of 304–305
Delaware 84
demand for water 117–22
   elasticity of 40–44, 122–6
   input demand 44–6, 138–41
   uncertainty in (*see* uncertainty)

361

demand side management (DSM) 129
discounting 58–63, 213, 244, 302
dissolved oxygen 71–2, 86
diversions 14
Dominican Republic 288
drinking water (*see* human health)
drought 4, 130–31, 173, 187, 288–99, 305–309
   index (Palmer) 307
   measures of 306–307
   water banks and (*see* water banks)

ecological impacts 81–2
economies of scale 48
efficiency 29, 57, 104–105, 190–92
Egypt 303, 345
Eiswerth, Mark 261, 262, 270
embedded cost rate structure 113–14
endangered species 192, 193, 253, 264–5, 267, 274
environmental Kuznets curve 93, 337
Espey, Molly 124, 125
evapotranspiration 6, 31, 120, 156
existence value 229
expected utility 176–8, 198
externalities 57

Federal Water Pollution Control Act (of 1972) 76, 83
fish consumption advisories 75, 87
floods 288–99
   protection against 290–91
   storage 130
flood control 292–6
   benefits and costs of 292–4
Florida 69, 82, 137
flouride 91
futures contracts 187–90

Ghana 341
giardia 80
Gisser, Micha 211, 212, 215, 218, 219
global warming (*see* climate change)
Griffin, Ronald 29
groundwater (*see* Chapter 7), 357
   contamination 225–8, 231–7, 238, 240, 241–2, 340
   Darcy's law 203
   law (*see* law)
   movement in 205–206

optimal extraction of 206–19
quality 232–7

Haiti 288, 315, 330–31, 338
Hall, Darwin 116
Hanemann, W. Michael viii, 111, 114, 121, 122, 124, 199, 256
Hanke, Steve 125
hardness 69
Hawaii 208, 209
hedonic property valuation 153, 255
Howe, Charles W. vii, viii, 27, 29, 63, 101, 302, 303
Howitt, Richard viii, 66, 157, 167, 172, 189, 190, 194, 257, 314, 315, 354
human health and use 11, 74–6
   and cancer risk 67, 68, 239
   and drinking water 72, 74–5, 77, 79, 83, 182, 225, 226, 227, 320, 334, 335
Hungary 327
hydroelectric power 275, 298, 299, 300, 355
hydrologic cycle 7, 58

Idaho 29, 309, 310, 311, 314
India 2, 319, 320, 321, 341, 347, 352, 356
Indonesia 202
instream flow 251–3
   laws (*see* law) 21, 22, 252, 266–7
   protection of 28, 192–4
   values for 258, 260–64
international conflicts 2, 18, 22–3, 343–7
irrigation 137
   technology 145–9, 151, 354

Jakus, Paul 87, 261

Kahn, Alfred 115
Kentucky 257
Kenya 321
Korea 334

Lake Tahoe (*see* Nevada)
Lambert, David viii, 279, 280
law 15–25
   groundwater 23–5

instream flow 28 (see also instream flow)
international 22–3
major U.S. legislation 21, 76–7, 83
Native American water rights 22, 276
prior appropriation (doctrine of) 19–20, 21, 266
riparian doctrine 17–18
rule of capture 23, 217
Loomis, John viii, 256, 261, 269, 305
Long Term Surface Water Treatment Rule 79
Lund, Jay 355

Maine 306, 308
marginal rate of transformation 61
market failure 57
  in agriculture 144, 161–2
metering (see pricing)
Mexico 158, 326, 356
Michigan 241–2
mining 19, 277–9
Missouri River 300
monopoly 105–108, 213
  regulated utility 105–106
Montana 75
Morris, John viii, 122, 126

navigation 298–300
Nevada 4, 6, 12, 128, 197, 243, 268
  Clark County 4, 243
  Lake Tahoe 13, 15, 68, 69, 72, 276
  Pyramid Lake 13, 15, 273, 274
  Reno 127–8
  Reno 1997 flood 127, 268, 288–9, 291
  Truckee River 15, 16, 29, 273–7
  Walker Lake 13, 267–73
New Mexico 205, 219, 227, 259
New York 118
Nigeria 92, 329–30, 345
non-market valuation 227, 230, 253–5

Ogallala aquifer 226
Ohio 79, 84
oil spills 81, 82, 254
option price 180, 195, 238, 239
Oregon 252

Pakistan, 319, 331–3, 356
passive use values 229
Philippines 93, 322, 323, 328–9
pollution 66–74
  nonpoint source 73, 155–7, 159, 160–61
precipitation 13, 107, 287, 306, 319
present value (see discounting)
pricing/price of water 100, 102, 109–14
  long run average cost pricing 114
  marginal cost pricing 111, 113, 207
  metering 125–8, 111, 173, 180
  peak load pricing 115
  per acre foot 100, 101, 140, 154, 155, 163, 277, 314
  ramsey pricing 114, 115
  shin pricing 120–21
privatization 339–41
producer's surplus 54–5
profit 53–4, 136, 164, 165, 181, 186
  maximization 139, 148, 186
property rights 16–17
public good 16

radon 79
rates (see value of water)
recreation (water-based) 87, 251–2
  value of water in 259, 269
return flows 10
risk 67–8, 88–90, 172–4 (see also uncertainty)
  of dying 194 (see also human health)
  risk premiums 185–7, 199
runoff 10
Russia 94, 336

Safe Drinking Water Act 76, 83, 89, 128
Saleth, Maria 28, 347
salinity 157–8 (see also total dissolved solids)
sanitation 321, 328, 332, 333, 339
Schuck, Eric 142, 146, 147
shadow price/value (see value of water)
Shaw, W. Douglass 87, 172, 196, 198, 270, 271, 280
supply of water 3, 103–105
  and groundwater 202, 206
  and uncertainty 181–4

Taylor, Lester 120
Texas 15, 79, 137, 154, 162, 204, 217, 243, 309, 356
Thailand 347
Three Gorges Dam 304, 342–3
total dissolved solids (TDS) 66, 70, 157, 268
total maximum daily load (TMDL) 77
transactions costs (*see* costs)
transfers 354–5
   interbasin 29–30
travel cost model 254, 258, 269, 279
Trelease, Frank 2, 16
Truckee River (*see* Nevada)
turbidity 71

uncertainty 62, 143, 172–99, 353
   in agriculture 163–7
   in demand 175, 178–81
Utah 306
utilities (*see* supply of water)

value of statistical life 90–91, 195, 290, 295
value of water
   in agriculture 136, 141–3, 152–5, 162–3
   average, per acre foot 100–102, 227, 277 (*see also* pricing per acre foot)
   marginal cost pricing 110
   marginal value 259
   rates 102–103, 108–17

shadow value 152
Virginia 18

Ward, Frank 258, 260–61, 269
Washington 81, 91, 264, 309, 327
wastewater 72
water balance 7, 31
water banks 190, 269–71, 309–15
water law (*see* law)
water markets 25–8, 100, 354
   transactions costs 63
Water Pollution Control Act 76, 83
water quality 74–81, 89, 95–6
   and agriculture 155–9
   and recreation 75
   and uncertainty 181–3, 194–8
water treatment 77–81, 103
   reverse osmosis 78
   treatment costs 78–81, 103–104, 182–3
West Bank 337–8, 344, 359
West Germany 344
Whittington, Dale 92, 329, 330, 331, 345
Winters doctrine 22
Wolf, Aaron 343

Young, Robert 155, 157, 258

Zilberman, David viii, 144, 147, 149, 150, 151, 160, 354
Zimbabwe 334–6, 354